Energy and Resources Financing

A Practical Handbook

Consulting Editors **Huw Thomas** and **Antony Skinner**

Consulting editors
Huw Thomas
Antony Skinner

Managing director
Sian O'Neill

Energy and Resources Financing: A Practical Handbook
is published by
Globe Law and Business Ltd
3 Mylor Close
Horsell
Woking
Surrey GU21 4DD
Tel: +44 20 3745 4770
www.globelawandbusiness.com

Print and bound by Gomer Press

Energy and Resources Financing: A Practical Handbook
ISBN 9781909416765

Table of contents

Introduction

Antony Skinner
Huw Thomas
Ashurst LLP

This book addresses the need for a practical guide to energy and natural resources financing in a time of rapid change in the energy and natural resources industries and the world of finance.

International resources companies are enduring a prolonged period of low commodity prices. In mature and frontier oil and gas basins, costs of extraction are increasing because of the technical challenges of exploiting the less accessible reserves – the days of 'easy oil' are at an end. At the same time, international oil companies (IOCs) have limited access to the still vast conventional reserves that are either held by national oil companies or are located in countries which IOCs cannot access due to civil breakdown, war or sanctions. The response of IOCs has been to examine closely their capital expenditure budgets across the energy chain.

Controversially, climate change campaigners claim that the majority of the reserves that the IOCs own may be stranded and to extract them would cause the global 'carbon budget' to be exceeded, thus tipping the planet into dangerous climate change.

Meanwhile the costs of renewable sources of energy supply such as wind and solar have fallen substantially, to the point where governments can justify withdrawing subsidies, albeit often out of fiscal necessity.

All this is in a world still feeling the after-effects of the global financial crisis. As a result of increased regulatory pressures, commercial banks are less able to make available the long-term loans that were previously the norm in project financings.

So what are the consequences for energy and natural resources financings? Some of the key developments are outlined below:

- A fall in the volume of financings for oil and gas assets across the energy chain. The oil price collapse has badly affected upstream financing and although, at the time of writing, lenders have generally been supportive of borrowers under existing facilities, there has been only limited new upstream financing activity. The cuts that IOCs have made to their capital expenditure budgets for midstream and downstream projects have also resulted in a decrease in project financings for pipelines, refineries and petrochemical plants. Companies looking for cheaper and more flexible solutions to monetise gas reserves are turning to floating LNG liquefaction solutions, and it is likely to be only a matter of time before we see the first successful financing of a floating LNG project;
- A fall-off in traditional forms of mining financing, including project

financing and high-yield bond issuance, forcing mining companies to embrace a range of alternative funding methods;

- A sharp upturn in the volume of financings for renewable energy projects, on both a single-asset and a portfolio basis;
- The prospects for nuclear energy improving in some countries, with the United Kingdom in particular seeing nuclear as a key means of achieving carbon reduction targets. Limited-recourse financing for nuclear projects, however, still looks a long way off;
- A move to mini-perm structures, where the loan life is limited to, say, five to seven years, well short of the project life, with a need for refinancing at the end of the initial term;
- For larger-scale financings, export credit agencies playing a critical role in plugging the gap left by commercial banks unable to lend on the longer maturities;
- The appearance of new sources of liquidity, such as pension funds and other institutional investors that are keen to lock in long-term stable returns. Some of these investors are still investing through traditional loan structures; others are investing through private placements or a combination of both; and
- A rise in the state capitalist model for the financing of infrastructure such as oil and gas pipelines, with Chinese state-owned entities in particular playing an active role.

No doubt many of the changes we are seeing are cyclical and, in due course, oil and gas financings will come back strongly, as may long-term bank lending. Whatever the challenges, this book provides a practical guide to achieving successful energy and natural resources financings across the spectrum.

Reserve-based lending

Nick Ross-McCall
Huw Thomas
Ashurst LLP

1. Overview

Oil and gas exploration and production (E&P) companies typically have many different equity and debt funding options at their disposal in order to finance their operations. With the exception of the majors and national oil companies, most players look to international commercial banks with specialist project finance or reserve-based lending (RBL) teams to supply the majority or a significant part of the debt funding for their projects. The defining feature of RBL is that the size of the facility is determined by reference to the current value of the borrower's oil and gas reserves rather than the strength of its balance sheet. Its look-forward nature means it is available to borrowers with little or no trading history.

The focus of this chapter will be on what is commonly called 'European RBL' or 'International RBL', the product used in most jurisdictions around the world, outside the United States and Canada where a different US RBL model applies. We shall see that the International RBL product is extremely flexible, being capable of adjustment to fit any point on a spectrum of borrower needs. These might range from a project finance style approach to a single-asset development, or to a corporate facility style approach to a portfolio of producing assets. This versatility is testament to RBL's continued prevalence over the last 30 years, with relatively low default rates considering the nature of the business and financial standing of its borrowers.

This chapter will give an overview of an RBL financing transaction from start to finish before examining the key principles underlying RBL and the key documentation features. It will then look at the scope of due diligence undertaken by lenders and common issues that arise, and progress to describing adjustments which can be made to the basic RBL product to meet special situations including mergers and acquisitions opportunities and decommissioning obligations. Next, the chapter will look briefly at other debt financing options available to E&P companies and how these might interface with an RBL facility, and describe the key differences between the International RBL and US RBL models. Finally, we will examine how to manage RBL facilities during a downturn in the oil and gas market.

2. History and development of RBL

2.1 US RBL model

RBL as a debt product has a fairly long and distinguished history. The US market predates the European/international market and is largely focused around Houston-

and Dallas-based lenders. It has developed largely in isolation, focusing on large numbers of modest onshore producing projects in the United States and Canada.

This chapter does not explore the US RBL model in detail but in section 8 below it does flag some of the key differences with the International RBL model.

2.2 Origins of International RBL model in the United Kingdom

The International RBL product originated in the United Kingdom with a focus on large offshore development projects. During the early years of the UK continental shelf industry in the 1970s and 1980s, the development of assets was financed either on the balance sheet by the majors or, where debt-financed by smaller players, involved financing a single asset on a project-finance basis. Projects were not, with the benefit of hindsight, particularly risky financing propositions because:

- fields were larger;
- loans were based on conservative reserve figures, leaving substantial cushions of reserves;
- sponsors were generally large companies; and
- decommissioning was a distant prospect.

As the North Sea basin matured, that type of financing largely became inappropriate for the generally smaller fields which were then being developed. At least as early as the 1990s (with a few deals even earlier) financing a portfolio of assets by way of a borrowing base facility became attractive to lenders as it de-risks the asset base; a deterioration in reserves at one field may be offset by upside from another and reserves on both producing and development assets could be used to finance development and even further exploration.

A number of factors drove a move in the United Kingdom from single-asset project financings to a portfolio or borrowing base structure, including:

- the assets under development in the UK continental shelf are smaller now (originally perhaps 100 million barrels or greater, but now more like 10 to 30 million barrels);
- technology risk has increased, with a greater reliance on enhanced recovery techniques to extract petroleum and yet also often reliance on ageing infrastructure for transportation;
- the field life of the assets being financed has become shorter (down to perhaps five years now as against 20 years at the high point of UK continental shelf discoveries), with decommissioning now a key issue;
- the single-asset approach is often not cost-effective for raising a relatively small amount of debt given the expense of putting together a quite complex and extensive finance document package.

Single-asset project financings still occur in the United Kingdom but multi-asset RBL facilities are now prevalent.

The portfolio approach of the borrowing base facility mitigates the risk of problems with one asset affecting the ability of the borrower to service the loan and permits a large enough loan to be raised with simple enough documentation, so as to make the exercise economically viable. In essence, an RBL facility seeks to match the loan size to the net present value (NPV) of future income from the portfolio of assets. That NPV calculation (and therefore the permitted size of the loan) is typically reassessed every six months during the tenor of the loan. If, for example, a new projection is produced on the basis of a lower oil price or the reserves are revised downwards, the borrowing base shrinks, and the borrower will be required to prepay the loans to the extent that the outstandings exceed the revised borrowing base amount.

2.3 Development of the International RBL market

In recent years, RBL facilities have been made available to small and mid-sized independents acquiring assets being divested by larger oil companies or developing new discoveries. As there is no strong parent company behind such a borrower, these have been secured primarily by way of a floating charge. Assuming the NPV is adequate to support the financing, the rest of the representation and covenant package is usually relatively light compared with what would be found in a full-blown project financing. Some commentators therefore regard RBL as thinly disguised corporate loans to sub-investment grade companies, and the defensive security as a means to justify the extra risk before credit committees. While there may be a nugget of truth in this for a small number of borrowers, the protection that the lenders receive through careful modelling and controls over the borrowing base cash flows usually provides legitimate differentiation for RBL as against plain vanilla corporate facilities.

RBL remains popular with borrowers today, primarily because of the flexibility and relatively favourable pricing that it provides. It enables borrowers to raise financing based on the value of their petroleum reserves. In the United Kingdom this is generally on a P50 basis for producing assets and on a P90 basis for development assets. RBLs are also attractive to borrowers in that the facility is revolving (ie, repaid amounts can be re-borrowed) and will often permit expenditure for general corporate purposes, so that the funds do not always have to be spent on the assets supporting the financing.

2.4 The European model goes international

In the last decade or so International RBL has spread rapidly from the North Sea to most major basins outside of North America, in particular across South East Asia, West and North Africa, the Middle East, Russia/Commonwealth of Independent States (CIS) and the rest of Europe. This has largely tracked the growth in international activities of independent companies.

Certain countries in the Middle East and North Africa, such as Oman, Egypt, Tunisia and Morocco offer strong potential for borrowing base-style lending. Despite the tight grip of the national oil companies, in particular in many parts of the Middle East, as fields mature there may be openings for independent companies to be allowed in to operate assets that the big players may consider not worthwhile, as happened originally in the UK continental shelf and in the Gulf of Mexico, and more recently in Indonesia. Such companies are likely to use debt financing to fund their activities.

West Africa has been fertile ground for RBL including large-scale developments in Nigeria and Ghana. South East Asia has seen progressively more activity. In any of these other territories where political risks are deemed to be higher than the norm, the lending criteria and terms for such deals may be commensurately more conservative, but this does not prevent deals from being successfully closed on the right terms.

London and Paris are now established as the premier international centres for upstream oil and gas financing (with other important bases including Geneva and Singapore). This is largely due to the historic development of the market by bankers based in London and Paris. Hand in hand with that is the fact that there are now many independent oil and gas companies headquartered in London which have activities around the world. In addition, a large number of consulting and advisory businesses have grown up in the same locations to support the deals. The lender community is wider than this and includes on occasion hedge funds and private equity funds, the World Bank (through the International Finance Corporation (IFC)), traders and even oil and gas majors.

South America and East Africa appear to be the next regions ready for the RBL technique. RBL is a flexible product and can be quite readily adapted for different jurisdictions, including:

- licence or production-sharing contract regimes;
- common law or civil law jurisdictions; and
- less developed or mature oil and gas territories.

The RBL structure even allows for producing assets in a mature territory to be placed in a borrowing base portfolio with more risky development assets from a newer territory.

3. Transaction overview

3.1 Initial steps

While the process for refinancing of existing RBL debt will be simpler, the first RBL facility for any E&P company will typically be a lengthy process requiring senior management's full involvement. However, the result – the introduction of relatively cheap senior debt into the capital structure leading to increased equity returns – is usually considered worth the effort.

Lenders undertake significant due diligence and so borrowers should gather as much information as possible to facilitate initial discussions, including reserves reports, field development plans, capital expenditure budgets, development contracting strategies, production histories and Know Your Client (KYC) information.

Lenders' origination teams, including in-house engineers, will conduct initial due diligence and develop or review a detailed cash-flow model. If this is considered bankable, a term sheet will be negotiated. This is usually produced by the lender, but can be a borrower-led exercise, particularly if the borrower wants to maintain competitive tension among multiple potential lenders.

3.2 Mandate letter

The next step is typically the signing of a mandate letter attaching the term sheet setting out the agreed terms prior to the execution of full documentation. Under the mandate letter, the lenders agree in varying degrees of certainty and conditionally, either to:

- take and hold a proportion of the total debt, in the case of a club deal; or
- underwrite all of the debt, in the case of a syndicated deal.

In a club deal, all the participant banks are known in advance of signing and agree the proportions of the debt they will hold. In an underwritten deal, one or more banks may agree to take on all the debt with the intention of selling it down (syndicating it) to other lenders in due course. The underwriters will benefit from a market flex clause in the mandate letter allowing them to make changes to key financial terms within agreed parameters, should syndication prove more difficult than expected.

In the RBL market, before the onset of the credit crunch, although a market flex provision would typically have been included in mandate letters, it was often restricted to only a right to change pricing, and then perhaps subject to a cap. Since then, in the relatively exceptional event of an underwriting, it has become more usual for the underwriters to insist on full market flex provisions to apply. In the context of the currently more prevalent club deal structure, market flex will usually not be relevant.

3.3 Full documentation

Once the mandate letter is signed, legal counsel are typically instructed for the lenders and borrower (if they have not been already), due diligence is completed by lenders and their advisers, and lenders obtain their final internal credit approvals. Credit officers will check that the proposed transaction meets financial return hurdles, that structure and security requirements are included in the documentation, and that downside sensitivity testing is carried out on the financial model.

The definitive finance documentation package will include, principally:

- the facility agreement;
- security documents;
- a security trust deed; and
- (if required) an intercreditor agreement and an accounts agreement.

In RBL deals where the only secured creditors are the RBL lenders and the hedge providers, the security trust and the intercreditor provisions can be incorporated in the facility agreement.

The key finance document is the facility agreement which will include the borrowing base mechanics described above and the following:

- *Representations and warranties:* These serve slightly different purposes to commercial contracts, such as sale and purchase agreements. Lenders are not particularly interested in suing for damages for breach of a representation, but rather want to force disclosure both before signing and on an ongoing basis, and to be able to call a default on breach of a representation. Many of the representations are deemed to be repeated on certain days throughout the life of the facility.

- *Covenants:* In classical project finance documentation these are extensive and are designed to give the banks control in relation to the basic management of the special purpose vehicle borrower and development of the project. There will also be extensive information covenants included on financial accounts and construction/production/reserves reports. In terms of weight and tightness of the covenant package, RBLs range from much less restrictive corporate finance style restrictions, to a package closer to a project financing for a hybrid borrowing base/project finance deal. This flexibility is one of the key strengths of RBLs as a robust financial product. Key covenants include restrictions on the borrower granting security over its assets to other creditors (a negative pledge), and restrictions on incurring other financial indebtedness, expenditure outside of an agreed model, disposals and acquisitions. Exceptions to these are always keenly negotiated. Financial covenants may also feature, particularly in corporate-style RBLs for larger borrowers.
- *Events of default:* These will include failure to pay, insolvency events, breach of representations or covenants or other terms of any finance document, and other more bespoke events relating to the borrower or its projects/assets. The occurrence of any of these allows lenders to accelerate the entire debt and enforce security. Banks also view them as a means of forcing the borrower to the negotiating table at a hopefully pre-emptive stage of the project if things go wrong, in addition to an opportunity to call for an immediate return of their money. Some bankers take the view that it is no bad thing if at any point in time lenders can point to a technical default under a facility agreement, but of course borrowers' counsel will make every effort to ensure that only genuine issues trigger an event of default.

Since the publication by the Loan Market Association (LMA) in the United Kingdom of a template English law syndicated loan agreement for investment grade and leveraged borrowers, the time taken agreeing mechanical and standard provisions of credit agreements has been greatly reduced. LMA-based documentation is always used in the European, and very often in the international, upstream oil and gas RBL market as a basis for negotiations.

3.4 Financial close

Lenders will insist on a range of conditions precedent (CPs) being set out in the facility agreement, which must all be satisfied or waived before first drawdown is permitted. The occurrence of CP satisfaction and first drawdown is typically referred to as financial close, but the phrase is sometimes used only to describe signing of the facility agreement. In RBL, these usually occur close together or even on the same day. Upfront fees are typically due to lenders on or within a short period of signing, rather than on satisfaction of CPs and so borrowers will want a high degree of certainty prior to signing that CPs can all be satisfied in due course.

3.5 Post-financial close

Lenders will monitor RBL borrowers closely on an ongoing basis up to final maturity or earlier prepayment of the loans. In development financings this can include monthly progress reports. In portfolio financings (with a balance between development and producing assets) monitoring focuses on updates to the financial model which are usually carried out every six months.

4. Basic principles of reserve-based lending and key documentation features

4.1 Cash-flow financing

The riskier a project, the more suitable it is for equity financing as opposed to debt financing. Debt providers will only lend on projects with a sufficiently low risk profile and clear cash flows to justify their expected low fixed returns. On the other hand, borrowers have a higher and uncapped potential return on their investments and a greater appetite for risk.

Debt financing is dependent on stable cash flows and traditionally is not appropriate for exploration and appraisal projects. During the frothy bank market before the global financial crisis, with debt providers being keen to establish relationships with new market entrants at an early stage in their business cycle, occasionally pre-development assets were capable of being debt financed. Since 2008, however, bank appetite for providing pre-development financing has diminished. The exception has been where high quality pre-development assets are financed as part of a portfolio of development and producing assets.

4.2 Projections and NPV calculations

RBL transactions essentially involve financiers lending against the NPV of future cash flows projected to be generated from independently audited oil and gas reserves of included fields. Calculation of the NPV and key financial ratios is achieved using an audited computer model to produce a projection through to the end of the life of the loan and beyond. The inputs for the model include relevant economic and technical assumptions. Usually, lenders provide economic assumptions such as forward curve petroleum prices and tax rates and the borrower provides technical assumptions such as

- capital expenditure (capex);
- operating expenditure (opex);
- decommissioning costs; and
- reserves figures.

Disputes over assumptions are often settled by using the technical bank's or majority lenders' (two-thirds by value of commitments) reasonable views, or, in the case of technical assumptions, by referring the matter to an expert for a quick determination.

The NPV is calculated by taking the projections of gross proceeds for each future period (usually six months) and then deducting projected expenses including capex, opex and taxes for such period and discounting the net amounts at a fixed rate of discount. The discount rate is usually comparable to or slightly higher than the interest rate payable on the loan, subject to a floor.

This initial projection is then redetermined periodically throughout the life of the facility, usually every six months, to provide the level of comfort required by lenders that the then current borrowings under the facility are covered by expected cash flows from the included fields. The reserves figures used in the computer model are usually taken from an annual independent reserves report and a semiannual update from the borrower's in-house engineers.

4.3 Debt sizing – borrowing base amount

The borrowing base amount is the term used to describe the maximum amount permitted to be drawn under the facility at any particular time. This must in any case be lower than the total commitments of the lenders at that time. The borrowing base amount is based on the NPV of certain cash flows, taking account of P50 or P90 reserves, divided by a denominator which differs depending on the cover ratio being used to limit the debt size.

P90 (or P1) and P50 (or P2) are shorthand for proved reserves and proved and probable reserves respectively under deterministic or probabilistic calculations (which usually give similar results). Typical definitions are:

- P90: those quantities of petroleum which have a 90% or greater probability of being recovered from the included fields (determined in accordance with the guidelines of the Society of Petroleum Engineers); and
- P50: those quantities of petroleum which have a 50% or greater probability of being recovered from the included fields (determined in accordance with the guidelines of the Society of Petroleum Engineers).

RBL banks are usually comfortable lending against P50 reserves for producing assets and P90 reserves for development assets. Development assets will have to pass the completion test defined by the banks, usually including production at commercial rates for at least six months, before qualifying as producing assets.

Of course, there is no certainty that the projected cash flows will be achieved. Economically recoverable reserves may be less, or expenditure may be higher than expected, for example if the geology of a field is more complex than anticipated, increasing the costs of development.

The borrowing base amount can be increased through commodity hedging, if the borrower enters hedging contracts ensuring a price per barrel higher than the price deck used by lenders in the projections to calculate gross revenues. The borrowing base amount can also be increased by bringing in more assets. This is usually permitted subject to two-thirds bank approval (by commitments), and likewise disposals or de-designation of borrowing base assets is usually allowed with two-thirds bank approval and subject to paying outstanding loans down to the reduced borrowing base amount.

The borrowing base amount is sometimes also increased by allowing capex add-back to be taken into account in NPV calculations where the projected capex spend on borrowing base assets in the next, say, 12 months is added back to the numerator in the NPV calculation. The usual rationale for allowing the add-back is that lenders are leveraging cash flows from assets rather than project NPVs and, therefore, upfront costs/capex should not reduce borrowing capacity if funded otherwise than from the cash flows (ie, including under the RBL facility itself).

4.4 Cover ratios and financial covenants

RBL lenders use cover ratios to size debt and to forecast the financial viability of a project. They are re-tested on a running basis in projections. The most important to an RBL lender are the PLCR and the LLCR (see below). Other uses of these ratios include:

- as a condition precedent to first drawdown;
- as a trigger to vary the interest rate;
- as a distribution block;
- as a tool to determine whether insurance proceeds must be applied in pre-payment of the facility as opposed to repair or reinstatement of an asset;
- as a drawstop preventing further utilisation of the facility; and ultimately
- as a trigger for an event of default.

(a) PLCR

The project life cover ratio or PLCR (also called the Field Life Cover Ratio or FLCR) is a key ratio, as banks focus very much on the life of the assets over and above that of the debt given that RBLs are typically five to seven years in tenor and usually refinanced well in advance of maturity. It is the ratio of the NPV at a relevant calculation date (usually every six months) of future projected net revenue during the life of a project to the principal debt outstanding (or projected to be outstanding) on that calculation date. Projections are run on a conservative post-tax basis with tax deductions only taken into account if capex-related allowances actually defer when tax is due on profits.

For debt sizing, the project NPV is typically divided by 1.5 so that lenders are only lending against two-thirds of the NPV.

The PLCR assists lenders in ascertaining the cushion available if the loan is not paid by the final maturity date and therefore the refinancing risk.

(b) LLCR

A loan life cover ratio or LLCR is the ratio of the NPV at a relevant calculation date (usually every six months) of future projected net revenue during the life of the debt facility to the amount of principal debt outstanding (or projected to be outstanding) on that calculation date. It is usually, but not always, included in an RBL as a determinant of the borrowing base amount where the loan life NPV is typically divided by 1.3. If included, the borrowing base amount will always be the lesser of the PLCR amount and LLCR amount.

There may be no loan life cover ratio in an RBL facility with a wide portfolio of borrowing base assets, on the basis that loans are not being matched against the NPV of a single asset. With the portfolio approach, there is a spread of assets which may change over time so the non-inclusion of an LLCR is agreed by lenders to meet borrowers' requirements for increased leverage, justified by this de-risking of the loan.

(c) ***DSCR***

A debt service cover ratio or DSCR is occasionally used by RBL lenders to gain comfort that the borrower will have funds available to make its debt payments on a current basis. It is the ratio of net revenue before payment of financing costs during a certain period (usually six months) to the financing costs due to be paid during that period. In RBL transactions, the debt service cover ratio is usually determined on a projected, rather than historic, basis, if at all. Even where not included in documentation, it will always be a feature that lenders are keenly aware of and will be looking at in the model.

(d) ***Other financial ratios***

Some RBL facilities for larger players incorporate ratio features from corporate style loans, with looser controls over the borrower group in exchange for corporate lending ratios, such as a total borrowings (gross or net) to EBITDA (earnings before interest, tax, depreciation and amortisation) ratio. Some deals go further and effectively become corporate facilities, leaving behind the RBL debt-sizing mechanics while maintaining a covenant package with the feel of an RBL facility. An advantage for borrowers is greater certainty over borrowing capacity which is determined annually based on past results and not susceptible to a quick drop after a price fall. Sometimes larger players can have both an RBL facility and a smaller corporate facility.

4.5 Reserve tail date

For additional protection, banks prescribe the date on which a certain amount (typically 20% to 25%) of the original reserves of the included fields remains as a longstop date for repayment of the loans, which may bring forward the final maturity date from the otherwise typical five- to seven-year term. This is known as the reserve tail date and protects the banks from relying on more speculative future recovery from the end of the life of the fields, allowing them to take a more robust approach towards abandonment costs. The traditional view is that decommissioning costs would be matched by revenue arising after the reserve tail date (though this may no longer hold true for some UK deals).

4.6 Control of borrowing base asset cash flows – project accounts

Control over cash flows in RBL transactions is achieved using secured bank accounts (usually known as proceeds or revenue accounts) through which all receipts relating to the relevant assets will pass. Under an agreed cash waterfall, withdrawals may only be permitted from these accounts to meet expenditures set out in the latest cash-flow projection (or to a set percentage over and above such figures, say 10%) and, subject to additional restrictions, surpluses after payment of finance costs and funding of any other relevant project accounts can usually be paid out as dividends and used for general corporate purposes.

Additional accounts might include:

- onshore and offshore accounts in jurisdictions where lenders are uncomfortable with all of the cash flows sitting onshore;
- cash lock-up accounts to which all free cash must be transferred in the event of certain cover ratios being breached;
- a debt service reserve account to which funds representing a certain period of debt service (typically three to six months) must be kept at all times;
- a completion reserve account to include a minimum balance to cover cost-overruns on development projects; and
- an equity reserve account in which equity monies are held to ensure an agreed equity to debt ratio is maintained.

4.7 Paying down to the borrowing base amount

As the borrowing base amount is recalculated periodically during the life of the loan, the facility will be a revolving facility (as opposed to a term loan which is typically only seen on single-asset project financing), but usually with the lenders' commitment reduced on six-monthly reduction dates. On a reduction date, the loan will need to be paid down to the lower of:

- the reduced commitment amount; and
- the borrowing base amount (be that PLCR-based, or the lower of PLCR- and LLCR-based).

In the past this has occasionally been only to the extent that the borrower has available free cash flow, as a nod to limited recourse project financing techniques, but borrowers now have to settle immediately, albeit perhaps within an extended grace period in the case of an unexpected drop in petroleum prices (and therefore the borrowing base amount) to the extent a pay-down is larger than previously projected in the model.

4.8 Hedging

RBLs always include a hedging policy. There may be requirements for hedging petroleum prices in respect of a certain proportion of projected production. In times of strong petroleum prices, borrowers have been largely successful in resisting specific requirements with the result that there is only a high level agreed hedging policy in the documentation, the only hard limits being on the maximum proportion of reserves which can be hedged so as to prevent over-hedging, with no minimum requirements. The hedging policy is usually permissive regarding interest rate and foreign exchange hedging and, unlike classic project financing, rarely mandates any such swaps.

4.9 Borrower group structures

A key issue when contemplating an RBL transaction is the position within the group structure of the company or companies owning the assets which are to be financed, and which companies within the group are to be borrowers and guarantors under the facility. This is easy enough in the case of a single-asset financing which may be undertaken by a special purpose company, as is typical in a classic project financing.

For a portfolio RBL, the assets are likely to be held by a number of field companies, at least some of which will also own non-borrowing base assets, for example exploration and appraisal assets.

In a whole group financing, every company in the group is a party to the loan documentation, providing cross-guarantees and security. This structure tends to be appropriate for relatively small cap companies with a significant proportion of development assets, where the lenders might expect the whole group to stand behind the financing. Or it may be appropriate for larger companies with a wide portfolio of assets which want to achieve beneficial borrowing terms more akin to a corporate facility.

The limited borrowing base group approach is used where there is a desire for only a certain sub-group in the corporate structure to be party to the loan documentation, and in this respect the loan takes on a quasi-project finance flavour, with typically no or only limited recourse to the parent or other parts of the group.

4.10 Non-recourse subsidiaries

The concept of non-recourse subsidiaries is used where there are companies located in the group structure such that they would otherwise fall to be obligors under the terms of the finance documents, but which the borrower wants to exclude from the reach of the facility. This is usually so that the relevant subsidiary can carry out – and finance – other projects independently. Restrictions are imposed under the finance documents which insulate the obligors under the finance documents from the creditors of the non-recourse subsidiaries and limit the dealings of the obligors with the non-recourse subsidiaries. These restrictions mitigate the risk of money leaking from the borrower group other than as a distribution permitted by the finance documents. It is rarely the case that it will be feasible to carry out a wholly non-recourse project financing in such a subsidiary, so consent of the RBL lenders is still likely to be required in practice for such a financing.

4.11 Security

(a) Typical RBL security package

In RBL deals, there is often a relatively light security package, including only perhaps share pledges, a charge over accounts (which will be located in a jurisdiction where appropriate security rights exist), assignment of insurances and hedging agreements and, probably, in jurisdictions which recognise the concept, a floating charge over the assets of the borrower. Since the global financial crisis, banks have generally become more conservative in approach and may be more inclined to require whatever security can be practically granted under local law such as assignments or pledges of key project documents and local insurances. We examine asset security in (b) below and insurance in section 5 below.

(b) Asset-level security and lenders' concerns

The lenders' main objectives when considering a security package are to:

- trump unsecured creditors;

- protect assets from actions by unsecured creditors;
- confer control of the company on a default; and
- enable sale of a company as a growing concern.

Often security is only taken defensively as, in practice, enforcement may be unrealistic, particularly over oil and gas fields where governmental consents to any sales or transfers will invariably be required (outside of the United States). Indeed, in many jurisdictions it is difficult, in practice, to take security over the licence, production sharing contract or concession due to the requirement for government and other counterparty consents.

In a classic project financing, lenders try to go further and ensure that effective security can be taken over all project contracts and that key project contracts remain in place in one form or another if and when lenders enforce their security. They achieve the latter by entering into direct agreements with key project counterparties to control termination of the underlying project documents. RBL lenders may be prepared to close a financing on the basis of no security being taken over the licence, production sharing contract or concession and other project agreements, or an undertaking from the borrower to use reasonable endeavours to obtain any necessary counterparty consent for the granting of security. RBL lenders do not typically require direct agreements or amendments to project documents. For assets on the UK continental shelf, lenders are comfortable with the history of the government's and other industry players' involvement. A more conservative approach may be necessary in other jurisdictions with less experience of international debt financings.

For English companies, cross-guarantees and security granted are likely to be of little use for lenders in appointing a receiver (the most bank-friendly type of insolvency practitioner) since sweeping changes in 2003. Banks have been willing to live with this, perhaps emphasising the point that their principal protection is through the operation of the borrowing base itself. However, this relatively relaxed attitude to security has been tested since the global financial crisis, with instances of RBL borrowers over-extending themselves by incurring excessive expenditure outside the context of the borrowing base assets. RBL lenders have greater incentive nowadays to take whatever security it is practicable to take.

(c) Security over licences in the United Kingdom

Petroleum assets on the UK continental shelf are managed by way of a licence-based regime with joint operating agreements (JOAs) entered into by the parties to a licence. The terms of the licences prevent the granting of security except with the consent of the Secretary of State, who in the past gave individual formal written consents to the creation of security over licence interests. However, in recent years this cumbersome process has been replaced by a general standing open permission, which is a consent by the Secretary of State to the creation of security over licences by way of fixed or floating charge, with certain notification conditions. The consent is stated to cover crystallisation of a floating charge into a fixed charge. A 2012 amendment clarified that any security whereby the licensee's interest in the licence is assigned on entering into the security is excluded from the permission, which applies to Scots law assignments in security. Under the RBL structure, usually only a floating charge will be taken over the licence interest and the borrower's interest under the JOA, which is permitted. Secretary of State consent would still be required on enforcement of the licence in relation to transferring it to another party.

Whether the co-licensee's consent would also be required would depend on the provisions of the JOA's assignment clause. Co-licensees may also have pre-emption rights under the JOAs which apply in such circumstances.

UK continental shelf licence security is only defensive in that it can prevent others dealing with assets, but not give effective control to lenders over the assets on enforcement. Nevertheless, it is superior to virtually any other jurisdiction (outside the United States) in that taking security is easy and in the context of enforcement there is a long history of asset trading in the United Kingdom with many potential buyers for distressed assets, and banks have a high degree of confidence that the Secretary of State will approve proposed transfers.

(d) Security in other jurisdictions

A floating charge is a common law concept available to lenders only in countries which have inherited an English law based legal regime. Given that many of the jurisdictions playing host to RBL financings nowadays are civil law based, it is often not possible to create floating security over the assets. Lenders would ideally like to see equivalent security, involving taking security in some form over the licence interests, contracts and other assets. In many jurisdictions this is difficult or even practically impossible and a cost–benefit analysis will be required to decide if it is worthwhile or practicable to take such asset security.

For example, in Norway the market view is generally that asset-level security is not worth taking because of the difficulty of obtaining consents and adjusting the finance documentation so that enforcement can only be taken on a Norwegian asset-related default. In the Netherlands there is a debate over whether even defensive security can be taken without breaking the relevant licence terms. In North African jurisdictions including, for example, Tunisia and Egypt, as well as in West African jurisdictions such as Gabon, it is possible in theory at least – subject to governmental and other counterparty consent – to take security over the production-sharing contracts or licences and other local law project agreements. However, the process for taking perfected security can be extremely cumbersome. North America has a different legislative set-up and, for onshore assets at least, asset level security can generally be easily granted.

4.12 Groupwide liquidity testing

Because of some bad experiences in the wake of the global financial crisis, RBL lenders now require group-wide liquidity testing. This focuses on any expenditure incurred across the borrower's wider corporate group, in the hope of controlling that risk. This typically requires a group-wide cash flow forecast to be produced every six months demonstrating that liabilities can be met when due over the next 12 months. This gives lenders advance warning of overreach on a group-wide basis, which is not always picked up in the model which focuses on the borrowing base assets.

4.13 Defensive features leading to a low rate of lender losses on RBL transactions

Debt sizing on RBL transactions is of critical importance to lenders, and many conservative features in combination make it unlikely that lenders will be left out of pocket in the event of a default. We have touched on some of these already but by way of summary:

- banks use forward curves of petroleum prices (the price deck) in the model which are more conservative than mid-market views, typically by at least 10–20%;
- banks use a reserve tail feature and so effectively refuse to lend against the final 20–25% of a field's or portfolio's reserves as at the date of the loan;
- banks use PLCR/LLCR mechanics as described to only lend against two-thirds of reserves or less;
- banks only lend against P90 reserves, or perhaps P50 reserves for producing assets, and may have discretion to risk (ie, decrease) reserves further than those contained in a third party reserve report; and
- banks discount cash flows by a rate that is typically at least as high as the weighted average cost of debt in the NPV calculations. Bankers may also build significant cost contingencies into the cash flows on development projects.

5. Bankability and due diligence

5.1 Bankability issues

It is often said that bankability is an art, not a science. As the requirements of borrowers have changed, so the market's view of what is a bankable structure has shifted to accommodate, so far as possible, those requirements. Examples include capex add-bank as mentioned above, a balloon repayment at maturity (so long as the cover ratios imply that a refinancing at maturity will be feasible) and adding limited borrowing capacity in respect of pre-development sanctioned reserves/resources, which has made a comeback into a small number of larger RBL and quasi-RBL facilities in recent years. The art is for an arranging bank to put together a deal which gives the borrower what it needs, but where any variation from the norm can be justified to ensure that the financing is still readily saleable in the bank market.

The lenders will need to be able to rely on a legal due diligence report prepared in respect of the assets being financed. This may involve commissioning a new due diligence report or updating an existing due diligence report (with a letter of reliance) which may have been prepared in connection with a listing of the company or the acquisition of those assets. In the latter case, a typical caveat in the reliance letter is that the report has been prepared for purposes of such a listing or acquisition, rather than the debt financing, but banks are usually attuned to this issue. Similarly, lenders will also typically commission technical and insurance reports and, as mentioned previously, will have reliance on an independent reserves report. We will look at a small number of key due diligence matters in more detail.

5.2 Licences/production sharing contracts/concessions

Lenders will focus on establishing title to the assets, and will seek comfort that the terms of any licences, production-sharing contracts or concession agreements (RBL techniques can be applied to assets governed by any of these) are sufficiently robust, free of restrictions on granting security over the assets and free from hair trigger defaults leading to counterparty termination rights. The due diligence report may also typically report on term, consideration, relinquishment, work obligations and profit sharing under production-sharing contracts. Debate can be had on the scope of previous transfers of interests over which due diligence should be undertaken, which can have a significant effect on the amount of work involved.

5.3 Joint operating agreements

The focus for lenders on JOAs is often the assignment clauses, particularly if the security package includes assignments of project agreements as opposed to just a floating charge. Usually assignment by way of security is permitted provided such security is expressly subordinated to the rights of the counterparties to the JOA (which is the case anyway). The due diligence report may also typically report on operatorship, insurance, work programmes, voting, default, and termination and decommissioning security.

5.4 Offtake/sales/marketing and transportation contracts

Lenders will focus on how secure the cash flows are for petroleum sales, and again on restrictions on creating security, and on the creditworthiness of the offtakers. Lenders will generally only count the reserves of a gas asset for debt sizing purposes to the extent they are satisfied with the offtake arrangements. Lenders will also be concerned, particularly for gas assets, that the hydrocarbons can be transferred from the site of production to either the nearest hub, processing plant, refinery or power station.

5.5 Public international law issues/treaties

Where an oil or gas field straddles a maritime boundary between two sovereign states (eg, the United Kingdom and Norway in the North Sea) then recourse may need to be had to relevant treaties governing the border. In some cases the countries may have agreed a general process on how to unitise the field. In other cases (perhaps in the Middle East or Africa), the borrower may be proceeding to exploit the field from one side of the boundary without a unitisation, but in compliance with the relevant treaty by for example only drilling further than the minimum specified distance from the border. In the latter case, lenders will need to make an assessment of the risk of a dispute arising which may interfere with the development of, and production from, the field.

5.6 Environmental and social issues

Environmental concerns and requirements vary from project to project but are always a critical issue for lenders, in part because of the reputational risk of being seen to fund an environmental disaster. Compliance with the Equator Principles is frequently a condition precedent and/or covenant requirement in RBL facilities. They seek to regulate the approach of financial institutions to environmental and social issues and are a voluntary code of conduct. Most commercial banks active in the RBL market have agreed to abide by them and this means that borrowers effectively have to comply with them too. The Equator Principles recognise that lenders are able to influence the environmental and social aspects of a project. They are substantially based on World Bank/IFC policies and apply in the case of project finance loans to projects with a total capital cost of more than $10 million or, in the case of project-related corporate loans (which is the category into which RBLs are more likely to fall), to facilities with a loan amount of at least $100 million.

The Equator Principles divide projects into three categories based on their likely environmental impact, and typically an environmental and social impact assessment (ESIA) is required. The ESIA examines potential negative and positive environmental and social impacts and recommends measures to prevent, minimise or compensate for them and to improve environmental and social performance. Affected groups, including indigenous people and local NGOs, must be consulted as part of the process and the final report must be published. In addition, an environmental and social management system (ESMS) and an environmental and social management plan (ESMP) may be required, which must draw on the conclusions of the ESIA and address mitigation, action plans, monitoring, management of risk and time schedules.

Lenders may impose documentary requirements such as proof of compliance with the ESMP and may require an independent environmental expert to be appointed to report on compliance.

5.7 Insolvency and administration

Insolvency risk and lenders' rights on insolvency, and in particular relating to the enforcement of security, are critical considerations for lenders and will vary depending on the jurisdiction(s) of incorporation of the borrower group, and potentially the jurisdiction(s) where the assets are located.

It is difficult to make any general statements but lenders tend to view common law jurisdictions more favourably than civil law jurisdictions. Reasons include greater certainty that contractual rights will be enforced as stated in documentation, and the existence of floating charge asset level security.

The security regime in the United Kingdom currently balances the law in favour of the appointment of an administrator and away from a receiver. In English law, an administrator acts for all of a company's creditors and tries to continue to run a company as a going concern, whereas a receiver acts in the interests of the security holders who appoint it.

Administration is seen by lenders as an inferior remedy, because when an administration order is made, enforcement of security and the institution or continuation of any legal process against the company without the permission of the court or the consent of an administrator is not allowed. Lenders are now entitled to appoint a receiver in only certain specified situations, none of which is likely to be applicable in the context of an RBL facility, except perhaps in the context of a single-asset project financing style transaction. This is due in part to the fact that North Sea projects have not typically included step-in rights for lenders. However, generally a floating charge will at least give lenders the right to choose the identity of an administrator.

5.8 Technical due diligence

Reservoir risk is typically one of the most significant for lenders and will need to be understood in detail, particularly on development heavy portfolios. The scope of technical due diligence required on an RBL deal will depend in part on whether arranging banks already have in-house engineers. Lenders may in any case need additional expertise, for example if there is a novel technical aspect to the development plan or if a particular recovery technique has not been attempted in the basin in which the asset is located. Also relevant will be the number and diversity of assets comprising the borrowing base and proportion of assets in production as opposed to a development.

5.9 Insurance due diligence

(a) Types required

Lenders typically commission a report by an insurance adviser covering insurances in place and whether they are considered sufficient given industry norms. Insurance typically required by lenders on upstream oil and gas financings during the operating phase follows a fairly standard energy package which may incorporate:

- property all risks;
- cost of control of wells;
- comprehensive general liability;
- marine hull;
- protection and indemnity;
- directors' and officers' liability; and
- all other insurances required by local legislation or the project agreements.

Development projects will, in addition, call for contractor's all risk insurance.

Lenders may also request delay in start-up and business interruption insurance, terrorism/sabotage insurance and (depending on the jurisdiction) political risk insurance to cover expropriation, non-convertibility of local currencies into hard currencies and breach of contract by a governmental authority or public body. These are expensive, and often successfully resisted by borrowers. MIGA, the insurance arm of the World Bank, is on occasion approached to insure against certain types of political risk.

The operator of a field would often take out the energy package insurance on behalf of the joint venturers, and the lenders will usually be satisfied with this arrangement.

(b) Recognising the lenders' interests

In the case of insurances taken out by the borrower, the lenders will require the security trustee on behalf of the lenders to be named as loss payee and possibly co-insured on property damage type insurances and additional insured on liability type insurances. In the case of insurances taken out by the operator on behalf of the joint venturers, the lenders should accept that this approach may not be practicable. As mentioned in section 4 above, lenders will also often take security over insurances, perfection of which usually requires notices to be served on each underlying insurer.

(c) ***Brokers' letters***

A typical condition precedent to an RBL facility is provision of a letter from the insurance brokers of the borrower confirming, at the minimum:

- the level of cover;
- that the insurances required by the facility agreement are in place and effective;
- that all premiums have been paid; and
- that the notations recognising the interests of the security trustee as required by the facility agreement have been endorsed on the policies.

Brokers should be able to provide such a letter, though it often requires negotiation as to the exact wording used.

(d) ***Reinsurance and cut-through***

Where local law requires that all or part of the insurances are taken up by local insurance companies, invariably lenders require that such risks be reinsured in a major foreign insurance market because the local providers may not be sufficiently creditworthy. A contract whereby the lenders can cut through the local insurance policy to the reinsurer is typically given, at least where governed by New York law, as this may be ineffective on the insolvency of the local insurer under English law. So it is often a requirement for the borrower or the banks to have an assignment by the local insurer of the reinsurance policy, or even a direct agreement with the local insurer and foreign reinsurer, whereby the foreign reinsurer would pay the borrower/banks direct. Cut-through arrangements in certain jurisdictions (eg, Thailand) leave a risk that if the local insurer becomes insolvent the reinsurer may also be faced with a claim from a liquidator and have to pay twice, so can be problematic to agree. RBL lenders will look at all the circumstances and may take a more relaxed view than project finance lenders, depending on factors such as the spread of jurisdictions of assets in the borrower base.

6. Optional extras to the basic RBL product

An RBL facility can be adjusted in a myriad of ways to meet borrower needs. We explore a handful in more detail.

6.1 Letter of credit facility for decommissioning security liabilities

RBLs often incorporate a letter of credit (LC) facility, the purpose of which is usually to enable a borrower to meet its decommissioning obligations. In some cases, an RBL facility can be predominantly or even exclusively for the purpose of posting LCs for decommissioning security. This has become a particularly acute issue in the UK continental shelf in recent years due to maturating assets and related infrastructure and a draconian legal regime which results in vendors, co-venturers and government all potentially requiring security to be given by new parties to a licence in respect of projected decommissioning costs. Lenders, larger co-venturers and, in particular, the government all take a cautious approach on the level of security to be provided. Purchasers and smaller co-venturers take the opposite view, as the costs of providing security result in a substantial liability on their balance sheets, limiting their ability to invest in new assets.

Fortunately, the introduction of a standard form decommissioning security agreement has largely mitigated the risk of having to post double or triple security, although top-ups are still not unheard of. Security in the North Sea is typically by letter of credit or, where the credit standing of the parent is sufficiently robust, parent company guarantee.

Another recent positive change is that the government has introduced the option for North Sea interest holders to enter into private law contracts with government, known as 'decommissioning relief deeds'. These guarantee that the current rate of decommissioning tax relief will be available in future. The introduction of decommissioning relief deeds is leading to a cut of 50% (or more for petroleum revenue tax (PRT) fields) in the amount of decommissioning security being required. Security was previously posted on a pre-tax basis as the view was that government could not be trusted not to reduce tax relief in future. This is a world first and it will be interesting to see if any other countries follow suit.

It will be interesting to see if debt facilities can be made available to companies backed up by the government's obligations to refund decommissioning costs, with principles similar to exploration financing facilities used by Norwegian companies effectively secured against a government commitment to refund 78% of exploration capex.

In an RBL LC facility, if decommissioning costs are included in the cash flows used to calculate the NPVs then the LC can usually be issued without counting towards the borrowing base amount, but still of course subject to the aggregate commitments of the lenders. Conversely, if the decommissioning costs are not included in the NPVs then the LC will count towards the borrowing base amount. The former can be advantageous to borrowers because the discount rate applied to the cash flows usually results in higher effective borrowing capacity.

Due to the usual operator's annual re-determination process as to decommissioning costs for a particular field, lenders may be requested to post an LC greater than that for which they have internal approval if the size of the abandonment liability under the decommissioning security agreement goes up. Conversely, if the re-determined decommissioning cost goes down, the borrower may be over-collateralising. A partial solution, offered by lenders who appreciate that an LC may be unlikely to be called on years before decommissioning work commences, is to document a base case cash collateralisation build-up requirement based on agreed ratios.

Getting the balance right between the lenders', borrowers' and government's interests is crucial as acquisition deals are being done, or potentially done, on more marginal fields where costs are finely balanced.

6.2 Senior stretch

Occasionally (and less frequently after the global financial crisis), senior debt in an RBL will be divided into base senior and senior stretch (or conforming and non-conforming) tranches, the stretch tranche being lent against a higher percentage of the NPV of future net revenues, with the excess being in effect the size of the stretch tranche. A higher margin and looser debt sizing ratios will apply to the stretch tranche. Usually only lenders with in-house technical skills tend to be able to lend over and above the base senior debt as they have the know-how to assess which assets can support the extra debt.

6.3 Private acquisition finance

The use of the RBL facility as a pure acquisition financing tool is now well established and, with many acquisition transactions being managed as auctions, and particularly with the addition of junior tranches, is well suited to maximising the debt available to the borrower. In this case the RBL can be sized based on the prospective assets and this structure has been seen, for example, in recent Nigerian deals.

A conventional RBL facility can also be used for acquisitions where it is based on a portfolio consisting predominantly of producing assets providing ample free cash flow over and above projected debt service.

In the scenario of the transformational acquisition undertaken by a small independent oil and gas company, the principal value will be found in the target assets. To avoid pre-emption and other contract and licence transfer issues and also maybe for tax reasons (eg, inheriting tax losses in the target), the acquisition will typically involve a share purchase of one or more asset-holding target companies. The lenders will want the target companies to give upstream security over their assets and a cross-guarantee covering any borrowings under the facility which, in certain jurisdictions, is restricted by laws relating to corporate benefit, financial assistance and reduction of net assets. In the United Kingdom, the giving of financial assistance by a private target company to an acquirer for the purposes of assisting the acquisition of the target's shares is no longer prohibited, which avoids the need for a costly whitewash procedure. Corporate benefit issues would still be relevant, but it should be fairly straightforward to demonstrate adequate corporate benefit for a subsidiary in securing the obligations of its parent, given support provided by the parent and the wider group to that subsidiary. In a large number of other jurisdictions, financial assistance, and the demonstration of corporate benefit, are more difficult issues. For example, in Norway upstream guarantees must be limited to the value of the loan outstanding received by the Norwegian subsidiary. Other European civil law jurisdictions and Nigeria pose similar issues, making asset level security difficult to take.

6.4 Public company bid financing

RBLs can on rare occasions also be used to fund bids for public companies and some particular considerations and risks apply in addition to those in the preceding paragraph.

(a) Conditionality

In recent years there has been a lot of consolidation among the numerous smaller independents including, in particular, those listed on junior stock exchanges such as the London Stock Exchange's Alternative Investment Market (AIM) and the TSX Venture Exchange in Toronto. A key factor in UK public company bids is the lack of conditionality that the lenders can place on the availability of funds, once the offer has been announced. Although the offer will invariably be made subject to numerous conditions, including no material adverse change in the target's business, in practice the UK Takeover Panel will not allow bidders to rely on them. Similarly, the bid financing facility agreement will contain some events of default, but in practice – other than in the case of insolvency of the acquirer's acquisition vehicle (which is unlikely, given that it will be a newco) and illegality – the banks would be required to fund through a default. This may be unfamiliar territory for oil and gas teams at banks which are not existing players in the public company acquisition financing market.

(b) Limited due diligence

An associated issue on a public company acquisition is the relative lack of ability, particularly on a hostile bid, to undertake due diligence over and above publicly available information. This may be adequate to allow the acquirers and their bankers to make a proper assessment of what debt structure the business will support, but it may be more challenging to use only such publicly available information to build the sophisticated computer model used by oil and gas banks on RBLs. Having said that, if the target assets in question are in mature basins, they may have been financed several times over in the past, so banks which are active in the market will have a good understanding of them. In practice, hostile bids are almost unheard of in the E&P sector, with acquirers generally carrying out a full due diligence process, partly due to the requirements of their funders.

6.5 Refinancings and amendments to key terms

RBL facilities are typically five to seven years with no prepayment fees. It may come as a surprise, therefore, to learn that they are usually refinanced far in advance of maturity. Lenders positively encourage this as they can recycle their capital and gain upfront fees more often (and more regularly than the bulk of the wider project finance market where tenors are often 15–25 years or longer).

Reasons for undertaking a refinancing include:

- a desire to lock in debt with as long a tenor as possible while markets are open;
- to achieve a better margin if assets have completed so that the asset portfolio is more weighted towards production; and
- to relax distribution restrictions allowing dividends to be paid to shareholders.

Special factors to consider on a refinancing include, in particular:

- if the syndicate of lenders is materially changing;
- the timing mechanics for repayment of the existing indebtedness;
- the release of existing security;
- the closure of existing bank accounts with the opening of new bank accounts; and
- the termination or novation of existing secured hedging.

There is a technical chicken-and-egg problem in that existing security cannot be released until the existing debt is repaid, but this can only be done from the proceeds of the new debt, which cannot technically be drawn while existing debt and security are in place. The usual solution is for the new lender to permit a utilisation request to be submitted on being satisfied that the existing indebtedness will be repaid and existing security released upon the first utilisation under the new facility being made.

If material changes are being made to an RBL facility by amendment, rather than a full refinancing, consideration should be given as to whether fresh security or guarantees are required. As material variations of the principal contracts can discharge guarantees unless consent is given to the variation by the guarantor, material variations are generally done with contemporaneous consent from all of the guarantors.

7. Other debt products and interface with RBL facilities

As mentioned earlier, borrowers have various debt finance options available to them. We examine some others here, including as to how they might interface with an RBL facility. Multi-source financings are becoming more common, even outside the United States and so, increasingly, subordination and intercreditor issues need to be understood by RBL banks.

7.1 Pre-development bridge financing

The debt options for a company whose portfolio consists only of assets which have been successfully appraised, but as yet do not have final development plan (FDP) approval are limited, particularly following the global financial crisis. The company may have already exhausted the equity markets. For example, London's AIM market, popular with start-up oil and gas companies, has not been consistently open to such companies in recent years. Borrowers can also turn to the now very select group of lenders willing to make available short-term bridge financing, the bridge to be taken out by way of an RBL at such time as the borrower has sufficient borrowing base capacity under standard NPV calculations when the assets have achieved FDP. This is seen on acquisitions, and in recent years on assets in Israel and West Africa.

Lenders providing such bridges need to be satisfied that everything is in place to ensure that the borrower will be able to bring its pre-development assets to FDP approval, and then onwards into production, at sufficient levels and within the right time frame to enable a refinancing within a satisfactorily short period, typically 12 to 18 months. Examples include in the case of oil to be produced from an inland location, lenders being assured that it will be feasible to transport that oil to market, or in the case of a gas field, if regulatory approval is required for the gas to be sold into a domestic market, lenders being assured that there is no reason why such approval will not be forthcoming. A bridge financing should be relatively quick and easy to complete, but a thorough due diligence exercise will need to be undertaken to satisfy the lenders on the refinancing risk. Terms, such as margin step-ups and cash sweeps, will encourage refinancing prior to the full term.

7.2 UDAB/PSF facilities and value given to pre-development reserves in RBLs

A further development on the bridge facility which appeared shortly before the onset of the global financial crisis but which has largely disappeared from the market in recent years was the undeveloped asset backed facility/pre-sanction facility (UDAB/PSF), providing bridge financing for pre-development assets, sometimes on a conveyor belt principle (for which see 7.3 below). A structure is established whereby assets are approved as UDAB assets when the lenders are satisfied (as described at 7.1 above) that they qualify for bridge financing. As and when the UDAB assets reach FDP approval, they are moved out of the UDAB facility, with an appropriate portion of the UDAB facility being repaid. The available amount under the UDAB facility is calculated in a highly conservative manner, with the lenders having a wide discretion as to determination of the reserves and NPVs attributable to those assets. Only a few US dollars per barrel value will be permitted and usually only strategically important assets seen as very likely to be sanctioned for development will qualify.

In recent years, this few US dollars per barrel for pre-development resources has returned in a small number of RBLs and quasi-RBLs for larger independents looking to push the amount of senior debt capacity.

There is no particular logic, at least under standard RBL metrics, for the value attributed to such resources, however lenders take the view that the relevant assets would realise at least that dollar amount if sold into the market.

7.3 RBL facility combined with UDAB/PSF

To mitigate the refinancing risk inherent in a UDAB facility, some borrowers put in place an RBL facility at the same time as the UDAB facility, the RBL facility standing ready to receive new assets (subject to the assets meeting specified acceptance conditions and majority bank approval) as they come off the UDAB facility conveyor belt. Alternatively, the UDAB facility may be put in place before the RBL facility, so saving the borrower commitment fees, but increasing the refinancing risk.

7.4 Other junior bank debt

Borrowers may supplement their senior debt with junior or mezzanine bank debt, typically on similar terms albeit with subordination to the senior debt on enforcement of security and perhaps also on repayment, and with debt sized using looser cover ratio tests and at a higher margin. Junior debt is often by way of term loan, rather than the classic RBL revolving loan. Sometimes hedge funds and private equity players provide junior debt, perhaps where the fund is also a shareholder in the borrower.

7.5 Second lien facilities

In the United States and Canada, second lien lending is a well-established market which has in recent years spread to the United Kingdom and the rest of Europe. However, this market has been largely closed, at least to upstream resources companies outside the United States, since the onset of the financial crisis. Second lien loans are seen as a response to a pricing gap in the capital structure that previously existed between senior debt and mezzanine/junior financing. Second lien debt is lien subordinated only, as opposed to debt subordinated mezzanine debt. This means a second lien lender is only required to turn over to the senior lenders proceeds from the enforcement of shared security rather than from any source, including before the enforcement of the common security. Other typical features are a longer maturity than the senior debt, a bullet repayment or limited amortisation and a higher margin incentivising early repayment (although RBL lenders may seek to control this).

In the US market, there are real advantages to the lenders from a bankruptcy law perspective in structuring the security rights in this way. In the United Kingdom this is really a distinction without a difference, so second lien debt is seen by some as an excuse for borrowers to replace classic mezzanine debt and its equity element with a pure subordinated debt tranche, albeit at similar pricing. Nevertheless, in terms of liquidity it is unfortunate that the US second lien market is still arguably missing a trick by not engaging with international oil and gas independents.

7.6 High yield bonds and convertible bonds

Depending on the state of the high yield and convertible bond markets (which are volatile and include seasonal variation), some independents have incorporated the issuance of high yield or convertible bonds as a key part of their capitalisation. The bonds may be listed or, more commonly for smaller companies, privately placed. They are often issued by a finance vehicle subsidiary with the benefit of a guarantee and (if convertible) capable of exchange into the equity of the parent company of the borrower group. An advantage is that investors view convertible bonds as quasi-equity so the covenant package tends to be rather light, and should not interfere with the ability of the group to raise senior bank debt. Even for non-convertible, high yield bonds, the covenant packages are rather loose. The bond debt is often injected at a higher level in the group than where the assets sit, which can obviate the need for an intercreditor arrangement, particularly if the bonds have a longer term than a co-existing RBL. In recent years, a handful of international companies have managed to tap the US High Yield Market and this trend is likely to continue, intermittently at least. These issuances tend to benefit from guarantees from the operating companies in the group, such guarantees being subordinated by means of an intercreditor agreement to bank lenders.

7.7 Norwegian bonds

The Norwegian bond market has long been a preferred source of finance for Norwegian E&P and oil field service companies, given the lighter terms and streamlined issuance process as compared with some other forms of financing. In the last few years this market has also become available at times for international sub-investment grade E&P companies, a small number of which have grasped the opportunity to issue fixed rate bonds at favourable coupons. However, the market is often closed.

As with other varieties of bonds, issuing companies considering such a bond need to weigh up what happens if developments do not go to plan. It may not be as easy to obtain consent from a group of non-bank lenders for a waiver or extension as it would be if dealing with just one bank or a fairly small syndicate of commercial banks. With Norwegian bonds being held in the bond clearing system through nominees, it can be a problem even identifying the beneficial owners of bonds. There is a much smaller but similar bond market in Sweden.

7.8 Raising debt by way of commodity hedging

RBL deals often comprise an element of commodity hedging to increase the borrowing base amount (assuming volumes are hedged at a price higher than the lenders' conservative price deck) and to give lenders comfort that sufficient revenue will be generated to repay debt. Typically, this is through cash-settled pre-paid put options with a counterparty with a sufficiently high credit rating (usually a bank, large trading firm or trading arm of a major oil and gas company). The hedging counterparty will rank equally with the senior RBL lenders and share in the senior security, albeit with constrained voting rights (usually arising only after the hedges have been terminated but payments remain outstanding) and limited rights to terminate the hedging transactions.

Recently, however, commodity hedging has been used on occasion to raise additional funding through the sale by borrowers of pre-paid call options or similar products, where the counterparty in effect pays up front for the right to acquire volumes in future at a cheaper rate than indicated by the forward price curve at the time.

This can give rise to concerns if the borrower's project suffers delay or the expected volumes are not produced, although insurance may mitigate these risks to an extent. If coupled with an RBL, the RBL lenders will want to take account of the call options in their model and ensure that, unlike in the case of normal senior ranking hedge liabilities, the call provider has only second ranking security and is subordinated through an intercreditor agreement.

7.9 Intercreditor arrangements

An intercreditor agreement will be required if funds are being provided from multiple sources which are not structurally subordinated. It may even be required in the case of structurally subordinated debt if its maturity is shorter than that of the RBL facility. RBL lenders dislike refinancing risk, both on RBL debt but especially on any other debt of the borrower. The agreement will typically cover permitted payments under the subordinated debt, which categories of lenders have to agree before any one group can accelerate any debt and take enforcement action and whether or not any group has a veto over a proposed exercise of discretion under other loan documentation with different lenders, and contain provisions on the sharing of recoveries and subordination. Intercreditor agreements can be difficult to negotiate and agreeing the main principles should be prioritised so as not to jeopardise the deal timeline.

As mentioned previously, new sources of debt (and equity) from multilateral agencies/export credit agencies (MLAs/ECAs), such as the International Finance Corporation and the European Bank for Reconstruction and Development, hedge funds, private equity houses, international commodity traders (and even the trading arms of oil and gas majors) and capital market investors have been increasingly available to stronger independents. These can lead to complicated intercreditor arrangements when done in conjunction with an RBL facility.

8. Differences between International RBL and US RBL models

This chapter has focused on the International RBL model. Some of the key differences in the US RBL model (used in the United States and Canada) are as follows:

- *Bankable reserves:* US RBL recognises proved, developed and producing (PDP) and proved development non-producing (PDNP) reserves, rather than the P90/P50 reserves of the International model. PDP and PDNP are as defined by the Securities and Exchange Commission (SEC) and equate approximately to P90 reserves. Sometimes a tiny proportion of debt can also be raised against proved undeveloped reserves (PUDs). This was all driven by SEC rules which, until recently, only permitted E&P companies to report on proved reserves.
- *Security:* US RBL facilities are typically secured by a mortgage on the relevant onshore leases. Security can be enforced without government approval. This is impossible in the vast majority of other jurisdictions where asset level security is defensive at best, taken to ensure that no one else can take the asset without lender approval. This allows US lenders to focus on the value of the collateral, rather than the certainty of future cash flows. Sometimes share security is not required, whereas it is seen as a critical part of the security package in International RBL.
- *Amortisation:* International RBL facilities typically have a fairly linear amortisation schedule after an initial grace period, whereas US RBL facilities often have bullet repayments where the entire principal amount is only repayable at final maturity (although interest will still be serviced throughout the loan life) and lenders take on significant refinancing risk. US terms are up to five years, whereas International RBL facilities are typically five to seven years.
- *Capital structure:* As US RBL takes limited reserves into account (see above) there are deep and competitive mezzanine debt, second lien facility and term loan B markets in the United States to fill the gap in lending capacity. Specialised mezzanine debt institutions dominate the former with the commercial banks seen in the RBL market rarely featuring. Listed borrowers often couple an RBL facility with a high yield bond, which can be secured or unsecured; second ranking if secured where an RBL facility is also present. Institutional investors such as pension companies tend to hold these bonds.
- *Debt sizing features:* In US RBL facilities there is no reference to PLCR or LLCR cover ratios. Banks have far more discretion to decide the borrowing base amount on a semiannual or even quarterly basis. They will give value to differing percentages of PDP, PDNP and PUD reserves, for example 100%, 75% and 50% respectively. They each assess this individually and can disagree with the amount proposed by the borrower or agent bank. Increases to the borrowing base amount must be approved by all lenders (as opposed to two-thirds by commitment in International RBL). Decreases must typically be approved by two-thirds of lenders by commitment. In addition, there is no reserve tail feature in US RBL facilities, projections are run on a pre-tax basis (except for royalties applied at the field level) and the price deck tends to be less conservative than in International RBL facilities.

- *Project accounts:* Project accounts and a regimented cash waterfall do not usually feature in US RBL facilities, although charges over key bank accounts are often included in the security package.
- *Representations and covenants:* US RBL facilities tend to have a lighter touch representations and covenants package, particularly regarding restrictions on financial indebtedness and hedging. An exception, however, is the US model's focus on project documents and controlling certain of the borrower's rights thereunder. The group-wide liquidity testing which is now ubiquitous in International RBL is not a feature in US RBL.

9. Managing an RBL facility through a downturn

This chapter has already mentioned the relatively low historic default rate in the RBL markets and hinted at some of the reasons for this. In summary, in the International RBL market at least, it is largely due to conservative debt sizing and detailed due diligence undertaken on project risks and likely cash flows. However, defaults do occur on occasion, particularly during downturns in international petroleum prices, and this paragraph offers the following list of factors which lenders and borrowers can consider in a stressed or default situation.

- Oil price downturns often provide a double hit to RBL borrowers. The borrowing base amount will be reduced at the next redetermination of the projection just at the time the borrower faces a liquidity crunch from falling revenues. Hedging production can of course be used to mitigate this risk but it can only be used to hold off pressure for so long. This issue can be more acute in the US market where banks have more discretion over the borrowing base amount, a less conservative price deck which is less suited to absorb real world price drops, and a superior security position which may make banks more ready to call a default in the knowledge that they have readily available enforcement options.
- The borrower may be able to cancel or reduce capex commitments on both exploration and development projects, and squeeze suppliers to achieve cost savings in opex. RBL lenders will expect borrowers to make every effort to minimise costs in a stressed situation. Other courses of action will be encouraged such as equity raises, refinancings, taking on new junior ranking debt and selling non-core assets.
- Defaults under RBL facilities may trigger cross-defaults to other debt facilities in the borrower group. Obtaining waivers for these, particularly from bond holders, can be far more onerous than from RBL lenders.
- Distressed debt traders, possibly with 'loan to own' strategies, may buy up debt in oil and gas companies, perhaps with no publicity if done through sub-participation, derivative or other synthetic products. They may be less willing to negotiate waivers than traditional RBL banks.
- Any hedging positions of a borrower may give rise to significant mark-to-market exposures, influencing lender behaviour depending on the security ranking of the hedging.
- In a stressed situation a restructuring of, or change of control in, a borrower may trip termination or pre-emption rights in licences, JOAs, PSCs and other

project documents. This can lead to a loss of assets with limited or zero compensation and negotiating related consents can use up a lot of management time. The US Chapter 11 bankruptcy process includes an automatic stay on terminating contracts but this may not be respected by counterparties with no assets in the United States, even though it purports to have worldwide operation.

- In many jurisdictions the nature of directors' fiduciary duties changes in a stressed situation from focusing on shareholders' interests to those of creditors. In addition, it can be easier for certain transactions, including the taking of security, to be set aside, at least until hardening periods have expired. Lenders will want to avoid effectively becoming shadow directors of their borrowers. Many oil and gas companies operate internationally and often a lowest common denominator approach is taken in terms of the laws of any relevant jurisdictions. Borrowers and their lenders will want to take specialist advice in such circumstances.
- Even if a particular borrower is not stressed, in a price downturn scenario its joint venture partners or key suppliers may be. This can be a source of additional risk, but also of opportunities.

10. Conclusions

The business of financing upstream activities is dynamic, with debt providers and their advisers adapting rapidly to the changing requirements of independent companies, enabling them to exploit the many new opportunities which are arising around the world. Being able to adapt tried-and-tested tools to new market conditions and new territories is where the exciting challenges lie for oil and gas financing specialists. The continued evolution of RBL as a way of catering to the wider needs of independents is a testament to this innovation and has kept RBL in pole position as a source of debt financing. Despite a small number of restructurings in the wake of the global financial crisis and, more recently, with the sharp fall in the oil price beginning in mid-2014, the credit history of the RBL market has remained robust and its future secure.

RBL techniques are being applied in new locations every year and RBL facilities are increasingly seen now as part of a complex capital structure, rather than the sole debt piece. It will be interesting to see how these two elements evolve and what happens as the International and US models increasingly come head to head – in particular in Central and South America and the Gulf of Mexico, where the last in particular is opening up to private investment and attracting interest from independents which might fund themselves in part through RBL debt.

LNG

Nikhil Markanday
Philip Thomson
Ashurst LLP

1. Introduction

1.1 What is LNG?

Liquefied natural gas or LNG is natural gas that has been supercooled to minus 161°C. At that temperature, it turns into liquid, reduces in volume by a factor of 600 and becomes capable of being transported by specially designed ships. On arrival at its destination, LNG can be converted back to its gaseous state.

The LNG industry thus offers a means of transporting gas (in liquid form) long distances by ship. It offers a means of monetising gas reserves that are located far from centres of gas demand. It also offers a means of supplying gas to industrialised economies with limited or no access to domestic or nearby sources of energy.

The first commercial LNG cargo was delivered from Algeria to the United Kingdom in 1964. In 2014, 239.2 million tonnes of LNG were transported,[1] with LNG deliveries representing approximately 10% of the world's gas consumption in 2013[2] with expected annual growth of 4.3%.[3] The biggest consumers of LNG have long been the industrialised but resource-poor economies of North-East Asia (Japan, South Korea and Taiwan).

As a result of growth in the volumes of LNG produced and sold and technological developments, the LNG industry has evolved from a niche industry dominated by the oil and gas majors and certain national oil companies supplying energy to a few resource-poor economies on relatively inflexible terms, to a larger-scale industry with a broader range of stakeholders supplying LNG to more economies and on more flexible terms. This development is expected to continue.

1.2 The LNG value chain

In simple terms, the LNG industry comprises a series of value chains with links as follows:

- gas production;
- gas transportation by pipeline to the liquefaction plant;

1 International Group of Liquefied Natural Gas Importers, "The LNG Industry in 2014", available at www.giignl.org/sites/default/files/PUBLIC_AREA/Publications/giignl_2015_annual_report.pdf.
2 World Energy Council, World Energy Resources 2013 Survey, available at www.worldenergy.org/publications/2013/world-energy-resources-2013-survey/.
3 BP Energy Outlook 2035, February 2015, available at www.bp.com/content/dam/bp/pdf/Energy-economics/energy-outlook-2015/Energy_Outlook_2035_booklet.pdf.

- liquefaction;
- transportation by LNG tanker; and
- regasification and delivery of regasified LNG to market.

Again, in simple terms, each link of the chain is dependent on the others. For example, if commissioning of the pipeline supplying gas to the liquefaction plant is delayed, it will be impossible to deliver regasified LNG to market (wherever that may be).

Having said that, as the LNG industry has grown and matured in recent decades, it has become more flexible. For example, in the case of a delay in commissioning of the into-plant pipeline, a liquefaction plant owner may be able to access cargoes in the LNG spot market in order to meet its obligations to deliver LNG to the regasification terminal.

Such mitigants may give practical comfort. However, sponsors wishing to monetise natural gas reserves by means of LNG will wish to see that there is a robust value chain which, after taking into account the costs (including capex, opex and financing costs) associated with each segment of the value chain, will allow regasified LNG to compete in the relevant downstream market.

1.3 Financing LNG infrastructure

The infrastructure that is unique to the LNG industry (ie, liquefaction plants, LNG tankers and regasification terminals) is capital intensive and can generate long-term stable cash flow. For these reasons, it lends itself to being project financed where the financiers rely on the cash flows generated by the assets being financed with limited support from sponsors.

While project finance has been the predominant financing technique, some infrastructure, especially in the regasification sector, has been financed on a corporate basis.

2. Structures

While trends have developed in the LNG industry regarding the structuring of projects, there is no one-size-fits-all model structure. Each LNG project must, by necessity, benefit from a bespoke structure. In principle, there are perhaps two fundamental structural issues which need to be resolved at an early stage when developing an LNG project. The first relates to the sponsor's appetite to invest at different links of the chain (ie, the integrated versus non-integrated structure) and the second relates to which stakeholder takes the risk and reward associated with ownership of the gas molecules (ie, the tolling versus merchant model).

A further structural issue to be resolved is the requirement to select the most appropriate corporate structure to be used in the gas production, gas transportation and liquefaction links of the LNG chain (although this can only really be resolved once the two fundamental structural questions mentioned above have been settled).

We explore these issues in more detail below.

2.1 How integrated along the value chain?

The threshold question for the largest sponsors is how far up and down the value chain will they invest. Some sponsors have sought to invest at all stages of the LNG value chain from well-head to the downstream market. However, in recent years, sponsors of the liquefaction and regasification infrastructure have increasingly been different entities operating different business models.

Even so, the issue remains whether the gas production, gas transportation and liquefaction links of the value chain are integrated into a single project (see Figure 1 below) or developed as separate projects with separate sponsors and linked only by contract (principally a gas supply agreement) (see Figure 2 below).

Figure 1: Fully integrated project

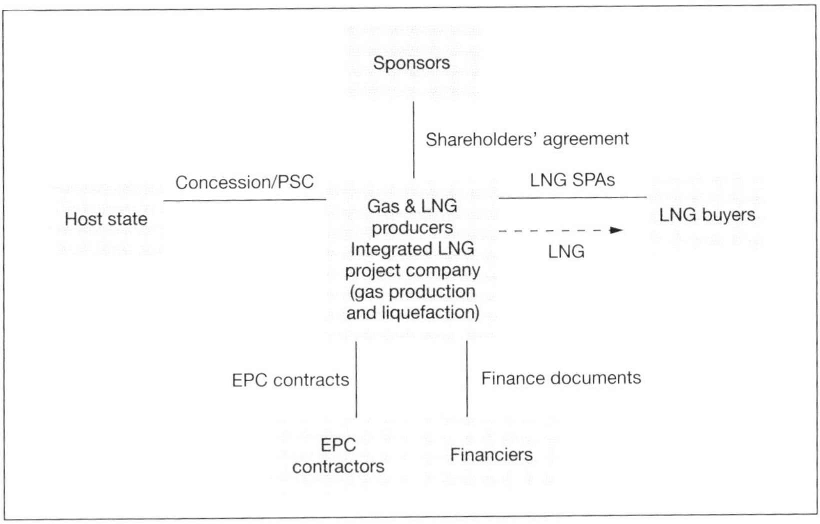

Figure 2: Non-integrated project

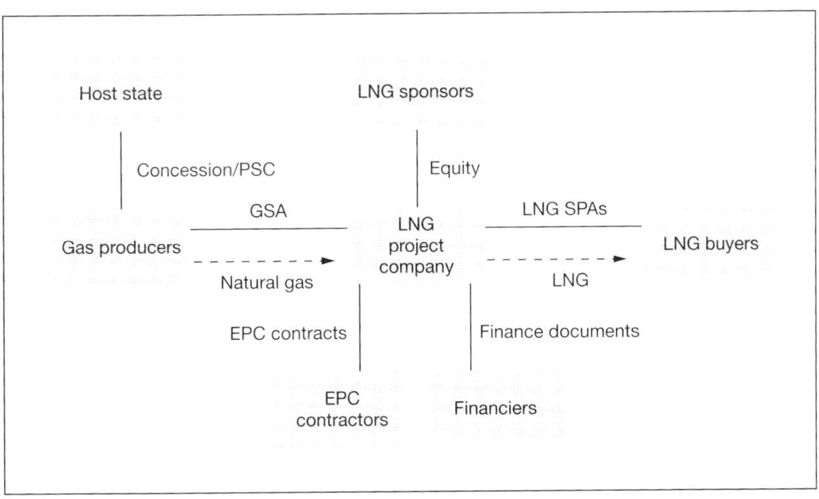

Factors influencing the outcome on this structural point include:

- whether the liquefaction plant takes gas from a single source or acts as an aggregator processing natural gas from multiple licence areas or blocks;
- the extent to which the sponsors developing the gas production project are aligned with those developing the liquefaction infrastructure;
- whether the sponsors can access a single pool of liquidity (even if from multiple sources) sufficient to finance both projects or whether they prefer to finance the two projects separately (in which case issues on project risk and the impact of those issues on potentially competing financiers will need careful analysis);
- whether the host country's regulatory regime applicable to exploration and production can apply to liquefaction, as well as the requirements of the host government in terms of backing into the assets; and
- the applicable tax regime.

As regards project financing, in principle, either structure can be made to be bankable, although the non-integrated structure in Figure 2 may raise additional complexities. For example, it will be necessary to agree the allocation of value between the upstream and liquefaction projects in the gas supply agreement. Likewise, the involvement of different financiers for the upstream development and the liquefaction plant will invariably lead to a more challenging implementation of the financing (see the intercreditor consideration point discussed at 3.4(d) below); whereas an integrated project structure lends itself to being financed by a common group of financiers. In an integrated project structure, all of the project assets and cash flows are integrated, developed and operated under a single concession with a single, common pool of security for the financiers.

2.2 Who takes commodity risk?

The second structural issue applies equally to the liquefaction and regasification infrastructure. That is, should the infrastructure owner also own the natural gas it is processing? The LNG project company in Figure 2 is operating on the merchant model because it is buying the feed gas under the gas supply agreement and selling the LNG under the LNG sale and purchase agreement.

Alternatively, the liquefaction infrastructure owner's business model may be to operate as a service provider. Under this model, it receives a fee for processing natural gas into LNG which is owned by a third party (ie, its customer). See, for example, Figure 3 as applied to a liquefaction project.

The same structural choice arises in the regasification segment of the chain, although the flow of the commodity is in reverse (ie, from LNG to natural gas).

Factors which can affect this point include:

- Risk appetite: The merchant structure implies a higher risk profile for the liquefaction infrastructure than the tolling structure. This is because, in principle, the project company is liable for failure to perform under the LNG sale and purchase agreement even if its non-performance is caused by the gas supplier's breach of the gas supply agreement. In practice, sponsors will seek

Figure 3: LNG tolling structure

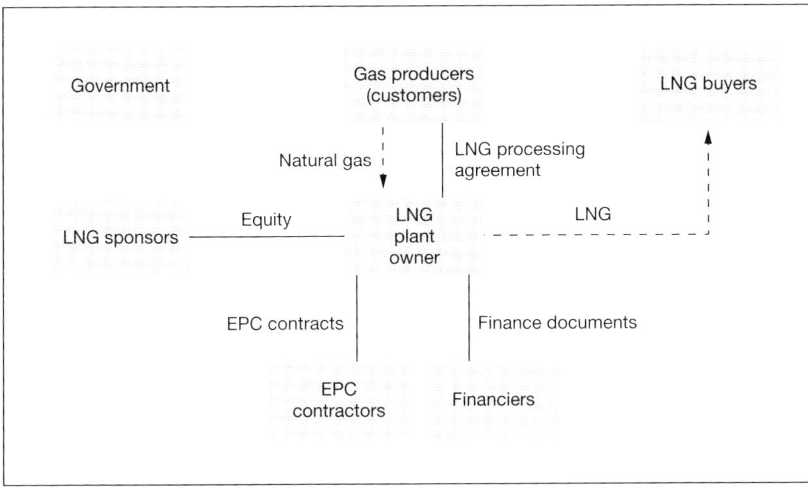

to mitigate this exposure by ensuring that the terms of the gas supply agreement and the LNG sale and purchase agreements are, as far as is commercially achievable, back to back. The tolling structure implies a lower risk profile because, provided that the infrastructure is available for use by its customers, the processing fee will be payable (and indeed in many cases the fee may be payable even if the infrastructure is unavailable due to *force majeure*).

- Regulatory issues: The applicable regulatory regime may influence the choice of structure. For example, in the European regasification sector, while the sponsors will often seek an exemption from the EU third party access (TPA) regime, the European Commission's approach is generally to link such an exemption to measures designed to maximise the utilisation of the regasification infrastructure through measures such as anti-hoarding or 'use it or lose it' provisions and provisions ensuring that dominant companies do not hold the lion's share of capacity. This may drive sponsors towards the tolling model. An exemption may also not be granted for 100% of the capacity.
- Tax: The tax regimes applicable to the merchant model and the tolling model are likely to be very different, reflecting the different activities being undertaken by the project company on each model.

Again, both the tolling and merchant models are capable of being made bankable. Given the different risk profiles of the two structures, financiers will need to undertake significantly more due diligence (and will want enhanced protections in the finance documents against a broader range of downside scenarios) on the merchant model than on the tolling model.

As a general rule, liquefaction plants tend to be structured on the merchant structure; and regasification plants tend to be structured on a tolling basis. We emphasise that there are plenty of exceptions to this general rule. For example, many of the liquefaction plants being developed in the United States are structured on the tolling model.

2.3 Incorporated or unincorporated?

Sponsors will also need to consider which is the most appropriate corporate structure for the project. In particular, is the liquefaction project to be structured as an unincorporated joint venture (UJV) or an incorporated joint venture (IJV)?

With a UJV, the sponsors hold their interests in the project directly and not through a project vehicle; and their relationship is regulated purely by contract. This is similar to the structure used in the upstream oil and gas sector where the parties' relationship is regulated by a joint operating agreement.

To finance a UJV, the sponsors may incorporate a finance special purpose company which raises debt and on-lends it to the sponsors in order to allow them to contribute an agreed percentage of their shares of project costs. Alternatively, individual sponsors may elect to raise debt at the sponsor level on the basis that the financiers' recourse is limited to their respective shares of the revenue stream received from the project.

With the IJV, the sponsors hold their interests in the project through one or more project vehicles in which the sponsors invest; and the sponsors' relationship is calculated by a shareholder or joint venture agreement as well as the applicable companies legislation. The IJV model is the model typically used to project finance assets in other sectors. In this case the debt is raised at the project vehicle level.

3. Financing considerations

3.1 Bankability of LNG project documents

In addition to bankability considerations related to the project structure as discussed in section 2 above, key areas for financier due diligence on LNG project documentation will be the legal regime of the host government, the gas sales agreement, the EPC contracts and the LNG sale and purchase agreements.

As with any project financed assets, the financiers will want the suite of project documents to work together to allocate risks to contractual counterparties and to leave the project with a clearly defined package of risks that the project is capable of managing and absorbing.

(a) Legal regime risks

In the context of a liquefaction project, a clear understanding will be needed on the legislative framework applicable to hydrocarbon exploration, extraction and export in the host country. Where the regime is not developed and tested enough for an investment on the scale of a liquefaction plant, the sponsors will seek to obtain an agreement with the host government covering matters such as:

- project identification and granting of applicable development rights;
- the participation of the host country's national oil company in the project;

- taxes, royalties and other fiscal provisions applicable to the project;
- support to be provided by the host government;
- local content and other similar requirements;
- environmental, social and labour requirements which will apply to the project; and
- the several liability of the project participants.

The sponsors and financiers will also be influenced by the track record of the host government in both existing gas projects and projects in other sectors and the project's ability to mitigate some of the political risks (see 3.2 below).

(b) ***Gas supply***

The financiers to a liquefaction plant will expect to conduct due diligence on the amount and status of gas reserves which are dedicated to the project and it would be customary to obtain appropriate warranty protection in this regard. There is often debate between sponsors and financiers as to the consequences under the project and finance contracts if the reserves prove to be insufficient. Sponsors will want to classify such an event as a *force majeure* while financiers will want to impose a make-up obligation on the sponsors to ensure that sufficient feedstock is made available to the liquefaction project to allow the project company to meet its LNG delivery commitments.

In the non-integrated project structure described in 2.1 above, the gas supply agreement will be the key document allocating value and risk between the upstream and liquefaction projects.

Financiers to the liquefaction project will prefer the gas supply agreement and the LNG sale and purchase agreements to be back-to-back, that is to leave the liquefaction project company with the minimum risk of liability to the LNG buyers related to the supply of gas.

Where this is not possible, financiers will carefully analyse the extent of any mismatch between the two projects and will require reassurance that the associated risks are properly mitigated.

US liquefaction projects are unusual in that they source gas from deep and liquid gas markets and can sell LNG on at a price linked to the gas market price. For this reason these projects do not need to be supported by a long-term gas supply agreement.

(c) ***EPC contracts***

How the construction arrangements are structured will depend on a number of factors. This issue is primarily driven by the scale and technical complexity of the construction arrangements and tax matters. For the larger LNG projects, a principal contractor will often enter into one or more construction contracts with separate onshore and offshore contracts, each of which form the construction contract package. This tax-splitting structure is used in order to minimise liability and onshore tax. Where a tax-splitting structure is adopted, appropriate bridging or umbrella agreements will then be needed to ensure that the project company is not exposed to interface risk between its offshore contract and onshore contract. For the financiers, construction risk can be mitigated through the provision of sponsor completion support, as discussed further at 3.4(a) below. Typically, key financier requirements in respect of the construction contracts can be summarised as follows:

- there should be contract price certainty, that is a fixed lump sum price (to the extent possible) with limited flexibility for the construction contractors to impose price increases;
- the project must be subject to a single turnkey construction contract, or where this is not possible (due to the size/complexity of the construction), a single principal contractor should take overall responsibility for the deliverability of the construction works;
- the contractors must be reputable with a track record and able to procure the provision of appropriate credit support in respect of their construction and defects remediation obligations;
- the contractor and project company must have the right to use proven technology for the life of the project;
- there should be a fixed programme and an appropriate delay liquidated damages regime will need to be agreed;
- the completion schedule will need to be achievable and the completion/performance testing regime robust;
- any aggregate liability caps and liquidated damages sub-caps will need to be carefully scrutinised. Certain liabilities (eg, those relating to death and personal injury) should be uncapped;
- appropriate and consistent indemnity and insurance regimes should be in place for the project company and all of the contractors on a project;
- the contractor will be expected to enter into a direct agreement with the financiers' agent providing for a standstill period on the contractor's right to take enforcement action against the project company, rights for the financiers' representative to step into the construction contracts to settle any sponsor breach, and ultimately for novation to a replacement sponsor.

To what extent the above is achieved will depend on the project-specific negotiations and the financiers' access to completion support. Ultimately, the financiers will derive significant comfort from the advice of their technical adviser.

Depending on the financing product being offered by export credit agencies (ECAs), the ECAs may need to confirm that the project's supply chain is consistent with their requirements for the sourcing of the construction works.[4]

(d) LNG sale and purchase agreements/offtake

As the global LNG market has become more liquid and more flexible, sponsors have become increasingly concerned to ensure that the offtake arrangements are flexible enough to allow the LNG to compete in the global market. At the same time, financiers have remained focused on ensuring that the offtake arrangements

---

4 See Clive Ransome's chapter on ECAs.

generate a robust long-term cash flow to ensure debt service. Striking a sustainable balance between them is a key challenge when structuring the offtake arrangements and negotiating them with offtakers.

Against this background, areas of particular focus from the perspective of financiers financing a liquefaction plant on a merchant basis will include the following.

Quantity: While the sponsors may wish to retain the flexibility to sell some of the project's LNG production on a short- or medium-term basis, the financiers will likely require a significant proportion of the plant's nameplate capacity to be committed to long-term take or pay sale arrangements.

In similar vein, where a buyer's downward quantity tolerance is agreed, financiers will wish to be satisfied that the project can continue to meet the agreed financial ratios where the buyer exercises the maximum agreed downward quantity tolerance in consecutive years.

Offtaker covenant: Assuming that the LNG sale and purchase agreement is structured on a take or pay basis, financiers will scrutinise the circumstances in which the buyer is excused its obligation to pay for LNG if it has not taken it (which is typically limited to circumstances of *force majeure* and seller's failure to deliver).

Likewise, financiers will wish to be comfortable with the creditworthiness of the offtaker and any credit support provider as well as the circumstances in which the offtaker may be obliged to provide additional credit support (eg, following a credit rating downgrade or a change in control).

Price: Long-term LNG sales are typically priced by reference to one or more recognised price indexes (eg, JCC and Henry Hub) with which financiers will be familiar. Financiers will scrutinise the project's ability to withstand a sustained period of low sales prices and will draw comfort from any floor (whether a hard floor or a soft floor such as an S or J curve) in the pricing formula.

Long-term LNG sale and purchase agreements are likely to contain provisions for periodic adjustment to the sales price to reflect changes in the market value (however determined) of LNG. Assuming that any such price review provision provides for both upward and downward flexibility, financiers are likely to want clarity around the trigger(s) for a price review and clear parameters around the price review procedure. Absent such clarity, given the increasing liquidity within the global LNG market, the outcome of a price review can be hard to predict.

Destination: Most long-term LNG sale and purchase agreements provide for delivery at one of a limited number of unloading ports with any diversions requiring the seller's consent and/or the sharing of any upside created as a result of the diversion. However, buyers are increasingly looking for the contractual flexibility to deliver to a wider range of markets both to take advantage of trading opportunities and to mitigate risk under a take or pay clause.

In some cases, export credit agencies will have requirements that a certain volume of LNG is delivered to specific countries, which can constrain the seller's ability to offer destination flexibility.

Controls on diversion and profit-sharing mechanisms can raise anti-trust issues, although financiers and sponsors will be aligned on wishing to ensure that there is no breach of applicable anti-trust law.

Liability and termination: Financiers will analyse carefully the seller's liability for breach of the LNG sale and purchase agreement (including in particular for failure to deliver LNG or the delivery of off-spec LNG), the circumstances in which the LNG sale and purchase agreement can be terminated (whether for default by either party or as a result of prolonged *force majeure*) and the liability arising on termination. The ideal position will be for any liability to be capped and for the seller's liability to be defined on a sole and exclusive basis.

Other financier protections: As with all key project documents, financiers will expect to take an assignment of rights under the LNG sale and purchase agreement and enter into a direct agreement with the counterparty.

3.2 Management of political risk

While political risk is not unique to the LNG sector, many liquefaction projects are located in countries which are perceived to present greater political risk exposure for both financiers and sponsors. Typical political risks encountered are:

- expropriation or nationalisation;
- politically motivated violence;
- change in law; and
- acts of government (eg, revocation of permits, imposition or change of currency exchange controls).

There are a number of options available to financiers and sponsors to mitigate political risk and often the parties rely on a combination of mitigation measures to derive appropriate reassurance to allow the project to proceed.

(a) ECA and multilateral agency (MLA) risk cover

There are a number of ECAs active in LNG project finance that provide protection to commercial lenders in respect of political risk. ECAs take an individual approach as to the level of cover they are able to provide and the range of cover for political risk is typically between 90 and 100%. Certain MLAs and ECAs are also prepared to provide insurance coverage for sponsors' equity investments. While not as common for LNG projects, it should also be noted that certain types of private political risk insurance may also be available, although in emerging markets the cost of business interruption insurance and political risk insurance cover is often prohibitive.

(b) Investment treaty protection

A bilateral investment treaty (BIT) may be in place between a sponsor's home country and the host country of the LNG project. The principle underpinning a BIT is that a foreign investment will not be subject to discrimination when compared with an investment by a host country. Note that a BIT does not directly protect debt investment. It should be noted that where there are considered to be deficiencies in the relevant BIT, the project can be structured to take advantage of additional BITs, for example by structuring the shares in the project through a holding company incorporated in a country which can take advantage of a more favourable BIT.

(c) ***Legislation***

It may be possible to mitigate political risk through legislation in the host country, for example through the existing legislation governing hydrocarbon exploration or through project-specific legislation designed to provide protection to foreign sponsors.

(d) ***Stabilisation clauses***

These clauses are intended to ensure the stabilisation of legal and fiscal regimes within which the project operates. These arrangements are helpful for mitigating political risks and providing compensation for host government breach; however, such clauses are susceptible to revocation by host governments who choose not to honour them.

(e) ***Offshoring of cash flows***

Sponsors may be able to keep much of the project cash flows offshore. A project's ability to do this will depend on the legal regime of the host country. Offshoring of cash flows will be challenging if, for example, there is a requirement for the proceeds of natural resources exports to be repatriated.

(f) ***Choice of governing law/venue for dispute resolution***

It is generally accepted that limiting the number of contracts to be governed by the law of the host country in an emerging market country will mitigate political risk. Stability is often provided by project and finance contracts being governed by English or New York law and for disputes to be resolved in the English or New York courts or by arbitration in a neutral forum.

3.3 Management of environmental and social risks

The construction and operation of LNG plants can present significant environmental and social risks. A failure to properly manage these risks can cause operational, financial and reputational risks both for sponsors and financiers. Increasingly, there has been international scrutiny and media attention on the ethics of financiers funding large resource projects in the natural resources sector.

To manage social and environmental risk, virtually all financial institutions have developed their own environmental and social standards for financing projects. While these standards are not instruments of international law, they set out what is accepted and expected conduct of public and private financiers.

Different categories of financial institutions have developed different standards to manage the environmental and social risks of financing resource projects, including LNG projects. Sponsors will need to be aware of the requirements imposed by the financiers, factor these requirements into their project activities even before the financiers have been appointed and, where relevant, abide by the requirements for the tenor of the debt.

The International Finance Corporation (IFC)'s Policy on Social and Environmental Sustainability and the IFC Performance Standards have set a benchmark for the assessment and management of environmental and social risks in relation to financing large-scale projects such as LNG plants. Prior to providing funding, an IFC borrower is required to provide information regarding social and environmental aspects of the project to the financiers and the proposed activities are then measured against the IFC Performance Standards. Each project is then categorised depending on whether the project poses a high, medium or low level of social and environmental risk. While the IFC is not usually involved in the financing of LNG projects, however, the key international standards outlined below, which will have direct application to the LNG industry, are largely modelled on the IFC Performance Standards.

(a) ***Equator Principles***

The Equator Principles (EPs) were developed by private commercial banks and were adopted in 2003 as a framework for addressing and managing the social and environmental risks of financing large-scale resources projects such as LNG projects. The most recent version of the EPs took effect on June 2 2013.

Currently 79 financial institutions from 35 countries have adopted the EPs and are designated as Equator Principles Financial Institutions (EPFIs). The EPs have also been adopted by four ECAs. EPFIs are required to implement the standards set out in the EPs in their environmental and social policies and include them in their procedures and lending requirements for certain loans.

(b) ***Common Approaches.***

The most recent agreement of the OECD Working Party on Export Credits and Credit Guarantees is the 2012 OECD Recommendation of the Council on Common Approaches for Officially Supported Export Credits and Environmental and Social Due Diligence (Common Approaches) which advises ECAs to undertake a due diligence of environmental and social issues in assessing applications for officially supported export credits for certain projects. A financier due diligence typically involves a review of the environmental and social impacts of the project activities based on information provided by the borrower as well as site inspections, interviews with employees and consultation with other stakeholders.

While different categories of financiers are subject to different standards, they share common themes and characteristics. Common to all the standards are the requirements:

- that projects be reviewed and classified according to their level of social and environmental impact;
- that public consultation with affected communities, including indigenous groups, occur as part of the assessment process; and

- that there is some level of public reporting by the financial institution regarding the implementation of the relevant standard.

3.4 Key provisions of the finance documents

(a) *Completion support*

In general terms, sponsor support in LNG projects can be broken down into the following categories:

- sponsor equity contribution obligation;
- completion support; and
- ownership retention obligations.

Equity contribution support and ownership retention obligations are general requirements of project finance transactions and, accordingly, are not discussed in any detail in this chapter.

It is customary in large LNG projects, and particularly where there is no lump sum turnkey construction contract, for sponsors to offer – and the financiers to require – completion support in the form of completion guarantees. Completion support is not intended to constitute a guarantee by the sponsors that completion will occur. Rather, completion guarantees are typically undertakings from sponsors to cover all of the borrower's debt service obligations until defined project completion milestones are proven to have been met through a process of physical and economic completion testing. In the event that the agreed project completion milestones have not occurred by a longstop date or in the event of a fundamental event of default (see below), the financiers can accelerate the debt and call on the completion guarantees for the repayment of the accelerated debt. The introduction of completion guarantees into the structure introduces a number of additional considerations requiring agreement between financiers and sponsors.

EPC contract: The fact that the sponsors have agreed to underpin the financiers' debt service payments until completion has occurred should mean that financier due diligence on the EPC contract(s) is reduced because the financiers can largely rely on the completion support package to mitigate their exposure to the construction risks. Unlike the customary position for a project without completion support, the financiers should not be looking to the EPC contractor and imposing a high liquidated damages regime for debt service or debt pay down. Accordingly, the introduction of completion guarantees should allow for more efficient EPC contract negotiation and a lower construction price. Completion support will not reduce the financiers' focus on certain matters such as environmental and social requirements or on export credit agencies' requirements for the sourcing of the project's supply chain.

Creditworthiness of sponsors: Financiers will scrutinise the creditworthiness of each sponsor providing the completion guarantees. Appropriate credit support enhancement will be required in the case of a deterioration in the credit standing of the completion support provider.

Event of default regime in finance documents: It is generally accepted that while the financiers' debt is covered by completion support, the financiers' ability to call an event of default under the finance documents should be limited to certain fundamental events of default while such support is in place. Sponsors will assert that the nature of the financing during the construction phase is more like a corporate financing. In practice, however, the categorisation of which events of default should constitute fundamental events of default is inevitably more complicated though it is not uncommon to restrict financier acceleration rights against the project as much as possible while the completion guarantees are in place and limit financier enforcement rights to calls under the completion guarantees. It should be highlighted that usually completion guarantees are structured as undertakings to pay in order to avoid the requirement of financiers having to first accelerate the debt in order to be able to enforce under a guarantee.

Completion testing: Typically the completion tests will focus on the core components of physical completion testing, a financiers' reliability test, an independent consultant report, the absence of default and financial testing. A key variable is whether the project is non-integrated and how the related project's completion is addressed. Where applicable, partial completion concepts (with appropriate completion support step-downs) will need to be considered.

Sponsor liability: As far as possible, sponsors will expect their completion support obligations to be several. Flexibility is often built into the finance documents allowing non-defaulting sponsors to voluntarily cure and pay on behalf of a defaulting sponsor. By doing so, the curing sponsor becomes entitled to the benefit of a proportionate amount of the defaulting sponsor's distribution payments and shareholder loan repayments (if any). This remedy allows the project to continue as normal without default.

(b) State participant involvement

In some LNG projects, the host government participates as a founding sponsor through its national oil company. Given the location of most liquefaction projects, the involvement of the host government may give rise to a few important considerations for financiers.

Funding arrangements: Financiers will want to ensure that their exposure to the completion support obligations and ongoing equity contribution obligations on the host government are sufficiently funded or credit supported.

World Bank Negative Pledge: Where the host government has outstanding World Bank group loans, the World Bank Negative Pledge (WBNP) contained in the IBRD General Terms will impact on the financing and security structure. The host government shareholding entity will be subject to restrictions on the creation of liens over public assets as security for external indebtedness resulting in priority to other creditors in allocation, realisation or distribution of foreign exchange. The analysis of the impact of the WBNP will be dependent on the structure and careful consideration will need to be given to any exclusions from the financiers' security package. A number of recently project financed LNG projects have successfully overcome the negative impact of the WBNP in the context of the overall collateral package afforded to financiers.

(c) ***Expansions***

Given the significant economies of scale that can often be realised by expanding an LNG project, sponsors often want the flexibility in the finance documents to expand through the addition of further LNG trains. Accordingly, the finance documents will govern the framework for such expansions. Typically, matters to be addressed will include the following:

- whether the expansion is to be constructed within the existing project or whether it constitutes a separate, ring-fenced project until its completion following which full integration into the original project will occur;
- the pre-agreed expansion conditions which, if satisfied, would by-pass the need for financier consent to any proposed expansion;
- the borrower's ability to select funding sources for the expansion from equity, third party debt financing, project cash flow (or a combination thereof); and
- the security structuring and intercreditor principles as between the existing lenders and expansion lenders (which is more relevant until the expansion is integrated into the original project).

Financiers will wish to scrutinise the additional contracts related to the expansion, including the LNG sale and purchase agreements and construction arrangements. Provided appropriate cover ratios are met and the expansion does not introduce new material risks to the original project, it is likely that financiers to the original project will have limited right to object to the expansion.

(d) ***Intercreditor issues***

Intercreditor issues are not unique to LNG project financings. This section highlights two particular issues often encountered on LNG projects.

Separate upstream and downstream financings: Where separate lender groups exist at the upstream and downstream links in the value chain, the lenders to the liquefaction plant will require an intercreditor agreement with the upstream lenders (and vice versa). The form of the relevant intercreditor agreement will vary depending on the project specifics. Fundamentally, the lenders to the liquefaction plant will need comfort that the upstream development will actually be completed and will not, for example, be terminated or subject to an enforcement process by upstream lenders. A key mitigant to lenders to the liquefaction plant is whether sponsor completion guarantees will be made available and whether the release conditions are dependent on completion of the liquefaction plant and also the upstream development.

Senior sponsor loans: The high cost of developing certain large-scale LNG projects may result in a funding gap as often more debt is needed than can be provided by financiers. Sponsors can step in to bridge the funding gap by providing loans to the borrower which rank equally with the other senior loans. The introduction of sponsor co-lending can avoid a delay to the project and its introduction is generally viewed positively by financiers as it raises financiers' confidence as to the viability of the project. The structuring of senior sponsor loans gives rise to additional consideration points from an intercreditor perspective including:

- the level of senior sponsor lender voting rights (which is likely to be limited to certain core entrenched rights);
- the switching-off of the senior sponsor lenders' right to information provided by the agent to financiers (or between the financier group);
- the ranking of the senior sponsor loan in the pre- and post-enforcement cash flow waterfalls and whether repayment constitutes interest only and if any distribution-type conditions apply, for example if certain project-related or sponsor-related events of default exist;
- the transferability of the senior sponsor loans and whether there is to be any stapling to the sponsor (or its affiliate's shareholding in the project).

4. Industry trends

Over more than 50 years, LNG has proved a reliable means of transporting energy long distances by sea and flexible enough to respond to numerous changes in the global energy market. We expect this successful track record to continue.

At the time of writing, there are perhaps three industry trends attracting particular attention:

- how LNG will penetrate and compete in new markets, many of which lack an established creditworthy offtaker. For example, there is significant interest in LNG to power projects in Africa and elsewhere;
- the impact on the global LNG market that will be seen as a result of the volumes of LNG that are expected to start coming to market shortly (principally from Australian and US liquefaction plants) as well as on the appetite for investment in further LNG infrastructure in the coming years; and
- the impact of floating LNG technology becoming established on a commercial scale and offering the means to monetise reserves that cannot be monetised by traditional LNG technology.

Project de-risking in financing oil and gas pipelines

Tom Dimitroff
Infrastructure Development Partnership LLP

1. Introduction

The price patterns established by trading oil and gas over time, as with other commodities, are cyclical. However, the development of infrastructure to enable the production, processing, storage, transportation and monetisation of oil and gas and related products is linear. Analysing and hedging the upward and downward movements of oil and gas commodity prices is fast-paced, and individual commodity traders can earn a fortune for their principals by taking decisions within a split second. Developing oil and gas infrastructure, on the other hand, is a long-term exercise that requires deep analysis and planning undertaken by large-scale, interdisciplinary teams. The resulting operational infrastructure will need to function with certainty and predictability over the long term – often for up to 40 or 50 years. The utilisation of oil and gas infrastructure is priced on the basis of the service provided rather than the value of the commodity. Project returns for infrastructure assets are calculated on the back of discounted cash-flow projections generated with precision over the life of an asset. Fluctuations in oil and gas prices will typically have no bearing upon project economics as they are targeted to deliver a 'utility' rate of return.

For the oil and gas trader, risk opens opportunity. For the infrastructure developer, risk is anathema. Indeed, risk within a project that is not extinguished or otherwise mitigated may lead to project delays, interruptions, cost overruns and, ultimately, to project failure because investors will invariably withhold financing. Project risk can also threaten serious adverse physical impacts. As with most infrastructure projects, developing an oil or gas pipeline involves a process of project de-risking. Indeed, before an oil or gas pipeline project can be financed, the paramount condition precedent is that the project has been fully and properly de-risked. But given the vast amount of global capital needed to develop infrastructure so as to keep pace with global GDP, is full de-risking the only correct approach to project development? Do funders and financiers place a different weighting on perceptions of political risk in the developing world versus other forms of macro and project risk in the developed world? What does it mean to de-risk an oil or gas pipeline project? What are the risk factors that can impede or even halt pipelines in development and operation? Why do strategic projects need to be fully de-risked before they may secure financing?

In answering these questions, there is a growing assumption that the approach taken by China to invest in infrastructure in the developing world (the Chinese state capitalist model)[1] is somehow structurally different to the approach taken by conventional strategic investors and institutional lenders (the conventional funding and finance model). In particular, advocates observe that the Chinese state capitalist approach is somehow more effective in its ability to respond quickly to local needs and to implement and construct projects faster. On the other hand, critics fear that Chinese state capitalist interests will begin to dominate regions of the developing world and exacerbate adverse project impacts on people, communities and the environment.[2] Nevertheless, critics will also concede that monies available under the conventional funding and finance model are grossly insufficient to meet the growing demands of developing world economies.

This chapter will begin by briefly examining some of the metrics driving development of and investment in global infrastructure in general and cross-border oil and gas pipelines in particular. The chapter will then turn to focus on the core market and project risk factors that are typically taken into account in developing and financing cross-border oil and gas pipeline projects. Principal de-risking considerations, tools and processes involved in structuring a financeable oil or gas pipeline project will be referenced. Differences in the way that Chinese state capitalist and conventional funding and finance approaches address project risk and project de-risking are observed. The chapter ends by examining 11 likely cross-border oil and gas pipelines, drawing a series of high-level conclusions regarding the Chinese state capitalist and conventional funding and finance approaches and by offering indicative policy recommendations going forward.

2. Global investment in oil and gas pipelines

2.1 Global infrastructure investment requirements

A January 2013 report by the McKinsey Global Institute estimates that $57 trillion in global infrastructure investment will be required between 2013 and 2030 in order to keep pace with global GDP growth.[3] This figure is significant as it exceeds the estimated value of current global infrastructure and is almost 60 per cent more than the $36 trillion invested in global infrastructure from 1995 to 2013.[4]

In developed and developing countries alike, the public sector has historically played a key role in the financing of infrastructure projects. In the latter, about 70% of infrastructure spending is publicly funded.[5] Public sources of funding are becoming increasingly strained, however, due to, among other things, rapid

---

1 Constituent component companies, institutions and agencies comprising the Chinese state capitalist approach include an array of state-owned oil and gas interests, the state-owned suppliers and contractors and the state development banks, including the newly formed Asian Infrastructure Investment Bank.

2 The strategic approach to project implementation pursued by the Russian state in conjunction with Russian state companies and international oil companies (IOCs) can also be described as 'state capitalist'. However, the execution of projects by Russian Federation interests has often followed the conventional funding and finance approach. For example, the Blue Stream and Nord Stream pipeline projects both fulfilled Russian Federation strategic objectives but were implemented using the core project de-risking approach outlined in this chapter.

3 Richard Dobbs and others, *Infrastructure Productivity: How to Save $1 Trillion a Year*, Rep. McKinsey Global Institute, January 2013. Web. August 18 2015.

4 Dobbs, *ibid.*

urbanisation and budget constraints in the wake of the 2008 financial crisis.[6] In line with these trends, Standard & Poor's have estimated an $8.4 trillion gap between the $57 trillion required for infrastructure spending through 2030 and the available public funds.[7] Accordingly, alternative sources of funding will need to be mobilised from international private sector investors and financiers in order to fill the gap.

The majority of the required infrastructure investments will be in greenfield projects in the developing world, although large-scale investment in the renewal and replacement of existing infrastructure in the developed world will also be required. According to research by Oxford Economics and published by PricewaterhouseCoopers, almost half of global infrastructure spending in 2012 was in developing countries, and this figure is expected to grow to about two-thirds by 2025.[8] China, which spent $503 billion on infrastructure between 1992 and 2011, is now the world's largest investor in infrastructure.[9] (During the same period the United States spent $374 billion.[10]) In addition, China has proclaimed that it will invest $1 trillion in new-build infrastructure in Africa by 2025.[11] In fact, while China is indeed the leader in trade with Africa, it still lags significantly behind the United Kingdom, the United States and Italy in terms of annual foreign direct investment in Africa.[12]

2.2 Oil and gas pipeline investment requirements

The overwhelming majority of global new-build infrastructure will be in the road, rail, power, water and telecoms context.[13] New oil and gas infrastructure, however, will continue to consume a meaningful share of the world's infrastructure spending notwithstanding current oil and gas oversupply and price fluctuations, because the long-term trend is that overall global demand for oil and gas will continue to rise inexorably over the next 25 years. Much of this demand growth will occur in the developing world – in particular in China and India, countries located at significant distances from the principal sources of low-cost hydrocarbons in the Middle East and Africa. Bridging the distance between these production sources and developing world consumption markets will require investments to develop new oil and gas

---

5 Georg Inderst and Fiona Stewart, "Institutional Investment in Infrastructure in Emerging Markets and Developing Economies", Rep. World Bank Group, March 2014. Web. August 18 2015.

6 Inderst and Stewart, *ibid.*

7 Michael Wilkins and others, "Global Infrastructure: How to Fill a $500 Billion Hole", Rep. Standard & Poor's Ratings Services, January 16 2014. Web. August 18 2015.

8 Oxford Economics, "Capital Project and Infrastructure Spending Outlook to 2025", report by PricewaterhouseCoopers, 2014. Web.

9 Richard Dobbs and others, "Infrastructure Productivity: How to Save $1 Trillion a Year", report by McKinsey Global Institute, January 2013. Web.

10 Dobbs, *ibid.* To further illustrate this point, see Lawrence Summers' recent editorial in the *Washington Post*, where he observed that during 2010–13 China poured more concrete than the United States did in the whole of the 20th century (see http://wpo.st/IcyfO).

11 Christopher Alessi and Beina Xu, "China in Africa", Council on Foreign Relations, n.p., April 27 2015. Web. August 18 2015. The facts, however, do not appear to bear this out. According to a recent analysis in *The Economist*, in 2012, total FDI into sub-Saharan Africa was $59.3 billion, of which $2.5 billion was from China, placing it behind the United Kingdom ($7.5 billion), the United States ($3.7 billion) and Italy ($3.6 billion).

12 See www.economist.com/news/middle-east-and-africa/21639554-china-has-become-big-africa-now-backlash-one-among-many.

13 *Ibid.* See footnote 3.

infrastructure and maintain existing facilities.[14] Accordingly, the two principal motivations for investing in oil and gas pipeline transportation infrastructure are to meet market demand growth and to address geopolitical risk factors that arise in the development of cross-border pipelines.

With respect to geopolitical risk factors, there are a number of elements that can motivate the development of cross-border oil and gas pipelines. To begin with, landlocked countries are more constrained in their import and export capacities, and pipelines are often the only pragmatic way for them to transport large-scale volumes of oil and gas. For example, Kazakhstan, Turkmenistan, Azerbaijan, Uzbekistan, Uganda, South Sudan and the Kurdish region of Northern Iraq are all landlocked producing states/regions entirely dependent upon cross-border pipelines to ship and therefore monetize their oil and gas production.

In addition, cross-border pipelines fulfil geo-strategic roles. For example, the one million bpd Baku-Tbilisi-Ceyhan (BTC) pipeline (and the parallel 10 bcma South Caucasus Pipeline (SCP)) completed in June 2006 formed the spearhead of US-backed energy policy to support the viability of the newly independent former Soviet republics. The pipelines were implemented with strong diplomatic support from the US government, which wanted to ensure that the new republics (Azerbaijan, Georgia and Kazakhstan in particular) would be able to export their resources without traversing the Russian Federation or relying on maritime shipment through the Persian Gulf.

A third facet of geopolitical risk is security of supply and export. Many regions around the world have insufficient domestic production of oil and gas to meet demand and therefore must rely upon imports to fill the gap. For example, the European Union and China have insufficient domestic production of oil and gas to meet their demand needs.[15] For them, the security of supply sources is thus an issue of national security. Similarly, key producing countries around the world have linked their production and export of oil and gas to particular markets via cross-border pipelines. Maintaining the security of these pipelines and market share is also a strategic priority. For example, more than 30 per cent of all gas consumed in the European Union is produced in the Russian Federation and exported by cross-border gas pipelines. Similarly, the majority of gas produced and exported from Algeria is destined for the European Union and delivered by cross-border sub-sea pipelines.

2.3 Disparities in pipeline funding and finance: developed versus developing worlds

Notwithstanding a clear need for comprehensive and sustained investment in infrastructure in the developing world (including in respect of oil and gas pipelines), available domestic public money is grossly insufficient to satisfy this need.[16] In

14 While the overwhelming majority of oil and an ever-growing amount of gas is transported from production source to consumption market by maritime tanker and LNG tanker, respectively, large-scale, new-build oil and gas pipelines will be needed to satisfy market demands.

15 In the case of security of supply, China has put into place cross-border oil and gas pipelines across a variety of countries around the world, including the following: oil pipelines across the Republic of Sudan (now the Republic of South Sudan and the Republic of Sudan); an oil pipeline from Kazakhstan to China; four gas pipelines from Turkmenistan to China; a parallel oil and gas pipeline from Myanmar to China; and, more recently, the 'Power of Siberia' pipeline development project.

addition, pure private sector financial investment in greenfield infrastructure development in the developing world is simply unavailable. Unfortunately, under the conventional funding and finance model, the early phases of project development are never debt-financed. Under this model, funding for early-stage project development may only be sourced from public money, international development aid, or equity-funded by strategic private sector investors/developers. Where developing world governments lack sufficient public resources for this kind of spending under the conventional model, they are, therefore, systemically at the mercy of external forces – through the aid agencies or private sector actors – who may or may not share the host government's strategic infrastructure priorities. These funders sometimes have strategic priorities at odds with those of the host government, but it is more often the case that they lack strategic vision. This potentially haphazard, externally driven, and piecemeal approach presents significant limitations to host governments and regional groupings of countries. Master-planning infrastructure prior to the development of individual projects is a more rational process for governments to meet their strategic priorities. Unfortunately, the focus of conventional funding and finance on individual projects can often frustrate governments in their efforts to deliver these priorities.[17]

Aside from a limited range of investments by sovereign wealth funds (SWFs), there are very few examples this author could identify of pure financial investments in greenfield (or brownfield) oil or gas infrastructure projects in the developing world. Instead, oil and gas production and related infrastructure projects in the developing world are typically sponsored and owned by strategic investors (ie, international oil companies (IOCs) and national oil companies (NOCs) or the host governments of the jurisdictions where the production and pipeline facilities are located).

In contrast, pure financial investment in the developed world is more common. For example, pure financial investment in the United States helped to drive an explosion of investment in upstream shale oil and gas production and associated infrastructure. At the end of 2013, the market capitalisation of the 107 Master Limited Partnerships (MLPs) operating oil and gas infrastructure assets was $464 billion in financial investment.[18] The implementation of this infrastructure investment has in part enabled oil production in the United States to increase by 1.2 million bpd in 2014 alone.[19]

When we move from the equity funding of infrastructure projects to debt financing, we find a similar disparity between the developed and developing world markets. Examples of debt financing of upstream oil and gas fields (ie, reserve-based

16 Analysts estimate that there is a spending gap of approximately $1 trillion per annum for developing economies – see www.ppiaf.org/sites/ppiaf.org/files/publication/PPIAF-Institutional-Investors-final-web.pdf.

17 Quasi-financial investors prepared to invest in oil and gas production and related infrastructure are Sovereign Wealth Funds (SWFs) where there is a strategic link between the SWF and the host government jurisdiction, as opposed to pure financial investors.

18 See www.cbreclarion.com/research/Documents/MLPs_Key%20Role%20in%20the%20U%20S%20%20Energy%20Renaissance_January%202014.pdf.

19 Between 2008 and June 2015, US crude oil production increased from 4 million bpd to 9.5 million bpd. See www.eia.gov/forecasts/steo/.

lending) in the developing world where commercial banks are prepared to lend without the support of multilateral, bilateral or other institutional participation and/or sovereign guarantees from the host government jurisdiction are available but limited. Commercial lending to oil and gas pipelines without such support is rare. Once again, examples of commercial debt backing upstream oil and gas projects and related infrastructure in the developed world are readily available. For example, accumulated commercial debt backing shale oil and gas investment in the United States since 2010 is estimated at approximately $550 billion.

As with equity funding, the main reason for the disparity between the developed and developing worlds in debt financing is the perception of elevated risk for projects in the developing world. While it is not disputed that actual and perceived political risk in the developing world is higher than in the developed world,[20] investment in upstream oil and gas and related infrastructure anywhere, including in the developed world, is not without material risk. For example, according to *The Economist*, 29 of the 62 exploration and production firms in the United States owe approximately $84 billion in distressed debt and account for 1.1 million bpd of oil production. Clearly, when decisions on deployment of capital and debt are being made, market actors place preponderant – and possibly undue – weight on the political risk in the developing world and less relative weight on the not insubstantial market risk in the developed world.[21]

3. Oil and gas pipelines: macro and project risk factors

The willingness of investors and financiers to commit monies to a project will follow from their ability to identify, hedge, allocate, mitigate or otherwise manage risk factors. As suggested above, the perception and treatment of risk associated with investment and debt commitments to oil and gas pipelines differs between the developed and developing worlds. In order to understand the different treatments, it is necessary to understand the different types of risk and importance ascribed to each. Risk in relation to oil and gas pipeline projects can be divided into two levels: the macro level and the project level. The following sections will examine each in turn in order to demonstrate their impacts on project development.

3.1 Macro risk

The term 'macro risk' refers to risk factors that extend beyond the context of a particular project. Volatile oil and gas commodity prices are thus one example of a macro risk. Between July and December 2008, the price of Brent crude oil dropped from $132.72/bbl to $39.95/bbl.[22] With the drop in the price of oil (and gas), capital expenditures (capex) on projects in the oil and gas sector dropped by more than 18% in the same period. A second example of macro risk is international sanctions, which

---

20 For example, see MIGA's assessment of principal constraints to foreign investment in the developing world – see www.miga.org/documents/WIPR13.pdf.

21 The fact that commercial debt was mobilised to finance upstream and related infrastructure projects exposed to commodities pricing (market) risk that manifested two times in less than a single decade has fascinating implications for the priorities commercial banks place on political and legal risk factors in the developed versus developing worlds.

22 See www.eia.gov/dnav/pet/hist/LeafHandler.ashx?n=pet&s=rbrte&f=m.

can halt projects in development or operation in sanctioned countries. For instance, recent sanctions against investment in or financing of upstream projects and trade in technology in Iran and the Russian Federation have prevented multiple projects from moving forward.[23]

Other examples of macro risk include:

- a sudden setback in aggregate demand or output;
- fluctuations in interest or currency rates; and
- volatility in the price of steel or the broader commodities market.

Safety and environmental factors can also represent macro risks. For example, the 2011 Fukushima disaster shut down the nuclear industry in Japan and subsequently in Germany and adversely affected nuclear power projects globally. Finally, the spectre of climate change can be seen as an emerging area of macro risk. In particular, legislation implemented by a growing number of governments to reduce greenhouse gas emissions and meet global targets may threaten investment in more carbon-intensive energy sources, such as coal (already being phased out in a number of states) and oil.

3.2 Project risk

In contrast to macro risk, the second level of risk, 'project risk', refers to risk factors that are unique to a particular project. Project risks can be further categorised into those that are external to the project sponsor(s) developing the project and those that are internal. External project risk factors are risk factors that challenge projects from sources outside of the project. These factors may include, among other things, commercial, funding and finance, political, legal, regulatory, fiscal, operational, security, safety, environmental, social and human rights factors. Internal project risk factors, on the other hand, are risk factors related to the enterprise risk management system implemented by the project sponsor(s) to identify, allocate, mitigate and manage external risk.

In order to establish a tangible basis for evaluating the sources and consequences of risk to actual cross-border pipelines (in development and operation), the author has reviewed 55 cross-border pipelines. The results of the analysis are summarised in Table 1.

As the table on the next page illustrates, political risk and commercial risk are, respectively, the first and second most frequent risks with the greatest magnitude of consequence for oil and gas pipelines in development and operation.

In examining the sources and consequences of risk for oil and gas pipeline developments and operations, it is important to note that while many project risk factors may appear to be external, there are very few that materialise in the absence of significant internal risk factors. Accordingly, developers should have robust governance systems in place to anticipate, identify and manage risk factors as they

23 The Iran–Pakistan–India gas pipeline has been delayed for years due to Iranian sanctions, notwithstanding the fact that Pakistan has a large and growing gas supply and demand gap. Similarly, drilling operations being undertaken by western IOCs in the Black Sea and Arctic have been halted due to sanctions against the Russian Federation.

Table 1: Sources and consequences of risk[24]

Source of risk	Pipelines in development			Total	Pipelines in operation			Total
Absence of applicable multilateral treaty or international principles on freedom of transit	0	3	0	3	5	0	0	5
Commercial (uneconomic or compromised economics)	7	7	2	16	3	5	3	11
Political (sanctions, embargoes, protests, failure otherwise to provide support)	12	5	2	19	9	8	2	19
Security (sabotage, terrorism, conflict, vandalism caused by a hostile third party)	2	7	0	9	7	4	0	11
Environmental or safety concerns/incidents	2	1	2	5	0	3	6	9
Human rights abuses	0	0	0	0	1	4	0	5
Community protests (labour, land rights, benefits, negative impacts on the environment)	0	1	1	2	0	7	0	7

Source of risk resulted in stoppage or cessation.
Source of risk resulted in significant delay or interruption.
Source of risk resulted in moderate delay or interruption.

appear in the normal course of business and in extraordinary circumstances. Failure to adopt and implement such systems may turn an external threat into an internal crisis with significant consequences to the sponsor company as well as the surrounding environment and communities.[25]

24 While technical risk is a critically important source of risk that can lead to serious consequences such as schedule delays and cost overruns (pre-completion) and operational, environmental and safety issues (post-completion), technical sources of risk are not included in the above table. For a more complete analysis and a complete listing of all 55 pipeline case studies, see http://jwelb.oxfordjournals.org/content/7/4/287.abstract.

4. Phases of project development and de-risking

Oil and gas pipelines are developed in successive phases, each of which brings different de-risking requirements. Projects begin with a feasibility study and progress to front-end engineering and design (FEED), construction and ultimately to operation and eventual decommissioning.[26] The first two phases (the feasibility study and FEED phase) involve clarifying and de-risking the business objective of the pipeline sponsor(s) to a point where they can take a final investment decision (FID). These phases are referred to jointly as the 'project development phase' and are typically funded through sponsor equity. Since these phases are the main sites of project de-risking, they will be the focus here. The principal activities associated with the conduct of a feasibility study and FEED and the relevant funding and finance considerations are set out below.

4.1 Project feasibility phase

In a cross-border pipeline development, the project feasibility phase typically includes, among other things, the following:

- initial political discussions between or among the host governments where the pipeline is proposed to be routed;
- a definition of basic design parameters, including routing and indicative capex and annual operational expenditures (opex) requirements;
- an understanding of the technical, geotechnical, environmental and social constraints;
- funding, ownership and development plans;
- consideration of the commercial structure, asset monetisation and/or exit strategy;
- definition of pipeline shareholding structure and internal governance;
- agreement on a pipeline tariff model(s) that will concurrently enable:
  - the sponsors to secure an appropriate economic return that will support the investment;
  - the users of the pipeline (the shippers) to have a certain, predictable and economic transportation tariff; and
  - the lenders (if any) to have a tariff that will support investment and/or debt financing;
- upstream due diligence and determination of indicative throughput scenarios and use of excess transportation capacity, including future use by

25 Examples of internal breakdowns in organisational behaviour and governance that led to catastrophic environmental damage and loss of life include the 2005 BP Texas City Refinery disaster (15 people killed and 170 injured) and the 2010 BP Deepwater Horizon (5 million barrels of oil spilled and 11 people killed). For root cause analyses that identify the foregoing 'internal risk', see the report of the BP US Refineries Independent Safety Review Panel (January 2007) available at www.bp.com/liveassets/bp_internet/globalbp/globalbp_uk_english/SP/STAGING/local_assets/assets/pdfs/Baker_panel_report.pdf and the Deepwater Horizon Accident Investigation Report (September 2010) available at www.bp.com/liveassets/bp_internet/globalbp/globalbp_uk_english/incident_response/STAGING/local_assets/downloads_pdfs/ Deepwater_Horizon_Accident_Investigation_Report.pdf.

26 The last phase involves the responsible decommissioning of the facility that typically includes a decommissioning plan as a condition to final permitting and the retention of funds within an account to fund the requisite decommissioning activities. As the final three phases represent the outcome of the de-risking, development and funding process, they are not discussed in further detail in this chapter.

the sponsors and/or access by third parties and the associated tariff for such use;
- identification and assessment of risk factors, sponsor appetite for risk and risk allocation, mitigation and management plans; and
- securing the required intergovernmental and host government concession and the applicable legal, regulatory and fiscal requirements.

In light of the above components, completion of the feasibility study should yield an integrated plan for the forward development, financing, construction and operation of the pipeline.

Where pipeline developers contemplate financing from commercial lenders or from multilateral lenders or export credit agencies (MLAs and ECAs, respectively), additional care must be taken to ensure that all development parameters can support the financing. At minimum, this should include the development of an initial funding strategy and finance plan and the planning for the acquisition of required rights to the land and the conduct of an environmental and social impact assessment (ESIA) in accordance with, among other things, the International Finance Corporation Performance Standards and applicable local laws.

4.2 Project FEED phase

Following the feasibility phase, the second phase of project development involves a rigorous process of de-risking the results of the feasibility study and otherwise fulfilling the activities required for the project sponsor(s) to take a final investment decision (FID) for the project. The de-risking process typically, among other things, includes the following:
- identifying all pre-completion risk factors that may delay, hinder or stop the project or escalate the cost of implementing the project;
- identifying all post-completion risk factors that may curtail, interrupt or halt the operation of the pipeline once completed; and
- developing and agreeing the main risk allocation, risk mitigation and risk management tools to address the pre- and post-completion risk factors identified.

The results of the risk identification and risk allocation analysis will inform the structuring of the principal commercial agreements that will support the implementation and operation of the project. The following agreements, among others, are standard:
- An intergovernmental agreement (IGA) signed between or among the host government jurisdictions where the proposed pipeline will be constructed and operated;
- A concession, host government agreement (HGA) or other form of public–private participation (PPP) agreement between the project company and each host government;
- A pipeline venture ownership agreement and structure, typically documented in a shareholders' agreement or unincorporated joint venture agreement and entered into between the sponsor(s)/owner(s) of the pipeline venture;

- A transportation agreement entered into between the project company offering transportation services in the pipeline and the shippers (users) of the pipeline and defining the terms of service and agreed tariff;
- An engineering, procurement and construction (EPC) contract (including a potential range of additional supply and construction contracts) entered into between the project company and the EPC contractor;
- An operations and maintenance (O&M) agreement entered into between the project company and the physical operator of the pipeline; and
- In the event of a debt financing, loan and related financing agreements entered into between the sponsor(s) and the lender(s).

The diagram shown in Figure 1[27] sets out the foregoing agreements supporting a pipeline built across two jurisdictions.

Figure 1: Agreement supporting a pipeline across two jurisdictions

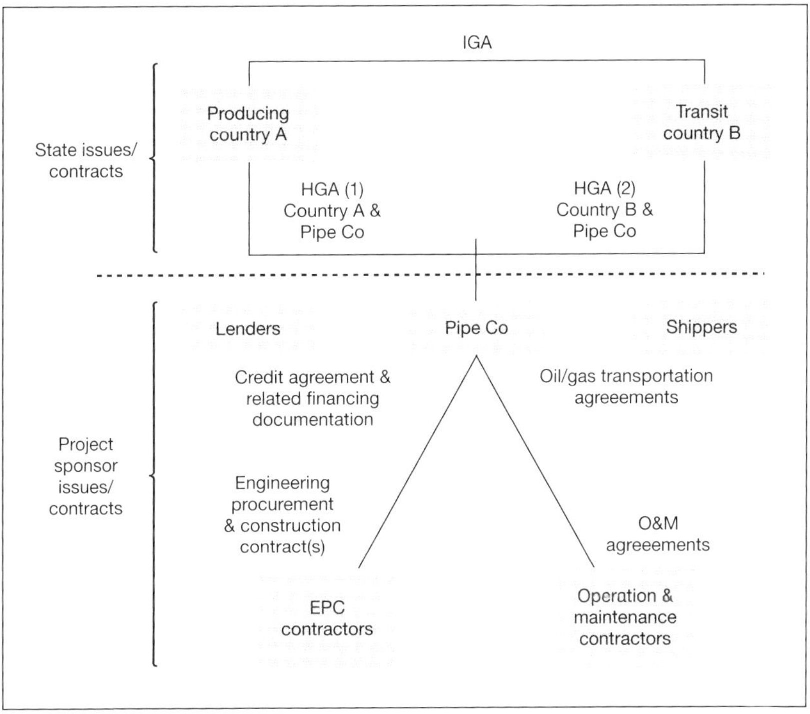

In addition to the foregoing de-risking activities, the FEED phase of the project will involve the sponsors undertaking, among other things, the following activities as a condition precedent to taking an FID:

- completing the detailed technical design of the pipeline;

27 See http://jwelb.oxfordjournals.org/content/7/4/287.abstract.

- entering into an appropriate concession, HGA or other PPP arrangement with the host government;
- obtaining most of the required rights to land (with a clear plan for obtaining the rest);
- satisfying all legal and regulatory requirements, including the obtaining of all required licences, permits, authorisations and approvals to construct and operate the project;
- completing the ESIA process;
- implementing the results of the risk allocation exercise by documenting and agreeing the requisite host government and commercial and finance agreements referenced above;
- issuing the invitation to tender to the EPC contractors and awarding and entering into the EPC contract; and
- in the event that sponsor equity funding is insufficient to support the full project construction, completing lender negotiations subject to completion guarantees and/or debt service undertakings from each shareholder on a several basis and seeking a first drawdown on debt post-FID.

5. State capitalist and conventional funding and finance models

Thus far, this chapter has briefly surveyed types and dimensions of oil and gas pipeline risk and the general phases of project development and de-risking. This section will now attempt to offer a high-level comparison of what appear to be two different approaches to funding and financing infrastructure development in the developing world: the state capitalist model and the conventional funding and finance model.[28] In order to compare the two models, this section will examine the strengths and weaknesses of each in regard to four key features of cross-border pipeline development:

- the mitigation of political risk;
- the advancement of host state development objectives;
- the attainment of project funding and finance; and
- the achievement of project sustainability.

5.1 Political risk mitigation

As referenced above, a distinctive feature of cross-border pipelines is the interdependency they forge between or among two or more sovereign host states. This state-to-state interdependency typically exists within a broader geo-strategic,

28 Funding and finance structures common to the state capitalist model include contractor finance (eg, the state finance underpinning the EPC contracts for the Turkmenistan–China gas pipelines), forward sales of oil (eg, much of the ongoing financing supporting infrastructure development and related government procurement has been supported by the forward sale of the Republic of South Sudan's allocated oil shipped through the GNPOC and Petrodar oil pipelines) and the financing of various infrastructure projects by means of oil-backed guarantees (eg, Angola, Venezuela and Kazakhstan upstream). Build, own and operate commercial structures are typical of the state capitalist funding and finance of infrastructure development across sub-Saharan Africa. For the purposes of this chapter, the two countries that espouse state capitalist interests are the People's Republic of China and the Russian Federation through their respective structures of state-owned and partially publicly traded entities and associated development bank interests.

historical, military, political, trade and macroeconomic context, which bears on the successful development and operation of a given pipeline project. Accordingly, a core and singular concern that needs to be addressed in a cross-border pipeline development is the political, legal, regulatory and fiscal risk that may arise from government action or inaction that can adversely impact the forward development, construction or operation of a pipeline. Collectively these risk sources are referred to here as 'political risk'.

Political risk in relation to a pipeline development has two principal dimensions: state-to-state (horizontal)[29] and a state-to-pipeline sponsor (vertical).[30] The former refers to risk posed between two or more host states and is best managed through the utilisation of IGAs. The latter refers to risk posed by one or more host states to the project sponsor(s), or vice versa, and is best managed through the utilisation of HGAs.[31] The diagram above in section 4, 'Simplified contracting issues: state issues versus project sponsor issues', illustrates these two dimensions of political risk: the horizontal relationship between the host states (A and B) and the vertical relationship between the host states and project company.

(a) Chinese state capitalist model

By and large, the Chinese state capitalist and conventional funding and finance models have yielded broadly similar results in achieving the horizontal alignment necessary to mitigate political risk.[32] However, in general, the state capitalist model tends to achieve the requisite vertical alignment more easily and more quickly. Indeed, aligning the interests of host states to those of state-owned companies is often a simpler task than aligning the more asymmetric interests of state and non-state actors.

Agreements under the Chinese state capitalist model will typically include stated and unstated enforcement mechanisms that can provide far more comprehensive project de-risking benefits.[33] For instance, Chinese state capitalist sponsors can tie pipeline development funding to loans backed by the forward sale of offtake or to

---

29 State-to-state (horizontal) political risk includes lack of political support, a failure by one state to grant interconnection rights to another, a failure to agree state-to-state income allocation, the imposition of transit fees by one state on another, misaligned standards, international sanctions or armed conflict.

30 State-to-pipeline sponsor (vertical) political risk includes lack of support from the national authorities for the project; a failure to issue permits in good time; a failure to secure rights to state land; a failure to assist in identifying owners and users of state and non state land; changes in law, regulations or fiscal terms; direct, creeping or indirect expropriation; denial of access to international arbitration; or a failure to enforce an international arbitral award.

31 A vitally important dimension of vertical legal and regulatory risk is the relative capacity of the local government to handle the regulatory and fiscal assessment and ongoing interface requirements in respect of the project. Often the sheer scale of project requirements dwarfs local government capacity. Consequently, the project risk factors (delay, in particular) relate more to capacity than to an unwillingness of the local officials to properly support the project.

32 With very few exceptions, cross-border oil and gas pipelines are supported by intergovernmental agreements entered into between or among the host states in support of the pipeline. One notable exception is the Nord Stream subsea gas pipeline, which links Russian Federation gas to Germany and the central EU markets, and was developed without an IGA.

33 Chinese state capitalist interests are able to leverage the dual nature (state and commercial) of their state-owned companies. On the one hand, state-owned companies function as commercial participants entering into commercial contracting arrangements with private sector interests. On the other hand, they can appeal to their ultimate sovereign owners that can in turn act in their capacity as states to advance and protect the interests of the state companies.

other benefits in the trade and military contexts. State capitalist interests can also advance state security of supply and security of export objectives that are not part of the ordinary mandate of private sector interests. On the other hand, state capitalist interests often do not seek separate HGAs when structuring their relationships with individual host states. Rather, vertical political de-risking tends to be wrapped into the horizontal arrangements.[34] This may limit the ability of the state-owned project company to effectively invoke vertical protections in respect of particular acts and omissions of the host state. The absence of an HGA may also complicate joint venture arrangements with IOCs or other forms of future private sector investment in the asset.

(b) Conventional funding and finance model

Although Chinese state capitalist enterprises may benefit from more straightforward and faster alignment with host states and more robust enforcement mechanisms to manage political risk (particularly horizontal risk), conventional funding and finance models have also been able to secure strong IGAs and HGAs to mitigate risk and facilitate pipeline development. For instance, the Chad-Cameroon pipeline, the BTC pipeline and all three constituent components of the Southern Gas Corridor (SCPX, TANAP and TAP) are supported by robust IGAs and HGAs. In addition, the BTC pipeline, and to a certain extent the Southern Gas Corridor, was developed with strong backing and diplomatic support from the US government. Despite the apparently greater alignment between state-owned companies and host governments under the state capitalist model, the conventional funding and finance model has also managed to mobilise state-to-state support often based upon geopolitical considerations. Nevertheless, neither private sector interests, nor the MLAs or ECAs that may back them under the conventional funding and finance model, can directly access the range of non-commercial benefits available under the state capitalist model.

5.2 Host state development objectives

Oil and gas pipeline projects can often advance broader development objectives for the states hosting a pipeline. For instance, pipeline development may enable host states to export previously unmonetised resources and thus promote macroeconomic growth. This is especially true for landlocked countries, whose export options are geographically limited. To illustrate the scale of growth that pipelines can fuel, consider the case of the Republic of Azerbaijan. Between June 2006 and 2012, the BTC and parallel SCP pipelines enabled Azerbaijan to export and monetise its oil and gas resources with phenomenal impacts on the country's GDP.[35] Other examples of

---

34 According to a 2014 Brookings analysis entitled "Africa in China's Foreign Policy", available at www.brookings.edu/~/media/research/files/papers/2014/04/africa-china-policy-sun/africa-in-china-web_cmg7.pdf, Chinese investment in Africa is "mingled with foreign aid to maximize feasibility and flexibility". Chinese government agencies and state enterprises "closely combine foreign aid, direct investment, service contracts, labour cooperation, foreign trade, and export". Brookings further observes that "the proliferation of China's commercial actors in Africa in recent years has made government supervision and management particularly challenging. Beijing's inability to cope with the rapidly expanding Chinese presence in Africa is exacerbated by the lack of political risk assessment and the absence of a comprehensive commercial strategy for Africa".

35 Azerbaijan's oil-related GDP exceeded 50 per cent in 2005 and 2006. See www.adb.org/sites/default/files/publication/27709/aze.pdf.

this sort of host government development impact include the gas pipelines recently implemented across Central Asia to deliver natural gas to China.

In addition to promoting broader economic growth, oil and gas pipelines can also determine which states are able to develop broader infrastructure plans and attract high-magnitude investments. For example, the Republic of Kenya is currently planning to develop integrated infrastructure involving $27 billion in port, power, road, rail, telecom and oil export pipeline projects. In addition, local officials anticipate that a duty-free zone, ancillary to the aforementioned infrastructure development, will spark broader community development. The anticipated result is an East African trade and transportation corridor, which analysts estimate could unlock in excess of $1 trillion in trade activity for the region.[36]

Where different developers seek to implement multiple interrelated infrastructure projects (as in the case of Kenya or the KRG), a master plan is a highly prudent condition precedent to the initial feasibility studies required in respect of the particular projects. The reason for this is the frequent interdependency between projects. For example, in order to construct a pipeline, a port and road network capable of receiving, storing, shipping and transporting the line pipe and other equipment is needed. An integrated master plan will identify project synergies and help avoid investment redundancies and other adverse impacts on people, communities and the environment. Unfortunately, many developing countries are not able to properly fund and undertake the level of strategic analysis and planning activities required. In addition, as noted above, the sheer scale of project development can often dwarf the capacity of the local government to appropriately regulate and administer the project, leading to project delays and at times complete paralysis.

(a) Chinese state capitalist model

Due to the fact that the Chinese state capitalist model operates on a direct state-to-state basis, it should be well suited to undertake and implement projects within a master-planned context.[37] In addition, state capitalist interests should also be well suited to provide direct capacity-building assistance to their local host government counterparts. In effect, a more direct relationship between the project interest and the governments' sovereign interests exist to provide targeted capacity-building assistance. Accordingly, the Chinese state capitalist model is in a better position not only to execute infrastructure master plans but to properly implement oil and gas pipeline developments within the context of a broader master plan. Unfortunately, despite this structural advantage, in practice, projects using the Chinese state capitalist model have not typically pursued master planning or other host country development agendas.

36 Another example of a critically important infrastructure development is the Kurdish Regional Government's development, construction and financing of an export pipeline that transcends the interests of any particular producer. The government's interest arises from the fact that the oil and gas production is not dependent upon a single oil or gas field, producer or strategic investor. Moreover, the KRG has an interest is ensuring that the main oil and gas export pipelines provide fair and equal access to shippers who may or may not be owner sponsors of the pipeline. This interest, while important to the KRG's broader development, does not align with the funding and finance requirements of the conventional funding and finance model and thus is unlikely to materialise where this model is applied.

37 Although, as noted above, the implementation of projects on a direct state-to-state basis will present a major barrier to private sector investment in specific aspects of the value chain.

This is largely due to the fact that these agendas are often misaligned with Chinese state interests (related primarily to secure access to commodity supplies) and to the interests of host country elites who may benefit directly and indirectly from patronage associated with the specific projects themselves.

(b) Conventional funding and finance model

Conventional financial investors tend to avoid investment in greenfield and brownfield oil and gas pipeline projects in the developing world. Western strategic investors backing greenfield pipeline developments (invariably upstream producers) invest in projects that maximise their upstream value. These goals are often inconsistent with the larger development goals of host states, including the need to master-plan interdependent projects and to accommodate a broader array of potential users (including non-investor shippers) of the operational pipelines (eg, oil and gas producers and shippers in the KRG). While commercial debt is available for oil and gas pipelines and other infrastructure in the developing world, debt capacity is often limited on a regional and sector basis and in no event will capital be loaned to developing world projects in the absence of international institutional participation. Finally, conventional funding and finance is provided exclusively on a project basis and, with the exception of multilateral development banks such as the African Development Bank, does not generally accommodate broader master-plan and more fundamental host government development objectives.

5.3 Project funding and finance

In regard to project funding and finance, a key difference between the Chinese state capitalist and conventional funding and finance models is that the latter requires full project de-risking as a condition precedent to debt financing, while the former often does not. Where developing world governments cannot afford this spending, it leaves private sector developers with the task of equity funding the front-end feasibility and FEED studies – sometimes with partial help from international aid agencies such as the World Bank or national programmes like the US Trade and Development Agency. Under the state capitalist model, in contrast, the process of project de-risking is not necessarily linked to the funding and finance of a project.

(a) Chinese state capitalist model

Under the Chinese state capitalist model, funding and finance decisions for projects may be largely de-linked from the de-risking process, obviating the need for many of the activities required under the conventional funding and finance model, as discussed below. For instance, a state capitalist enterprise may agree to fund all five phases of a pipeline project (feasibility, FEED, construction, operation and decommissioning) in exchange for the forward sale of oil or gas or another form of oil-backed repayment guarantee. In another scenario, a state contractor may agree to fund the feasibility, FEED and construction phases of a project, provided that the work on these phases is contracted to the EPC contractor in question.

By compressing and reducing the due diligence and rigour associated with the feasibility and FEED de-risking process, the state capitalist model may appear to save time and reduce project cost, but by failing to adequately de-risk, projects developed in this manner are exposed to escalated project as well as sponsor risk. For example, using a form of contractor finance, the host state (and other project sponsors) may be deprived of the merits of the competitive tendering process. This may give rise to bribery and other corrupt practices in the contract award process, as well as relinquishing host state leverage over, among other things, EPC contractor cost, local content and quality of performance. Ultimately, the result may include lower quality infrastructure and adverse impacts on people, communities and the environment.[38]

(b) Conventional funding and finance model

Under the conventional funding and finance model, debt will typically not be made available to a pipeline venture prior to completion of the feasibility and FEED phases. This places emphasis upon projects sponsored by strategic investors with deep pockets promoting single, large-scale infrastructure developments. As noted above, pure financial investors will not typically invest in greenfield infrastructure projects implemented in the developing world regardless of whether they have been fully de-risked, and they certainly will not fund pre-FID development activities.

Conventional western funding and debt financing is possible in the developing world, but funding will be limited to strategic investors, and debt finance will only be disbursed after the following activities, among others, have been performed:

- The FEED study is complete, a lender-compliant tendering process has yielded an acceptable EPC contractor and equipment, and supplies and services are appropriately procured from suppliers/countries that support any tied debt facilities associated with particular ECAs;
- A project has been developed in accordance with agreed international technical, health, safety, environment, human rights and other standards, and compliance has been independently assured;
- The principal commercial agreements (the shareholders' agreement and the transportation agreement) ensure that the project cash flows are developed to yield acceptable commercial returns;
- The finance case has been tested to support minimum debt service coverage ratios (DSCR) over the life of potential loans, and the initial loan life coverage ratios (LLCR) are appropriately calibrated to the project debt capacity;

---

38 For an indicative, non-exhaustive set of examples, see www.wsj.com/articles/sri-lanka-halts-chinese-backed-construction-project-1425564657A. Work on the $1.4 billion Colombo Port City was stopped after local government inspectors looked into allegations of corruption and other contract irregularities. – see www.wsj.com/articles/SB10001424052970204138204576601980264218492. In 2011, the Myanmar government suspended work on a $3.6 billion hydro-electric project after public outcry over environmental impacts – see www.stimson.org/images/uploads/Yun_Issue_Brief1.pdf. Chad shut down China National Petroleum's operations after the company dumped excess crude oil in ditches near the capital – see www.nytimes.com/2013/09/18/world/africa/china-finds-resistance-to-oil-deals-in-africa.html?_r=1. Gabon withdrew an oil field permit from a subsidiary of the Chinese Sinopec because of environmental concerns – see www.bloomberg.com/news/articles/2013-06-06/gabonese-judges-to-arbitrate-over-addax-field-seizure. Other examples include the construction of the GNPOC and Petrodar pipelines by Chinese contractors. The pipelines straddle the Republic of Sudan and the Republic of South Sudan and are owned 40 per cent and 41 per cent, respectively, by CNPC. The oil flows have helped fuel internal conflict that led to the secession of the Republic of South Sudan in 2011, the halting of oil flows through the pipelines between January 2012 and May 2013 and 18 months of civil war in the Republic of South Sudan.

- The financing agreements, security arrangements and guarantees are fully executed;
- An IGA and relevant concession or other form of HGA or PPP arrangement have been entered into between the host states and the sponsor company;
- All licences, permits and authorisations have been secured from the host states; and
- The project has otherwise been fully de-risked, and all sponsor actions needed for FID to be issued have been taken.

The rigour and process requirements for the feasibility and FEED studies under the conventional funding and finance model add enormous complexity and professional service engagements from local and international counsel, as well as other technical, investment banking, environmental and social advisers. The consequence of this is that the timing required for the conduct of the feasibility and FEED phases of the project is extended, along with the quantum of funding. On the other hand, the rigour of the due diligence, process requirements and standards should ensure a higher quality, more transparent and sustainable project.

5.4 Project sustainability

As noted in the previous section on project funding and finance, the rigour and complexity of the cross-border pipeline development process differs between the Chinese state capitalist model and the conventional funding and finance model. These differences may influence the ultimate sustainability of projects developed under the two models. In particular, projects developed under the conventional funding and finance model, with relatively more demanding de-risking requirements, are likely to be more sustainable in the long term than those developed under the comparatively less stringent state capitalist model. Project sustainability is also essential to support long-term debt as sustainability reassures lenders that their debt will be repaid over time.

(a) Chinese state capitalist model

Under the Chinese state capitalist model, oil and gas pipeline projects are likely to undergo a less complex and less rigorous development process than projects developed under the conventional funding and finance model. While the relative simplicity of the process can save time and money in the short term, as already noted, challenges to project sustainability will likely emerge in the longer term. Specifically, product quality performance and lifespan, project economics and respect for affected people, communities and the environment may be compromised. Indeed, not only does the lack of rigour associated with the state capitalist model tend to yield inferior results and create adverse host state impacts, but the absence of rigorous processes to, among other things, properly de-risk projects has undercut the productivity of the investments and saddled the home state with 'mountains of non-performing' loans.[39]

---

39 See *Fortune* magazine, available at http://fortune.com/2014/12/01/china-investment-losses-infrastructure/.

(b) ***Conventional funding and finance model***

In contrast to project development under the state capitalist model, development under the conventional funding and finance model is characterised by more robust due diligence and transparency requirements, especially where projects are implemented by publicly traded IOCs. While the more complex process may require more time and money in the short term, it helps ensure that the project secures greater and more sustainable value in the long term.

5.5 A high-level comparison of the two approaches to funding and financing pipeline developments

On the surface, the Chinese state capitalist approach to implementing infrastructure development projects, including oil and gas pipelines, in the developing world has appeal. By conflating distinctions between sovereign and commercial relationships, certain aspects of cross-border and host government political risk that may otherwise present insurmountable impediments to a commercial enterprise operating in the developing world are mitigated. In addition, the conflation of investment and aid and the pre- and post-completion dimensions of project development also appear on the surface to yield projects that can be implemented more quickly and with fewer process constraints than may otherwise be the case using a conventional funding and finance approach. Finally, Chinese state capital can also fill at least some of the gap between the need for capital and capital available to fund required infrastructure in the developing world.

However, the apparent advantages presented by the Chinese state capitalist approach are often little more than shortcuts to responsible project management and implementation. Projects that are funded without proper de-risking are by definition risky projects, and the track record of projects implemented under the Chinese state capitalist approach generally bears this out. Over time, an increasing dissatisfaction with the Chinese state capitalist approach will likely develop in the host states as well as in China – especially as investments prove to be wasteful.[40] Moreover, the recent commodities downturn and slowing of the Chinese macro-economy are likely to further this trend going forward.

On the other hand, the conventional funding and finance approach is structurally limited in its capacity to respond to the needs of developing countries to master-plan multiple and interdependent infrastructure projects. In addition, the sheer scale of the funding required eclipses the available debt capacity of development institutions that have frequently mandated capacity limitations on a regional and a sector basis, for example it is highly unlikely that there is sufficient global debt capacity to fund more than one East Africa oil export pipeline.[41] Moreover, financial investors, who may

---

40 *Ibid.*

41 Prior to the outbreak of civil war in the Republic of South Sudan, the government had advanced plans to pursue alternative export pipelines via the Republic of Kenya and the Federal Democratic Republic of Ethiopia and the Republic of Djibouti. In addition, the respective upstream operators in the Republics of Kenya and Uganda have been debating the routing for oil export pipelines via the territories of the Republic of Tanzania. (Total is currently exploring this option as an alternative to various routings across the Republic of Kenya. It is highly unlikely that more than one oil export pipeline will be developed due primarily to constraints in global debt capacity.)

otherwise have the capacity to fill some of the gap in available capital, will simply not commit to invest in greenfield or brownfield projects in the developing world.

Table 2 summarises some of the broad conclusions that may be drawn by comparing the two models.

Table 2: State capitalist and conventional funding and finance approaches: a high-level pros/cons snapshot

Project development factor	Chinese state capitalist approach	Conventional funding and finance approach
1. Political risk	• Easier to align interests of state enterprises and host state governments and de-risk political components. • Wider array of enforcement mechanisms available to manage political risk. • Most effective in contexts where the state capitalist countries (Russia/China) have clear strategic interests (eg, to control export markets and access secure supplies oil and gas and other raw materials). • However, direct state-to-state arrangements may preclude other forms of future private sector investment in the asset	• More difficult to align asymmetric interests of state and non-state actors but no funding or finance without political de-risking. • Nevertheless, there is a core track record of examples where political alignment between and among transit states in cross-border pipelines has been achieved under a conventional funding and finance model.
2. Host state development objectives	• Better positioned to engage in master-planning integrated infrastructure beyond the scope of a particular oil or gas pipeline project. • Better positioned to engage in government capacity-building tailored to deliver project development needs.	• Less likely to fund master planning, less likely to engage in strategic planning that considers the broader state development context and less likely to debt finance feasibility studies. • Aside from the power sector, pure financial

continued on next page

Project development factor	**Chinese state capitalist approach**	**Conventional funding and finance approach**
2. Host state development objectives *continued*	• No restrictions on funding any phase of project development including feasibility and FEED studies. • Primary concern in state capitalist model is to secure export markets (Russia) or to secure access to oil and gas and other commodities (China).	investment unavailable for greenfield and brownfield infrastructure in the developing world. • Commercial lenders will not debt finance greenfield infrastructure projects in the developing world without development institutional support. • Primary concern of equity funding of oil and gas pipelines is to maximise upstream value.
3. Funding and finance	• Projects are developed in less time and, in theory, at a reduced cost. • Value to host governments is often compromised by lack of transparency, bribery and other forms of corruption and reduced leverage over project implementation, resulting in escalated cost. • EPC contractor finance often results in lower quality and a lack of local labour and overall local content. • Large-scale monies have been made available apparently without rigorous de-risking and other process and due diligence requirements.	• More time-consuming due primarily to de-risking process. • More costly as the de-risking due diligence, compliance with standards and finance negotiations take time. • Greater transparency and rigour in contractor selection, project implementation and standard of execution, yielding (in general) a higher quality outcome. • Pure financial investors unwilling to fund and commercial lenders unwilling to extend credit in the absence of international institutional guarantees.

continued on next page

Project development factor	Chinese state capitalist approach	Conventional funding and finance approach
4. Sustainability	• General deficiencies in project de-risking/due diligence. • General lack of attention to local labour and local content. • Insufficient attention to capacity building. • General failure to mitigate adverse impacts on people, communities and the environment. • Escalated costs get passed to host state often through build own operate and transfer (BOOT) models resulting in reduced long-term value to host state. • Deficiencies in sustainability.	• Greater rigour in project de-risking and implementation. • Higher standard of project implementation. • Greater attention to adverse impacts on people, communities and the environment. • Higher levels of transparency, community consultation and attention to grievances. • Enhanced overall sustainability also assures lenders that debt obligations will be fulfilled over time.

6. A glimpse forward at likely future cross-border pipelines

Over the course of the next decade at least 11 major cross-border oil and gas export pipelines will be developed across multiple regions in both developed and developing countries around the world. Table 3 summarises the likely approaches and risk factors, the likely rigour of the de-risking processes to be undertaken and the likelihood that host government development needs will be met by the various projects. Of the 11 projects referenced, at least nine will be developed in the developing world but of these only two to three are likely to use the Chinese state capitalist approach. All projects will encounter core risk factors to a greater or lesser extent, although project risk factors are likely to be uniformly more acute for projects in the developing world. Finally, the projects presenting the least likelihood of meeting host government needs will be those developed in the developing world. This is particularly concerning as it is in the developing world where the greatest need for the pipeline infrastructure is found but also the greatest vulnerability to adverse impacts.

Table 3: Likely future cross-border oil and gas pipelines

• Pipeline development • Parameters • Developed/ developing world location	• Funding/finance approach	• Likely risk factors • Rigour of de-risking process	• Likelihood that host government development needs are met
• Power of Siberia gas pipeline[42] • 61 bcm • Developing world (Russia–China)	• State capitalist • TBD	• Commercial (gas pricing offered by Chinese interests) • De-risking process unknown.	• The project will contribute to Chinese domestic security of supply. • Russia may not get the most competitive gas pricing terms, namely those offered by EU markets.
• Turkmenistan –China gas pipelines • 90 bcm (maximum combined capacity of lines A-D)[43] • Developing world	• State capitalist • Likely contractor financing and forward gas sales • Developing countries	• Commercial/ market risk (gas price) • Overall project de-risking will likely lack rigour.	• The remaining (fourth) pipeline will further alleviate security export dependency for this landlocked producer of gas. • However, the overall long-term contribution to Turkmenistan's sustainable development is questionable including master-planning (to date revenues have been deployed to build a 'marble Ashgabad').

continued on next page

42 See http://www.gazprom.com/about/production/projects/pipelines/ykv/.
43 See www.energycharter.org/fileadmin/DocumentsMedia/Thematic/China_and_the_ECT_2015_en.pdf.

• KTCS (Kazakhstan–Azerbaijan–BTC) oil export system • 500,000 bpd[44] • Developing world	• Conventional funding and finance • Equity/potential project finance	• Project complexity and commercial transportation terms • Project de-risking will be fit for purpose.	• Enormous cost of production due to governance break-downs and lack of appropriate regulation (Kashagan). • KTCS will provide export optionality to Kazakhstan but the project presents logistical and commercial challenges.
• Southern gas corridor • 10 bcm (expandable to 20 bcm)[45] • Developing and developed world (Azerbaijan–Georgia–Turkey–Greece–Albania–Italy)	• Conventional funding and finance • Equity (SCPX) and project finance (TANAP, TAP)	• Project complexity, market risk (gas price and EU demand) project cost and security. • Appropriate project de-risking on all components	• The degree to which the project contributes to regional sustainability will depend upon political risk and master-planning efforts in Turkey and the Southern Balkans (Albania, Macedonia, Kosovo and other IAP countries). • Regional Kurdish issues will continue to present security and other challenges to KRG and Turkey.

continued on next page

44 See www.chemie.kz/en/news/02-11-2009news-chem/.
45 See www.tap-ag.com/the-pipeline.

• East Africa oil pipeline • 250,000–300,000 bpd[46] • Developing world (Uganda–Kenya)	• Likely conventional funding and finance[47] • Project finance (if conventional)	• Political, lack of capacity, legal, regulatory and fiscal risk and absence of master planning • Appropriate project de-risking if conventional funding/finance	• Much will depend upon master-planning, transparent investment, proper project de-risking and attention to environmental and community needs. • A Chinese state capitalist approach (in particular absence of master-planning, proper project de-risking and extensive community consultations) would be harmful to people, communities and the environment and the sustainable development of the East Africa region.

continued on next page

46 Indicative estimates based upon combined Uganda and Kenya onshore production and personal involvement with the project(s).

47 Given the recent fall in commodities prices (generally), and the price of oil in particular, the slowdown in Chinese macro-economy and the fact that investment has not yet been committed, it is unlikely that a Chinese state capitalist approach will be pursued; however, a possibility remains that Uganda and Kenya will pursue this approach with Chinese interests, especially given CNPC's substantial interests in Uganda and broader Chinese infrastructure commitments in East Africa.

• Turk Stream Gas Pipeline • 63 bcm[48] • Developing world (Russia-Turkey)	• State capitalist • TBD	• Commercial and political • Likely appropriate project de-risking	• The extent to which this project will deliver value for Russia and for the European Union is questionable as this new-build pipeline is not being developed to deliver significant new gas sources but to redirect existing flows around the Ukraine.
• KRG–Turkey oil and gas pipelines • 1M bpd / 20 bcm[49] • Developing world	• State capitalist • TBD/raising funding may be challenging.	• Political (sovereign status of KRG), corruption and security risk • Grossly insufficient project de-risking	• KRG will need to mobilise significant international debt to compensate upstream investors and to properly master-plan expansion of its oil export. • The development of a new gas export system will be needed. • The commercial and de-risking process and structure for the oil export pipeline will need to be retrofitted in order to mobilise international funding/finance.

continued on next page

48 See www.south-stream-offshore.com.
49 Based upon indicative estimates and personal engagement with the project.

• Iraq–Jordan oil pipeline • 1M bpd • Developing world	• State capitalist • TBD • Raising funding may be challenging.	• Security risk, corruption, political • Unknown but unlikely to be sufficient de-risking.	• Strong need for Iraq to develop additional export capacity according to a country-wide master plan. • Degree to which resulting pipeline infrastructure is fit for purpose will be entirely dependent upon master-planning and project de-risking.
• Iran–Pakistan –India gas pipeline • 22 bcm[50] • Developing world	• State capitalist • TBD • Raising funding will depend upon timing of sanctions release.	• Sanctions, master-planning, security, political risk and community risk factors • Unknown	• There is a dangerous gas supply demand gap emerging in Pakistan so the new pipeline is badly needed. Supplies will also be needed in India but whether a cross-border system will be allowed over the Pakistan–India border is debatable. • Lack of proper project de-risking would create adverse impacts on people and communities.

continued on next page

50 See www.gulfoilandgas.com/webpro1/projects/3dreport.asp?id=100730.

• US–Mexico gas pipelines • Up to 14 TCF via multiple pipelines[51] • Developed world	• Conventional funding and finance	• Commercial • Rigorous project de-risking	• Pipelines will help to support delivery of gas to enable Mexico's emergence as a global manufacturing powerhouse. • Cheaper gas feedstock will help support Mexican manufacturing competitiveness.
• Keystone XL oil pipeline • 830,000 bpd[52] • Developed world (Canada–US)	• Conventional funding and finance • Developed	• Political • Commercial • Rigorous project de-risking	• Will provide a vehicle for Canada to monetise its landlocked oil sands resource (although netbacks for Canada may be enhanced by refining heavy oil in Alberta and exporting finished products). • Public relations management as environmental and social issues should be, in effect, manageable.

7. Conclusion

Clearly, the rigour associated with project de-risking should be regarded as an indispensable component to the funding and financing of all infrastructure developments, including in the context of cross-border oil and gas pipelines, regardless of whether they are implemented in the developed or developing world. In addition, a creative approach to addressing the need to mobilise funding and finance and the actual and perceived political risk associated with cross-border pipeline projects, as well as other types of infrastructure developments in the

51 See www.eia.gov/todayinenergy/detail.cfm?id=20992.
52 See http://keystone-xl.com/about/the-keystone-xl-oil-pipeline-project/.

developing world, will need to be found. Towards this end, the OECD governments, through their various aid and development agencies, could consider directing aid towards master-planning new-build infrastructure. For example, the interrelated infrastructure being proposed by the Republic of Kenya in its LAPSSET corridor is a strong candidate for this type of aid. In addition, international aid agencies and institutions such as the International Finance Corporation, the Multilateral Investment Guarantee Agency and the European Bank for Reconstruction and Development could concentrate their efforts on increasing their capacity to implement guarantees to absorb political risk to enable the deployment of greater amounts of private sector commercial debt. Host governments in the developing world will need to explore further public–private partnerships and seek to provide international equity and debt capital assurances in the form of sovereign guarantees.

I would like to thank Winifred Andersen for her comprehensive research and editorial work on this chapter and Troy Edwards, William Browning, Richard Herbert, Chris Schulten, Alexandre Chavarot, Peter Sloan and Madeleine Dimitroff for reading through the draft and offering excellent comments, edits and additions.

Refinery and petrochemical projects

Clive Ransome
Milbank, Tweed, Hadley & McCloy LLP

1. Introduction

Refinery and petrochemical projects are typically large, expensive, complex and technically demanding. They tend to have long construction periods of up to five years; their capital cost means that sponsors must have deep pockets, a proven track record in managing the technology required for any particular project and the market reach to sell complex products to sometimes geographically diverse, sophisticated and competitive markets. Refinery and petrochemical projects normally require significant debt; this typically comes from a wide range of lenders, export credit agencies (ECAs) and multilaterals. The debt mix will normally depend to a large extent on the sourcing of key process technology. Lengthy construction, commissioning and testing processes would mean that the borrower is not able to start operating and generating the cash flows required to service its loans for a number of years after first utilisation – this means that interest costs during the construction phase are high and long terms are required in relation to the debt to enable sponsors to achieve reasonable rates of return on capital invested. Projects of the scale typically found in this sector often require different tranches of financing from multiple sources such as:

- multilateral and bilateral development agencies;
- ECAs;
- international and local commercial banks; and occasionally
- Islamic financiers.

The objectives of sponsors and the concerns of lenders in refinery projects are broadly similar to those in other types of infrastructure projects. Often the sponsors must obtain financing on a highly leveraged basis, and a project's lenders will want to ensure the sustainability of a revenue stream sufficient to pay down project debt with adequate debt service coverage. However, despite the fact that there are many similar issues in project financings, refinery and petrochemicals projects frequently raise special issues – these are explored below.

Different providers of debt finance often have different perspectives, requirements and capabilities. As a result, negotiating a common set of financing terms and conditions can be difficult and time-consuming. There will often be differences in the tenor and pricing of the different tranches. It is sometimes difficult to address all the intercreditor issues which may arise, particularly in recent years those presented by the preferred creditor status of multilateral development banks.

This chapter reviews recent developments and trends in the refining and petrochemical industries and the sourcing of financing for these projects and outlines some of the typical financing terms and key requirements for the limited recourse financing of such projects. While refinery and petrochemical projects present somewhat different issues, they share many common features and for that reason we have chosen to cover both industries in this chapter. In recent years, key sponsors have sought to improve margins on refining projects by integrating refineries with large-scale petrochemical projects – we set out as a case study later in this chapter the market-leading Sadara petrochemicals project in Saudi Arabia as an example of a fully integrated large-scale refinery and petrochemical project.

2. Refining crude oil

There are two types of crude oil – sweet crude and sour crude. Sour crude contains relatively high levels of sulphur so normally requires treatment before it is ready for the refining process. This makes it more expensive to refine. Sweet crude is the industry standard and includes, for example, Brent Crude and West Texas Intermediate.

Crude oil can be light or heavy. Most simple refineries have a preference for light crude because it requires less processing. The density of crude is described as its API (American Petroleum Institute) gravity. This is an inverse measure of a hydrocarbon liquid's density as compared with that of water. The higher the API gravity, the lighter the crude. Crude with gravity below 27 degrees is considered to be heavy crude. By way of example, Basra Light Crude as sold by Iraq's Ministry of Oil in recent years has fluctuated between 28.1 and 32.2 degrees; the Basra Heavy blend has an API of around 23.6 degrees.

Where facilities are available to do so, difficult types of crude are often blended to produce an average API density, and sulphur content, which are more attractive to purchasers.

The role of a refinery is to produce physical and chemical changes in crude oil and other feedstocks. This is achieved through a series of specialised manufacturing processes. One of these processes is distillation – the separation of heavy crude oil into lighter groups (called fractions) of hydrocarbons.

Refining oils is basically simple chemistry. Crude is heated usually to around 350°C, and the vapourised petroleum is pumped into a fractionating tower. The products of heated crude rise up the tower, cool down and its components condense back into distinct liquids, collected in a series of collection trays. Lighter liquids such as kerosene and naphtha collect near the top of the tower; the heavier ones (such as lubricants and waxes) fall to the bottom. The different resulting liquids are described as "fractions".

One key fraction produced through the refining process is fuel oil. This is used for heating or for diesel fuel in the automotive industry. Another is naphtha, used in gasoline and also as the primary source from which petrochemicals are derived.

In addition to the various fractions, distillation results in heavier residues remaining after lighter fractions are extracted. Heavy residues contain carbon and hydrogen which can be used to produce more complex compounds and, ultimately, to create useful products. These are generally processed using high temperatures and low pressures.

Following distillation some products (such as jet fuel) are virtually ready for use. Most products, however, are not yet finished and further heating, pressure and chemical catalysts are required to make them into marketable products. Naphtha and by-products of the oil refining process (such as ethane and propane) are feedstocks which are processed using an operation known as "cracking". Cracking is the process of breaking down heavy oil molecules into lighter, more useful fractions. When a catalyst is used, the process is known as "catalytic cracking".

Cracking produces new products. These form the building blocks of the petrochemical industry – olefins (mainly ethylene, propylene and butadiene) and aromatics, named for their distinctive perfumed scent (mainly benzene, toluene and xylenes). These new products are then processed in petrochemical plants. The steps required for transforming olefins and aromatics into useful, more specialised, products varies depending on what the required final product may be.

Refineries can be simple or complex. The complexity of a refinery is assessed through its "Nelson Complexity". A refinery's Nelson Complexity assigns a complexity factor to each major piece of refinery equipment based on its complexity and cost in comparison to simple crude distillation, which is assigned a complexity factor of 1.0.

The complexity of each piece of refinery equipment is then calculated by multiplying its complexity factor by its throughput ratio as a percentage of crude distillation capacity. Adding up the complexity values assigned to each piece of equipment, including crude distillation, determines a refinery's complexity on the Nelson Complexity Index (NCI).

A simple refinery which involves only a distilling column, a cat reformer and some treating of gas and distillates might have an NCI of 2.1. A complex refinery may involve a cat cracker, an alkyline plant, a thermal cracker, a gas plant and hydrotreating and might have an NCI of 8–12. A very complex refinery may involve a hydrotreater, a variety of crackers, a vacuum distiller and a delayed coker and might have an NCI of 15 or above.

Figure 1: Typical yields from a barrel of light sweet crude

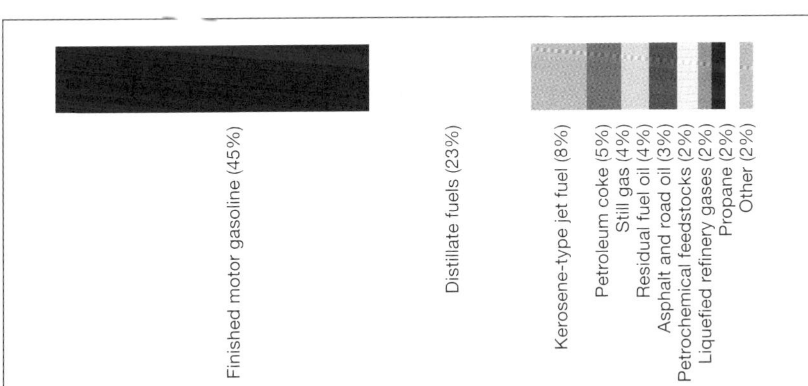

3. Petrochemical feedstocks

Petrochemical feedstocks are the various hydrocarbons derived from the refining of oil, gas and coal. These hydrocarbons are further refined to produce petrochemical products. They are the building blocks of the petrochemical industry.

Feedstocks are converted into a range of chemical products with a wide array of uses. At the feedstock stage, they are usually known as "intermediates" – the intermediates are then processed into plastics, liquids and resins which ultimately are turned into marketable products. Some feedstocks are used in the direct production of petrochemicals, such as methane, benzene, toluene and xylenes (benzene, toluene and xylenes as a group are referred to as "BTX" in the petrochemicals industry). Ethane, propane, butanes, naphtha and gas oil are optional feedstocks for steam crackers which produce intermediate petrochemical feedstocks. Other examples of intermediate feedstocks include ethylene, propylene, butenes and butadiene.

Gas and oil are by far the most common starting points for feedstocks – they are readily available and can be processed efficiently. As a result, petrochemical companies often build petrochemical plants close to oil and gas refineries – operational costs, such as transportation, are reduced as a result, and often major infrastructure such as ports, railways and roads can serve more than one plant. Coal-derived feedstock is predominantly methanol, obtained from a coal-to-liquids process. Coal can also be gasified to produce feedstocks.

Methane, ethane, propane and butanes are mainly obtained from natural gas. Naphtha and gas oil, as well as benzene, toluene and xylenes are obtained from petroleum refineries. Ethylene, propylene and butadiene are the basic building blocks of all olefins (also known as alkenes) and these form the basis for many common products.

Synthesis gas (also known as syngas), is gas obtained from synthesising hydrogen and carbon monoxide. This can also be converted into feedstock. Syngas can also be an intermediate by-product developed during the processing of ammonia, methanol, synthetic petroleum or synthetic natural gas. Petroleum by-products which might otherwise end up as waste can be conserved as feedstock. During the gasification refining process, any material which contains carbon can normally be processed and used.

Since feedstocks and the end products vary, there are many different petrochemical production technologies. An ethylene-producing plant is most likely to use catalytic cracking, a technique that uses high pressure and high temperatures to crack natural gas. By contrast, a methanol-producing plant uses a reforming process, using high temperature steam, medium pressure and a catalyst to produce products.

Oil, gas and coal are still in reasonable supply in many parts of the world and are, at the time of writing, comparatively inexpensive. Alternative sources for petrochemical feedstocks have been developed over the years, however – feedstocks can be produced from sugar cane, corn and other organic agricultural sources. The use of food for fuel is controversial in some countries but remains a viable alternative for countries with few fossil fuel resources but space for large-scale agriculture.

4. Feedstock and geography

Feedstock supplies vary between different regions. Supply trends change with time. Ethane feedstock supply has decreased in the Middle East and Canada in recent years. New oil and gas discoveries have impacted on the petrochemical industries of the United States, Brazil and Canada. The United States and Brazil have benefited from recent discoveries of shale gas and pre-salt reserves.

In Canada, ethane production has reduced in recent years because of reduced natural gas supply from the Western Canadian Sedimentary Basin. The Canadian petrochemical sector is now focusing on the discovery of bituminous oil, which now accounts for more than 50% of the country's crude oil production for meeting future feedstock needs.

The petrochemical sectors of Saudi Arabia, Iran and Qatar have traditionally used ethane as the main petrochemical feedstock, but securing new ethane supplies has become difficult because of the high demand from existing petrochemical plants and the energy sector and major expansions of existing plants (such as Saudi Arabia's PetroRabigh Project). Petrochemical plants in the Middle East are usually based on naphtha feedstock.

Natural gas production has increased in Saudi Arabia, Iran and Qatar but not sufficiently to meet all demand. Despite the increases in natural gas production in Saudi Arabia and Iran, ethylene capacity has increased even more. Qatar's ethane production has been restricted because of a moratorium on its North Dome gas field.

The largest petrochemicals producers at the turn of the millennium were the United States, Western Europe and Japan. Over the last 15 years a number of Asian countries including South Korea, Singapore and Taiwan have significantly expanded their petrochemicals production capabilities. Lately, Saudi Arabia and Kuwait have built extensive new capacity. These new facilities are aimed at servicing the fastest-expanding petrochemical markets – China, Latin America and the Middle East. The emergence of China's shale gas and coal industries has also changed the face of the world's feedstock supplies. This ongoing development in China will support the country's growing economy.

5. Recent industry trends

The last decade has seen many changes in the refining and petrochemical industries. There has been a significant decline in the refining industry in Western Europe and the United States, but both industries have grown significantly in non-OECD countries. Many major oil and gas companies have sold off or mothballed their refineries, but other oil and gas companies are building new refineries in China and the Middle East and integrating them closely with upstream activities. In the last five years, major financings have included:

- the PetroRabigh Expansion Project (Saudi Arabia);
- Sadara (Saudi Arabia);
- the Jubail Refinery (Saudi Arabia);
- the Egyptian Refinery Company Refinery (Egypt);
- the Guru Gobind Singh Bhatinda Refinery (India);
- multiple extensions of the Jamnagar 2 Refinery (India);

- the Paradip Refinery (India);
- the 10+ expansion of the Grupa Lotos Gdansk Refinery Expansion (Poland);
- the SOCAR Turcas Aegean Refinery (Turkey); and
- the Nghi Son refinery (Vietnam).

The bulk of new project financed refineries to be built between 2015 and 2020 are likely to be located in non-OECD countries, particularly in India, the Middle East and North Africa and the Asia Pacific region.

There has also been significant recent change in the petrochemical industry. Natural gas prices in the United States have plummeted as a result of the shale gas boom and the United States now produces some of the world's cheapest natural gas (the primary feedstock for most petrochemical projects). A decade ago high natural gas prices forced many petrochemical companies to shut down or scale back their operations; now the United States has become one of the most attractive destinations for investment and many new petrochemical plants are expected to be constructed there within the next decade. Major new gas discoveries have been made in difficult parts of the world, most notably ENI's recent supergiant gas discovery at Zohr Prospect in the Egyptian Mediterranean (which could have a major impact on refining, LNG production and the petrochemicals industry in Egypt).

The petrochemical industry is also continuing to develop plants in other jurisdictions which benefit from low feedstock costs. There continues to be a high level of development of petrochemical plants in the former Commonweatlth of Independent States, but sanctions against Russia and Russian entities have caused the collapse of US and European support for new oil and gas projects in Russia. Countries such as Kazakhstan and Uzbekistan have progressed polyethylene and polypropylene projects aimed at Far East markets with extensive investment and finance from key Korean and Chinese investors and ECAs in particular.

6. Recent trends in the sourcing of debt finance

After the onset of the financial crisis in 2007, commercial banks scaled back their lending to energy and infrastructure projects, including refining and petrochemical projects. This problem has been compounded by banking downgrades and Eurozone instability, which have had a disproportionate impact on European banks, traditionally the dominant commercial lenders in project finance. Moreover, the increase in capital requirements introduced by Basel III may make it more expensive for commercial banks to use their capital to support long-term financings. Increasingly, commercial banks are allocating their scarce capital to key relationship clients.

Fortunately, ECAs and multilateral development banks (such as the International Finance Corporation, European Bank for Reconstruction and Development, Asian Development Bank, African Development Bank and Inter-American Development Bank) have increased their lending to energy and infrastructure projects. As refinery and petrochemical projects tend to source services, equipment and works from a wide range of OECD countries, it is often possible for sponsors to adopt a contracting strategy which ensures that a large portion of the services, equipment and works are sourced from countries whose ECAs are willing and able to support their exporters by providing financing for such projects.

ECA financing can either take the form of direct lending or the guarantee or insurance of loans provided by commercial banks under covered loan facilities. The pricing and tenor of ECA financing tends to compare favourably with other sources of financing. Under the OECD's Arrangement on Officially Supported Export Credits, ECAs are able to extend loans with a tenor of up to 14 years from the starting point of credit (or provisional acceptance of the relevant facility), which (depending on the duration of the construction period) can equate to a debt tenor of 18 years door-to-door. In many large-scale downstream financings, ECA direct and/or covered facilities account for the majority of the debt finance.

Multilateral development banks have also played an increasingly important role in financing refining, petrochemical and other energy and infrastructure projects in emerging markets. Through their A Loan/B Loan loan structures, they are able to extend the benefits of their political strength and – in some cases – preferred creditor status to international commercial banks and make it more attractive for such banks to participate in a financing, particularly one with long tenors.

7. Key financing terms for a downstream project

7.1 Debt sizing and equity commitments

The ultimate debt capacity of a refinery or petrochemical project will depend on its underlying economics and on the results of various sensitivities that have been run through the financial model. Typically, the sponsors and lenders will run sensitivities for changes in certain key variables such as interest rates, feedstock prices, project costs, technical performance, product prices and operating costs. Although the results of such economic and sensitivity analysis will vary from project to project, most recent projects in the refining and petrochemical sector that have been financed on a limited recourse basis have been so at a debt to equity ratio of 70:30 or 65:35. Typically, the sponsors fund their equity commitments through a combination of share capital and deeply subordinated shareholder loans.

7.2 Equity funding

Sponsors typically prefer to fund their equity in proportion to the senior debt, while lenders normally prefer that the sponsors fund their equity upfront. Often this issue is resolved by having the sponsors fund a portion of their equity up front, with the balance being funded on a fully committed basis in proportion to senior debt.

7.3 Completion and completion support

In almost all refining projects and in most petrochemical projects, the sponsors are required to give a completion guarantee (or debt service undertaking) in relation to the repayment of the project loans if project completion is not achieved by an agreed long-stop date. Project completion is usually defined to be the date when:

- the refinery or petrochemical facility has:
  - been commissioned and achieves substantial or provisional acceptance

    under the relevant engineering, procurement and construction (EPC) contract or contracts;
  - satisfied the agreed performance and reliability tests demonstrating over a period of time that it can reliably operate in accordance with certain performance criteria;
  - met certain financial tests;
  - received all required governmental approvals and licences to operate; and
- the project company has:
  - complied with all applicable covenants (including any covenants relating to environmental or social matters) under the relevant finance documents;
  - funded a debt service reserve account to the required level (typically an amount equal to six months' debt service); and
  - satisfied certain other customary conditions to project completion.

As the financing will typically become non-recourse to the sponsors after it is achieved, the definition of project completion is often subject to considerable negotiation.

In some projects it has been possible for the sponsors to provide for the lenders to drop the requirement for a completion guarantee (or debt service undertaking) and to replace it instead with a capped contingent equity facility under which the sponsors agree to contribute more equity to the project company if there is a project cost overrun or the project company is required to buy down a portion of the senior debt if the project does not achieve the performance guarantees assumed by the base case projections. There is an important link between the EPC structure for refineries and petrochemicals projects and the completion support which lenders will require. In older, simpler financings lenders often required the sponsors to secure a robust lump sum turnkey EPC contract from reputable, experienced and creditworthy contractor(s) and to actively manage construction risk. In the larger, more complex (and recent) financings split EPC contract packages has become the norm. In sizing a contingent equity facility, lenders (with the assistance of their technical adviser) will take into account:

- the risk of a delay in achieving provisional or substantial acceptance;
- the risk that there will be a cost overrun;
- the level of contingencies set out in the approved project budget; and
- the risk of the refinery or petrochemical facility not meeting the technical performance guarantees assumed by the base case.

7.4 Debt amortisation

Refining margins and petrochemical product prices tend to be cyclical. As a result, the loan repayment profile for most refinery and petrochemical financings is designed to give the project company some flexibility so that in good times it can repay principal more quickly and in lean times principal can be repaid more slowly. This flexibility is effected by having two amortisation schedules: a mandatory loan amortisation schedule which must always be met to avoid being in default, and a target loan amortisation schedule which the project company must meet to the extent that it has sufficient excess cash flow after covering:

- operating costs;
- taxes;
- interest;
- commitment and other lender fees;
- principal payments required under the mandatory repayment schedule; and
- the funding of certain reserve accounts.

The project company will be barred from making any dividends, distributions or payments on subordinated shareholder loans to the sponsors if at the relevant time it has not achieved the target loan amortisation schedule.

7.5 Expansions and expansion financing

It has become the norm for sponsors to seek to hardwire the potential for expansion of refineries and petrochemical plants into an initial financing. This may involve inserting into the initial common terms agreement expansion criteria and the concept of permitted additional debt – this has been a contentious subject in the larger Middle East projects in recent years.

8. Potential debt sources for financing refineries and petrochemical projects

8.1 Commercial banks

Refinery and petrochemical projects have traditionally been financed by commercial banks, in part because these sources have had substantial experience in non-recourse and limited-recourse financing in oil and gas, mineral, power and other infrastructure projects. This has meant that commercial banks are well-versed in both the process and substance of project financing. Nonetheless, as a result of the general contraction of credit in the commercial bank market, there are fewer active commercial banks in the project finance market willing to lend on a long-term basis in emerging markets across the globe.

The ability of international commercial banks to participate in refinery and petrochemical projects in emerging markets may also be affected by the regulatory environment in the bank's home jurisdiction. If banks in the United States, United Kingdom, Europe or Japan are required to set aside significant reserves in connection with loans to such projects, the loans may not produce sufficient risk-adjusted returns to be economically attractive. Accordingly, innovative structures, including debt for equity and debt for debt swaps, may need to be devised to alleviate such requirements.

These sorts of issues being faced by international commercial banks heighten the importance of local banks, capital markets and multilateral agencies as keystone lenders to emerging markets refinery projects.

8.2 Multilateral agencies/export-import banks

In the emerging markets, multilateral agencies and ECAs are playing a critical role in the development and financing of major projects. These agencies are described in Clive Ransome's chapter on ECAs; the most active in recent years include the World Bank, International Finance Corporation, Asian Development Bank, Export-Import Bank of the United States, Japan Bank for International Cooperation, Overseas Private Investment Corporation, Multilateral Insurance Guaranty Agency, Korea EximBank, UK Export Finance, SACE, Coface and Euler Hermes. While many of these entities do not have sufficient resources to meet the enormous capital requirements needed to develop a major refinery or petrochemicals project alone, they have other significant attributes, including:

- the capacity to provide both equity and debt;
- the ability to provide political risk insurance to sponsors, suppliers and lenders; and
- the ability to furnish soft risk protection for projects that might otherwise be unfinanceable due to political risk considerations.

The long-term effectiveness of multilateral agencies and ECAs in promoting petrochemicals and refinery initiatives will ultimately depend on their ability to mobilise other sources of capital (normally through international commercial banks, local institutions and specialist funding entities such as pension funds). The multilaterals and ECAs act as a catalyst to private sources of capital from banks, institutional investors and the public capital markets. Financing an emerging market refinery or petrochemicals project without multilateral or ECA support has become very difficult since the 2007 financial crisis.

8.3 Capital markets, Islamic finance and *sukuk* issues

Projects have long sought access to the bond and commercial paper markets, generally backed by a commercial bank or other type of guarantee. Projects now are seeking access to such markets without any form of credit enhancement. Islamic finance and *sukuk* bond issues are the most significant new development in the refineries and petrochemicals financing sector in recent years – the *sukuk* issues on the Jubail and Sadara financings are the largest ever achieved in the market to date. Integrating these structures into a multi-sourced financing has raised a number of new technical, commercial and practical issues – these are explored in more detail in the Sadara case study at the end of the chapter.

Tapping the public markets involves certain trade-offs which must be recognised at the outset. An important consideration for a public market financing is the inflexibility involved in such financing during the construction phase. Structuring a project financing for the public market also requires attention to all potential material contingencies. In a private deal, experienced lenders are generally equipped to address unanticipated problems which may arise, normally monitoring a project through an independent engineer. The lenders are closely involved during the construction phase, often providing consents and waivers to borrowers as unanticipated issues arise. By contrast, in a capital markets context, it may prove difficult for sponsors to obtain waivers or to amend agreements which are sometimes necessary during the construction phase of a complex project. Typically, concerns about liability make trustees for bondholders reluctant to take discretionary action and it is impracticable to get bondholders to grant consents and waivers. As a result, public capital market deals often have fewer covenants and controls than bank deals, to reduce the likelihood that individual investor consents will be required.

Another important issue is the negative carrying cost of unspent bond proceeds during the construction period. Bank loans are drawn down on a monthly basis as construction of a refinery project advances. With a public deal, a borrower receives all of the money at closing and is required to invest the portion not immediately used in short-term investments. That means the borrower has borrowed at the significantly more expensive long-end of the yield curve, but is earning very little on the money invested at the short-end.

Normally a project will need to be rated for its bonds or rates by one of the recognised international ratings agencies (Standard & Poor's, Moody's or Fitch) to be successfully placed in the public market. To achieve an investment-grade rating for a public deal covering construction and operation requires a strong contractual framework, full disclosure of all potential risks and very thorough due diligence. In recent major Middle East projects *sukuk*s have been successful, but are normally issued a short time after the main financial closing of the initial debt facilities – this has enabled them to use the certainty and availability of the initial funding to incentivise *sukuk* investors.

9. Criteria for assessing financeability

9.1 Risk categories

In a project financing, the lenders look primarily to the cash flows of the project they are financing instead of to the credit of the sponsor(s) of such project. Potential lenders will conduct extensive due diligence on any refining or petrochemical project to ensure that all relevant risks have been identified and addressed. Some of the key issues which lenders to a refinery or petrochemical project would expect the sponsors to address are as follows:

- feedstock supply risk;
- market, pricing and offtake risk;
- completion risk;
- technology risk;
- operating risk;
- legal risk;
- currency risk;
- political risk;
- environmental risk;
- taxation;
- governmental assistance.

The extent to which these risks should be addressed depends upon the financing parties involved, the country in which the refinery or petrochemicals project is located and the relevant by-product. While comprehensive coverage of these risks would be ideal, in reality the allocation of risks is the subject of extensive negotiation and compromise.

(a) ***Feedstock supply risk***

Feedstock is essential to keep a refinery or petrochemicals plant running. Most plants are designed to include limited on-site storage, so continuity of feedstock supply is usually important. The risk with respect to feedstock supply is that there may not be an uninterrupted or sufficient supply. Deliveries of feedstocks and other inputs in the refining process (such as catalysts, electricity, natural gas and hydrogen) can be interrupted by a variety of events, including:

- shortages of shipping vessels;
- closures of pipelines supplying the project or refinery;
- embargoes; and
- other national or international political events.

Although in many cases alternative feedstocks or materials will be available from other suppliers or through different methods of delivery, lenders generally expect to be protected against feedstock supply risk, typically by insisting on a long-term feedstock contract entered into with a reliable supplier, with the provision for credit support and the payment of adequate damages in the event of non-performance. The arrangements will differ depending on how the feedstock is to be delivered (pipeline or tanker) and the flexibility of the facility to process different feedstock. For example, an inland petrochemicals project which relies on gas delivered by pipeline will have more onerous supply guarantees than a seaboard refinery with its own jetty which can process a wide variety of crudes. In any event, what the lenders will want to see is certainty of supply, a reasonable credit in the feedstock supplier, and a contractual structure which is designed to incentivise the feedstock supplier to perform (and to penalise the supplier appropriately if it fails to do so). While lenders may be willing to accept market pricing for feedstock, they are not normally prepared to take risk on feedstock volume. Feedstock supply agreements therefore often generally impose deliver or pay obligations on the supplier so that liquidated damages are levied if there is a failure to deliver. The term of the feedstock supply contracts is customarily a few years longer than the final loan maturity date under the loan facilities.

(b) ***Market, pricing and offtake risk***

Lenders will want to ensure that there is a robust market for the product slate to be produced by the relevant refinery or petrochemicals plant. Lenders generally seek the advice of a market consultant to evaluate and opine on the strength of the market and the project company's marketing strategy – the marketing report for both types of project is a crucial piece of commercial due diligence. Unless the target markets are perceived to be generally robust, the lenders may require the project company to enter into long-term offtake contracts for some or all of its products with creditworthy offtakers – this can be very difficult or impossible to achieve in the most valuable target markets such as Japan, Korea and South East Asia. Unlike the supply side, take or pay obligations in offtake contracts have not been the norm in many projects in recent years.

Offtake purchasers are often a wide range of trade and market purchasers of different types ranging from airport fuel suppliers to petrol and diesel sellers through to small lubricants suppliers to the automotive industry – so a diverse range of credits. Sponsors and lenders rely upon the proceeds of offtake to satisfy debt service, meet fixed costs and provide equity returns. Lenders will require legal assurance through the sales contracts that the purchasers will perform their payment obligations in a timely manner during the term of the financing, but also that the project's products are priced in a manner which is competitive in the relevant market or markets and sufficient to support the project's cash-flow requirements. Both the purchase price for hydrocarbon feedstock and the sale price for products are likely to be determined under the relevant contracts by reference to a market price; the lenders will want to ensure that the margin between the two sets of prices is likely to be sufficiently large to ensure that the refinery or petrochemical facility will generate enough cash flow to service their loans, as well as to pay dividends to the sponsors. In analysing and running sensitivities on project cash flows, the lenders will look not only to the pricing formulas set out in the feedstock supply and product sale agreements, but also at historic and projected global and regional margins for the products in question.

Market-based pricing requires exhaustive due diligence. Markets and prices for petrochemical products are driven by factors beyond the control of the sponsors and lenders, including:

- the aggregate demand for crude oil and feedstocks (which fluctuates with changes in economy and price);
- the impact of energy conservation efforts;
- international political and economic events; and
- refinery utilisation rates within the particular derivative-product industry.

It is difficult for lenders to insulate themselves fully against market-based risks. Commodity hedging can provide protection against a declining (or advancing) market through:

- price floors (and ceilings);
- provisions which increase an offtaker's minimum quantity commitment to counterbalance declining prices;
- sponsor support agreements (such as the subordination of any sponsor claims under feedstock supply agreements); and
- other margin stabilisation mechanisms.

These structures are designed to shift the risk of declining (or advancing) market prices to either or both the offtakers and the sponsors.

Where lenders can be persuaded to accept the risks associated with market-based pricing, it generally tends to be the case that:

- the lenders believe that the market price of the product will remain within a narrow, predictable band of volatility;
- the lenders believe – on the basis of expert marketing advice – that the refinery or petrochemicals project will be a low-cost and high-profit producer

of the relevant product, thus providing a margin to insulate lenders from price fluctuations; and

- the project has strong and experienced sponsors – the nature of the sponsors' involvement in the project, such as high levels of equity investment and/or indications that the project is of a strategic nature, help increase the lenders' confidence that the sponsors will continue to support the project should market conditions deteriorate.

(c) Completion risk

The lenders, as well as the sponsors, will want to ensure that the project is built on time and in accordance with the performance parameters set out in the base case. If completion of the refinery or petrochemical facility is significantly delayed or if the facility is unable to meet the performance standards contemplated by the base case, the project company may have difficulty generating the cash flow required to make principal and interest payments with respect to the loans when due.

To mitigate this risk, lenders in the past sometimes required the project company to enter into a fixed price turnkey EPC contract with a reliable, experienced and creditworthy contractor. Under this type of structure the contractor would be required to guarantee the completion of the project by a specificed date and give performance guarantees, including:

- a guarantee of throughput;
- guarantees of process unit efficiencies;
- a guarantee of the product slate the refinery or petrochemical facility is capable of producing; and
- a guarantee of utility consumption.

If the contractor fails to complete the project by the required date, the EPC contract would normally provide for the contractor to pay delay liquidated damages. Where performance falls short of the guaranteed performance levels, the EPC contract would provide for performance liquidated damages to be paid by the contractor (subject always to overall limits to the aggregate quantum of liquidated damages). After an extended period of delay, delay liquidated damages would hit their cap and the EPC contractor would face the risk of having its EPC contract terminated for its default. Similarly, performance liquidated damages apply only to limited shortfalls in performance. Performance above a defined minimum level will be mandatory and no buydown by the EPC contractor would apply to such shortfalls.

The market has, however, in recent years moved away from the single point of contact turnkey contract through a main contractor who wraps all subcontractors. Technologies continue to change; it is often difficult or impossible in practice for a contractor to wrap a technology provider who will be providing limited guarantees or contractual commitments in relation to specific process technology. The cost of wrapping risks can be prohibitive. As a result, in the larger and more complex projects split EPC packages have become the norm – by way of example there were almost 100 EPC packages in the Sadara project.

As mentioned above, the lenders will also require that the sponsors provide a completion guarantee undertaking or alternative completion support (such as a debt service undertaking) until project completion is achieved. As with many other types of project, there is an important link between the structure and strength of the EPC arrangements and the scope and extent of sponsor support the lenders will require. The weaker the sponsor completion support, the more robust the transfer of risk onto the contractor under the EPC contract needs to be (and vice versa).

(d) Technology risk

Lenders will want to ensure that the refinery or petrochemical facility uses process technology which has been tested and proven on a commercial scale, and generally at the scale of the project in question. This is not typically an issue for a refinery project since most of the processing methods currently used in the refining industry have been in commercial use for several decades. Occasionally this has, however, been an issue for petrochemical projects. For example, gas to liquids technology is relatively recent and some gas to liquids projects have experienced difficulty in achieving the performance levels required to satisfy the lenders' project completion test.

Petrochemical projects often use a variety of processing techniques. Process units for certain types of technology are produced by relatively few manufacturers; often the warranties and liabilities process manufacturers are prepared to provide are limited and difficult to negotiate. The project company will enter into licensing and technology transfer agreements with the leading licensors of the relevant process unit technology. The track record of licensors and their technology is particularly important as the licence and technology transfer agreements are normally subject to limited recourse against the licensors and have low relative caps on liability when compared with the damage to a project (and its revenues) caused by failed process technology.

(e) Operating risk

As oil refining and petrochemical production are specialised activities, the lenders will want to ensure that the project company has the technical and practical ability and physical resources to operate and maintain the relevant facility once it has been completed efficiently and effectively. As project companies are generally special purpose companies with no prior history, the sponsors need to demonstrate that the project company will have appropriate expertise and resources available to it on commencement of operations. If the sponsors cannot demonstrate that the project company will have such capability in time, the lenders will require the project company to enter into an operation and maintenance agreement with an experienced third party operator whereby such third party agrees to perform the operation and maintenance of the facility. It is not uncommon for lenders to encourage sponsors without a track record in operations to form a joint venture with a company with substantial experience in the relevant industry.

(f) Legal risk

Project participants – especially lenders – need comfort that if any problems arise there is a well-developed body of commercial law, an independent judiciary and an expedient legal process to resolve such disputes. The legal framework should recognise arbitral awards and foreign judgments and allow for enforcement of contract rights and collateral security interests by lenders following default.

Emerging market governments can offer further certainty and reliability to sponsors and lenders by allowing mediation or arbitration in a neutral forum. Since government or government-controlled entities will often be party to any such dispute, assurance of an impartial, fast-track forum for dispute resolution – located outside the host country – will increase the confidence of lenders and sponsors in the security of their investment.

Where possible, sponsors and lenders will want the project agreements to be governed by the law of a jurisdiction that has an internationally recognised body of commercial precedent, rather than local law. At least as far as security documents and enforcement of collateral over assets located in the host country are concerned, sponsors and lenders have to date accepted local legal risk provided that disputes in respect of such laws are resolved by arbitration in a neutral forum.

A further complication arises where the party to the agreement is a government or a government-controlled enterprise, since this type of entity may be reluctant to agree to foreign governing law and, in any event, may enjoy sovereign immunity. Even if a sovereign entity were to agree to foreign law, any foreign judgment that is later obtained may not be enforceable against that entity in the host country. Therefore, it is advisable to either obtain a waiver of the government entity's sovereign immunity or agree to local law, provided that any disputes are resolved by arbitration in a neutral forum.

Lenders will want comfort that the project company and the project will operate in a legal and fiscal framework which is stable. If the agreements that document the project cannot be enforced in the host country, then the lenders will have no confidence in the contractual framework for the project. Likewise, the lenders will want to ensure fiscal stability. In preparing their financial model, the lenders will make certain assumptions about the fiscal regime that will apply to the project company and the project. If those assumptions turn out to be incorrect, then the project company may not generate sufficient after-tax net income to service the loans.

If the project is sited in a country with a stable and well-developed legal system, lenders are often willing to take this risk. However, if the project is sited in an emerging market with a developing legal and economic system, lenders will often insist that the project company or sponsors enter into an implementation agreement or host government agreement with the host country which stabilises the fiscal regime (and sometimes the legal regime) applicable to the project company and project and contains an undertaking to issue any required consents or approvals. The implementation agreement often includes undertakings from the sponsors and/or the project company to invest a certain minimum amount in the project, provide training to local employees and, to the extent competitive in terms of price and quality, give preference to local suppliers and vendors. The implementation agreement or host government agreement would also include language allowing the lenders to rely on such stabilisation and other undertakings and to step into the shoes of the project company and enforce such undertakings if their loans went into default.

Host government and implementation agreements exist in many countries, including Turkey, Uzbekistan, Vietnam, Indonesia and across West Africa. To support the Nghi Son refinery project in Vietnam, the Vietnamese government entered into a government guarantee and undertaking agreement which sets out the applicable currency, legal, taxation and offtake regimes for such a project. Likewise, the government of Uzbekistan entered into an investment agreement to create legal and fiscal stability for Uz-Kor's gas to chemicals project in Uzbekistan.

(g) Currency risk

Lenders are likely to provide the bulk of debt finance in US dollars. Lenders will be keen to see that the project company has access to hard currency to service its loans. The project company is also likely to incur at least some of its operating expenses in US dollars.

It is market practice for the purchase price for refinery products and some petrochemicals products to be denominated and paid in US dollars. Where offtake is purchased in other currencies, hedging mechanisms can be adopted to mitigate currency risk. These arrangements will need to address the availability, convertibility and rate fluctuations of foreign currency. Currency availability and convertibility guarantees can sometimes be obtained from a host government or central bank. As stated above, conventional ECA cover will normally include currency unavailability and inconvertibility. Where the offtaker's payments are denominated and payable in local currency, it may be possible to include some form of exchange rate indexation in the offtake price to shift the risk of adverse currency movements from the project to the offtaker.

(h) Political risk

In cases where the refinery project being undertaken in a country is the first of its kind to involve substantial foreign investment, lenders may be unwilling to absorb certain risks of a political nature. This is particularly the case where the investment is in a sector which was previously government controlled. Lenders will also want to ensure that, to the extent possible, political risks – including the risk of expropriation, nationalisation, revocation of licences and approvals, government interference, political violence, terrorism and civil war – are mitigated so far as practicable. In some jurisdictions these risks can be mitigated by the host government entering into an implementation agreement with respect to the project. Implementation and similar agreements should ideally provide for international arbitration in the event of a dispute.

Other types of political events may be partly covered by political risk insurance. Events for which such coverage may be available include:

- sabotage;
- war;
- confiscation;
- expropriation;

- nationalisation;
- indirect interference (eg, creeping expropriation);
- revocation of permits;
- discriminatory taxation; or
- regulation against the project or project sponsors or incidental interference (eg, governmental actions affecting feedstock supply or the transportation thereof).

Political risk insurance is generally provided by ECAs as outlined above. Political risk insurance is, however, normally limited in amount and is not available for all countries.

There are other alternatives to mitigate political risk (so-called "soft political risk insurance") which require no government involvement. These include forming a joint venture with a local company, ensuring extensive local participation in the refinery project, including a multilateral agency in the financing or ensuring that the syndicate of lenders is from a broad range of countries (including the host country).

(i) Environmental risk

All lenders will be concerned to see that due diligence is performed on the environmental and social risks and that the project is structured so as to limit these risks to the greatest extent practicable. Multilateral financial institutions such as the International Bank for Reconstruction and Development and the International Finance Corporation (which are both part of the World Bank group) have over recent years set the template in international projects for environmental due diligence and compliance. Under World Bank standards, proposed projects are classified into one of three categories depending on the type, location, sensitivity and scale of project and the nature and magnitude of their potential environmental and social impacts, with category A projects having the greatest environmental and social impacts and category C projects having the least. Most greenfield refinery or petrochemical projects are likely to be considered category A projects.

Under the World Bank approach, the project company or an independent third party expert must have consulted in a structured and culturally sensitive way with the indigenous peoples and local NGOs in the region of the planned refinery or petrochemical facility. A full environmental and social assessment, normally in the form of a study, must be prepared to examine the project's potential positive and negative environmental impacts, and recommending any measures required to mitigate environmental impacts and improve environmental performance. An environmental management plan must also be prepared by the project company or a third party expert that draws on the conclusions of the environmental and social assessment and addresses issues such as mitigation, action plans and management of risks.

More than 70 commercial banks, representing over 85% of the commercial bank project finance market, have adopted the Equator Principles under which they agree to comply with the World Bank's approach to environmental and social issues (including the World Bank's performance standards) for projects in excess of $10 million. Therefore, even if no member of the World Bank group is involved in the financing of a refinery or petrochemical project, it is highly likely that some of the other lenders will be required to comply with the Equator Principles. OECD ECAs have also adopted a common approach to environmental and social issues which is similar to that of the World Bank.

(j) Taxation

Potential liability to interest withholding, stamp and other types of applicable taxes is as important to project economics as the more common issues of depreciation and deductibility of expenses. Interest-withholding tax is normally levied on payments of interest to non-residents (ie, foreign lenders); stamp or real estate taxes may be assessed on the principal amount of the debt; and other types of taxes may be levied on local companies (including the project company) which have foreign ownership. If the government wishes to reduce the capital and operating cost of the project, and thereby to reduce the cost of the refined product, it may consider granting appropriate exemptions.

(k) Governmental assistance

The commitment and allocation of resources, both labour and financial, which are required to develop, finance, construct and operate an international refinery or petrochemicals project are substantial. Often in such projects there are long lead times before achieving milestones such as financial closing and so sponsors often seek assurances from the host government which give them exclusive rights to negotiate for the construction, ownership and operation of such project for a definite period.

In addition, a sponsor will want to ensure that the government gives it all necessary property rights, access to transportation, land and, if required, sea access to the project site in order to carry out all construction and operation activities.

Typically, in countries where permits and government approvals under local law are subject, in part, to governmental discretion, sponsors and lenders might also seek positive support and assistance from the government in obtaining – and maintaining – all necessary permits and approvals required for the construction and operation of the refinery or petrochemicals project.

In some countries, foreign insurers are prohibited from offering insurance locally. Project participants will be reluctant to rely on coverage from local insurance companies which in some instances may be small, relatively inexperienced and unknown in the international market and therefore an unsatisfactory credit risk. Two possible measures to mitigate insurance concerns are to obtain insurance from the local insurance companies and reinsure those risks offshore with international insurers (this measure may have a substantial cost impact), or to seek an exemption from the government for insurance coverage for the project from foreign insurers.

Other related issues that may need to be addressed in enhancing the financeability of a project include obtaining exemptions from any restrictions or duties on the import of spare parts and equipment necessary for the construction of the refinery or petrochemicals plant. Frequently, in addition to local labour, sponsors will need qualified expatriate personnel to construct and operate the project. Therefore, governments might agree to assist and support the sponsors in their efforts to obtain work permits and visas for such personnel.

Undertakings of this nature typically appear in some form of development or implementation agreement between the sponsor and the host government which is generally signed before the introduction of lenders to the process. Alternatively, such undertakings could be included in the document that sets out other agreed assurances.

10. Case study: Sadara integrated chemicals project

10.1 The Sadara chemical complex

The Sadara complex is located in the Royal Commission for Jubail and Yanbu's Jubail Industrial City II, the largest industrial complex of its kind in the world, in the Eastern Province of the Kingdom, approximately 100 kilometres northwest of Dammam. When completed, the complex will be one of the world's largest integrated chemical facilities; the largest ever built in a single phase, and will comprise 26 fully integrated manufacturing units. The construction of Sadara benefits from its proximity to the well-established industrial infrastructure at Jubail. However, the sponsors have had to bring order to the huge complexity, inevitable when developing so many units concurrently on a greenfield site. In naming Sadara as its 2013 Deal of the Year, US Ex-Im was able to cite the involvement of approximately 70 contractors from the United States alone.

Two main alternative contract models, LSTK and EPCM/LSPB, were used across a series of construction packages, using the sponsors' experience of project management and planning to reconcile uniquely complicated technical and engineering issues, including intellectual property (IP)-sensitive technology licensing issues, together with the rigorous market expectations relating to customary environmental and social requirements, and procurement eligibility considerations applicable to the OECD-compliant tranches of the financing. Construction of the project commenced in the second half of 2012 and the first production units are expected to begin to come on line in the second half of 2015.

The Sadara complex will use ethane and refinery liquids, such as naphtha, as feedstock and, by using best-in-class technologies to crack refinery liquid feedstock, it will introduce new specialty chemical plants and businesses as well as new value chains to the Kingdom. It is configured with a mixed feed cracker and an aromatics plant as the key feed process units. These units will produce: ethylene and propylene from ethane feedstock and naphtha feedstock; and very high-purity benzene and toluene from pygas and purchased benzene and toluene, as the four primary hydrocarbon intermediate product streams for the derivatives process units. More expressly, performance products will include polyurethanes (isocyanates, polyether polyols), propylene oxide, propylene glycol, elastomers, linear low-density polyethylene, low-density polyethylene, glycol ethers and amines, and total production will amount to approximately 3 million metric tons per year of high-value added chemical products and performance plastics, which are anticipated to generate approximately $10 billion per year in revenues.

Sadara will market products to customers located within the Kingdom and the Middle East area, and, initially, a Dow subsidiary will have the exclusive right and obligation to market the products outside of the region (under separate product marketing and lifting arrangements for each product) using Dow's extensive global distribution channels.

Some of the complex contractual structures resulting from the construction, operations and technical issues described above are illustrated in the simplified overview on the following page.

10.2 The financing

In nurturing the Sadara concept through the global financial crisis, the sponsors were always likely to have to match the uniquely complex commercial contracting, technical and engineering project challenges described above with an unprecedentedly diverse project financing strategy, devised with the assistance of the Royal Bank of Scotland plc and Riyadh Bank as financial advisers.

The sponsors released their 400-page draft financing term sheet to the ECAs and Public Investment Fund (PIF) in August 2011. Milbank, as international legal adviser to the creditors, together with Greengate as financial adviser to the ECAs and PIF, and Ernst and Young/AHB as independent chartered auditor to the Federal Republic of Germany, assisted with the due diligence process over the initial review period before term sheet negotiations between the sponsors and the ECAs/PIF were largely concluded in three very constructive all-party meetings between February and April 2012. To enable the lenders to respond effectively to the sponsors' schedule, they agreed to organise themselves into distinct work-streams encompassing technical, environmental, market and modelling issues, in each case coordinated by designated agencies or advisers. In the meantime, the sponsors had finalised a bridge financing with the PIF, which was signed in May 2012, shortly before the sponsors took the financing term sheet, largely agreed with the ECAs and PIF, to the commercial bank market on May 28 2012.

10.3 The *sukuk* issuance

At around the same time as the launch to the commercial bank market, the sponsors embarked on an ambitious plan to issue a *sukuk*. The *sukuk* was the second-ever project finance *sukuk* to launch in the Kingdom, after the $1 billion SATORP issuance in 2011, and is the largest publicly listed *sukuk* to date. The *sukuk*, which was priced at 95bps over six-month SAIBOR and has a tenor of 15.75 years, was 2.6 times oversubscribed and was sized at SAR 7.5 billion (equivalent to $2 billion).

(a) *Structure of the* sukuk

The structure of the *sukuk* is shown below and utilises a *musharaka* arrangement which is essentially a Sharia-compliant partnership arrangement between Sadara and a special purpose issuer. The issuer contributes the proceeds of the *sukuk* issuance to the *musharaka* which is applied by Sadara to procure certain project assets in accordance with the procurement agreement. Sadara contributed its rights in the land lease to the *musharaka*, which added to the complexity of the transaction from

Figure 2:

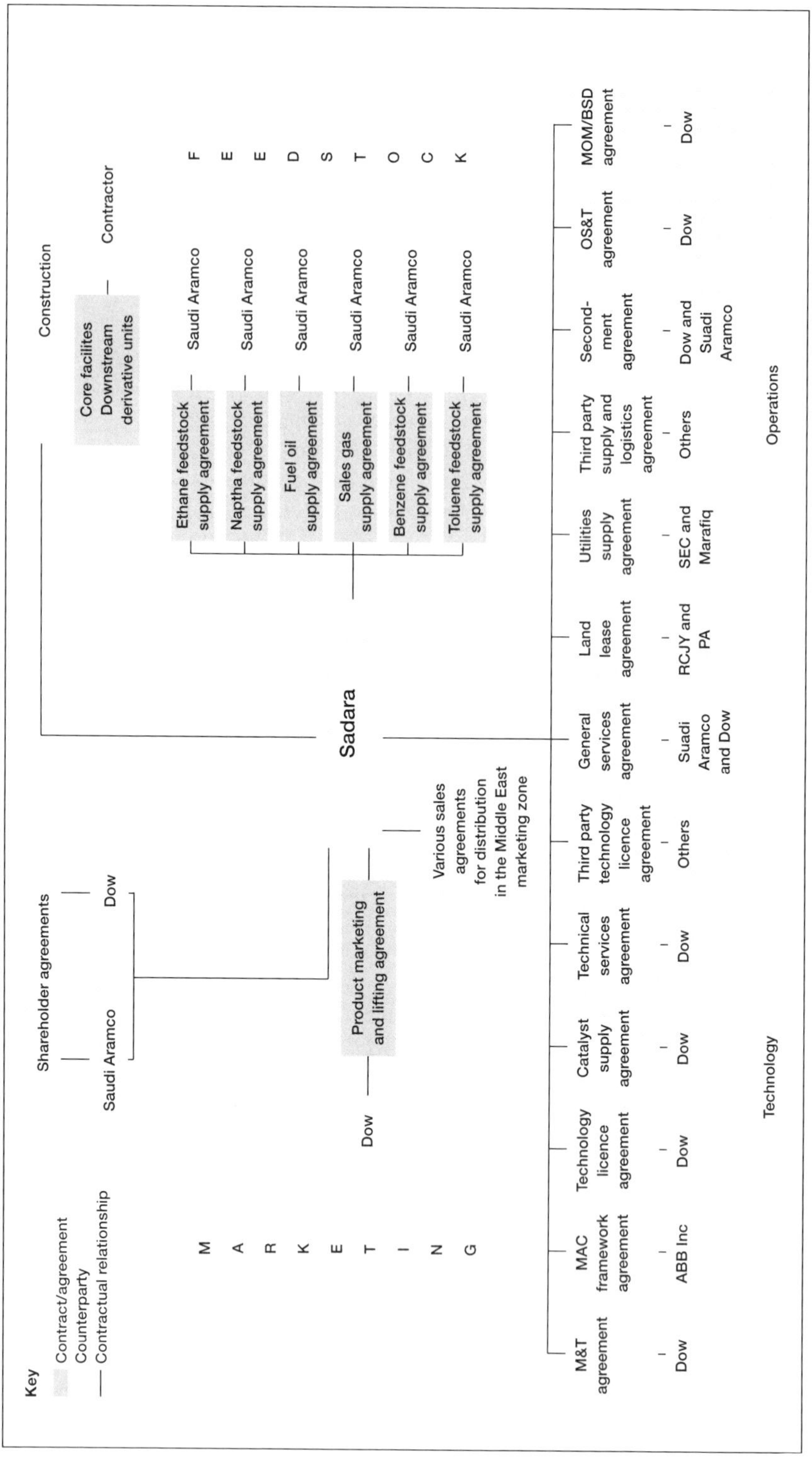
Key
Contract/agreement
Counterparty
Contractual relationship
Shareholder agreements
Saudi Aramco
Dow
Construction
Core facilites
Downstream
derivative units
Contractor
M A R K E T I N G
Dow
Product marketing and lifting agreement
Various sales agreements for distribution in the Middle East marketing zone
Sadara
Ethane feedstock supply agreement
Naptha feedstock supply agreement
Fuel oil supply agreement
Sales gas supply agreement
Benzene feedstock supply agreement
Toluene feedstock supply agreement
Saudi Aramco
F E E D S T O C K
M&T agreement
MAC framework agreement
Technology licence agreement
Catalyst supply agreement
Technical services agreement
Third party technology licence agreement
General services agreement
Land lease agreement
Utilities supply agreement
Third party supply and logistics agreement
Second-ment agreement
OS&T agreement
MOM/BSD agreement
Dow
ABB Inc
Others
Suadi Aramco and Dow
RCJY and PA
SEC and Marafiq
Dow and Suadi Aramco
Technology
Operations

a Sharia and Royal Commission for Jubail and Yanbu perspective. The project assets are then leased to Sadara under a forward lease agreement. Rental payments are paid by Sadara to the *musharaka*, and then on to the issuer for payment to the *sukuk* certificate holders in accordance with the terms of the certificates. The certificates benefit from the completion guarantees during the pre-completion period of the project.

(b) The split-closing regime

The project financing had many unprecedented features, with one of the most notable being that the *sukuk* was closed on April 2 2013, which was after the sponsors had received debt commitments from the commercial banks, but over two months before the rest of the initial senior debt was signed on June 16 2013 and closed on June 30 2013. Termed as a "split-closing", the sponsors were keen to ensure that once the other initial senior debt was ready to sign, the affirmative consent of the *sukuk* certificate holders would not be required for the amendment and restatement of the finance documents (now reflecting the terms subsequently agreed between Sadara and the other senior creditors). A mechanism was put in place so as to provide confirmation to the *sukuk* certificate holders prior to the second signing date that the proposed amendment to, or restatement of, the relevant finance documents on the second signing date would not affect certain key rights of the *sukuk* certificate holders. Aside from structuring and documenting this complex arrangement, adequate safeguards to protect the rights of the certificate holders had to be negotiated between the joint lead managers and the sponsors, including requiring the redemption of the certificates at par if the rest of the initial senior debt had not been signed within a specified period from the *sukuk* being closed, preventing certain key intercreditor rights of the certificate holders from being amended and restricting any amendments which would adversely impact the commercial deal for the certificate holders. In addition, the split-closing regime, together with the associated risks, also needed to be disclosed in the prospectus in order to comply with the applicable disclosure rules.

The split-closing regime allowed the sponsors sufficient flexibility to then continue to negotiate the finance documents with the ECAs and commercial banks and to establish also the size of the debt allocations for the ECAs and banks once the final issuance size of the *sukuk* was known. The regime also meant that the signing of the rest of the initial senior debt would not be delayed by having to wait for a vote of the *sukuk* certificate holders. No such vote was necessary and the main project financing closed on schedule.

10.4 The main financing

The negotiation of the finance documents for the main financing continued apace even while the *sukuk* was being negotiated. In order to ensure that the marketing of the *sukuk* was not adversely affected, it was necessary to ensure that the rights of the *sukuk* certificate holders were aligned with other providers of initial senior debt.

The commercial deal included a number of features of note, listed at (a)–(g) below.

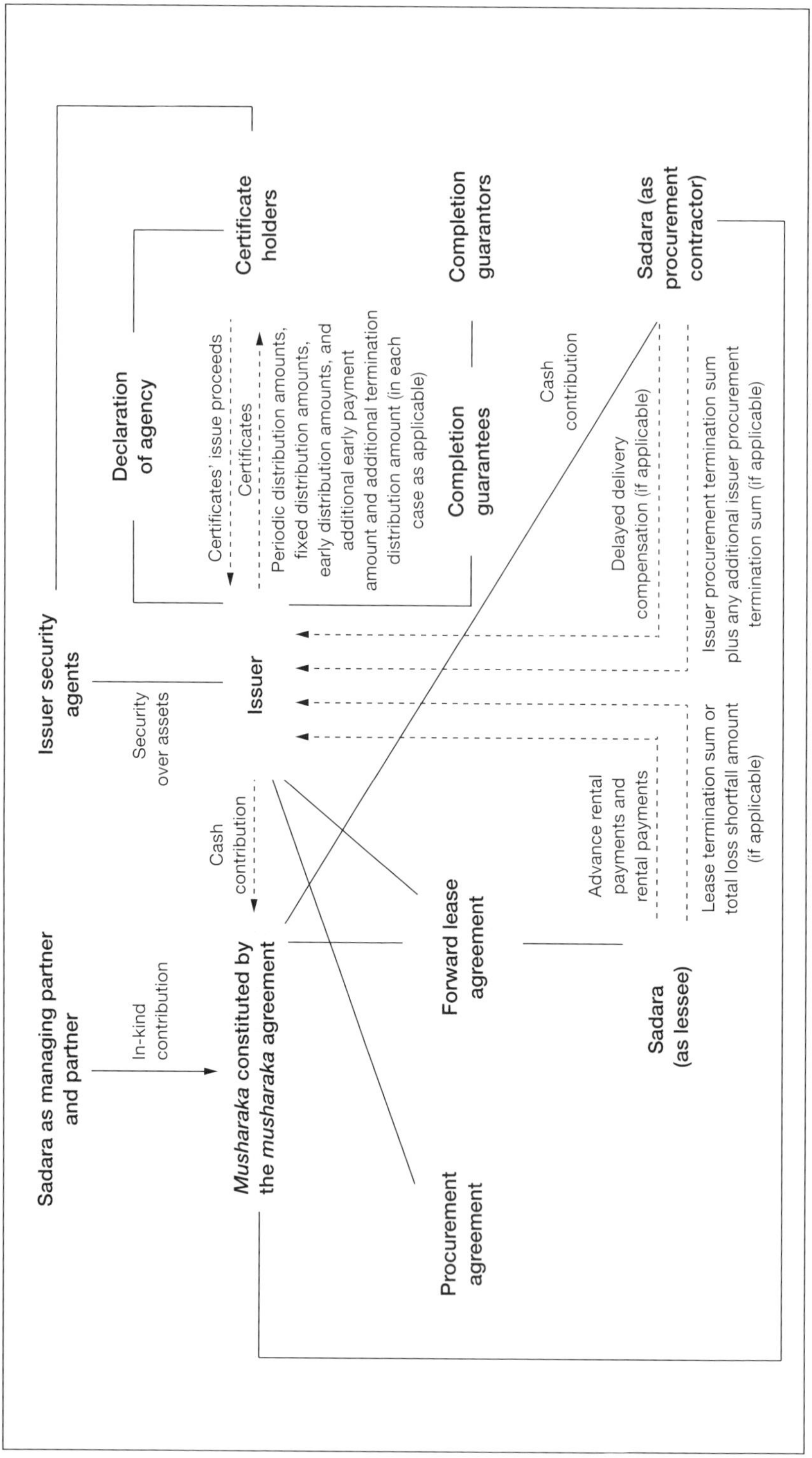
Sadara as managing partner and partner
In-kind contribution
Musharaka constituted by the musharaka agreement
Issuer security agents
Security over assets
Cash contribution
Issuer
Declaration of agency
Certificate holders
Certificates' issue proceeds
Certificates
Periodic distribution amounts, fixed distribution amounts, early distribution amounts, and additional early payment amount and additional termination distribution amount (in each case as applicable)
Completion guarantees
Completion guarantors
Procurement agreement
Forward lease agreement
Sadara (as lessee)
Advance rental payments and rental payments
Lease termination sum or total loss shortfall amount (if applicable)
Cash contribution
Delayed delivery compensation (if applicable)
Issuer procurement termination sum plus any additional issuer procurement termination sum (if applicable)
Sadara (as procurement contractor)

Figure 3:

(a) *The initial senior debt*

In September 2012, for the purposes of the Sadara project, US Ex-Im agreed to grant its largest ever commitment of approximately $4.975 billion. ECA-direct loans were also subsequently granted by FIEM (of Spain) and K-Exim (of Korea), in addition to a direct loan being granted by PIF.

Coface (of France), Euler-Hermes (of Germany), K-Exim and K-sure (both of Korea) and UK Export Finance (through the Export Credits Guarantee Department) agreed to provide ECA risk policies to cover commercial bank tranches in dollars and, in some cases, Saudi Riyals, and the commercial banks provided uncovered loans in the same currencies, including a letter of credit facility in the Saudi Riyal facility.

In addition to the conventional debt facilities, the sponsors arranged both *istisna-ijara* and *wakala-ijara* facilities with 11 Islamic finance institutions named as mandated Islamic lead arrangers, which facilities were made available as part of the main project financing ultimately signed and closed in June 2013.

(b) *Additional senior debt*

Petrochemical facilities often seek the flexibility to either debottleneck an existing plant or adopt new processes or plant to adapt to changing market conditions or opportunities. Sadara has sought similar flexibility and to allow this to occur, subject to, amongst other conditions, financial ratio testing. Sadara will also have scope to incur additional senior debt for various purposes, including expansions and partial refinancings.

(c) *Pre-completion net revenues*

As commercial operations are expected to commence with respect to certain plant units well before the scheduled project completion date of December 31 2017, the treatment of revenues prior to completion was the subject of some focus. Scope was included to permit the use of such revenues to:

- pay project costs;
- refinance equity contributions; and
- make shareholder distributions, subject to certain conditions.

(d) *Creditors' reliability test*

In light of its significance as a completion condition, particularly given the magnitude of the project financing, the creditors' reliability test was always likely to be an area of significant negotiation, but the particular complexity of the Sadara complex, with its 26 separate units, made this an area which required careful consideration. To enable the efficient agreement of the concept, particularly in light of the intellectual property relating to the technology being tested, a separate technical and legal working group was established to agree an appropriate and detailed test. The 26 units were grouped into three envelopes and subjected to integrated performance testing and a 60-day completion, operation and reliability test within a 90-day testing period, to be completed within a reasonable period of time.

(e) ***Sponsor commitments***

Saudi Aramco and Dow are required to continue to own Sadara (65:35) prior to the project completion date except that the financing documents envisage an initial public offering (IPO) of up to 30% of Sadara. After completion, the sponsors are generally required to maintain a 20% share in Sadara reflecting their deep involvement in the project as, in the case of Saudi Aramco, the feedstock supplier, and, in the case of Dow, the main technology licensor and marketer.

(f) ***SIDF facilities***

Although not participating as initial senior debt, the financing envisages that the Saudi Industrial Development Fund (SIDF) may join the deal on customary SIDF terms, which include first-ranking asset security and restricted tenor, but is subject to an assignment of the residual proceeds of security granted to SIDF.

(g) ***Intercreditor issues***

Given the scale and the range of the financing facilities, intercreditor issues were of particular sensitivity and were a matter of detailed negotiation once the finance plan became settled.

In light of its particularly large commitment, it was considered important to recognise the voice of US Ex-Im and, given their role as anchor creditors in the term sheet negotiations, the other ECAs, which led to the incorporation of a voting concept requiring an ECA majority (ie, a simple majority of the ECAs, which simple majority must generally include US Ex-Im) in favour of a range of qualified majority decisions, which generally incorporate matters that would customarily be super-majority or all-lender decisions. This concept was of particular relevance given the scope for additional senior debt described above (generally capped only by reference to ratio testing and capable of therefore substantially diluting the voting rights applicable to initial senior debt).

One area of particular additional complexity as an intercreditor matter was the treatment of the original *sukuk* issuance and the scope for an additional *sukuk* financing or a conventional bond issuance in the future. As a general matter, consistent with many capital market issuances, the *sukuk* certificate holders benefit from a somewhat more limited range of voting rights than do the ECAs and PIF. The rights afforded the certificate holders did, however, have to recognise their interest in participating in important decisions. This interest had to be balanced with the overarching aim of ensuring that the decision-making process for the project financing continued to function in an effective and efficient manner.

10.5 Big, complicated and flexible

The most notable features of the Sadara financing are its size, its complexity and the flexibility it affords the sponsors to adapt the business to an evolving world. To achieve a successful deal, the sponsors dedicated deep financial and technical resources, mobilised strong advisory teams and invited the participation of many of the world's leading ECAs and other financial institutions. Chemicals projects top the list of challenging assignments in all circumstances, but when combined with huge scale and a broad array of financing tranches and options, Sadara did much to redefine the limits of the possible in project finance.

Financing power and renewables projects

Nacim Bounouara
Antony Skinner
David Wadham
Ashurst LLP

1. Introduction

Financing a thermal or renewable power project on a project finance basis follows the same set of non-recourse principles and structure as other project finance transactions. Figure 1 on the next page sets out the classic project finance structure adapted for a power project.

However, in order to understand how to finance a thermal or renewable power project, you first need to understand the project you are financing in terms of applicable regulatory regime and power generation technology. There are common themes that apply across all power project financings, but there are also subtle differences that are specific to each jurisdiction and each power generation technology. Set out below in section 2 is a summary of the key features of the evolution of the electricity industry and in section 3 is a summary of each power generation technology.

Section 4 describes the key financial considerations of funders of a power project to ensure that such a project is bankable and the economic and financial parameters are workable. One important aspect of the bankability of a power project is the due diligence exercise carried out by funders and this is described in section 5.

Sections 6 and 7 highlight the key features and terms of the financing of power projects and section 8 considers some of the recent developments in the power financing market following the 2008 global financial crisis.

Section 9 looks at some of the key structural issues funders will consider when looking at the construction arrangements. Finally, section 10 concludes the chapter by covering important land-related considerations applying to any power project financing.

2. The electrical evolution

2.1 Developing gas and electricity markets

As a general rule, electricity markets follow a structured path of evolution. In less developed markets, as a country develops and the need for a national electricity supply emerges, a single party – usually the government or a government-owned entity – will be responsible for gas supply, power generation, transmission and distribution of the electricity and the supply of electricity to consumers. At this early stage, project finance is the logical fund-raising tool to facilitate investment, as the

Figure 1: Project finance structure

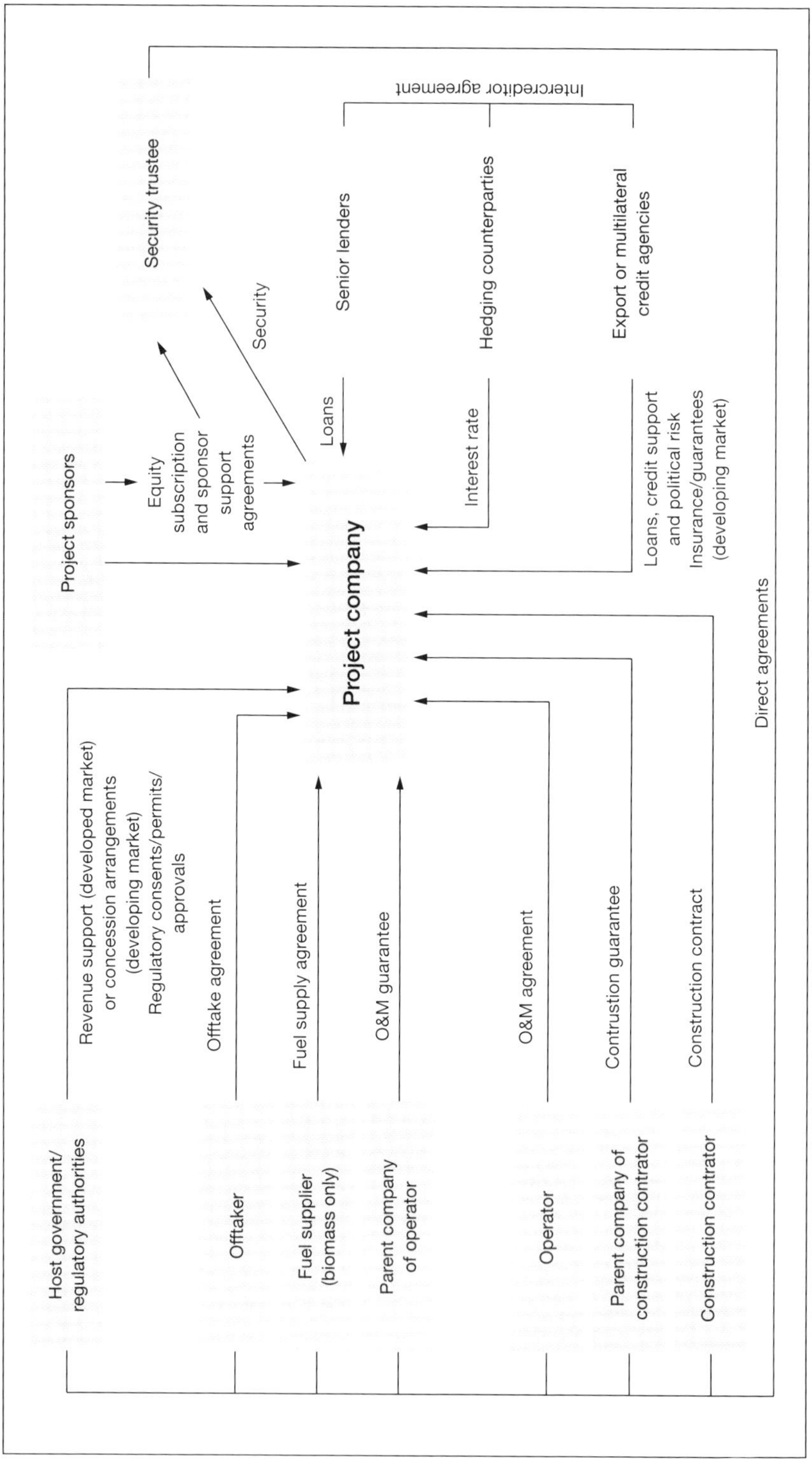

relevant government or government-owned companies may not be able to raise sufficient funds on a corporate basis either through the bank or capital markets. Depending on the rating of the relevant government, even project finance may require the involvement of multi-lateral lenders or export credit agencies because commercial banks and markets will not take uncovered risk on the relevant institutions.

Power generation is seen as the first link in the electricity supply chain in which to create an opportunity for private investment. Abu Dhabi provides an excellent example whereby the government of Abu Dhabi created an opportunity for foreign investment in its electricity sector. In the late 1990s we saw the first independent power project (IPP) in Abu Dhabi. Under this structure, the Abu Dhabi Water and Electricity Authority (ADWEA) went out to tender for overseas investors to bid to build, own and operate a large-scale gas-fired power and water desalination station in Abu Dhabi.

Under this structure the bidders were asked to provide a technical solution and to bid for the price of power they would charge to sell capacity and output to an ADWEA affiliate. The successful bidder entered into a shareholders' agreement with another ADWEA affiliate and formed the project company to undertake the project on the basis of equity provided by the successful bidder and ADWEA, alongside significant project finance debt provided by commercial banks. ADWEA has now developed over 13,000 MW of capacity using this model and there are a number of successful IPP programmes based on this model or on similar models throughout the region, including in Bahrain, Jordan, Kuwait, Oman, Qatar and Saudi Arabia, to name a few.

Arguably, this IPP structure makes for a simple financing because the project is reliant on a single government-owned counterparty (or sometimes multiple government-owned counterparties) for key commercial elements of the project, including long-term fuel supply, grid connection and long-term power offtake, as well as land. Being government-related, such counterparties are also able to provide the project company and its investors with certain protections against changes in the law and other political (uninsurable) risk. While this single point responsibility is helpful, it does nonetheless put the relevant government at the centre of the transaction and sponsors and lenders will therefore need to be satisfied that the relevant government entities have sufficient creditworthiness to stand behind their various fuel supply, power offtake and other obligations.

2.2 Market evolution

As the gas and electricity markets in a country develop, then it is likely that the government will look to move away from its direct involvement and a private company or companies will become the gas suppliers and power offtakers and ultimately the suppliers of power to consumers. For transmission and distribution, this is normally the last part of the electricity supply chain to be privatised because it is a natural monopoly and so even if the sector is privatised, it is likely that there will be only one company taking the responsibility of the high voltage transmission network with perhaps different distribution companies for the lower voltage distribution networks for different regions, as is the case in the United Kingdom.

It may take some time in the electrical evolution of a country before there are multiple suppliers of gas and offtakers of power. While there is only one party responsible for the supply of gas and/or purchase of power, this gives rise to the risk of a stranded asset following an event of default affecting the project regardless of how it was caused.

If there is a default by the gas supplier or, more likely, power offtaker (particularly where there is any government control over these entities), then sponsors and lenders would look to make sure that the defaulting offtaker is required to purchase the power project by way of a termination payment for an amount equal to the outstanding debt and a return on equity. Where there is an event of default by the project company, it is then more difficult to justify that the non-defaulting offtaker is required to purchase a defaulting asset. This is often a hotly debated topic. In most jurisdictions in these circumstances there is typically an option for the government to purchase the relevant power plant, but in such a circumstance the price to be paid by the offtaker is linked to the amount of outstanding debt so the shareholders who have invested equity in the project will lose their investment. This is justifiable because the termination has been caused by a project company event of default. This is the prevailing model, although not all models provide for such a termination payment structure. Indeed, in some jurisdictions such as Oman, the project company has no express right to terminate for offtaker default and must simply sue for damages in the event of government default (principally non-payment).

As a country evolves and establishes a track record for the successful construction and operation of IPPs, then the government may seek to refine the risk allocation slightly, pushing more risk towards the private sector on the basis of a proven track record generating investor confidence in the sector. However, for so long as fuel supply and long-term power offtake remain in government hands, the changes to the model will remain fairly limited.

2.3 Market liberalisation

The final stage of this electrical evolution is one of market liberalisation. At this stage, there are multiple buyers and sellers of gas and power. In the United Kingdom, for example, power and gas are now commodities which are traded. You do not need a licence to trade power and gas in the United Kingdom and there are specific commodity traders and investment banks who trade power and gas in a very sophisticated market.

In the United Kingdom, power is monitored on a half-hourly basis, each half-hour being a 'settlement period'. Generators, suppliers, large consumers and traders of electricity all have energy accounts under what is called the 'Balancing and Settlement Code'. For each settlement period, each party must ensure that its energy account shows a zero balance. This means that a party has generated or bought the same volume as it has consumed or sold.

For physical generators, the credits to their account will be made by way of a physical meter attached to the account which records the level of generation for that settlement period. The debits from their account are likely to be by way of contractual notifications to the system administrator to debit a specified quantity of electricity from their account and credit it to a specified buyer's account. Therefore, it is imperative that a generator knows how much it will generate in a given settlement period so that it can sell the correct volume of electricity.

For physical consumers, the debits from their account will be made by way of a physical meter attached to the account which records the level of consumption for that settlement period. Converse to generators, the credits to their account are likely to be by way of contractual notifications to the system administrator to credit a specified quantity of electricity to their account and debit it from a specified seller's account.

For non-physical traders, credits and debits will be by way of notification to the system administrator. Therefore, it should be more straightforward for a trader to make sure its credits and debits are matched and its account will show a zero balance at the end of the relevant settlement period.

If a party's account does not show a zero balance at the end of the settlement period, that party will be in imbalance and will be required to pay to or receive from the system administrator a cash out price determined by the system operator. This reflects the fact that if there is a negative balance on the account, the party is short and sold more than it bought and therefore needs to buy the shortfall from the system. If there is a positive balance on the account, the party is long and sold less than it bought and therefore needs to sell the shortfall to the system.

The above is a high level summary of a very complex system, but it goes to show the complexities of financing a project in a liberalised market. The general view among lenders is that this type of imbalance risk should not rest with the project company. If there is a long-term tolling agreement or power purchase agreement (PPA) attached to the project, this generally passes the imbalance risk on to the toller/offtaker in most cases. Where there is no such long-term contract, the imbalance risk may sit with the project which adds to the uncertainty of the project revenues and increases the risk to the project.

It is worth noting that in a liberalised market the gas supply regime is as sophisticated as the power offtake regime. Therefore, the comments made above with respect to imbalance risk for power apply equally to imbalance risk for gas. One key difference, however, is the fact that power cannot be stored and therefore needs to be generated and consumed almost simultaneously which is why settlement periods are generally short and are somewhere between 15 minutes and one hour. However, gas can be stored and therefore the physical pressures of balancing supply and demand are slightly more relaxed. Therefore, the period over which a party's gas account needs to be balanced will be longer and, in the United Kingdom for example, the equivalent settlement period is 24 hours rather than 30 minutes.

In a liberalised market where there are many buyers and sellers of gas and power, the stranded asset concern of a single offtaker market does not apply. This materially impacts the termination compensation provisions of gas supply agreements (GSAs), PPAs and tolling agreements. Increasingly, these contracts are viewed like any other commodity trading contract. There is an ongoing debate as to whether power and gas are financially or physically settled in the United Kingdom. The ultimate penalty for non-delivery is the payment of a penalty fee to the system operator and it is the system operator who is responsible for physical deliveries. Everyone else is financially motivated to perform.

In the United Kingdom and Europe, power and gas can be traded using industry standard trading contracts such as:

- an International Swaps and Derivatives Association (ISDA) Agreement;
- a Grid Trade Master Agreement (GTMA) for power;
- a National Balancing Point (NBP) contract for gas;
- an International Emissions Trading Association (IETA) Agreement for carbon emissions; and
- a European Federation of Energy Traders (EFET) Agreement for European gas and power.

These contracts generally work on the same principles of having a generic master agreement with a schedule which is filled in to reflect the general commercial terms between the parties and a confirmation for each trade which sets out the exact terms of the relevant trade.

These trading style contracts also use a similar form of termination compensation calculation which is based on a mark-to-market calculation. This means that the non-defaulting party calculates what it expected to pay and receive for the term of all outstanding trades under the agreement and compares that with what it would have to pay for the same terms in the market at the date of termination. This may be a positive or negative amount. If the amount is positive (ie, the non-defaulting party would have to pay a third party to receive the same terms) then the non-defaulting party will claim its loss from the defaulting party. If the amount is negative (ie, the terms under the existing trade(s) are better than those available in the market at the date of termination) the non-defaulting party may have to pay a termination amount to the defaulting party. This is called a 'two way termination payment'.

Even the more bespoke GSAs, PPAs and tolling agreements in liberalised markets still have similar mark-to-market style termination payments. However, when a project has been project financed, it is generally too abhorrent to lenders to consider that, at the time they lose their offtaker, their borrower may be required to make a termination payment to the defaulting offtaker. There is also the issue of where the money would come from to pay such a lump sum. Therefore, lenders often require a one-way termination payment only.

The fundamental principle of project finance is that the party best placed to bear the risk does so. Therefore, in certain situations, no party to the project considers it is best placed to bear the risk of political *force majeure* events. In which case, some form of political risk insurance may be required to make the project bankable.

3. Overview of power generation technologies

3.1 Gas-fired power projects

Gas is one of the cleanest and most efficient forms of power generation from fossil fuel, in particular when it is used in a combined cycle gas turbine (CCGT). This is where a gas turbine is used to generate the electricity and the residual heat is used to drive a steam turbine.

For a CCGT project you need a party to supply the gas, in certain jurisdictions you need a party to supply the carbon allowances and you also need a party to purchase the power. The interface between these contracts is key to understanding the risk profile of the project. This will also impact the financing terms. The nature of the gas supply and power offtake contracts will also be dictated by the stage of electricity evolution of the country in which the project is being developed.

When considering the tenor of any financing, banks will want to make sure that the tenor of the tolling agreement (and indeed GSAs and PPAs as discussed below) will be at least as long as the tenor of the debt. Banks will also require the term of the project contracts to be longer than the term of the debt so there is a tail beyond the scheduled debt repayment profile during which the project will still be generating revenues to service any residual outstanding debt.

3.2 Contractual structure

(a) Tolling agreements

The most conservative form of contractual structure for a gas-fired plant is a tolling agreement under which a single party supplies all the gas and carbon and purchases all the power. The toller under the tolling agreement takes market risk with respect to gas and power price and demand risk that the power from the power station will be required at the right price.

Under a tolling structure, the generator will be paid an availability fee for being available regardless of whether it generates any power. This availability fee will need to be sufficient to cover all fixed costs of the project including debt service (interest, principal and fees), a return on equity and fixed operation and maintenance costs. The generator will also be paid an energy fee when it generates to cover variable costs associated with generation.

The toller will have control as to when to instruct the project company to generate electricity and the project company will be required to generate at the levels instructed. The despatch instructions from the toller will need to take account of the technical parameters of the power station, such as how long it takes to fire up the power station and ramp up to the required level of power output. If the project company fails to deliver the power it has been instructed to deliver, it is likely to incur some form of liquidated damage to the toller or at least forfeit some of its availability payment because it is not in fact available to generate.

If a tolling agreement is not available, then the next most conservative approach is a long-term fixed (or indexed) price gas (and if applicable, carbon) supply agreement and a separate fixed (or indexed) price PPA. A full risk analysis will need to be carried out in order to identify any residual risk that sits with the project company with respect to risks that arise under each of the GSA and PPA. For example, if the gas supplier fails to deliver gas when required, the project company will either have to source gas from an alternative supplier and claim from the contracted gas supplier the increased cost of procuring replacement gas, or if the project company is not able to source alternative gas, it will also need to be compensated for loss of power revenue for not being able to generate power due to the lack of gas.

Conversely, if the power offtaker does not take the power when required, the generator may have liability to the gas supplier for failure to purchase gas. This liability will need to be passed through to the power offtaker.

The allocation of risk in a default scenario is reasonably clear cut in that the defaulting party should compensate the non-defaulting party for any losses. However, in circumstances of *force majeure*, risk allocation becomes more complex particularly when you are having to take into account political *force majeure*. If the counterparty(ies) to the GSAs and PPAs (and also tolling agreements) are government entities, then there is a strong argument that such entities should take political *force majeure* risk, but if they are private companies or only partially government-owned companies, this makes for a more complicated discussion as to who is best placed to bear the risk or potentially some form of political risk insurance may be required.

(b) GSA/PPA structure

Under a GSA/PPA structure, it is still important that the project is not exposed to market demand risk. Therefore, you either look to create a payment structure whereby the offtaker pays an availability fee for the plant being available and an energy fee for when it is required to generate (and this energy fee will need to be sized to cover the cost of gas), or you can create a take or pay structure under which the power offtaker is required to offtake a minimum quantity of power each year (and potentially on a more time-granular basis). If the power offtaker does not take the minimum required volume of power over the specified time period, it is required to pay for the power as if it had taken it to ensure the project receives the required level of revenue for the year.

This structure will also need to tie into a similar take or pay requirement under the GSA. One will also need to consider how a take or pay structure – which may be annual – ties in with a semi-annual payment requirement under the finance documents. The two may need to match.

(c) Merchant structure

The final type of contractual structure available for CCGT projects is a merchant structure. Under this structure, the generator takes demand risk and market price risk and, as a result, is exposed to demand and price fluctuations. This is the most risky structure and sits least well in a project finance context. There are examples of merchant projects with a mix of success and failure due to reasonably volatile power and gas prices around Europe, particularly as the influx of renewable power increases.

3.3 Mitigation and risk analysis

Project finance is based on principles of certainty. Therefore, not to have certainty of price for power or gas or an exposure to demand risk leaves massive risk at the project level. Project finance lenders are unlikely to accept this risk profile without serious risk analysis and mitigation requirements.

The first mitigation technique will be to require a far lower gearing of the project than one would see on other project finance transactions. The classic debt to equity ratio for a project finance transaction is somewhere between 70:30 and 80:20. For a merchant project, that ratio is far more likely to be at the 50:50 level.

Other mitigation techniques may include a requirement for the borrower to enter into a contracted position with respect to gas supply and power purchase for a specified period of time going forward. The borrower could have a rolling strategy which requires, for example, 50% of gas supply and output to be contracted for delivery in three years' time, 75% to be contracted for delivery in two years' time and 100% to be contracted for delivery in one year's time. This is a simple example but one which has been used on project financings.

It is also important to note that generally a borrower/generator will be required to lock in the power price, the gas price and the carbon price at the same time so the borrower has locked in its 'clean spark spread'. This is the difference between the price of power and cost of gas and carbon in generating that power.

3.4 Location

For gas-fired power stations, the location of the project will also have an impact on the type of gas supply contract. In liberalised markets, the gas is likely to be delivered from the gas network so there will be many suppliers and the specification of gas will be just what it is as it is distributed from the gas network. In some jurisdictions, the country may have a plentiful supply of in-country gas and therefore the local gas supplier will be able to deliver gas from his gas reserves, in which case it is likely that an analysis of the gas reserves will be required.

However, for countries with no local gas network or gas supplies, a gas-fired power project may have to rely on the import of liquefied natural gas (LNG). Nikhil Markanday and Philip Thomson's chapter on LNG considers financing of LNG projects in more detail, but for the purposes of this chapter, readers should be aware that shipping LNG over long distances is expensive and requires specialist ships. In order to finance a gas-fired power project which utilises imported LNG, lenders will require a long-term LNG supply contract. It is debatable as to whether it will be possible to secure a fixed price for the LNG supply and therefore the cost of LNG may need to be a straight pass through cost to the power offtaker under the PPA.

Another key factor for LNG power projects is the fact that the LNG needs to be regasified before it can be used by the power station. For early LNG power projects, this required the construction of a permanent regasification terminal which increased the capital cost of projects and therefore increased the ultimate tariff for the power produced. As technology has advanced, we are increasingly seeing floating storage regasification units (FSRUs) being used. These are giant ships which sit just offshore and the LNG tankers connect to these ships and unload their cargo. The FSRU regasifies the LNG when required by the power station and stores the LNG in the meantime. Again, this is discussed in more detail in the chapter on LNG.

3.5 Coal-fired power stations

Coal-fired power stations are one of the oldest ways of generating electricity. In the

United Kingdom, 31%[1] of the electricity supply is still generated from coal. However, many of the coal-fired power stations are old (some more than 40 years old) and there has been a raft of EU and domestic legislation which has been introduced over the last few years which means that many of the coal-fired power stations in Europe will need to be closed down by 2016[2] in order to meet EU air quality legislation.

Furthermore, in the United Kingdom, legislation has been passed that effectively means that there will be no new coal-fired power stations built in the United Kingdom unless they benefit from a carbon capture and storage (CCS) facility which effectively makes the power station emissions free. There are a number of CCS facilities under development in Europe, but the United Kingdom has a geological advantage and therefore the potential to become the world leader in CCS. At the time of writing, there are no commercial-scale CCS projects under construction but there are a number of proposed projects.[3]

However, coal power is still a significant feature of new power stations being built elsewhere in the world, particularly in the developing countries. In China alone, it is recorded that the country is constructing one coal power plant every week, with 39 gigawatts added in 2014 or three 1,000 megawatt units every four weeks.[4]

With respect to the likely contractual and financing structure of a coal-fired power station, all the comments made above with respect to gas-fired power stations apply equally to coal, with one notable exception. Coal is a solid and stable substance, which means that it is relatively easy to transport over long distances and store on site. Therefore, the imbalance risk associated with gas does not apply to coal. The key issue for coal is ensuring that sufficient quantities of coal are available to meet the electricity output profile of the power station. Lenders – being conservative in nature – will require stockpiles to be built up so that even if no coal was delivered to site for an extended period (say 30 days), the power station would continue to be able to generate. It is likely that stockpile requirements will be higher during winter (or summer, in hot climates), when power demand is higher and adverse weather is more likely to impact the ability to deliver coal to the site.

With respect to the coal supply contract, coal is generally seen as a readily available commodity with a global supply chain. Lenders may therefore be slightly more relaxed over the requirement to enter into a long-term coal supply agreement as long as a conservative assumption for coal price and transportation costs is built into the financial model. Alternatively, it may be possible to enter into a coal price hedge to swap a floating price under a coal supply contract to a fixed price. Commodity hedges are discussed further in Kerion Ball's chapter on hedging.

One will also have to consider whether the coal supply can be met from domestic supplies or international supplies. For international supplies, one will also have to consider the likely available suppliers depending on the type of coal required. For example, if the particular coal specification of a power station requires coal from a particular country, then a long-term supply contract may be required by lenders to

1 See www.energy-uk.org.uk/energy-industry/coal-generation.
2 See www.energy-uk.org.uk/energy-industry/coal-generation.
3 See www.ccsassociation.org/why-ccs/ccs-projects/current-projects/.
4 See www.theecologist.org/News/news_round_up/2773053/chinas_fossil_fuel_emissions_fell_3_in_2014.html.

lock in the price, but this may also give rise to the risk of political *force majeure* or sanctions applying to the source country depending on the country of origin.

Furthermore, due to the fact that burning coal emits more greenhouse gases than burning natural gas, if applicable in the particular jurisdiction of the project, the cost of carbon emissions will be more material. We refer above to the 'clean spark spread' with respect to gas. For coal, the equivalent term is the 'clean dark spread'.

3.6 Wind farms and solar parks

When financing a wind farm or solar park project, you need to be aware of some distinct features of wind and solar projects. The first is obvious in that there is no fuel supply to worry about. Once built, the raw material for generating electricity (ie, the wind or sun/irradiation) is free. Therefore, there is no fuel supply contract. This also impacts the PPA. Due to the fact that the wind/sun/irradiation is free, a generator will want to ensure that it is generating every moment it is able to when the wind is blowing at the right speed or the conditions are sufficiently bright. Therefore, under the PPA, the offtaker should be required to accept and pay for all power generated by a wind farm or solar park.

The need for a power offtaker to accept and pay for all power generated is compounded in countries (eg, the United Kingdom) which implement a green certificate regime. Under these regimes, generally, the generator is issued with a green certificate for generating green power. With the generator able to sell the green certificate, it has a strong interest in wanting to maximise its generation in order to maximise revenues. In most cases, the purchaser of power will also be the purchaser of the green certificate but this is not essential and there may be separate offtakers for each.

On a global scale, a feed-in tariff regime rather than green certificates is more common. Under a feed-in tariff, a single body – either the transmission operator, a supplier or a government body – will purchase all power generated by a wind farm or solar park at a published tariff, or bid for a fixed tariff for a specified period of time. This provides price certainty to generators and funders alike and derisks the project from market price and demand fluctuations.

There have been widely publicised events such as those in Spain under which the Spanish government retrospectively reduced the feed-in tariffs. This caused outrage among developers and funders who had built wind farms and solar parks and invested debt and equity on the assumption of receiving a set price for a set period. Therefore, if the feed-in tariff can be hard-wired into a binding contract with compensation provisions, this would be preferable. Indeed, in most non-liberalised countries, the feed-in tariff will be incorporated into the PPA with a state-owned offtaker, as discussed above, and so developers and funders can take comfort from the binding nature of the PPA.

We discussed in section 2 above the concept of imbalance risk, particularly in liberalised markets. Imbalance risk for wind and solar parks is compounded due to the intermittent nature of the supply. It is therefore important to pass the imbalance risk on to the offtaker in order to make a project bankable. From an offtaker's perspective, they will charge a premium for taking this imbalance risk which is likely to be implemented by way of a discount to the market price of power. Further, the offtaker will want to ensure that it has as much information as possible in order to manage its exposure to imbalance risk on a real time basis.

This can be achieved by the offtaker being given access to the SCADA feed. This is a live supervisory control and data acquisition system which shows the ongoing output of the wind farm or solar park. Also, the offtaker will require regular updates as to the availability of the wind farm or solar park so that it can calculate the likely output from the facility based on its own analysis of the current and forecast wind or irradiation conditions.

The only liability a generator should accept is if it fails to provide access to the SCADA or updates of its availability and outages affecting the facility. The generator would usually require some form of grace period of at least a couple of hours and this risk should ideally be passed through to the operator of the facility. The level of this liability is likely to be linked to the imbalance charges incurred by the offtaker as a result of not receiving the power it had expected.

For renewable projects based on intermittent generation such as solar and wind, detailed data with respect to wind speeds and solar irradiation is gathered and analysed. For wind projects, the data needs to be very local to the wind farm and is likely to be based on data collected by a wind mast erected on the site at least one or, preferably, two or more years before the date of financial close. For solar projects, irradiation levels can be based on more regional data.

Once the information has been collated and analysed, projections are then made on a P50 and P90 basis. This is the probability that the output generated by the wind farm or solar park will be over a specified level for a specified period of time (usually on a 10-year basis). P90 gives rise to a 90% probability of exceedance and is therefore reasonably certain. P50 gives rise to a 50% probability of exceedance and is therefore a more aggressive assumption. The impact of this P50 and P90 data is discussed further at section 4 below.

3.7 Biomass and energy from waste

To date, there have been fewer banked biomass projects than other renewables projects. This is primarily because of regulatory uncertainty surrounding governments' policies and just how green biomass projects are and also concerns over creditworthy and sustainable fuel suppliers.

A biomass project is generally seen as a cross between a wind project financing and a coal project financing. Clearly, there is a solid and stable fuel supply as with coal, so the comments made above with respect to coal supply apply equally here. However, biomass supply is still relatively new as a global industry and therefore there are only a few large suppliers of biomass and, generally, funders are not comfortable taking a long-term credit view on these suppliers. This has given rise to issues for the availability of long-term debt funding for biomass projects and we have seen the need for export credit agencies and other government support to make these projects bankable.

Biomass itself is a baseload technology (ie, the biomass power station can operate all the time with limited starts and stops) but with controllable despatch so the plant can be switched on and off depending on power price because the fuel supply is a cost to the project (unless it is a waste project in which case the waste biomass may itself generate revenue for the project company). However, unlike with coal and gas projects, a biomass project is likely to benefit from some form of green subsidy, whether a green certificate or feed-in tariff. Therefore, a low power price may not in itself deter generation if the impact of the green subsidy means it is still economic to generate even with low power prices.

For a waste to energy plant, it may be that the project has to continue to generate in order to burn the waste it has been paid to take. There may be environmental or planning constraints on how much waste (fuel supply) the generator is allowed to store on site at any one time. In any event, the generator may have take or pay obligations under its fuel supply agreement to further incentivise it to continue to generate even in a low power price environment.

Interestingly, PPAs for biomass plants are generally based on wind PPAs with an obligation on the offtaker to take all power produced by the generator with no rights of the offtaker to control the despatch of the plant. This is a good deal for generators and so the trade-off is that the PPA is likely to include some controls over annual output because failure to achieve a guaranteed output level (typically 70–80% of the total output of the plant over a year assuming a 100% generation profile) will give rise to some form of liability on the generator. This is because the offtaker is working on the basis that it will receive a steady output of baseload generation. Unlike with intermittent generation such as wind and solar, the offtaker will have assumed only a limited exposure to imbalance charges in its financial model. If the biomass plant is not operating as expected over a year, this puts greater pressure on the offtaker with respect to imbalance risk and the offtaker therefore looks to pass some of the risk back to the generator. This risk to the project will need to be analysed from a technical perspective to ensure that it is adequately passed on to the operator of the plant.

4. Debt sizing and the financial model

A fundamental element to any power project financing is how much lenders are willing to lend. It is not as straightforward as a sponsor saying, "my capital cost is £100 million and I would like a debt to equity ratio of 75:25, therefore I would like to borrow £75 million." Funders will look at it differently and say, "what debt service (principal and interest) can you afford to repay on each payment date assuming a debt service cover ratio of say 1.7:1?"

A debt service cover ratio is the ratio of net cash flow to debt service (interest and principal) over a specified period. What this means for debt sizing is that for each year during the operating life of the project, you calculate the projected revenues of the project company and deduct operating costs for that year. You will then divide the projected revenues for that period by 1.7 to work out what debt service the project can afford. This is calculated through a detailed Excel-based financial model.

The financial model will make various assumptions about the revenues that will be generated by the project based on P50 and P90 generation figures (for wind or solar projects), the availability payment or take or pay level for gas or coal-fired projects and either the power price specified in the PPA or a market-based power price determined by a market adviser.

The financial model will also make certain assumptions as to operating costs based on the prices set out in the operating budget and the operation and maintenance contract. The funders can then model the likely net cash flow of the project over the life of the project. Often, the funders will only account for revenues which are contracted under a PPA. Therefore, even if the actual life of the asset is 20 years or more, if the PPA is only for 15 years, the funders will only account for 15 years of revenue in the financial model.

It is an iterative process run under the financial model which is analysed by the sponsors, funders, technical adviser and even a model auditor, but eventually the sponsors and funders will agree on the financial model and therefore determine the total amount that can be borrowed.

For projects which benefit from a long-term fixed price PPA, the financial model and ratios should be reasonably straightforward because the revenues can be readily ascertained for the life of the debt (subject to agreement on indexation and technical availability and output profiles). To complicate matters further on projects which are exposed to a merchant risk with respect to price, funders will apply a risk weighting on revenues for debt sizing purposes. For fixed revenues, funders will likely require approximately £1.30 of projected revenues for every £1 of debt service in any period (ie, a debt service cover ratio of 1.30:1). However, for merchant revenues, funders will likely require approximately £1.80 of projected revenues for every £1 of debt service (ie, a debt service cover ratio of 1.80:1). The reason for this is that merchant revenues are far less predictable and therefore funders require a larger buffer so that even if prices fall significantly, there will still be sufficient cash in the project at any time to afford to repay debt.

Any debt service cover ratio of less than 1:1 means there is insufficient cash in a period to service debt which would clearly be unacceptable to funders as it means a certain non-payment event of default. Therefore, the funders will also run what they call 'sensitivities' under the financial model. These are events used to stress test the economics of the project to calculate what the consequence would be if certain events occur. Sensitivities include changing the assumptions with respect to operation and maintenance costs, breakdowns, an increase in inflation or an increase in any unhedged portion of LIBOR. In projects which rely on merchant revenues, funders will run sensitivities at the lowest price of power likely to occur based on market expert advice.

In all cases, what the funders are looking for is to test what series of unfortunate events need to occur before the project is at a lower than 1:1 debt service cover ratio.

For renewable projects based on intermittent generation such as solar and wind, as discussed above, detailed data with respect to wind speeds and solar irradiation are gathered and analysed. Projections are then made on a P50 and P90 basis.

Funders are generally comfortable applying a P50 assumption for base case debt sizing, but they will run a sensitivity on a P90 basis, again to stress test the economics of the project. In most cases, funders will run a sensitivity on a P90 output and on merchant projects a low price scenario and require that this gives rise to a debt service cover ratio of greater than 1:1 in every calculation period.

The funders will also have certain other requirements to limit the amount that can be borrowed. This may include a maximum debt to equity ratio, an average debt service coverage ratio and a minimum debt service cover ratio.

Another ratio that is often used by funders both at the debt sizing stage, but also on an ongoing basis throughout the life of the project, is the loan life cover ratio (LLCR). This is the ratio of the net present value of net cash flow over the term of the PPA to the total debt outstanding. The net cash flow is usually discounted at the same rate of interest that applies to the loan itself. Again, a ratio of around 1.3:1 is common.

Above, we have focused on the financial model, revenues and costs for the purposes of day one debt sizing. In addition, these inputs are used to calculate debt service cover ratios and loan life ratios throughout the life of the project. These ratios are used to determine how the project is performing compared with how it was expected to perform and can act as an early indicator of potential performance issues.

One would generally expect to test financial ratios every six months on calculation dates once the project is operational. For debt service cover ratios, the finance documents are likely to contain a one-year look back debt service cover ratio test (an historic debt service cover ratio or HDSCR), a one-year look forward debt service cover ratio test (a projected debt service cover ratio or PDSCR) and a loan life cover ratio test looking forward to the end of the term of the debt (or in the case of hard mini-perms, as will be discussed below, looking forward to the notional profile of the debt).

The historic debt service cover ratio will use actual data based on revenues and costs accrued as at the calculation date. However, the projected debt service cover ratio and the loan life cover ratio will still need to use assumptions as to future revenues and costs. Therefore, there will be some debate when drafting the documents as to how and when these assumptions should be updated. There are generally technical, economic, market and wind/solar assumptions. The technical and economic assumptions should be reasonably non-controversial and will be based on the operating performance of the plant and macro-economic conditions such as inflation and tax. However, there is a general nervousness on the part of borrowers to adjust the wind or solar and market price assumptions.

For the wind and solar assumptions, borrowers will argue that lenders have agreed to lend based on the P50/P90 projections which they signed off on at financial close. These projections are likely to be based on a 10-year average. Therefore, if there is one bad wind/solar year, statistically this means that this will be compensated for by a good wind/solar year in the future. To update the wind/solar assumptions too regularly cuts through the 10-year average projections. This argument sometimes succeeds, but will depend on the reliability of the wind/solar data at financial close. The longer the data that has been used to generate the P50/P90 projections, the more reliable the data should be. Conversely, if relatively limited data was available at financial close, funders have a stronger argument that assumptions should be updated more regularly.

With respect to market price assumptions (which are only relevant if the price under the PPA is linked to market price), market experts generally update their long-term power price projections at least annually. Therefore, it is likely that funders will want to use the most up-to-date market price forecasts for the purpose of calculating forward-looking revenues. Borrowers may concede this point but are mindful of the cost involved in procuring forward-looking power curves.

5. Experts and due diligence

Project finance of power and renewables projects is inherently conservative. Therefore, funders will carry out comprehensive due diligence on the project to identify the key risks associated with the project and how best to mitigate those risks. The following experts are likely to be appointed to carry out due diligence in relation to the project.

5.1 Market adviser

As discussed in section 4 above, for projects which do not benefit from fixed prices and which are therefore exposed to market price fluctuations, funders will require a market adviser to provide an analysis of future power prices. They may also be asked to advise on the future price of certain renewable benefits or gas. These experts will produce forward curves based on low, medium and high price situations and the funders will use these forward curves in their financial model for the purposes of their base case and also to run sensitivities. The forward curves are sometimes specific to the site of the project itself as this will then take into account local as well as national factors in determining the forward price for power.

Even though great emphasis is placed on the forward curves of power, market advisers do not guarantee that these curves will be accurate and it would be very difficult to bring a claim against these advisers if their predictions prove to be wrong.

5.2 Technical adviser

The funders will appoint a technical adviser to review all technical aspects of the project including the design, specifications, financial model and also the contracts associated with the project. The technical adviser will be asked to sign off that the output and availability of the project assumed by the sponsors, particularly in relation to the financial model, are correct. The technical adviser will also be asked to sign off on the fact that the cost assumptions for operation and maintenance are correct. Finally, the technical adviser will be asked to comment on the technical aspects of the project contracts to ensure that the contracts reflect the technical design of the plant and feed correctly into the financial model.

It is not unusual for the technical adviser to act as environmental and social adviser to the funders in emerging markets. In this capacity, the technical adviser will review all environmental and social aspects of the project to ensure that they comply with any requirements imposed by the funders.

The technical adviser will generally prepare an extensive due diligence report for the funders. A technical adviser can be sued for negligence, but will generally look to cap his liability at a modest level.

On wind and solar projects, a technical adviser will be appointed by the funders to analyse the wind or solar data the sponsors are using for the purposes of the financial model and, in particular, the P50 and P90 projections which are fundamental to the financial model. Clearly, the longer the period the data has been based on the more reliable it will be deemed to be.

5.3 Legal advisers

Funders' legal advisers will be appointed to advise in relation to the finance documents but also to carry out detailed due diligence on the underlying project documents. As with most project finance structures, the contractual framework is a house of cards and if one contract does not work properly or does not interface with the other project contracts, the whole house of cards – the project in this case – will come tumbling down. Funders' legal advisers will carry out a risk analysis of the project contracts and advise funders of risks that could threaten the revenue stream of the project such as delays under the construction contract or performance of the plant (ie, not achieving guaranteed levels both at the end of construction and during operation).

Funders' legal advisers will review the PPA and identify risks which could impact the revenue received under this contract, including:

- failure to accept power;
- failure to deliver power both in the short and long term;
- termination; and
- compensation on termination.

All this will need to be considered in the context of the relevant jurisdiction and applicable electricity regime. The interface between the PPA and any fuel supply contract will also be key in order to identify any residual risk that sits with the project company.

5.4 Insurance adviser

The insurance adviser will be asked to review the insurance policies that the project company is proposing to put in place to ensure they meet market practice and adequately cover likely physical damage, third party liability and revenue replacement. The insurance adviser will also be asked to review the project contracts to ensure that any indemnities being provided by the project company and any other liabilities of the project company are insurable and disclosed to the insurers.

The finance documents are likely to contain an extensive schedule which sets out which insurances the project company is required to maintain during construction and operation. This will set out levels of insurance, who is to be an insured party and various lender endorsements which are required to be included on the various insurance policies.

6. Non-recourse financing and security

Like any other project financing, financing of power projects is usually made on a non-recourse basis. This is a fundamental principle for this type of financing. Lenders will therefore rely on the cash flows expected to be generated by the project in order to be paid interest and repaid principal of the debt. No recourse to sponsors should be expected from lenders (other than to the extent of the equity committed by sponsors in accordance with the agreed debt to equity ratio). Debt sizing and due diligence (as mentioned above) are therefore critical to ensure that the fundamentals of the power project are sufficiently strong to allow for the required level of debt to be put in place and a sufficient return for sponsors.

Lenders will, however, have full recourse to the project. To this effect, lenders will require a full security package over all assets of the project and the shares of (and shareholder loans to) the project company. The full security package will allow lenders to enjoy a preferred position in comparison with unsecured creditors and, more importantly, to have the ability to sell the project and/or the project company in a default scenario in order to be repaid in full.

The structuring of the security package will depend on the location of the project. Indeed, security over an asset will need to follow the rules applicable to the jurisdiction of the country where such asset is located. In some countries (eg, England), a debenture would allow lenders to take a full floating and fixed charge over all assets of a project company located in England (including the rights of the project company under all agreements governed by English law). In addition to a specific security over the shares of the project company (and shareholder loans made to it) granted by the shareholder(s) of the project company, lenders would benefit from a security over all assets of a project company through one single security document.

In other countries, the structuring of the security package is very different. For example, in relation to power projects in emerging markets, security equivalent to the English law debenture would not usually be available and a full suite of security documents governed by local law will be required to cover all assets of the project located locally. Lenders would also require that some of the assets be held offshore (or governed by English law); this is usually the case for reinsurance policies with acceptable reinsurers (as it is not unusual to see a requirement under applicable local law for insurance policies to be arranged locally), some of the account banks, key project documents such as the engineering, procurement and construction (EPC) and operation and maintenance (O&M) agreements (and their associated bonds and other credit support), hedging arrangements and, depending on the local rules for enforcement, security over the shares of a specific 'holdco' which will be holding the shares of the local project company. For such offshore assets, additional security documents will be required.

Direct agreements allowing lenders to step in and/or novate the underlying agreement to a third party to ensure that such underlying agreement remains in place at all times – including after enforcement in a default scenario – are common. Lenders would typically require direct agreements covering the PPA, the fuel supply agreement (if applicable), the land related agreement, the EPC and O&M agreements and other material agreements depending on the specifics of the power project.

A detailed legal analysis of the regime applicable to the security package (including direct agreements) will be required to ensure that lenders are comfortable with the rules on enforceability and therefore the strength of their security package which is a key concern for lenders from a credit risk perspective.

7. Finance documentation

The usual first step on the financing of a power project is for lenders and sponsors to agree a term sheet summarising the key features of the financing of that project and a mandate and/or commitment letter pursuant to which lenders may agree to arrange (and, in certain cases, fund) the project subject to conditions and upon terms that are usually highly negotiated. This step is necessary to help lenders obtain their required internal approvals on a fast-track basis according to agreed key principles for the financing.

Once such a step is complete (or, later in a bid scenario, if and when the sponsors are awarded the power project), lenders and sponsors move to full documentation which would include one or more facilities agreements (depending on the tranching of the financing), possibly a common terms agreement if there are various tranches which cannot be accommodated through a single facilities agreement, an intercreditor agreement (if not incorporated within the common terms agreement), an equity subscription agreement, an accounts agreement, security documents, hedging arrangements and fee letters.

7.1 Facilities agreement/common terms agreement

The main finance document is the facilities agreement (if there is no common terms agreement). This agreement would include:

- mechanical and other provisions relating to the lending of the funds such as the amount and purpose of the loan;
- calculation of interest;
- drawdown mechanism;
- repayment schedule (provisions of which are usually based to a certain extent on the template English law syndicated loan agreement for investment grade and leveraged borrowers published by the Loan Market Association (LMA));
- environmental and social provisions and insurance requirements specific to the power project; and
- representations and warranties, covenants and events of defaults which are negotiated between the parties and described below.

(a) Representations and warranties

The main purpose of representations and warranties in the context of a project financing is to force a borrower to disclose certain facts or events which are deemed important to lenders and otherwise to represent a set of facts which are correct as at the date of signing/financial close. Such facts or events would typically cover various aspects of the project company, the project and the project assets. They may include but are not limited to: authority to enter into the transaction documents; validity of the transaction documents; no withholding of tax or tax deduction; no litigation; financial statements; full disclosure of information; insurances; consents and authorisations; shareholding of the project company; sanctions; occurrence of *force majeure*; and other project-related events.

Representations and warranties are made by the project company (and in certain cases the sponsors) on the signing date/financial close and repeated for some of them (typically those which are not covered by a covenant which is to be complied with at all times) from time to time including before any money is advanced by lenders and on interest payment dates.

A breach of such representations and warranties will trigger an event of default giving lenders the ability to accelerate the loans and ultimately enforce their security.

(b) Covenants

Covenants are effectively the tools for lenders to control the project company's business and the project. In power project financings (like other project financings), covenants are very detailed and highly negotiated between the parties to strike the right balance between the need for lenders to have such control and the ability for sponsors to run and develop the project in an efficient manner.

Positive covenants (ie, what the borrower must do) and negative covenants (ie, what the borrower must not do) regulate various aspects such as compliance with laws, consents and transaction documents, access to the project for lenders and their advisers, tax and accounting, environmental and social covenants, working capital, additional financial indebtedness and guarantees, suspension and abandonment, budgeting, transactions with affiliates, variations to works, distributions, and project specific covenants resulting from lenders' due diligence findings.

A breach of such covenants will trigger an event of default giving lenders the ability to accelerate the loans and ultimately to enforce their security.

(c) Events of default

Events of default entitle lenders to accelerate the repayment of the debt, cancel their commitments and/or enforce their security. Such consequences effectively mean that sponsors have lost the project and, not surprisingly, the negotiation of such events of default is probably the most difficult part of the financing process.

Typical events of default would include failure to pay, breach of covenants or representations, insolvency, breach of certain levels of financial ratios (eg, loan life cover ratio and debt service cover ratio usually on a historic basis only), illegality and other important events affecting the transaction documents and project/assets related events such as failure to complete the power project by a certain date (which is typically shorter than the longstop dates to complete under the PPA and the EPC agreement) or forecast funding shortfall (ie, a gap in the funding plan to complete the project most likely due to unexpected cost overrun).

Depending on the severity of the event of default, a grace period may be available to give the project company a period of time to remedy the event before it becomes a full-blown event of default. During this remedy period, a default will be deemed to have occurred and the project company will not be permitted to draw down debt or make distributions.

7.2 Intercreditor arrangements

Intercreditor arrangements are made between senior creditors involved in the power project which comprise third party lenders providing funds to the project company and hedging providers which usually rank equally with those lenders. Intercreditor arrangements regulate various aspects of the relationship between senior creditors such as:

- voting and decision making;
- enforcement of the security;
- distribution of proceeds post-enforcement; and
- appointment of a security trustee (or security agent).

Negotiating intercreditor arrangements is not an easy exercise, in particular where it involves senior creditors having different interests: lenders versus hedging providers or Export Credit Agencies (ECAs); or multilateral lenders versus commercial banks or financial institutions. A complex funding structure will necessarily lead to complex intercreditor arrangements.

In addition, to the extent that there are any junior creditors in a project (eg, sponsors, mezzanine lenders), they will be required to sign intercreditor arrangements in order to contractually subordinate their rights against the project company to those of the senior creditors (ie, except for highly regulated permitted payments to those junior creditors, the project company will be prohibited making any payment to them until the senior debt has been discharged in full).

7.3 Equity subscription agreement

The equity subscription agreement is a key agreement for lenders and sponsors. This agreement regulates the level, form and timing of equity contributions that will be required to be made by sponsors in the project company. Depending on the credit standing of sponsors and corporate structure of the shareholding, lenders may require credit support to cover such obligations to contribute equity. Such credit support would usually take the form of an on-demand parent company guarantee if the guarantor is acceptable to the lenders or a letter of credit from an acceptable issuing bank which has a specified minimum credit rating from a recognised rating agency.

The equity subscription agreement will also cover other aspects pertaining to sponsors (if such aspects are not covered in the equity subscription agreement, they will need to be covered elsewhere in the documentation) such as any restriction to transfer directly or indirectly shares in the project company applicable to one or more sponsors during the construction phase and the operational phase.

7.4 Accounts agreement

Project accounts are highly regulated in project financings given that such financings are non-recourse to sponsors and lenders will be relying on the cash flows generated by the project company. Typically, the project company will need to open and maintain a certain number of defined project accounts – which will be secured in favour of the senior creditors – to enable it to run its business and discharge its obligations towards lenders but will be prohibited from opening other accounts. The most common project accounts needed in power project financings include the following:

- a disbursement account: where loans and equity proceeds are credited and which is used to pay construction and other project costs during the construction phase;

- an operating account: where revenues and other proceeds are credited during the operational phase and which is used to make payments relating to the project in accordance with an agreed cash flow waterfall. A typical cash flow waterfall would provide for such payments to be made in the following order of priority:
  - permitted capital and operating and maintenance costs;
  - interest and fees on the senior debt;
  - principal of the senior debt;
  - mandatory prepayments and any associated hedging termination payments;
  - reserving of the debt service reserve account;
  - reserving of any maintenance reserve account;
  - voluntary prepayments and any associated hedging termination payments; and
  - distributions;
- insurance and compensation accounts: where insurance proceeds and compensation payments (eg, performance liquidated damages) received by the project company are credited and which are used for very specific purposes subject to conditions to be satisfied (eg, to reinstate the project following the occurrence of an insurable event or prepay the debt);
- reserve accounts: such as the debt service reserve account where an amount equal to the next scheduled payment of interest and principal in respect of the debt will need to be built up over time and/or maintained to the credit of such account or the maintenance reserve account where an appropriate balance (set following input from lender's technical adviser) will be required to be maintained to pay for costs associated with maintenance works that need to be done from time to time and which have not been passed down to third parties such as the O&M contractor; and
- a distribution account: which will be credited only if a certain number of distribution tests (including with respect to certain levels of financial ratios such as loan life cover ratio and debt service cover ratio on a historic and projected basis) are met by the project company.

Other project accounts may be necessary depending on the specifics of the power project. As mentioned above, certain project accounts may need to be held onshore and others offshore, in particular power projects in emerging markets where lenders would usually require this to mitigate local risks.

7.5 Security documents

For more detail on security documents, see section 6 above.

7.6 Hedging arrangements

As mentioned above, lenders rely primarily on the cash flows generated by the power project and will therefore require visibility and certainty regarding revenues generated, and costs borne, by the project company. Any potential element that could reduce such cash flows will need to be eliminated or at least mitigated. Interest rates and foreign exchange currency risks are elements that lenders would usually seek to mitigate through hedging arrangements entered into by the project company.

Loans provided by lenders to fund power projects will usually bear a floating interest rate using a benchmark such as LIBOR or EURIBOR plus an agreed margin. Hedging floating interest rate exposure will ensure that the project company will only have to pay a fixed interest rate to one or more hedging providers instead of the floating interest rate that is required to be paid by the project company to lenders. The project company is thus insulated from the risk associated with potential movements in interest rates over the life of the project.

Loans provided by lenders and equity contributed to fund power projects will be denominated in one or more currencies. If there is any currency mismatch between those sources of funding and the project costs that are required to be paid by the project company during construction, foreign exchange currency hedging will be required to be put in place. Hedging foreign exchange currency will ensure that the project company will have to pay only one or more agreed amounts denominated in a given currency (using the proceeds of the loans and/or equity received) to one or more hedging providers instead of equivalent amounts in another currency (ie, the currency required to pay the relevant project costs) using a pre-agreed currency conversion rate. The project company is thus insulated from the risk associated with potential movements in the relevant currency conversion rate.

A hedging policy is usually included in the facilities agreement (or the common terms agreement if there is one) which specifies the hedging levels and products required to be put in place by the project company.

Hedging providers are typically classified as senior creditors with regard to the project company and would rank equally with lenders and benefit from the same security package. It is not uncommon to see in power project financings hedging providers also being lenders or affiliates of lenders and in certain cases this stapling is a requirement negotiated between lenders, hedging providers and sponsors.

See also Kerion Ball's chapter on hedging which describes in more detail the form and content of hedging arrangements.

7.7 Fee letters

Fees payable to the banks or financial institutions in various capacities are recorded in fee letters. Fee letters would usually cover the payment of:

- an arrangement or up-front fee to the arrangers shortly after signing of the documentation/financial close or upon first disbursement of the loans;
- an agency fee to each bank or financial institution performing an agency or trustee role; and
- a bank account fee to the account bank if such payment is not already regulated by an account mandate between the account bank and the project company.

Provisions relating to commitment fees payable to lenders instead of their obligation to make loans available for drawing by the project company are usually included within the facilities agreement, although some lenders such as certain ECAs would require the inclusion of those fees in separate fee letters.

Other fees may be payable as agreed between lenders and sponsors.

8. Recent evolution of key financing features

Power project financings have not been immune to the effects of the 2008 global financial crisis. Like other structures of financing, power project financings went through difficult times. Stricter regulations on banks and their lending requirements which came into force since 2008 have had a significant impact on the financing of power projects. Innovative ways of funding had to be considered and key financing features had to evolve to permit the continuing financing of power projects and to cater for the increased need for more power across the world. The key notable changes are outlined below.

8.1 Tenor

Long tenor financings have become more difficult for borrowers to obtain, in particular from commercial banks and financial institutions, as a result of stricter regulations on banks and their lending requirements. Prior to 2008, it was not unusual to find tenors ranging between 15 and 25 years linked to the duration of the PPA excluding a negotiated tail.

In recent years, the use of soft and hard mini-perms has increased. A diagrammatic representation in Figure 2 sets out the differences between hard and soft mini-perms.

Figure 2: Hard and soft mini-perms

(a) Hard mini-perm

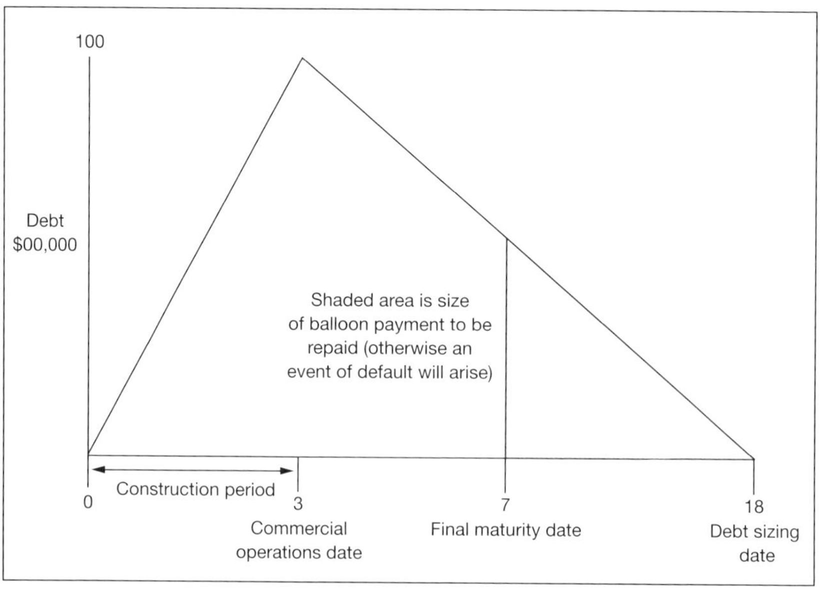

(b) Soft mini-perm

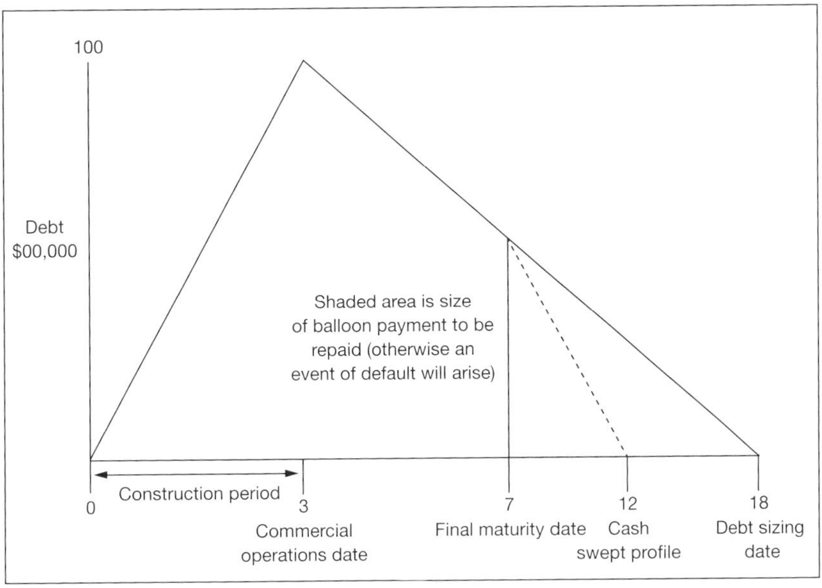

Under a mini-perm structure, the debt is sized over the same term as with a long-term financing and a notional repayment profile is created again on the same basis as long-term debt. However, a hard mini-perm requires the full debt to be repaid within a short period of time (typically three to four years post-completion) which gives rise to a balloon repayment on the final maturity date.

A soft mini-perm allows for a longer tenor with a sweep by lenders of all or a substantial portion of any cash available for distributions to sponsors, starting typically three to four years post-completion in order to repay the debt in full earlier. Combinations of both hard and soft mini-perms can also be found on the market. The objective of the mini-perm structure is to ensure that the debt is refinanced at the earliest opportunity after the beginning of the operational phase once construction risk has been eliminated. This puts additional pressure on sponsors to find a refinancing in a slightly improved but still challenging financing environment.

8.2 ECAs and multilateral institutions financings

Since 2008, there has been an upsurge in power project financings involving ECAs and multilateral institutions, in particular in emerging markets. At a time when sources of funding were scarce, ECAs and multilateral institutions stepped up their funding commitments to allow for companies to continue the development of their business in the power sector. Multilateral institutions such as the International Finance Corporation and Asian ECAs such as Japan Bank for International Cooperation (JBIC), Nippon Export and Investment Insurance (NEXI) and the Export-Import Bank of Korea (KEXIM) have been extremely active in the Middle East,

Asia and Africa in recent years. The primary purpose of multilateral institutions is to lend to projects in the developing world where raising financing is more challenging due to increased political risk. ECAs are usually involved to the extent that a sufficient level of goods and/or services used for the purposes of a project is produced in or delivered from their home country.

The involvement of ECAs and multilateral institutions in project financings has a direct effect in the structuring of a project, its financing and the documentation. Indeed, such institutions will have mandatory policy requirements which will need to be met by any power project seeking their involvement. Such requirements vary from institution to institution but would usually include stricter environmental and social requirements, developed sanction-related provisions, detailed reporting and increased access to the project/assets, and in relation to ECAs, a minimum level of content or shareholding held by a sponsor from the home country.

It is also not unusual for ECAs and multilateral institutions to provide financing to a project whether through direct loans or political risk covers alongside commercial banks or financial institutions. Intercreditor arrangements between those different groups of lenders in such cases are highly negotiated and complex.

8.3 Project bonds

The use of project bonds as a way to fund power projects is a recent trend and is a direct consequence of the shortage of long-term financings available from the lending market and higher project funding costs for banks resulting from the implementation of the Basel III regulations.

Project bond financings, however, face a certain number of challenging issues including:

- the investors' lack of appetite for construction risk and the need to have project bonds wrapped by a third party (eg, Infrastructure UK (IUK) in the United Kingdom) to address this concern;
- the 'negative carry' issue being the higher interest payable to the bondholders on project bonds which are typically issued up front compared with the interest earned by the project by investing the proceeds of such bonds until they are required to fund project costs over the construction period;
- the implementation of effective decision-making procedures for bondholders;
- the pricing and deliverability – including with respect to tenor – of project bonds are certain only upon issuance of the project bonds themselves which does not fit with any requirement from a procurer to obtain fully committed financings in the context of a bid process; and
- the difficulty of implementing this funding solution in a certain number of emerging markets not sufficiently mature/sophisticated to accommodate this alternative way of funding.

By way of comparison with the infrastructure market, the use of project bonds in the power sector remains underdeveloped. Lending remains at this stage the most common option to fund power projects. However, project bonds constitute a developing alternative debt funding solution which is expected to increasingly compete with traditional lending structures in the power sector.

9. Construction document: bankability issues

In parallel with any work stream associated with the finance documents, funders will also need to understand and be comfortable with the construction arrangements pursuant to which the power generation technology is to be built. The documentation put in place will vary depending on which of the differing technologies summarised in section 3 above is to be adopted but it is possible to identify some common themes.

9.1 Risk transfer and procurement structure

Funders will need to consider the balance between the transfer of risk away from the borrower special purpose vehicle (SPV) to the construction supply chain and the risk premium charged by the supply chain. The more risk assumed by the contractor, the higher the risk premium. Conservative sponsors and funders will want to see a blanket engineer, procure and construct (EPC) wrap of construction risk, however such an approach may not always offer best value for money.

Certainly, for onshore wind projects it is no longer the case that an EPC wrap with the usual single point of responsibility for all construction-related matters is necessary. Instead, it is now common to see separate contracts for the supply of turbines and certain electrical and data analysis equipment on the one hand, and for the balance of plant (eg, site access roads, turbine foundations and any modifications to existing civil infrastructure/bridge strengthening works) on the other. The borrower/SPV itself manages the interface risk between these two contracts either using the internal management resource of an affiliated group company or by buying in the necessary know-how under a technical adviser appointment.

For offshore wind projects, the cost of an EPC wrap is considered prohibitive and therefore it is common for the contract packages to be split with as few as four and as many as 20 depending on the experience and risk appetite of the developer.

For gas-fired power stations the EPC wrap of construction risk remains the favoured approach notwithstanding that certain work streams may be procured under separate contracts (eg, construction of gas supply lines).

9.2 Performance security

Funders will also take a keen interest in the forms and amount of security offered by the various construction contractors. Funders will expect to take an assignment of these instruments as part of their overall security package. A typical security package will include:

- an on demand advance payment bond equal to the value of any advance payment;
- an on demand performance bond (or in the United Kingdom, an adjudication bond) for approximately 10–15% of the contract price in place until completion;

- an on demand warranty bond for approximately 5% of the contract price from completion until expiry of the defects period which is generally the period from takeover of the plant until two years following takeover during which time the contractor is required to make good any defects at his own cost.

10. Key elements of real estate and financing

Real estate is specific to each jurisdiction. This section 10 is written in the context of a project located in England.

A funder will want to ensure that the borrowing developer has a good and marketable title to the land on which the project has been, or is to be, constructed. The funder's legal advisers will occasionally investigate title themselves but the preferred route is for the developer's legal advisers to provide a Certificate of Title in the latest form prescribed by the City of London Law Society on which the funders can rely. This will then be reviewed by the funder's legal advisers who will also provide to the funders an overview report on the Certificate of Title on which the funders will also rely.

Funders are usually more risk averse than developers and will want to know that any potential risks to the project arising from the title have been addressed. There may be a need for the developer to take out insurance if there are any outstanding title issues that could potentially impact upon the project, however remote those risks may be. If the developer already has any title insurance in place, the funder will want to ensure that there is a sufficient level of indemnity cover and that the benefit extends to successors in title to the developer, as well as mortgagees.

Funders will need to ensure that the Certificate of Title is used appropriately in the context of the wider technical due diligence undertaken in respect of the project site. The interface between what rights the project needs from an operational perspective against what rights the site benefits from legally is key. The Certificate of Title contains a range of confirmations from the developer which can assist this process. Funders should seek appropriate warranties from the borrower in the finance documents as regards to the accuracy and completeness of such confirmations.

The Certificate of Title should not deal just with the underlying freehold title but also with the terms of any lease that has been or will be granted to the developer and the funders will want to see that the lease:

- permits all works to be undertaken by the developer;
- grants to the developer all rights that will be required both for construction and the ongoing running of the project; and
- contains no unusually restrictive covenants or conditions that could prevent the project being operated in the event that the security is ever enforced.

The funders will also be concerned to ensure that the lease does not prohibit charging or that if consent to charge is required from a landlord, it is already in place before the financing is completed. Hybrid leases are also common in projects of this nature and contain a range of provisions, some of which real estate practitioners would normally associate with long leasehold interests (eg, limited alienation control) and others with shorter-term rack rent leases (eg, strict alteration controls and more complex rental structures). This can create a tension between the interests of the landlord and the funders, particularly around forfeiture/re-entry rights. It may be necessary to negotiate a direct agreement between the landlord and the funders to solve these issues and to ensure the funders' position is fully protected.

Some projects will involve the distribution of resources such as the electricity produced at the property and in such cases the funders will require the Certificate of Title to cover not just the land on which the project has been constructed, but also any adjoining land on which connecting cables need to be laid to ensure that the resources can connect into the national grid system. Ideally, all consents to lay cables and wayleaves to permit their future retention and maintenance on adjacent land will have been granted prior to any funding being in place. However, it is not unusual in renewables projects for documentation to follow the event, particularly where a distribution network operator is involved who will want to see that the cables have been constructed before they will enter into a formal wayleave agreement. In such instances, the finance documents are likely to include a condition subsequent requiring the developer to negotiate and complete a wayleave agreement with a distribution network operator within a specified period of time.

There may also be a sub-station lease where electricity generated by the project will be fed into the grid system. If this is offsite, then the funders will need to know that the sub-station is entirely within the ownership of the district network operator so that there is a clear route of title from the property to the national grid system. If the electricity sub-station is onsite, then the funders will be concerned to ensure that the terms of the lease, under which the developer holds the land, permit the construction of a sub-station and usually the subsequent grant of an underlease to the district network operator. The nature of such sub-stations does not always allow for a self-contained underlease to be granted (and in some instances the district network operator may not want to enter into a lease), so the funders will want to see that the lease also allows the developer to share the use of the sub-station with the distribution network operator in the event that one half of the structure is controlled by each party.

When the funding has been completed, the funders will need to ensure that any security over the project site (where located in England) is registered at the Land Registry. The funders' legal advisers can apply to register a charge but it is preferable for the borrower's legal advisers to undertake to the funders that they have obtained clear priority searches at the Land Registry in the name of the funders and that, following registration of a charge against the borrower at Companies House, they will apply to register the charge as a first ranking security against the property and will pay all necessary fees.

There may be circumstances, for example where a loan is being made to a parent company (such as in holdco portfolio financings) and the premises are held by a subsidiary company, where there may not be a direct charge over the property itself as the security is taken at the parent company level. Other than registering a charge at the Land Registry, however, the funders will take every other action as if security were being taken so that they have the reassurance that if the security is ever enforced at parent company level the benefit and burden of the project operated by the subsidiary company can be passed to another third party who can operate it clear of any title issues.

Nuclear power

David Wadham
Ashurst LLP

1. Introduction

In the electricity industry worldwide we take it for granted that, in many countries, the private sector owns and operates power generation facilities. We also take it for granted in many jurisdictions that private capital and, in particular, third party equity or debt finance has been used to finance the construction of those power generation assets. The private sector, including private financial institutions, understand and are willing to assume the risk of constructing, owning and operating, or financing, generation assets that deploy a wide range of technologies, including the conventional technologies of oil, coal and gas-fired generation, through to all forms of renewable energy including wind and solar and taking in new hybrid technologies such as biomass and energy from waste.

However, with the exception of the United States, the development, ownership, financing and operation of nuclear generation facilities largely remains the preserve of the state or institutions owned by the state. The role of the private sector in the ownership and operation of nuclear power, and in particular the role of third party finance in the financing of that generation capacity, remains limited.

2. Nuclear power: the specific issues

This chapter assumes that, based on the information given in Nacim Bounouara, Antony Skinner and David Wadham's chapter on financing power and renewables projects, the reader is already broadly familiar with the development and financing of power generation facilities. The relevant points made in that chapter about the development of power generation for the most part apply equally to nuclear: the sponsor or funder of a nuclear power station will need to understand and allocate many of the risks that apply to conventional or renewable power generation, such as construction risk, fuel supply risk and offtake risk. But the developer or funder of a nuclear power plant faces an additional set of complex and unique challenges.

Some of the key challenges include:

- complex national and international regulatory regimes dealing with nuclear liability and other matters such as non-proliferation and safeguards;
- extremely high capital cost and long construction periods;
- complex and often first-of-a-kind (FOAK) technology;
- political and regulatory risk over an extremely long project life; and
- significant decommissioning, waste management and disposal costs.

Taken together, these factors give rise to a set of project challenges for nuclear developers and funders that is intrinsically more risky and complex than traditional power project development. There is no single easy solution to these issues or a single template for nuclear development and, indeed, a number of these factors and the appropriate solutions vary significantly from country to country.

This chapter seeks to examine some of the challenges facing the development and financing of nuclear power. First, we consider the sponsors and funders of nuclear power projects and how the characteristics of nuclear power plant development influences the nature of the sponsors and the available funding sources. Then we consider some of the key project risks that are somewhat unique to nuclear power project development.

3. Sponsors in the nuclear sector

3.1 State involvement

In most jurisdictions, the ownership and operation of nuclear power facilities has traditionally been, and remains, the preserve of the state and state-owned corporations. The capital costs involved and the liabilities associated with nuclear facilities have simply been costs and risks the private sector cannot take. According to the International Atomic Energy Agency (IAEA) in 2015 there were approximately 437 operational reactors in the world with 378 GW of net capacity. With the exception of the United States, the vast majority of these reactors are owned and operated by state utilities or by companies that are privatised former state utilities, often still with a significant degree of retained government ownership. These include companies such as EDF in France (58 reactors) and Rosatom in Russia (34 reactors).

Strong state ownership is still largely applicable to the newer generation of reactors that are in construction: the capital cost of a typical nuclear plant with one or two reactors is still typically too high for all but the largest utilities. In 2015 according to the IAEA there were reportedly 68 reactors with a total capacity of approximately 66 GW under construction. China has by far the greatest number of reactors in construction (25), followed by Russia with nine. However, in these countries the construction and financing of nuclear power is largely a national affair, where the state or a majority state-owned utility is developing nuclear plants based on nationally owned technology.

3.2 Private investment in nuclear power

However, there are signs in some countries of a subtle shift in the developers of, and the role of debt finance in, nuclear power plants. A number of countries with limited natural resources or with large energy demands have started seriously to consider the potential benefits of low-carbon baseload power that nuclear power would generate and have launched international tenders for the development and construction of nuclear generation capacity. Countries that fall into this category include the United Arab Emirates and Turkey, with others considering this route. At the same time, we have seen in more liberalised markets a willingness to develop and construct the latest generation of nuclear independent power producers (IPPs), often prompted by concerns around the long-term impact of fossil fuels. Such countries include the United Kingdom and Finland. These projects are interesting because they involve the development and construction of nuclear power plants led by sponsors, and deploying technologies from outside the host country.

The other interesting shift is in the identity of the lead developers or sponsors. Projects are no longer necessarily being led by the resident state utilities; we are seeing manufacturers competing for the opportunity to export their particular nuclear technology. The Korean and Chinese manufacturers are seeking new markets for their technology (although this can involve complicated discussions over IP rights given the original genesis of some technologies). Equally, two countries with the largest proportion of nuclear generation, Japan and France, recognise that the future new-build opportunities in their home market are limited and are therefore seeking to keep domestic manufacturing bases alive by exporting technology. This is particularly true of Japan in the wake of Fukushima, where we see manufacturers such as Hitachi and Toshiba (Westinghouse) aggressively pursuing new-build opportunities in other countries.

As it stands, we are therefore at an interesting point where we see private, or at least partly private, institutions which may or may not be utilities beginning to take the lead in developing new-build nuclear projects, albeit with strong state support.

4. Who are the funders of new-build nuclear?

If the identity of the sponsors is beginning to change, is this reflected in the funding techniques or the providers of funding?

4.1 The bank market

To date, unlike with other forms of power generation, the commercial bank market has shown little appetite for financing nuclear power plants on a limited- or non-recourse basis. The project financing of nuclear power plants requires the provision of large sums over long tenors against the backdrop of complex and often unique project risks. What is more, since the global financial crisis of 2008 and with the impact of the Basel III banking regulatory changes, the number of banks prepared to lend big on long-term energy projects has reduced. That is not to say that IPPs (conventional or renewable) do not get financed or that mega-energy projects cannot raise project financing in the commercial bank market, but in many senses nuclear project finance catches the weaknesses of both. Electricity generation is essentially a national undertaking, with electricity rarely crossing borders and paid for at source in local currency; and yet the capital costs of a nuclear power project are akin to a mega oil project such as a new refinery or petrochemicals facility, whose products are globally transportable and paid for in dollars and whose project development is backed by a strong state sponsor or national or multinational oil company, with revenues and resources way beyond the dreams of the typical IPP developer or national electricity company.

Add to that the challenges of the large capital expenditure and an ultra-long tenor to maximise the operational life, and all the challenges of the liability issues associated with nuclear power, and it is easy to understand why commercial banks have struggled to become overly involved in the sector.

4.2 The bond market

As the bank market has struggled to digest the large volume of infrastructure to be built across the world, there have been efforts in various markets to bring the bond markets more into infrastructure finance. However, while the longer tenors achievable in the bond market would sit well with the long operational life of a nuclear power plant, the same issues around the identification and allocation of risks as apply to commercial banks will apply to bondholders too. Additionally, the bond market does not cope well with construction risk, both in terms of the appreciation of that risk and then responding to events occurring during construction, and construction risk on nuclear projects is considerable (see below).

4.3 Multilateral institutions

Multilateral financing institutions, such as the International Finance Corporation (an arm of the Word Bank) and the various regional development banks, such as the Asian and African Development Banks, are heavily involved in infrastructure finance. However, nuclear power is a sensitive political subject and so most multilateral institutions are for policy reasons not involved in the financing of nuclear generation, although the European Investment Bank is more flexible in its approach to nuclear.

4.4 Export credit agencies and state-related funders

To the extent new-build nuclear is not funded directly by the relevant national government or by the balance sheet of the large (state-owned) utility company, debt funding is likely to come from export credit agencies or state-related funders.

An export credit agency (ECA) is a government-owned financial institution established to support the export of that country's goods and services. Most OECD countries have an ECA and, indeed, a number of other countries too. The provision of ECA finance is informally governed by the OECD Arrangement on Guidelines for Officially Supported Export Credits, known as the "Arrangement". Current participants include the European Union, Japan, the Republic of Korea and the United States and the Arrangement covers the export of goods and/or services which have a repayment term of two years or more.

The support normally takes one of two forms:

- direct lending; or
- a contractual guarantee or insurance policy to support lending by commercial banks.

In other words, an ECA may either lend itself or cover others for the risks of lending on terms permitted by the Arrangement. Most ECAs operate on the latter basis, although a number of institutions, such as the Japan Bank for International Cooperation, Korea Export Import Bank and the United States Export-Import Bank offer the possibility of direct lending. Clearly, in view of the large sums involved, the ability of some ECAs to create additional pools of liquidity by deploying their own capital is helpful.

There is a specific "sector understanding" set out in Annex II of the Arrangement covering nuclear power plants. Importantly, the sector understanding sets out a longer repayment term for nuclear power plant financing than is available for other lending (ie, an 18-year repayment term as opposed to a standard 12-year term). There are also other repayment terms linking to fuel supply, spent fuel disposal and enrichment and fuel management.

Crucially, in the context of nuclear plant financing, ECAs being arms of government have an ability to assume and manage the political risks associated with nuclear to a far greater extent than commercial banks. ECAs have a policy goal of supporting a country's export of goods and services that operates in tandem with any economic analysis of a particular project. Additionally, through government-to-government contact, ECAs have a way of assessing and mitigating or influencing political risk. It is not uncommon to see that while a particular ECA is assessing an investment in a specific project in a particular country, there are various government-to-government meetings taking in place in the background and perhaps even some form of inter-governmental memorandum of understanding on inward investment being negotiated and signed.

It is perhaps no coincidence that the countries with strong nuclear manufacturers also have active ECAs. In relation to the Abu Dhabi nuclear programme being undertaken by ENEC on the basis of contracts signed with Korea Electric Power Corporation (KEPCO), it is understood that the – as yet unimplemented – debt package for that project has a significant element of direct K-EXIM financing. Equally, it is expected in the UK context (and elsewhere) that JBIC, one of the most active ECAs, will play a strong role in supporting the export of the rival Hitachi (ABWR) and Toshiba/Westinghouse (AP 1000) technologies.

ECAs, while significant, are however by no means the only form of government support. China is currently the world's most active new-build nuclear market and is dominated by so-called state-owned enterprises (SOEs), such as China General Nuclear (CGN), China National Nuclear (CNNC) and State Nuclear Power Technology Corporation (SNPTC). However, in relation to their domestic activities, each of these SOEs enjoys strong support in the form of project level lending from Chinese state banks. The likes of China Development Bank and Industrial and Commercial Bank of China are frequently engaged by the SOEs to provide project-level debt, although the debt is more akin to corporate financing rather than non- or limited-recourse debt.

Another example would be the United Kingdom, where Infrastructure UK (IUK), an arm of the UK government established by HM Treasury in the aftermath of the financial crisis to stimulate and support investment in UK infrastructure, is playing a significant role in the current UK nuclear new-build programme. IUK operates by providing a guarantee to commercial debt providers such that it assumes the full risk associated with a particular project. In the case of the Hinkley Point C project being developed in the United Kingdom, IUK has offered in return for a guarantee fee to provide a substantial guarantee such that long-term bonds of that value can be sold into the bond market in tranches to fund construction. The cost of those bonds will be broadly equivalent to UK government debt plus a slight premium, as effectively those bondholders will be taking UK government risk (with project risk being assumed by IUK). It is worth noting that the issuance of the IUK guarantee in support of Hinkley Point, together with the contract for difference supporting the sale of the plant's output, was considered to constitute state aid for European Union purposes and was notified to, and approved by, the European Commission. As at the time of writing, the Austrian government has challenged in the European Court the European Commission's decision to approve the state aid measures. It will take some time before the outcome of this challenge becomes clear (see more below).

5. Funding nuclear development pre-FID

One of the challenges facing nuclear development is the length of the development phase before the sponsors take their final investment decision (FID). Many of the challenges are not unique to the nuclear sector: the would-be sponsor of any conventional or renewable power project needs to acquire land, get a grid connection and secure a long-term offtake for the power generated. But the scale of these standard tasks for nuclear power plants goes significantly beyond that of conventional projects. The planning process for nuclear power plants understandably goes way beyond that required for conventional generation. Acquiring the necessary land and obtaining the relevant land consents is an extremely complex process. Equally, there is a world of difference between acquiring access to grid, for example, for a 70 MW wind farm when compared with a two rector 3 GW nuclear plant. Likewise, selling the electricity generated by a 5 MW solar park with an anticipated useful life of 25 years is an altogether different proposition from finding a route to market for 3 GW of power operating baseload over perhaps 60 years. It should therefore be evident and of no surprise that nuclear projects take much longer to develop than their conventional or renewable counterparts.

Some of these risks may be mitigated if the development opportunity takes the form of a host government-sponsored tender, but the development timescales and costs of new-build nuclear are not for the faint-hearted. At the time of writing, EDF's Hinkley Point C NPP has been in development for several years, with FID scheduled for later in 2015, at an estimated pre-FID cost of circa £2 billion.

In terms of financing these pre-FID costs, there is little option but for sponsors (including manufacturers) to assume these costs, hoping to sell down some of their equity (at a premium) at or around FID and bring in some element of debt to refinance some of these costs.

6. Funding nuclear development post-FID

Once the lengthy pre-FID development phase has been successfully negotiated, then there is a degree of certainty to the project that permits sponsors to consider a wider range of funding options. At this point in a conventional power project's life cycle, the sponsors may well have successfully put in place a non-recourse financing, with the project's construction being funded under a highly leveraged (eg, 80:20 debt/equity) model, with sponsors at risk for their base equity and a small amount of cost overrun (contingent) equity only, and with funders willing to accept no recourse to sponsors (other than for their equity) on the basis of a strong construction contract and looking to the debt to be repaid from the proceeds of the sale of electricity under a long-term power purchase agreement (PPA).

However, the characteristics of a nuclear project mean that funders cannot easily apply the high leverage, non-recourse structure of a conventional IPP to its nuclear equivalent.

7. Key risks for the financing of nuclear projects

As mentioned above, many of the risks faced by developers of nuclear plants are the same as those faced by developers of conventional and renewable plants, even if on a larger scale. But what are the key risks that make nuclear such an inherently different proposition? We analyse these risks below in three stages:

- construction risks;
- operational/decommissioning risks; and
- general risks.

8. Construction risks

8.1 Contracting strategy

The first major difference with conventional IPPs lies in the likely construction contracting strategy to be adopted and its impact on the project's bankability.

It goes without saying that non- or limited-recourse funders to a power project are at their most vulnerable during the construction phase: at this point the power plant is not operational and not producing revenues to pay down the debt being incurred as the plant gets built. Any funder will therefore look very carefully at who the construction contractor is and assess their technical capability and financial strength. The funders will also examine closely the contracting strategy, wanting to ensure that there is clear responsibility (and recourse) for failures in construction.

Most conventional IPPs are developed and constructed on the basis of a fixed price, turnkey construction contract with a major contractor, in many cases the manufacturer of the power generation turbines. Funders are therefore able to derive a great deal of comfort from the fact that there is single point responsibility from a reputable and solvent entity to construct the plant to a fixed specification by a fixed date and for a fixed price. These obligations are backed with significant delay and performance liquidated damages to keep equity and debt providers whole in the event of delays or performance shortfalls. In a disaster scenario, these remedies are typically supplemented by some form of rejection regime entitling sponsors (or more typically funders) to put a substantially non-performing plant back to its contractor in return for repayment of the contract price (ie, the transaction can be effectively unwound).

However, in the case of nuclear plants, for reasons of sheer cost and risk, it is extremely difficult to replicate this turnkey construction contract structure that underpins conventional IPPs. Whereas a large gas-fired plant may cost in the region of, say, $1 billion (and the above structure requires the contractor to assume a liability equivalent to that construction price), the capital expenditure for a nuclear plant may be ten times that amount. It is evident that there are very few companies with the size or commercial appetite to construct, on a lump sum single contract basis, a $10 billion nuclear plant.

The different cost and risk profile necessitates different contracting strategies. While there is no fixed approach, one can perhaps distinguish between two broad approaches. The first is to try to maintain some element of the turnkey approach with the sponsors still seeking to limit the number of contracts, possibly even still to a single contract, but with some of the elements of that contract at a fixed price while others may be on a cost plus or target price basis (with associated pain share/gain share mechanism). The other approach would be a more multi-contracting strategy, with the plant owner placing multiple contracts for the plant's construction and commissioning and supervising that process itself or appointing an architect engineer to do so. The former is the approach being adopted on the Baraka NPP in the United Arab Emirates, whereas the latter is the approach being adopted by EDF on its Hinkley Point C project in the United Kingdom. Both approaches have their own merits and disadvantages. For example, the single contract approach still pushes a considerable degree of risk away from the project company and obliges the contractor to assume a considerable degree of interface risk. However, the contractor will charge a hefty premium for doing so. The architect engineer approach allows a more flexible and reactive approach to construction on the part of the owner and may succeed in reducing hefty risk premiums being charged by contractors, but clearly there is a very significant degree of interface risk being assumed by the owner itself with far less protection in the way of liquidated damages to offset time and performance issues.

Whichever approach is taken, it presents the funders with risks that are not present in a conventional IPP construction: the project vehicle to which funders are lending is exposed to a degree of cost and interface risk that cannot easily be assumed by a thinly capitalised, debt-heavy project special purpose vehicle (SPV).

The overall result is therefore likely to be the requirement from funders for sponsors to provide some form of completion support or contingent equity. This additional equity is likely to be far in excess of the cost overrun equity typically made available by sponsors of a conventional IPP, which could be as little as 2.5–5% of project cost. Funders of a nuclear facility are likely to require that the principal sponsors provide some form of completion guarantee for the plant, for example remaining responsible for the costs of all debt service until such time as the plant enters commercial operation. Contingent equity would fulfil a similar function, being available to supplement base equity and meet any cost overruns or the costs of a delay in construction. In either case, the quantum of this support could be considerable, perhaps even equivalent to the sponsor's original base equity commitment.

8.2 Construction period, cost overrun and delay; technology risk

Irrespective of what contracting strategy is adopted, a nuclear construction presents a considerably different risk profile to the construction of a conventional or renewables plant.

A typical construction period for a solar farm or an onshore wind farm might be only a few months, whereas a typical construction period for a combined cycle gas-fired plant may be 36 months. From a funder perspective, the shorter the construction period, the better: this is essentially a dead period when no revenue is being generated and considerable interest during construction (IDC) will either accrue or have to be serviced from another funding source. However, the typical construction period for an NPP may be in the region of 60 to 84 months. Combined with the greatly increased capex, the challenges to project economics posed by the construction period and expenditure of an NPP are evident. While the financing costs of an NPP during a long construction phase are high, they can to some extent be largely quantified. However, the additional challenge from a lender perspective is the risk of cost overruns and delays.

Substantial delays in the construction of renewables plants are relatively rare; even on large-scale complex combined cycle gas-fired plants, delays of more than a couple of months are unusual and lenders can be comforted that delays of many months should be fully covered by heavy delay liquidated damages. However, while one should not generalise, the complexity and scale of nuclear plants has led many prominent NPPs to suffer major delays on a scale beyond those typically encountered by conventional plants. Additionally, based on the possible contracting strategies outlined above, there is unlikely to be single point of responsibility for that delay or, indeed, cover in the form of delay liquidated damages for the project vehicle and its lenders.

Again, this delay and cost overrun risk is not one funders will bear and so, to the extent the risk is not borne by the contractors, sponsors will need to assume this risk, either by making sure there is available very substantial cost overrun equity or through some form of sponsor completion guarantee.

An additional complication is the question of technology risk. Whatever the technology, be it renewable, conventional or nuclear, funders typically want to fund only proven technology, preferring equity to take the risk on prototype plant design. However, this can be a difficult requirement to satisfy in the nuclear sphere where the number of reactors in development, relative to, say, conventional gas turbines, is far fewer. Additionally, national regulators, such as the UK Office for Nuclear Regulation (ONR), may require design changes to be made to the existing (proven) reactor design during the licensing process. This FOAK risk is one which is difficult for lenders to bear. Indeed, in the State Aid approval decision issued by the European Commission in respect of the Hinkley Point C NPP, it was noted that the financing had been structured such that sponsors (and not funders) took this FOAK risk.

9. Operational/decommissioning risks

9.1 Power offtake

Once the plant is built, it needs to generate and sell electricity to be able to pay down debt and pay a return on equity. These arrangements for the sale and purchase of electricity will, of course, depend on the organisation of the relevant national electricity market. As explained in Nacim Bounouara, Antony Skinner and David Wadham's chapter on financing power and renewables projects, how the generator sells its electricity will depend on to what extent the generation sector has been liberalised. In non-privatised and/or developing markets, the electricity is likely to be sold to a single state-owned bulk purchaser of electricity. Rather than being a payment per megawatt hour of electricity delivered to the grid, the payment structure might be based on a so-called capacity (availability) payment model, where the generator is paid a capacity (availability) payment for making the plant available (and which payment covers the plant's fixed costs of construction, operation and return) coupled with an output payment (covering the variable costs of operation) for the electricity generated to the extent the plant is dispatched. In fully liberalised markets, the plant output will simply be sold to one or more private purchasers of electricity, be they traders or suppliers.

In non-privatised or developing markets, the developer of a nuclear plant will have secured a long-term power purchase agreement to sell the electricity generated. If the plant has been built in response to a government-initiated tender, the terms of that PPA may well have been set at the outset and the price fixed as part of the tender process.

However, a liberalised power market presents a considerable challenge to the developers of a nuclear plant. Electricity may be bought and sold (traded) on a spot or relatively short-term basis. Longer-term PPAs may be difficult to negotiate and will be with private sector participants, not state companies, and these participants will have difficulty accepting an extremely long contract term, perhaps 15 years at most, and one for a plant which does not become operational for the best part of a decade. The owner of a nuclear plant, and especially its funders, will be looking for a reliable long-term purchase of the plant's output to pay down the considerable capex incurred in the plant's construction. If the plant does not benefit from a long-term PPA, the generator will have to put in place arrangements to trade its own power in the market place or appoint someone in the market place to do so on its behalf. That person will need to put in place a trading strategy, selling the plant's output through a combination of forward trades and spot and short-term selling. This is a considerable task as nuclear plants are relatively large compared with other sources of power generation and so the generator will need to secure sales arrangements for 1200 MW or considerably more of generation capacity. These arrangements will need to be robust and will be subject to considerable scrutiny by any funders as the generator is taking exposure to the power market, the so-called merchant power risk.

An additional complication in a liberalised market will be that the costs of building a new-build nuclear plant may make it difficult to compete in the market with existing baseload generation, be it gas-fired, coal-fired, or indeed nuclear, which has largely or fully amortised its initial construction cost. Some form of subsidy mechanism may need to be put in place to support the project in return for generation of the large quantities of low-carbon power the project provides.

The most recent (and prominent) example of such a mechanism is the United Kingdom's contract for difference (CfD) regime. The CfD regime is applicable to various forms of renewable generation, as well as nuclear. It operates much like a typical contract for difference derivative instrument. At the outset of the contract, a "strike price" is set (by competitive tender for most renewable technologies but by bilateral negotiation for nuclear projects) and the government-owned counterparty to the CfD pays the generator the difference between a specified market price (referred to as the "reference price") and the strike price for each MWh of electricity generated.

If for any period the reference price exceeds the strike price, then the payment reverses such that the generator repays the difference to the CfD counterparty. The CfD term is set at 15 years for most projects, but is open to negotiation in the case of nuclear projects, with the CfD for Hinkley Point C being set at 35 years.

The introduction of a long-term nuclear CfD is a key element in securing investment into UK new-build nuclear for private sector participants and the scheme has attracted considerable interest, not least because it has been the subject of intense scrutiny under the European State Aid approval process. The European Commission issued a decision approving the Hinkley Point C CfD (and associated IUK financing) in October 2014. At the time of writing, the Commission's decision has been appealed by a number of renewables generators in Europe, as well as most controversially and notably, by the Austrian government. The outcome of the appeal will take several years, but most commentators think it is unlikely even in the most extreme case to result in a complete invalidation of the CfD mechanism.

9.2 Opex and the nuclear fuel cycle

Securing a long-term reliable and price-stable supply of fuel is of course a concern for lenders on any conventional IPP. The same is true of a nuclear power project, but there are additional complications associated with the procurement of nuclear fuel on the international market and its treatment.

The transport of nuclear fuel gives rise to concerns from a non-proliferation perspective, as indeed do the enrichment of nuclear fuel and the reprocessing of spent nuclear fuel.

As with the question of liability for nuclear damage, funders will need to assess whether the host country is party to the relevant international treaties and conventions, as well as assessing the local regime for the procurement of nuclear fuel. Other issues that will arise in relation to fuel supply include the following:

- Inter-relationship between fuel fabrication and the construction and commissioning process: reactors require a specific type of fuel that is packaged in a particular way. There is therefore an inherent link with the reactor's commissioning process as it would be an unenviable situation if a plant performed poorly during commissioning and each of the construction contractor and fuel supplier sought to blame the other for the problems. As a result, it is commonplace for the fuel for at least the first fuel reload to be supplied by the contractor.
- Diversity: to minimise political risk, funders will also want to see a fuel strategy which encourages diversity of supply. Uranium can be sourced from a number of countries, some of which do not have consistent records of political stability, so funders will want to ensure that the fuel supplier has access to uranium from a number of sources. This may mean in practice that funders may wish to look through the construction or fuel supply arrangements and have a degree of scrutiny of and indeed possibly control over, underlying supply arrangements.
- Long-term price risk: commodity prices, including for uranium, are not entirely predictable and, as a result, the costs of operating the nuclear plant can fluctuate

over time. Mitigating this risk is not easy, but funders will want to explore ways of doing so, either by passing the costs of any increase in fuel through to the purchaser of power or by seeking ways in which the fuel supplier can retain price risk (at least for a certain period) and itself hedge the risk (eg, if it has a much larger portfolio of plants to supply and operate) even if this means the IPP purchasing fuel at a price above the prevailing market price.

9.3 Decommissioning risks

One final area of risk that is markedly different from that applicable to conventional or renewable generators, is the area of the costs and liabilities associated with decommissioning a nuclear plant. At the end of its working life, a nuclear plant will need to be safely decommissioned and its radioactive elements stored. This will involve the decommissioning of the plant, the management on-site for a relatively long period of spent fuel and intermediate-level waste, before the eventual transfer of radioactive waste to a long-term storage facility and the rehabilitation of the site.

Given that the operational life of an NPP could be 60 years or more, it is unlikely that any funders involved in the funding of the project during its construction will have any interest in the plant by the time of its decommissioning phase. However, it is clear that the generator will need to accrue considerable reserves during its operating period in order to meet its liabilities during the decommissioning period.

The question of decommissioning costs and liabilities is a crucial one for the host government. After interim storage at site, spent fuel will need to be stored in a suitable facility for hundreds of years. Such periods of time run way beyond the time horizon of private sector sponsors and funders and indeed make it inevitable that there is some degree of government involvement with decommissioning and waste management. The host government will therefore want to make sure that, even if the private sector developers and funders are not ultimately responsible for long-term storage, such costs have been factored into the project's costs and returns and appropriately reserved such that a future government is not left to foot the bill for the storage of nuclear waste or indeed the plant's decommissioning.

In the United Kingdom, this issue was brought into sharp focus by the collapse and subsequent renationalisation of British Energy which left the UK government with huge liabilities for decommissioning of British Energy's fleet of reactors in the United Kingdom. Partially as a result of this experience, the Energy Act 2008 introduced a comprehensive regime requiring operators to establish a funded decommissioning plan to meet the full costs of decommissioning, waste management and disposal and for the funds to be held in, and invested by, a separate, bankruptcy-remote SPV.

It is clear, therefore, that the nuclear project's operating model will need to take into account the need to reserve for decommissioning and waste costs. This can give rise to some interesting questions for lenders, who would typically expect to rank as senior and secured as against all a power project's other creditors. However, in practice, a host government will be keen to ensure that the appropriate funding of a decommissioning and waste storage fund will take priority over the claims and controls of debt providers.

10. Risks that apply throughout the life of the project

10.1 Legal and regulatory risk

Unlike conventional power generation, which is regulated very much on a national basis, nuclear power is also subject to a complex web of international conventions and treaties. Potential funders to a nuclear power plant, particularly in a new nuclear state, will need to conduct thorough due diligence to understand how the host country has committed itself to international agreements, as well as the rights and responsibilities of those involved in nuclear power generation under national law and indeed the risks to which they, as funders, may be exposed.

Nuclear power cannot be developed by one state in isolation. A state thinking about implementing a nuclear power programme will need to enter into multilateral and bilateral agreements and cooperation arrangements with other countries. In addition to becoming a member of the International Atomic Energy Authority (IAEA), a state developing a nuclear programme will be expected to accede to a broad range of nuclear instruments covering matters such as:

- non-proliferation (of nuclear weapons);
- nuclear safeguards;
- nuclear accident protocols;
- conventions regulating the provision of assistance in the case of a nuclear emergency;
- spent fuel and radioactive fuel management; and
- conventions regarding liability for nuclear damage.

Potential funders to a nuclear programme will want to understand how a new nuclear state has committed itself to the above matters.

Furthermore, funders will then need to understand the national regime for nuclear legislation. A host state can be expected to exercise tight control over nuclear power generation and funders will need to understand the applicable national regime. A number of the original nuclear states have national nuclear regimes that to some extent pre-date, and even influenced the development of, the international regimes (eg, the US Price-Anderson Act of 1957) while others are more recent. Given the cross-border nature of nuclear liability, there is great benefit in a harmonisation of regimes and, indeed, in an effort to assist countries implementing a nuclear power programme in 2003 the IAEA published its *Handbook on Nuclear Law* and then in 2010 its associated *Implementing Legislation*. These publications assist potential legislators in providing a checklist of issues to be covered and the correct implementation into national law of the prevailing international conventions. Nonetheless, notwithstanding the desirability of harmonised cross-border legislation, it is impossible to expect a one-size-fits-all approach to such a complex matter and funders will therefore need carefully to perform due diligence on the national regime to assess it for compliance with, and deviations from, international norms.

10.2 Liability for nuclear damage

One specific concern for funders will be the question of liability for nuclear damage.

In conducting its risk analysis, one of the fundamental concerns of a bank or any other funding institution will be its exposure to third parties in the event of an accident causing nuclear damage. As incidents such as Chernobyl have demonstrated, the question of nuclear damage is one that is unfortunately not contained within national borders and therefore the analysis of liability for nuclear damage will need to examine not only the prevailing liability regime in the host state, but also an examination of the regime in neighbouring states and indeed in any state with some involvement in the project.

There are two main international conventions dealing with liability for nuclear damage, the Paris Convention on Third Party Liability in the Field of Nuclear Energy (Paris Convention) and the Vienna Convention on Civil Liability for Nuclear Damage (Vienna Convention). The Paris Convention is only open to OECD members, although Turkey has sought and been granted consent to join. The Vienna Convention was originally dominated by a number of East European countries with interests in nuclear power and has a broader geographic base, with recent adherents to the civilian nuclear market, such as the United Arab Emirates, having also acceded to this convention.

Both these regimes seek to deal with liability for nuclear damage in a similar manner, adhering to six basic principles:

- The designated operator of a nuclear installation is exclusively liable for nuclear damage;
- Strict no-fault liability applies to the operator;
- Liability is limited in amount;
- Liability is limited in time;
- There is appropriate coverage for the operator's residual liability; and
- There can be no discrimination between claimants based on nationality, domicile or residence.

The adherence to these principles is important to funders, in particular the channelling of liability to the designated operator and the limiting of liability.

However, not all states are party to one of these conventions. Some nuclear states such as the United States, Canada and Japan have their own third party liability regimes. Other states, particularly those with no interest in, or a positive dislike of, nuclear power will not be party to these regimes. This lack of total coverage inevitably complicates the risk analysis for funders. What if ionising radiation from a plant in country X is blown by the prevailing winds into country Y? How will the courts of country Y react to a claim for damage brought in that country? Will they take action or will they respect the sole authority of the courts of country X?

In short, understanding the potential liability flowing from a nuclear accident at a new plant will involve a complex analysis of the host country's implementation of international regimes as well as those of adjacent countries, and an analysis of the likely behaviour of foreign courts as regards assuming jurisdiction.

Irrespective of the results of this analysis, funders may wish to seek additional contractual protections from a host government. Nuclear law is complex and, if the relevant law is new, there may be a degree of uncertainty as to how certain provisions will be interpreted in practice. Depending on the country in question, there may also be uncertainty over the capability of the judiciary to analyse complex questions of law and fact in a consistent and predictable manner and, indeed, there may be additional uncertainty complicated by the need to interpret liability provisions through the prism of the applicable local law. In these circumstances, particularly in the context of a government-launched tender, funders may at least want to explore the possibility of some form of backstop indemnity under a known law to supplement any newly created liability regimes.

Irrespective of the cover afforded by the host state under the applicable liability regime, funders will need to consider the residual liability borne by the project company. For example, when 2004 Protocols to the Paris Convention and the Brussels Supplementary Convention enter into force, the minimum residual liability for the designated operator will rise to €700 million in Paris Convention countries. Funders to projects in such a country will need to understand how this liability can be met, either from specialist insurance markets or by some other form of financial security.

10.3 Political risk

It is evident that investing in nuclear power entails a significant degree of political risk. This of course is true to some extent for investment in power generation generally; in OECD countries in particular, the subject of which type of generation mix to pursue is never far from the headlines as policy makers try to balance the competing demands of reliability, affordability and environmental sustainability.

However, scrutiny of nuclear power is particularly intense and indeed post-Fukushima a number of countries have undergone a reversal in nuclear policy that has had a major financial impact on the owners of nuclear plant. For example, in Germany the decision was taken in 2011 to phase out all nuclear generation by 2022 and the sudden decision has given rise to a number of legal challenges from German energy companies which have been hit hard by the decision.

How political risk is treated depends very much on the nature of the electricity market in a given country. In a developing country, where private sector participation in the power sector is underpinned by long-term implementation agreements and/or PPAs with the host government, it is customary for the generator to benefit from strong political risk protection clauses which would typically provide a broad change in law protection, allowing the generator to be compensated for the effects of the change in law and, in extreme situations, terminate the PPA and recover adequate compensation. However, in OECD/liberalised markets, there is often very little in the way of political risk or change in law protection for conventional and renewables generators: there is often no contract between the generator and a government entity, with any subsidy regime taking the form of a statutory framework.

In this context, it is worth noting that the United Kingdom's recently introduced CfD regime (which applies to both renewables and nuclear generators) has taken the form of a bilateral contract between a government entity and the generator, with one of the reasons for the private law contract being that it potentially conferred greater rights (protection) in respect of change in law: the standard form CfD benefits from extensive (albeit carefully drafted) change in law protections. It is thought that the bespoke nuclear CfDs will encompass a greater degree of (nuclear-specific) change in law protections. These protections are a logical investor response given the legislative and policy changes that have adversely impacted the nuclear and broader renewables industry in certain countries.

11. Conclusions

In its 2009 report, *The financing of nuclear power plants*, the Nuclear Energy Agency of the OECD concluded that "Corporate finance is the most likely applicable model for new NPPs" and that:

It appears that there is very little likelihood in the foreseeable future to finance a new NPP by using non-recourse or 'project' financing and that debt investors are unlikely to be willing to provide significant funding for a nuclear plant without recourse against the balance sheet of a strong and creditworthy utility.

By and large, the NEA's conclusions have so far proved correct. However, there are signs of a changing market for NPPs. Large state utilities are no longer the only sponsors of NPPs, with manufacturers increasingly playing a role. With strong ECA support in the background, it will be interesting to see how this new generation of sponsors can take the financing of the next generation of nuclear power plants forward.

Mining

Barry Irwin
Allen & Overy LLP
Peter Wilkes
Allen & Overy

---

1. Introduction

Recent years have been challenging times for mining companies seeking to raise finance. Lower commodity prices have put equity values under pressure and consequently some of the traditional sources of funding for the mining sector are constrained, forcing mining companies to consider a broad range of alternative funding methods and combinations of different sources to satisfy their funding needs.

Traditional bank debt and capital market bond issues are still vitally important and will remain so. However, farm-ins, strategic partnerships and joint ventures, royalty financing, streaming and offtake financing have become more common as sponsors find it difficult to raise traditional debt on favourable terms and are either unable or unwilling to raise equity at prices they see as substantially dilutive to their existing shareholders. Junior miners and explorers have been particularly hard hit due to their traditionally heavy reliance on equity markets to undertake small capital raisings to fund their drilling and development programmes. Majors are also feeling the pressure as evidenced by the spate of full or partial divestments and even withdrawals from projects in an attempt to reduce costs and improve shareholder returns.

In this chapter, we provide a summary of most of these various forms of financing, both the traditional and the less common. However, mining finance is a broad and sometimes arcane area of law and practice, and it is therefore beyond the scope of this chapter to provide an exhaustive analysis of all types of mining finance. So what follows is necessarily descriptive; it does not address all the possible means of raising capital or the many complexities and nuances which are a feature of all the different forms. Many of the funding methods adopted in the mining sector are not unique to the sector. However, there are some unique or noteworthy features to the approaches employed in financing the mining sector and we will touch on some of these in this chapter.

2. Financing and the mining project life cycle

Some of the financing techniques discussed in this chapter can be, and routinely are, adopted across the various stages in the life of a mining project, while others tend to be restricted to only parts of the cycle. This is represented diagrammatically in Figure 1 on the following page.

Figure 1: Financing and the mining project life cycle

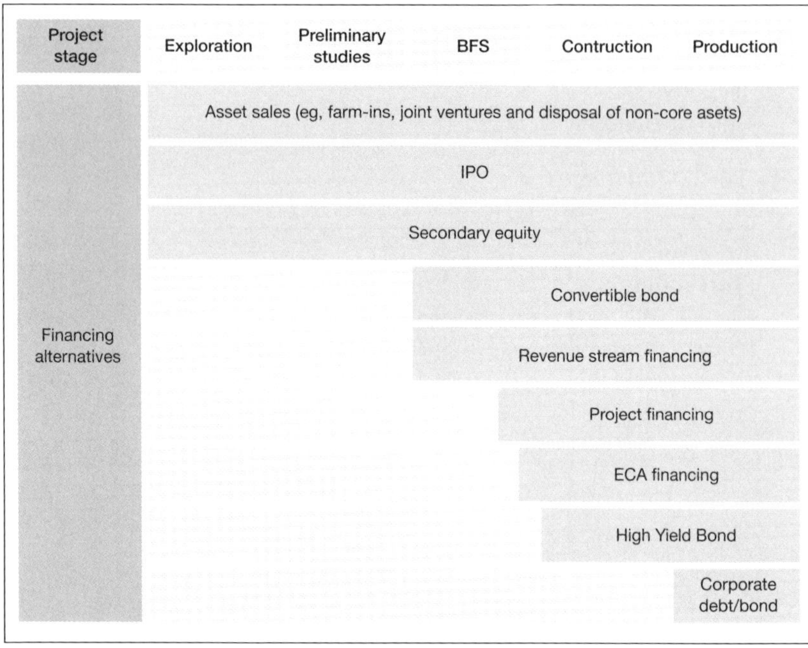

3. Mergers and acquisitions as a source of financing

The sale of an interest in a mining project is a common mechanism for raising funds and reducing the costs and risks to the sponsors of development. The exploration phase of a mining project can be expensive and is necessarily speculative, but it is only the beginning. The costs of completing a drilling programme, undertaking a preliminary economic assessment and then a bankable feasibility study (BFS), plus converting exploration permits into mining leases or concessions and obtaining other necessary approvals, all require substantial capital, to say nothing of the costs of achieving full development and production. Consequently, many junior explorers decide to sell down an interest in their projects to form strategic alliances or joint ventures in order to unlock the necessary funding. Indeed, in times of low commodity prices this may be the only feasible option for the juniors. The farm-in agreement entered into by Rio Tinto with Antipa Minerals Ltd is an example of a junior miner selling down an interest in a project. Under that agreement, entered into in 2015, Rio Tinto has the right to earn up to a 75% interest in Antipa Mineral Ltd's Citadel gold project in Western Australia by funding A$60 million in exploration expenditure over 10½ years.

Selling down interests in projects is not limited to junior miners. Many mid-tier miners and even the majors are divesting interests in their mining assets to reduce costs, spread risk and raise funding. Larger mining companies will permit other miners to farm-in to non-core assets as a means of maintaining an exposure to exploration while minimising the high risks inherent in funding exploration. In

2011 Chinalco Yunnan Copper Resources Ltd entered into farm-in agreements to acquire up to a 60% interest in three Rio Tinto copper exploration projects in Chile by incurring up to US$71 million in exploration expenditure. For larger projects that have reached the decision to mine and are facing the significant costs associated with the development phase, mining companies of all sizes may look to sell down an interest to one or more other miners or mining investors to share the costs and associated risks of development. In 2012 Roy Hill Pty Ltd sold interests in its multi-billion dollar iron ore mine and port and rail infrastructure project which led to three investors, namely China Steel Corporation, Marubeni Corporation and POSCO, holding a 30% interest between them. Also in 2012 Rio Tinto completed the sale to Chalco (a listed subsidiary of the Aluminium Corporation of China (Chinalco)) of a 47% interest in the Rio Tinto subsidiary that holds the interest in the undeveloped Simandou iron ore project in the Republic of Guinea, Africa.

3.1 Investors

The range of participants providing funding through the acquisition of a full or partial interest in a mining project includes:

- major mining companies, to take advantage of the exploration work undertaken by juniors before the real value uplift;
- major and mid-tier companies seeking to diversify their geographical exposure or to move beyond a single commodity or a limited number of commodities;
- financial investors such as private equity funds, hedge funds, sovereign funds and new corporates backed by such funds, typically by acquiring minority stakes without operatorship;
- commodity traders, often by acquiring a minority interest as a means of obtaining insight into a project, to secure supply or – increasingly – to move their businesses 'upstream';
- state-owned enterprises (SOEs) which are mining companies looking for security of supply for the benefit of the state; and
- other state-owned or privately owned enterprises (such as steel producers and power generators) looking to secure long-term offtake arrangements.

Generally, the typical investor will require either some level of de-risking such as completion of drilling programmes or a BFS to establish a resource base, and possibly the current owners having reached a decision to develop and mine, or they may require a high level of control over the project, often disproportionate to the investment.

3.2 Structures

A divestment of an interest in the project can be structured in various ways, including, but by no means limited to:

- an outright sale of all of the assets comprising the project;
- the sale of all of the shares in the project company;
- a placement of shares in the parent company (particularly if it is listed);
- the sale of some of the shares in the project company and the formation of

an incorporated joint venture (typically the approach in Indonesia and many other jurisdictions);
- the sale of a partial undivided interest in the assets and the creation of an unincorporated joint venture (often, but not exclusively, the approach in Australia and Africa); or
- the sale of a partial interest in the project and the formation of a partnership (typically in North America).

3.3 Farm-ins

The sale of a partial interest is often structured as a 'farm-in'. These are in most, if not all, jurisdictions almost entirely creatures of contract and so there is infinite scope for variation, but there are some basic principles which are common to many farm-ins. It is also important to note that the common practice – to the extent that there is one – can vary considerably from one jurisdiction to another. A conventional farm-in will typically incorporate at least some of the following elements:

- the acquirer agrees to fund a fixed amount;
- the funding is often in stages in accordance with an approved programme and budget;
- the funding is over an agreed term;
- the funds are applied towards project exploration and/or development costs to advance the project to an agreed stage;
- often the investor assumes responsibility for the work, effectively taking on the operatorship;
- in exchange for funding, the investor earns an agreed percentage interest in the project (or in the shares in the project company);
- sometimes, the investor is obliged to make milestone payments as well as bearing the cost of the work required to 'earn in';
- usually, upon completion of at least the initial stage of funding (but sometimes over several stages), the investor will have a right to exercise an option to have the earned interest vest, or to withdraw and walk away from the project;
- in the case of a farm-in at the development phase, the cost for earning the interest is generally higher than at the pure exploration stage, reflecting the fact that some de-risking has occurred through the exploration and preliminary economic assessment; and
- staging the investment usually results in the cost to the acquirer being higher than an outright purchase up front.

In a farm-in arrangement, the acquirer's funds are invested directly into the project as opposed to being paid to the owner for their own use.

As noted above, farm-in arrangements can be structured so that the party earning the interest has flexibility to withdraw from the arrangement, generally at certain agreed stages. In 2013, Vale International Holdings exercised its right to withdraw from a farm-in agreement with Goldminex Resources Ltd relating to exploration tenements in Papua New Guinea. Under the farm-in agreement relating to the

Citadel gold project referred to above, Rio Tinto has the option to withdraw following an initial 18-month programme requiring it to sole fund A$3 million of exploration expenditure.

3.4 Advantages

Some of the advantages of a farm-in are as follows:

- From an existing owner's perspective, a farm-in will enable it to minimise costs through the earn-in period.
- The owner may also have flexibility to dilute to a minimal interest or to exchange its residual interest for a royalty interest.
- Farm-in agreements avoid the need to deal with volatile equity markets or incur debt on unfavourable terms.
- Farm-in agreements can be a particularly attractive option for a company which considers that the market is undervaluing its shares. Entry into a farm-in agreement on favourable terms can be seen as external validation of the project and have the effect of re-rating the company.
- For a major selling down an interest in a project, a farm-in can send the message to the market that the company is streamlining and re-focusing its business.
- Given that a farm-in is a contractual arrangement, it is structured through direct negotiations between the parties, so the parties are free to tailor arrangements to suit the specific assets and their specific circumstances.
- Unlike debt funding there is no requirement to maintain minimum cash flows or credit ratings.
- A farm-in can be less dilutive than an equity raising.
- A farm-in can allow companies to take advantage of each other's strengths. For example, a junior miner can benefit from the knowledge base, cash reserves and specialised staff and technology of larger, more established mining companies, whereas larger mining companies can benefit from the junior's ability to take on higher levels of risk and their greater knowledge of local exploration assets.
- Larger strategic partners can often assist with obtaining bank debt for the development of the project. One of the key terms of the 50:50 joint venture announced in 2006 between Anshan Iron and Steel Group Corporation (Ansteel), one of China's largest steel producers, and Gindalbie Metals Ltd, a junior Australian mining company, was the provision of assistance by Ansteel to Gindalbie to obtain both debt and equity funding for the development of their Karara iron ore project.
- Subject to the laws of the jurisdiction where the project is located, it may be possible to structure the farm-in arrangement so that the costs funded by the acquirer are 100% tax deductible.

3.5 Issues to consider

At the time of negotiating the farm-in agreement, it is appropriate and prudent for the parties to agree the terms of the associated joint venture or partnership agreement. Issues to be considered by the parties negotiating those agreements include:

- when the interest will vest (eg, at commencement, progressively against agreed milestones or at the end of the earn-in period);
- how long the earn-in period should be (ie, the acquirer may seek a longer period to contribute its funding and the owner may seek a shorter period);
- whether the farm-in is to all minerals which may be discovered in or produced from the relevant tenements, or limited to a single mineral (both being quite common);
- the control over spending during the earn-in phase – ideally this will be in accordance with an agreed programme and budget, but the acquirer may seek a level of flexibility if it is sole funding;
- whether it is to be an incorporated or unincorporated joint venture;
- valuation issues – given the early stage of the project, these can be complex, presenting challenges in agreeing the amount required to be paid and the percentage interest to be earned;
- the decision-making regime and reserved matters requiring approval of both parties (or of parties holding a relatively high percentage interest in the project);
- deadlock breaking mechanisms, which may range from quite complex 'Russian Roulette' clauses, forced trade sale or auctions, put and call options, expert determinations or mediation, to the relevant decision simply not being passed;
- transfer and pre-emption rights;
- dilution and whether there is a right to elect to dilute or whether it is a consequence of failing to meet a cash call;
- dispute resolution processes (ie, arbitration versus litigation);
- exit mechanisms; and
- the sharing of risk, responsibility and liability.

Special care needs to be taken where the interests of the parties may not be aligned. The objectives of a junior explorer may (and often do) differ from those of a major mining company, with the risk that the junior may be outspent and diluted out of the project.

Almost without exception, an acquirer will consider it essential to conduct technical, financial, environmental and legal due diligence reviews. These can be complex, time-consuming and expensive as the acquirer will need to be comfortable with all aspects of the project. Often government approval will be required for the transfer of an interest in the underlying tenements. In addition, as the parties are forming a partnership or an incorporated or unincorporated joint venture, they need carefully to consider the financial and technical status, the cultural fit and reputation of the other party.

The flexibility and potential complexity of farm-in arrangements, together with the inherent requirement that the parties work together and achieve certain synergies, gives rise to a potentially higher execution risk than would be the case for a traditional capital raising. Consideration also needs to be given to the possible impact on future funding, including by building in mechanisms to permit participants to grant security interests over their respective project interests in favour of future financiers – or collateral agents and security trustees – and agreeing intercreditor principles to the extent that the participants have granted each other cross-security.

4. Equity funding options

Equity funding through initial public offerings (IPOs) and secondary or follow-on issues is a vital source of capital for mining companies throughout the mine life cycle. It is particularly important for explorers and junior miners as their access to other sources of funding is limited. But it is equally important during the construction and development phase of the mining project as debt funding will generally be available to fund only between 55% and 70% of the total development costs of the mining project. For example, in 2015 TMAC Resources Inc completed an IPO on the Toronto Stock Exchange raising C$155 million, which together with funds under its US$120 million senior secured term loan facility, will be used to develop its Hope Bay gold project in Nunavut.

Equity can also act as the funding source of last resort, as a means to address cost overruns or of de-leveraging in tightening markets (recognising that the dilutionary effect on shareholders may be a negative but necessary consequence in some circumstances).

4.1 Stock exchanges and listing

Key stock exchanges for mining companies are the London Stock Exchange (LSE) (where the largest miners such as BHP Billiton, Rio Tinto, Glencore and Anglo American are listed), the Toronto Stock Exchange (TSX) and the Australian Stock Exchange (ASX). Also significant are the Johannesburg Stock Exchange in South Africa for African mining projects and the New York Stock Exchange for major mining companies, including those seeking a secondary listing. The Hong Kong Stock Exchange is also growing in importance for mining companies given the importance of China as a buyer of mining product and investor in mining projects.

Each exchange has initial and ongoing listing requirements which must be met for companies to be admitted to, and maintain their listing on, the relevant exchange. The TSX also operates the TSX Venture Exchange and the LSE operates the Alternative Investment Market (AIM), which together with the ASX are more accommodating for smaller mining companies, particularly those with no or limited producing assets. To be admitted to AIM, there is no requirement for a minimum market capitalisation or trading history. For the ASX, the company must:

- have a minimum of A$3 million in net tangible assets (including funds raised through the IPO but after deducting the costs of the fund raising);
- have a market capitalisation of at least A$10 million (post-IPO); or
- have aggregated profit from continuing operations for the last three full financial years of at least A$1 million plus consolidated profit from continuing operations for the 12 months to a date not more than two

months before its admission application of at least A$400,000 and must still be profitable.

For the TSX Venture Exchange, depending on the stage of development of the company's projects, the company will either be a Tier 1 or Tier 2 company. A Tier 1 company must have C$2 million in net tangible assets, adequate working capital to carry out its work programme for 18 months and C$200,000 of unallocated funds. Tier 2 companies must have adequate working capital for 12 months and C$100,000 of unallocated funds. There is no net tangible assets requirement for a Tier 2 listing.

Junior miners may seek an initial listing on AIM or the TSX Venture Exchange, and then move to the main board of the LSE or TSX after developing their project and growing into an established operating miner. Further, after listing on one exchange, companies may seek a secondary listing on one or more other exchanges. Typically this is motivated by a desire to obtain exposure to a broader range of investors or a deeper equity market, but may also arise because the company has acquired new projects in different jurisdictions and certain exchanges may be seen as more supportive of those jurisdictions (eg, LSE/AIM may provide a deeper market for projects in Africa than the ASX alone).

4.2 IPO process

A listing will typically be completed as part of an initial public offering which will require a prospectus or offering circular. The specific disclosure requirements and liability regimes differ across the jurisdictions depending on the exchange on which the listing is being sought. However, generally, there is a requirement to disclose all information which may be material to an investor's decision whether to invest or to make an informed assessment of the assets and liabilities, financial position, profits and losses and prospects of the company.

Any IPO will involve a thorough due diligence process to ensure and verify disclosure of all material information and ensure that the disclosure is not misleading or deceptive by inclusion or omission. Directors, as well as the company itself, may be liable for a failure to meet the disclosure regime or for misleading and deceptive information. The due diligence process is intended to protect against such liability. Independent experts will be called upon to provide reports which may include an independent accountant's report and an independent technical expert's report on the mining project and its reserves and resources.

The IPO may also include an underwriting agreement or dealer management agreement by which brokers are appointed to manage the offer process in exchange for a fee, typically based on a percentage of the capital raised.

4.3 Standby equity

Standby equity facilities provide an alternative to the usual methods of equity raising, through rights issues and placements. Under a standby equity facility, the mining company has an option to issue up to a set number of shares to the facility provider by way of a series of issues over a set time frame, which may be a period of months or more than a year. The facility provider agrees to subscribe for the shares at a set price but the issuer has the option of whether to undertake share issues. Given the standby nature of the facility, the issuer is usually entitled to elect not to make any share issues during the term of the facility without suffering a penalty.

4.4 Advantages

While an IPO is costly and time-consuming, once a company is listed it has access to a liquid market of investors through secondary issues such as placements, rights issues and share purchase plans, which are typically faster and cheaper and can often be carried out on a low documents or no documents basis. The ability to raise funds in the equity market quickly provides a potential avenue to reduce debt exposures and repair a balance sheet in a declining market.

A key consideration for companies undertaking capital raisings is the potential dilutionary effect on existing shareholders, which is particularly an issue in declining markets. Once listed, a company is required to comply with a range of additional regulatory requirements, including the requirement to keep the market fully informed about all information relating to the company and its assets which may be material to investors.

5. Convertible notes

Convertible notes are a familiar source of finance for most mining companies. They are a form of hybrid instrument which combines both debt and equity characteristics. They sit in the capital structure above shares and, depending on their terms, until converted are equal with or possibly subordinated to senior and other subordinated debt.

Convertible notes are typically issued to institutional investors by mining companies with established operations. For example, in March 2015 Paladin Energy Ltd, an Australian uranium miner, completed the issue of US$150 million senior unsecured convertible bonds to institutional investors with an interest rate of 7% per annum and due in 2020. The need to service interest payments dictates that convertible notes may not be suitable for issue at an earlier stage in a mine's life cycle. Having said that, convertible notes are often used by junior mining companies to raise funds at or about the bankable feasibility study or construction phase, through the issue to cornerstone investors, resource-focused private equity funds or small groups of seed capitalists. For example, in 2014 Sundance Resources Ltd announced the raising of A$40 million by the issue of convertible notes to Wafin Ltd, a company controlled by a resources sector investor. The proceeds raised were to be used to progress the debt and equity financing of the Mbalam-Nabeba iron ore project in Africa. The convertible notes were unsecured, with no interest and if not converted must be redeemed by the company at 130% of their face value 36 months after their issue.

Convertible notes can be an attractive source of capital during a rising market or even a volatile market as they provide downside risk protection, through the requirement to repay the loan component with an interest rate return, but potential upside in a rising market through increases in the value of the equity.

5.1 Key features

A convertible note is a loan or debt instrument with the lender having the right to convert the debt to equity. It may be in the form of one instrument or a loan with a separate warrant or option. The interest rate may be fixed or floating. It may be structured to be redeemable only by the issuer as a means to qualify for equity accounting treatment. It may also be possible to structure the instrument so that it achieves equity credit for ratings agencies, although this may not be the case for typical convertible notes issued to institutional investors in the international market.

The conversion price is generally determined based on the market price immediately prior to announcement of the issue. So the price is market driven and not known until close to the issue date, which increases execution risk. The conversion price is usually a slight premium over the market price. The higher the premium over the then market price the longer the investor will want to hold and have the right to convert and the higher the coupon expectations (ie, it will trade more like debt). The coupon will usually be lower than interest available on straight debt.

The convertible note instrument will include anti-dilution provisions to adjust the conversion price for future restructures, share issues and activities of the company which would dilute the return to the investor. Convertible notes may be secured or unsecured. Notes issued into the international market typically include a negative pledge requiring security to be granted to the note holders if the issuer undertakes similar capital raisings on secured terms.

5.2 Issues to consider

Issuers of the convertible notes need to consider the securities laws of their jurisdiction which may apply to the issue of shares on conversion of the debt to equity. In addition, if it is proposed to make a public offering of the convertible notes, consideration needs to be given to whether the offer will be limited to institutional investors or will include retail investors. A key factor in determining whether to include retail investors will be the time and costs involved in complying with the securities laws in the jurisdiction where the offer is to be made. Securities laws in different jurisdictions may apply to the offer either of the debt instruments or the securities to be issued on conversion, or both. If applicable, those laws may require prospectus-like disclosure documents or regulatory approvals, and may impose potential liability on issuers and their directors. An offer to institutional investors will typically qualify for relevant exemptions from such laws. For this reason, most convertible note issues in the international market are made as exempt offers to institutional investors. Convertible notes issued under such offers may be listed on a stock exchange to meet the requirements of certain investors whose charter restricts them to investing in listed instruments or to provide liquidity for secondary trading. In Europe, the stock exchanges of Ireland or Luxembourg are often used, as well as London. In the Asia Pacific, the Singapore stock exchange is commonly used.

Issues to be considered by companies issuing convertible notes include:

- the potential dilution of shareholders due to the equity option being priced at pre-convertible note prices;

- the coupon, which requires cash flow;
- in some jurisdictions, listed companies can issue a limited percentage of their share capital each year without shareholder approval. If this is applicable to the proposed issue, then the option element of a convertible note reduces this placement capacity;
- execution risk around timing and pricing, and the risk of last-minute changes to pricing (margin and/or conversion premium);
- the default risk in a declining market and the associated refinancing risk; and
- negative reactions of markets to convertible notes depending on pricing.

From the investor's perspective, it is important to bear in mind that if the share price does not rise, then the fixed coupon return will generally be lower than straight debt.

5.3 Advantages

One advantage for an issuer in issuing convertible notes is that it provides another potential source of finance which, particularly for a bilateral convertible note, can be negotiated and concluded relatively quickly. Also, the terms can be flexible and often do not contain the same level of covenants and restrictions as straight debt. In addition, the coupon will often be lower than straight debt and the instrument can be structured to sit above equity but below other debt.

From an investor's perspective, the key advantage is that it provides downside protection through the fixed income element even if the share market declines, with a potential upside through the equity conversion at prices set at the time of entering into the convertible note.

6. Royalty and streaming financing

Both royalty and streaming arrangements are financing methods available to mining companies in the bankable feasibility or pre-project development phase as well as during the production phase. In each case, the funding is based on proven reserves. Traditionally, if employed, royalty and streaming arrangements provided only a relatively small portion of the overall funding required for project development. However, more recently, royalty and streaming companies have been able to raise significant amounts of capital and, therefore, in some instances have been able to provide a significantly larger portion of the total funds required to develop a project. For example, as part of the consideration for its 2012 acquisition of a gold and silver stream from Inmet Mining Corp's share of the Cobre Panama copper project, Franco Nevada agreed to provide an upfront deposit of US$1 billion to be used to finance a portion of Inmet Mining's US$4.8 billion share of the development costs of the project.

These revenue-based funding arrangements are an alternative to a dilution of shareholders' interests at an early stage of development through equity issues or a farm-in.

Royalty investment companies include Franco-Nevada Corp, Royal Gold Inc, Anglo Pacific Group, Callinan Royalties Corp, Premier Royalty Inc and Royalco

Resources Ltd. Other royalty investors include resource-focused private equity funds. Streaming companies include Silver Wheaton Corp and Sandstorm Gold Ltd, as well as Franco Nevada and Royal Gold Inc.

6.1 Royalties structure

The basic structure of royalty financing involves the purchase by a third party from the mining company of a royalty right in return for the payment of an upfront purchase price. The payment is upfront in the sense that typically it is paid in the expectation that the project will be successfully developed and, in time, produce income. The royalty comprises a right to receive a fixed percentage of the future proceeds from the sale by the mining company of the mineral product extracted from the relevant mining project. There are a range of different royalty types, including:

- a gross revenue royalty;
- a net revenue royalty (ie, based on profit);
- a net smelter return royalty (gross revenue less a pro-rata share of certain mining and transportation costs, that is cash flow that is free from operating and capital costs); or
- a percentage of product produced taken in kind.

Arguably the simplest is the gross revenue royalty as it avoids potential disputes as to the costs to be deducted from the revenue generated by the project. Net smelter return and net profit royalties are more common in North America. In some instances, net profit royalties may be structured so that the royalty is not payable until the mining company has recovered from net profits its capital costs and all pre-production costs (although this may be more common in the oil and gas sector than the mining sector and is similar to a free-carried approach to mining joint ventures).

The royalty is usually for the life of the mine, and any sale of the mine by its owner will be subject to an undertaking by the mining company to cause the buyer to assume the obligation to pay the royalty. Sometimes a royalty is structured so that the mining company has the option to buy back the royalty right if the royalty holder seeks to sell the royalty. In 2014 Silver Wheaton entered into an agreement for a 1.5% net smelter returns royalty on Chesapeake Gold Corp's Metates gold-silver project in Mexico under which Chesapeake has a right to buy back two-thirds of the royalty for a five-year period and a right of first refusal if Silver Wheaton elects to sell the royalty.

One of the critical issues is to ensure that the royalty interest flows with the project and binds future owners, which also provides protection against insolvency risk. In some jurisdictions it is possible to register the royalty interest against the mining title so that the royalty enjoys priority over other creditors and binds purchasers of the mining title. However, this is by no means the case in all jurisdictions and will depend on the law of the jurisdiction where the project title is located. Where the royalty interest itself is not an interest in land, the royalty holder typically seeks a security interest or lien over the mining title to which the royalty relates.

The key terms of the royalty agreement will include:

- the percentage rate of the royalty;
- how it is calculated;
- the amount of the purchase price for the royalty;
- the minerals or mining product to which the royalty relates;
- the mining area from which the products are to be extracted and on which the royalty is payable;
- if and how the payment obligation is secured;
- stapling of the royalty to the underlying tenements and associated assignment rights; and
- possibly, a right of pre-emption for the mining company to buy back the royalty if the royalty holder proposes to transfer it.

6.2 Streaming arrangements – structure

Under streaming arrangements, the investor provides an upfront payment to the mining company for the right to buy a fixed percentage or amount of future production from the mining project.

Streaming arrangements are most common in North America and with North American-based streaming companies. They are often structured so the percentage of the product which is the subject of the streaming arrangement is only a small proportion of the project's anticipated total production to ensure that the project owner's and the streaming company's interests are aligned.

The product which is the subject of the streaming arrangement may be the mineral produced from the project or a by-product of the mining operations, such as precious metals produced from base metals mines (eg, gold produced from copper mining operations). The removal of this product and the associated revenue from the project's return can have a negative impact on the project's operating costs resulting in a higher mining cost (and, in times of low commodity prices when there is a strong focus on being a producer low in the cost curve, this is a relevant factor).

Typically, the investor in a streaming arrangement undertakes to buy an agreed percentage of future production for cash at the lesser of an agreed fixed price or the market price prevailing at the time of delivery. So, there is usually an upfront payment and then payments at pre-determined prices on actual production. In 2015 Silver Wheaton agreed with Vale SA to purchase an additional 25% of the gold production from Vale SA's Salobo mine in Brazil for an upfront cash payment of US$900 million and ongoing payments of the lesser of US$400 and the prevailing market price for each ounce of gold delivered under the agreement.

The upfront payment may be structured as a deposit and if future sales at the fixed price are lower than market price then the difference may be credited against the deposit. Generally, any deposit remaining at the end of the term is repayable by the mining company as a means of providing protection against poor performance of the mine.

Streaming arrangements will usually have a term equal to the life of mine. The key provisions to be negotiated include:

- the amount of the upfront payment;

- the fixed price;
- the term;
- the percentage of product to be purchased; and
- the method of delivery.

Streaming arrangements typically do not give rise to an interest in the project tenements and therefore, absent a security interest or lien, the streaming company ranks with other unsecured creditors. If a purchaser of the mining project does not agree to sell the product to the streaming company on the same terms, then the streaming company may only have a claim against the former owner. For these reasons the streaming company should consider taking security over the relevant project, which may not be complete protection but will go some way to protecting its interest.

Tax and accounting treatment are a key consideration when structuring the streaming arrangement and will to an extent depend on the laws of the jurisdiction where the project is located or where the streaming arrangement is enforceable.

6.3 Royalties and streaming arrangements – advantages

From a mining company's perspective, some of the advantages of royalty and streaming arrangements as a means of financing include the following:

- They are not traditional debt and have no interest payments, which is attractive to miners particularly pre- and during project development, given the lack of revenue for meeting debt service obligations.
- They can operate as external validation or endorsement of the mining project.
- The arrangements have flexible contractual terms which can be agreed and executed relatively quickly and with limited documentation (usually only a royalty or streaming agreement and any associated security or lien).
- They are covenant-light compared with traditional debt facilities, with very few covenants and events of default (including no financial covenants and no penalties for construction delays).
- There is no obligation to pay for or deliver product until production, so the miner only pays if it has the revenue or product (although depending on the structure this may have a negative impact on the profitability of the project).
- The investor takes production and commodity price risk.
- There is no dilution of shareholder equity and no dilution of ownership in the project (although they indirectly reduce shareholder returns by reducing total revenue).

6.4 Royalty and streaming arrangements – key considerations

It can be challenging for a mining company's management to determine the true cost of a royalty, namely the value of the loss of future cash flow. What might seem reasonable at the time of receipt of the purchase price might seem less so when the royalty payments significantly exceed the original purchase price.

It is important for the mining company to consider its future funding needs.

Having a secured royalty or streaming arrangement in place can add complexity when negotiating with bank financiers who typically require a first priority lien or security position. Having said that, financiers familiar with financing the mining sector are often comfortable with a prior ranking secured royalty or streaming arrangement. The mining company should ensure that the royalty or streaming arrangement does not restrict the ability to raise future secured financing and should agree the intercreditor principles with the royalty or streaming company at the outset. Under future funding arrangements the royalty payment should be treated as an operating cost in the cash flow waterfall, but future financiers may press for subordination.

For both streaming and royalty arrangements, the streaming or royalty company is not obliged to contribute to funding of expansions, but nevertheless shares in the benefit of any expansion if it is within the agreed mining area.

The streaming or royalty company has no direct control over the management or operation of the project and therefore its due diligence will focus on the technical strength of the project, the management team's capability, political risks and other factors which may impact the ability to obtain a stable long-term return on its investment.

Streaming or royalty companies generally have a lower cost of capital due to their ability to access funds in markets not as readily accessible to mine development companies and they can often fund through tax-effective structures.

7. Offtake – prepayments and receivables financing

In the context of financing the development of a new project, offtake agreements are a critical element. For non-exchange traded commodities, or bulk commodities such as iron ore or coal, financiers will often want the project to be supported by a long-term offtake agreement which provides certainty as to a revenue stream to service the debt. Multiple offtakers will spread the credit risk on the offtakers and improve bankability of the project. For London Metal Exchange (LME)-traded commodities such as gold, financiers may require the miner to enter into commodity hedging agreements (typically using an ISDA Master Agreement) to hedge against the risk of fluctuations in the commodity price and lock in the price in line with the base case financial model.

7.1 Prepayments

Aside from ordinary hedging of commodity price risk, financiers will also enter into prepayment agreements with mining companies under which the miner will receive an advance payment against the future delivery of the commodity to be produced. Such arrangements are usually documented under ISDA Master Agreements or the financier's own form of prepayment agreement. They are usually only available to producing mining companies and will usually be provided on an unsecured basis.

As an alternative, offtakers and commodity traders (as well as financial institutions in some instances) have on occasion (often in times of high demand) provided significant prepayments to miners under otherwise standard offtake agreements. Such prepayments are set off against future deliveries of product on an agreed amortisation basis, with a discount or fee also deducted in lieu of interest charges. Typically these are unsecured and with no covenants beyond the usual terms of the offtake agreement. The offtaker is therefore exposed to insolvency risk as an unsecured creditor for any rebate due on the prepayment if the miner fails to meet its delivery obligations. The miner is generally not willing or able, due to the constraints of its other funding arrangements, to provide general security for the obligation to deliver product in the future. Offtakers look to have recourse to the product as and when it is produced but this does not provide security until the product is produced and then there may be disputes as to which product is the subject of the relevant security. Consideration also needs to be given to the rate of amortisation and how to manage the risk that a falling commodity price may result in the sale price for a shipment of product being less than the amortisation payment due to be set off against that shipment. Notwithstanding these issues, prepayments can be a viable alternative source of financing available to producing mining companies.

In August 2012, Paladin Energy entered into a long-term offtake agreement for the supply of uranium to Électricité de France SA with deliveries to be made between 2019 and 2024. The agreement included a US$200 million prepayment.

Offtakers have also been known to provide credit support for developing projects as a means of securing supply. Such support may be in the form of completion guarantees or other forms of limited guarantees or separate loan funding, often at a lower cost than bank debt funding due to the ability of the offtaker to obtain margin through the offtake pricing.

7.2 Pre-export or receivables financing

Pre-export and receivables financing are forms of secured lending to mining producers where the mining company assigns the receivables under its offtake contracts to the financier in exchange for payment from financiers. In 2010 JBIC and Sumitomo Mitsui Banking Corporation provided a US$150 million loan to Vietnamese coal miner, Vietnam National Coal Mineral Industries Holding Corporation Ltd (Vinacomin) which was secured over the receivables under coal offtake contracts between Vinacomin and its Japanese offtakers.

Often funds will only be advanced against confirmed orders or shipments and therefore the funding is a form of cash flow management by which the mining company receives advances from the bank at the time of shipment as opposed to having to wait until payment of the invoice.

Issues to be considered include the ability to assign the receivables by way of security – or an absolute assignment – under the terms of the offtake agreement. Perfection of the assignment depends on the laws of the jurisdiction where it is enforceable but is often achieved by serving notice on the offtaker and directing the offtaker to make payments directly to an account with the financiers. The financiers will not want there to be set-off rights under the offtake agreement and will want to limit early termination rights.

Sometimes this type of financing is structured with commodity traders as initial offtakers, who in turn sell to end offtakers. Under this structure, security may be given over the original offtake agreement with the commodity trader as well as the offtake agreement between the trader and the end offtaker. Through these structures the receivables can remain offshore in the trader's collection account or be paid direct to the financiers in an offshore account. This mitigates the currency control and local legal risks which may be inherent in emerging jurisdictions. However, some jurisdictions require funds to be repatriated on a timely basis to the mining company's onshore account.

This alternative source of funding is only really available for established producers which can demonstrate a sustained period of delivery, established reserves to support on-going production and low credit risk on their offtakers.

8. Debt funding – project finance

8.1 Structure

Debt funding from commercial banks is a vitally important – and the largest – source of finance for the mining sector. For sponsors seeking to develop a mine, project finance is typically their preferred funding structure. Project finance is debt provided to a special purpose company which owns the project (or the operator of the project) and where repayment is dependent on the revenue to be generated by the project. Under a true project finance structure, the lender's recourse is limited to those revenues, the project assets and the shares in the project company. On the other hand, in corporate lending a group company will act as borrower and may be guaranteed by other members of the corporate group, and the lenders will have recourse to all of the assets of the borrower or the corporate group, if it is guaranteed.

As true project financing isolates the risks associated with development of the project and servicing the debt to the project, without exposing the full balance sheet of the sponsors, it is particularly attractive for developing mines in higher risk emerging markets. For this reason major mining companies which would typically elect to fund the development of mines in their home jurisdiction from corporate revenue and lower cost corporate debt, may turn to a project financing when developing a mine in an emerging market.

8.2 Sponsor support

In practice, it can be difficult for mining companies to obtain project finance on full 'non-recourse' terms, and the sponsors will often be required to provide one or more forms of "sponsor support". Most often this will include a completion guarantee by which the sponsors guarantee repayment of the debt, with the guarantee being released on project completion. Other forms of sponsor support include debt service undertakings by which the sponsor undertakes to pay for debt service in the event of a shortfall or failure to pay by the borrower, which undertaking may be subject to a cap. Alternatively, the undertaking may be structured as a mandatory buy down of the debt where the sponsor undertakes to pay or buy down debt to sustainable levels at completion.

Project financing can usually be raised to fund approximately 60% of the total construction costs of a project with the balance of funding being contributed through equity, quasi-equity, subordinated debt or a combination of such sources. The equity component of project financing may be able to be structured as a debt-funded equity bridge loan guaranteed by the sponsors and to be repaid at project completion. This approach can improve shareholder returns by delaying the timing of the equity contribution allowing equity to be raised after the value uplift arising from project completion. The ability to obtain such funding will generally depend on the creditworthiness of the sponsors, although some private investment funds or cornerstone investors may provide equity bridge loans on a project basis.

8.3 Key considerations

The due diligence and documentation for project financing is complex, time-consuming and therefore relatively costly. The fees and interest rate for project finance are higher than corporate debt, reflecting the higher risk. Transaction costs will typically be funded as part of the project finance. A requirement of project financing is that a structure be established which ensures that all of the development and construction costs are fully funded to achieve completion of the construction and get into full production.

Lenders will engage technical consultants to review and advise on various aspects of the project, including the mine model and reserve and resource position, to verify the viability of the proposed mining operations and mine life. The base case financial model will be approved and form the basis for approved spending on development costs. If the mine includes processing or beneficiation facilities, consultants may report on the design and capabilities of those facilities. Insurance, including potentially in relation to political risk, is also important and independent consultants may report on these aspects.

Title to the mining area and perfecting security are a key focus of the due diligence. The mining title may be in the process of being converted from an exploration (or other forms of) permit to a mining lease or a concession. Depending on the jurisdiction, the sponsors may also be negotiating a mining convention or state agreement with the local government. Ministerial or governmental approval may be required for the construction and development of the project in addition to other regulatory approvals, including under environmental legislation. Managing these processes and obtaining these approvals can be time-consuming and become a "gating" item to satisfying conditions precedent to drawdown for the project finance.

The form and methods of perfecting security will depend on the laws of the jurisdiction where the project is located. In some emerging markets, structures may be adopted under which offshore holding companies and offshore accounts and insurance policies are used as a means of addressing what may be perceived as deficiencies with local security laws. Some jurisdictions, such as African jurisdictions based on Napoleonic laws, can be debtor protective on enforcement, or the available effective security can be limited and may not cover future debt claims. However, common law jurisdictions are more lender-friendly and generally adopt self-help enforcement regimes more in line with the English law approach.

8.4 Contracting and risk allocation

Of fundamental importance to project financing is appropriate risk allocation. The due diligence will focus on the contracting strategy to be adopted by the project. Ensuring that robust contracts with creditworthy counterparties are in place for all material aspects of the construction and operations phase (eg, fuel, electricity, water and other consumables) is critical. Similarly, offtake arrangements which lock in the revenue are also critical. For exchange-traded metals, the financiers may require a percentage of production to be hedged to fix the commodity price and remove commodity price risk. Interest and exchange rate hedging may also be required. For bulk commodities and other minerals which are not exchange-traded, the lenders will usually require enforceable offtake agreements with creditworthy counterparties, although in some circumstances they may be prepared to assume market risk (with the benefit of an expert's report on the market).

For construction, the lenders prefer an engineering procurement and construction (EPC) contract for a fixed sum with liquidated damages for construction delays. However, engineering procurement and construction management (EPCM) contracts may also be used with multiple underlying contracts. The risk allocation across these contracts will be carefully reviewed by the lenders and their advisers, who will focus on the scope of work, standards of care, treatment of delays, damages, *force majeure* events, indemnities, dispute resolution, the ability to take security over the contract and the creditworthiness of the counterparty. For material contracts, the financiers will require direct agreements with the contractors giving the financiers step-in rights to cure defaults by the borrower and hold the contracts in place to complete construction.

8.5 Covenants

A project finance facility will include very tight restrictive covenants limiting the ability of the special purpose company to:

- incur debt;
- grant security or liens;
- dispose of assets;
- pay distributions;
- undertake activities other than the project;
- enter into contracts other than project-related agreements;
- vary project documents; or
- pay costs outside the base case financial model.

Key risks during the construction phase of a mining project include cost overruns or delays in achieving project completion. A range of mechanisms may be adopted to mitigate the risk of cost overruns and delays. The base case financial model will include contingencies for delays and cost overruns. In addition, the financiers may require a standby facility, letter of credit facility or funded blocked account to be put in place or a contingent equity contribution from the sponsors.

Drawdowns under the project finance facility will typically be progressive against cost invoices and will be approved by a technical adviser for the financiers, provided that at each drawdown a cost-to-complete test can be satisfied.

8.6 Term and refinancing with corporate debt

Project financing for mining projects is usually shorter term than for infrastructure projects, creating some pressure to refinance shortly after project completion. In addition, miners will be incentivised to refinance after the project has reached the production phase to move from the restrictive covenants in their project financing facility to the more flexible covenant regime of a typical corporate debt facility. How flexible those covenants may be will depend on the borrower's or sponsor's level of ongoing reliance on the project.

Once the mining company has an established history of operations and/or has diversified to multiple projects, debt funding may be available on corporate terms. Such terms will still include restrictions on debt incurrence and the creation of security interests, and will often include financial covenants or ratios such as debt service coverage ratios, leverage ratios and tangible net worth covenants. The corporate facility may be secured or unsecured and will often be provided to the corporate group on the basis that material subsidiaries are guarantors. If the company has an investment grade credit rating, then the covenants are less restrictive, often limited to a negative pledge.

8.7 Development financing institutions and export credit agencies

Development financing institutions (DFIs) and multilateral agencies provide funding support in the form of direct loans, equity investments and risk guarantee instruments to the private sector to further the economic development of developing countries and emerging economies. They are government-owned entities (often multiple governments). Multilateral agencies include the World Bank Group (IFC and MIGA), the European Bank for Reconstruction and Development, the Asian Development Bank and the African Development Bank.

Developing countries typically present higher risks both at a project and country level. Commercial banks may not be in a position to bear these risks, and DFIs therefore provide an important role in bridging the gap. DFIs require strict compliance with social and environmental standards (such as the Equator Principles), labour standards, local participation in the project and anti-bribery and corruption standards. The time and costs incurred in completing diligence on such projects and negotiating documentation with the DFIs and their advisers can be significant. However, the support provided by DFIs or multilateral agencies can lower the cost of bank debt provided for the project.

Most developed countries have one or more export credit agencies (ECAs), which are government agencies initially established to provide support to transactions which would increase the export of goods or services from their country. ECAs also play an important role in providing financial support to the mining sector. In some instances, absent the ECA support, the sponsors of a project may not be able to raise sufficient funding to develop the project.

ECAs provide support in the form of direct loans, or insurance or guarantee cover in relation to goods or services meeting certain criteria as a means of increasing exports from their home country. This form of ECA support is referred to as "tied" because the goods or services must be provided to the relevant mining project. ECAs also provide "untied" support where the development of the project is seen as beneficial to the ECA's home country. This may be because the project produces commodities of strategic importance to the ECA's country or because an entity from the ECA's country is the offtaker for the project or has an equity interest in the project. As with tied support, untied support may be in the form of direct loans or insurance or guarantee cover. Traditionally, ECAs were important in providing political risk cover for projects in higher risk countries. However, following the global finance crisis, ECAs have to an extent stepped in to fill some of the funding gap that has arisen from the constriction of the traditional bank debt market, particularly for very large projects such as Roy Hill Pty Ltd's US$7.2 billion project financing for the development of its iron ore mine and port and rail infrastructure project in Australia. This project involved five ECAs and 19 commercial lenders. The ECAs provided or supported more than 60% of the total facility.

Advantages of ECA support include that the tenor of ECA funding is often longer than that which commercial lenders are able to provide, or the cost of the commercial lenders providing loans for the same term is higher than sponsors are prepared to pay. ECA participation can also be crucial in endorsing the project and encouraging participation by other lenders. However, ECA involvement can increase the time it takes to finalise documentation and achieve financial close due to the need to comply with the ECA's sometimes differing eligibility criteria, operating guidelines and internal approval requirements and the additional due diligence requirements. Like DFIs, ECAs undertake thorough due diligence in relation to, and require strict compliance with, social and environmental standards (such as the Equator Principles).

The involvement of ECAs can also increase complexity in relation to the intercreditor arrangements that need to be negotiated to regulate arrangements between the different classes of financiers. As with all financiers, the voting arrangements under the intercreditor agreements are important to ECAs, and they will seek control in relation to certain decisions.

A relatively recent example of DFI and ECA support for a project financing is the US$823 million project financing in 2010 of the Boleo mining project in Mexico. The syndicate of financiers included Export-Import Bank of the United States, Export Development Canada and Korea Development Bank which together provided US$723 million of the debt funding, with the balance being provided by a group of commercial banks.

9. Debt capital markets issuances

The debt capital markets are an important source of finance for the mining sector. Bonds can sometimes be used to finance greenfield projects, although they are more often used to refinance project finance facilities after project completion. In addition, the debt capital markets are an important ingredient in the multi-source debt capital structures being adopted by mining companies with operating projects. Of the major mining companies, Rio Tinto, BHP Billiton, Anglo American and Vale SA each have a range of bond or note instruments issued in the international debt capital markets.

The US market is the largest market, and for this reason bond issues will often be in the form of 144A/Reg S exempt offerings. Rule 144A is a safe harbour exemption under US securities laws for the resale of unregistered securities to qualified institutional buyers (QIBs) within the United States. Regulation S is a safe harbour exemption for certain offers and sales of securities outside of the United States. These exemptions allow access to and re-sales within the large US institutional investor market without the complex requirements of registration under the US securities laws.

Established mining companies which frequently issue debt instruments in the international capital markets may establish medium-term note programmes, known as MTN programmes, which permit them to issue a wide range of debt instruments quickly, cheaply and frequently. There are a range of different types of bonds issued in the international capital markets including Eurobonds, foreign bonds and global bonds.

Bonds may be listed to increase the market for possible investors to include those whose charter limits them to investing in listed instruments. Exchanges often used in Europe include Luxembourg, Ireland and London, and in the Asia Pacific region include Singapore.

The bond market is a deep market for long-term capital. A bond instrument can be a fixed interest or floating rate instrument, and can provide attractive pricing compared with bank debt in the local market of the issuer, although this varies between project bonds, high-yield bonds and investment grade bonds.

9.1 Project bonds

Project bonds used to finance the development of a greenfield project will have most of the features typical of a project financing. They will be fully secured with tight restrictive covenants based on a base case financial model. Unlike a bank facility, all of the proceeds for a bond issue are received on closing of the issue. Accordingly, the funds will be paid into a blocked account with withdrawals permitted only to meet approved costs and subject to satisfying cost-to-complete tests. Debt service will be required to be fully funded for the construction phase and will be held in blocked accounts. In 2006 Fortescue Metals Group Ltd issued fully secured project bonds to raise approximately US$2 billion to finance the development of its greenfield iron ore mine and port and rail infrastructure project in Australia.

9.2 High-yield bonds

Bonds issued by miners with established operations may be secured or unsecured, although they are often unsecured. Sub-investment grade bonds are issued to the high-yield market and the covenants applying to the issuer and restricted subsidiaries will typically include restrictions on:

- certain payments and investments;
- incurring indebtedness;
- granting liens or security interests;
- asset sales;
- transactions with affiliates;

- sale and leaseback transactions;
- agreements restricting payments of dividends; and
- consolidations or mergers.

Early repayment by the issuer is typically subject to a 'non-call' period and a 'make-whole' payment which may step down over time. There may be a requirement to redeem the bonds on a change of control which has a negative impact on the issuer's or bond's credit rating.

Of critical importance to the issuer are the 'baskets' or exceptions which they are able to negotiate to the restrictive covenants which, for example, will permit them to enter into certain limited credit facilities, finance lease transactions and asset sales. Certain covenants may be suspended if the bonds achieve an investment grade credit rating.

9.3 Investment grade

Unsurprisingly, investment grade bonds contain fewer restrictive covenants, often limited to a negative pledge on granting liens or security interests and restrictions on consolidations or mergers. Early repayment or redemption may be made at any time without penalty. There may be a requirement to redeem on a change of control if it results in a credit rating downgrade.

9.4 Process

The process for issuing bonds in the debt capital markets involves the preparation of an offering circular which is prepared by the issuer with the assistance of an arranger/underwriter. The level of disclosure varies depending on whether the bond is a project bond, high-yield bond or investment grade bond, but generally the level of disclosure is higher than an information memorandum for a syndicated debt facility. Liability attaches to the issuers – and potentially sponsors – in relation to the issue of the offering circular. Due diligence is carried out in conjunction with preparation of the offering circular. In the United States, counsel for the issuer and counsel for the arranger/underwriter each issue opinions providing negative assurance in relation to the offering circular. A comfort letter is also obtained from the issuer's auditors, generally based on accounts which are not more than 135 days old.

9.5 Key considerations

The bond markets can be volatile, which increases execution risk given the need to prepare the offering circular, including the detailed description of the bonds, and to complete due diligence prior to launching the transaction in the market.

There are higher carry costs with bond issues as compared with syndicated bank debt because all of the proceeds are raised on closing of the issue. Often bond covenants will be tested on an incurrence basis and will not operate as maintenance covenants, which can be an advantage to borrowers in a deteriorating market.

Due to the fact that bonds are widely held, it can be costly and time-consuming to seek consents and waivers when compared with seeking consents under syndicated bank facilities which are more relationship-driven. It will usually be necessary to obtain a credit rating for a bond issue, which involves time and costs. Indeed, the time and costs incurred by issuers completing their first bond issue can be significant, although subsequent issues can generally be completed more efficiently.

Traditionally the bond market has been more suited to longer-term infrastructure projects. However, both major established miners and emerging mining companies have turned to the bond market as a source of capital for mining projects with large-scale capital needs.

9.6 Term loan B

The term loan B market in the United States is a high-yield market comprising institutional investors such as commercial banks, mutual funds, insurance companies, pension funds and hedge funds. There is some overlap with the high-yield bond market.

Term loan B funding is structured under a syndicated facility agreement and will require an information memorandum but will typically involve less detailed disclosure than a bond offering circular. Security will be subject to the laws of the jurisdiction where the borrower or its assets are located. Lenders are generally responsible for their own due diligence. A rating is invariably required. The interest rate is typically a floating rate with maturities being between five and seven years. The loan may be amortising or with a bullet repayment and generally may be prepaid at any time without penalty. Covenants will often include maintenance-style covenants, although it is possible to negotiate covenant structures with covenants based on incurrence tests only.

Mining companies which have raised funds through term loan B facilities include Fortescue Metals Group Ltd and Atlas Iron Ltd, both Australian iron ore producers.

10. Other issues of note

10.1 Funding non-integrated projects

The development of large-scale bulk commodity mines with heavy reliance on road, rail and port infrastructure to get their products to market, including in particular in emerging markets such as Africa, raises the issue of funding for mining and associated infrastructure projects on a non-integrated basis.

For such funding to be achieved, it is necessary to ensure that inter-project agreements allocate each risk to the individual project best able to mitigate that risk and to economically incentivise each project to perform in a manner beneficial to the other projects, while mitigating risks. This not only involves take-or-pay arrangements but also structuring the pricing/fee/tariff arrangements so as to provide appropriate returns to ensure that each project remains motivated to achieve its primary goal of getting its project into operation in the most timely and cost-effective way. Key issues to be considered include:

- payment timing mismatches and associated working capital concerns;

- managing the risks of delays in one project adversely affecting another project; and
- managing intercreditor risks in a way that minimises the risk of the lenders to one project being able to collapse the other projects.

Consideration may be given to paying funds into trust accounts or to paying agents and establishing working capital facilities to cover short-term liquidity or cash flow issues, for example where the mine is not able to get product to the port due to a shutdown on the rail project.

Protective mechanisms to be considered include the possibility of taking second ranking security in favour of the lenders to the other projects and robust step-in rights if one project defaults in its obligations to the other projects. Clearly, ship-or-pay and take-or-pay arrangements are an important consideration to ensure a revenue stream to the other projects. Restrictions may be imposed on the activities of each project so that additional risk is not introduced which may negatively impact the other projects.

Force majeure needs to be appropriately allocated and to be structured to provide appropriate relief. Funding two or more interdependent projects on a non-integrated basis increases the complexity and risk analysis for managing cost overruns and delays (eg, will they be funded and how and will costs be passed back to the 'responsible' project?).

Funding on a non-integrated basis permits the funding to be sized for the particular project which can be advantageous in a constrained banking market. It also allows different ownership between the projects, which may increase the range of investors for one project over the others. For example, a port and rail infrastructure project will attract a different class of investor to a straight mining or an integrated mining and infrastructure project. However, the hurdles to be overcome to enable the projects to be funded on a non-integrated basis are significant.

11. Conclusion

In these challenging times in the mining sector, it is more important than ever for the management of a mining company carefully to evaluate the costs of capital being raised, its flexibility and its impact on current and future availability of alternative sources of finance. Avoiding the dilutive impact of an equity raising by undertaking the sale of a strategic stake in a mining project or the sale of a royalty may appear sound at the time; however, the loss of the future revenue and the introduction of a joint venture partner may have significant implications for future financing and limit the sources of future capital available to the company. Equally, relying solely on syndicated bank debt as the source of funding for a mining company may not be the optimal use of the company's balance sheet.

It is becoming more common for mining companies to draw on multiple sources to finance their development costs and operations, often with a mix of equity or quasi-equity instruments, syndicated bank debt, bonds and other sources which may include equipment financing, or some of the various forms of offtake and revenue financing referred to in this chapter. To ensure that the company is adequately financed and manages its balance sheet in a cost-effective and efficient manner, it is important that there is an understanding of:

- the range of alternatives available;
- the advantages and disadvantages of each; and
- which is best suited to the different phases of a mining company's life cycle, the resources of the company and the current and likely future market for its products.

High yield financings

Anna-Marie Slot
Ashurst LLP

1. Introduction

According to an S&P Dow Jones Indices report, from 2007 to 2013 the global debt market increased from $70 trillion to $100 trillion, an increse of 43%. The corporate bond market has almost tripled in size since 2001. At the end of 2014, the energy sector represented approximately 15% of the Credit Suisse High Yield Index. This sector includes companies in Exploration and Production (E&P), Midstream and Pipeline, Refining, and Service and Equipment. Companies such as Tullow Oil Plc, Kuwait Energy Plc and Ithaca Energy Inc have all included bonds in their capital structures. What are high yield bonds and why should you consider them in your financing structure? One reason is the versatility bonds offer to companies in the industry in terms of covenants, repayment schedules and interest payment dates.

Although bank financings and bond financings can come in many forms, several key differences between bank debt and high yield bond debt are set out below:

Aspect	**Bank**	**High yield bond**
Covenants	Maintenance (usually tested quarterly)	Incurrence (tested when the company takes various actions)
Repayment	Amortising	Bullet
Interest payments	Quarterly	Semiannual
Interest rate	Floating	Fixed

By way of background, high yield bonds developed in the United States in response to restrained liquidity for 'fallen angels', that is, companies that had been investment grade but lost their investment grade status. As a result of the downgrade, these companies faced increasing difficulty in accessing the bank markets for their financing needs. The particular nature of high yield and what sets it apart from other financing sources, such as traditional bank loans, results from the structure of its covenant package. The covenants are incurrence based, meaning they are tested when the company takes certain actions but are not tested on a scheduled basis like maintenance covenants. Therefore, there is no ongoing affirmative obligation to provide a certificate to the financiers confirming compliance with a set of pre-agreed ratios such as a leverage test, consolidated net worth or capital expenditure limitations. The covenants work in an opposite manner, permitting many actions of the company and only requiring testing when the company is taking an action that could affect the overall credit that the investors evaluated on day one as described in the offering memorandum. This may include incurring additional debt or making dividend payments or making significant changes to the company's structure such as a merger. Given the nature of the covenants, the underwriters and the company work together to understand the needs of the company over the duration of the bond as well as taking into consideration the type of business that the company operates in and the ongoing requirements of the industry. The underwriters then craft a covenant package that is in part market standard and in part built to accommodate the anticipated growth path of the company for the duration of the bond while maintaining debt servicing capability.

This chapter gives an overview of the major covenants including a brief discussion of particular aspects of high yield bonds used to finance resources companies. It concludes with some points for consideration in adding a high yield bond to a company's capital structure. The chapter will focus on the process for offerings of high yield bonds pursuant to an exemption from registration in the United States rather than US registered deals.

2. Process and structure

2.1 Process

A bond usually involves a capital markets offering in which the company approaches investors to obtain financing through the use of a prospectus or offering memorandum. The offering memorandum describes the company and the terms of the bonds being offered. For companies outside the United States, and indeed for some US companies, the offerings are typically made pursuant to an exemption from registration in the United States, most typically through Regulation S or Rule 144A. The type of offering, and therefore type of investor able to purchase the bonds, drives the level and types of disclosure. For example, critical components of disclosure in an E&P transaction are the reserve reports including proved and probable reserves. Historically, the US Securities and Exchange Commission (US SEC) requirements for issuers in the oil and gas industry to disclose their reserves differed from practices elsewhere in the industry. On December 31 2008, the US SEC adopted significant revisions to its rules bringing them more into line with the market practices and technological changes that had occurred in the industry in the period from the mid-1970s through to the 2000s.[1] One significant change was the ability to disclose probable and possible reserves in addition to just proved reserves.

1 Modernization of the Oil and Gas Reporting Requirements, US SEC Release Nos 33-8995; 34-59192 (December 21 2008).

In addition to industry-specific reports and information, the offering memorandum will include:

- information about the company;
- its consolidated financial statements (usually covering the last three years and any interim period from the last audited financial statement, but the specifics of what needs to be included is again driven by whether the offering is made pursuant to Rule 144A or Regulation S and the identity of guarantors, if any);
- a discussion of the company's performance during the financial periods presented;
- risk factors highlighting risks to the investor arising from the industry;
- the geographic location of the company's assets and operations; and
- any risks specific to the company itself or the bonds being offered.

The process of issuing a bond depends on a number of factors including scope of disclosure and availability of information but typically can be as short as 10–12 weeks for companies that are organised and engaged in the process. There are transactions that have been done more quickly in the context of Regulation S only offerings or for experienced issuers. There are also transactions that have taken more time to get to market.

In most offerings, the issuers will also go through a ratings process in which one or more of the international rating agencies will review the company and the terms of the bonds and provide a rating of both. These ratings will affect the pricing of the bond as higher rated companies will generally be able to issue a bond at a lower interest rate than similar companies with lower ratings. The culmination of preparing and finalising the offering memorandum and the ratings process will be a roadshow where the company as issuer will meet certain investors globally, depending on whether the offering is being made pursuant to Rule 144A and/or Regulation S, to offer the bonds for sale.

It should be noted that, as a capital markets instrument, bonds are subject to the conditions of the capital markets and particularly of the high yield markets. The markets themselves respond to international events such as the continuing restructuring of the Greek debt as well as macroeconomic events such as quantitative easing by governments around the world. Indeed, at times, the high yield markets have gone for long periods without a successful offering or when only the highest ranked issuers were able to successfully complete their offerings at an interest rate they would accept.

2.2 Ranking and status of bonds

High yield bonds can be senior notes, senior subordinated notes or subordinated notes. Senior subordinated bonds and subordinated bonds are contractually subordinated by their terms to certain other debt. Bonds can also be structurally subordinated through being issued at a holding company or other intermediate company above the operating company in a corporate structure. If bonds are issued at a holding company which is above the company that owns the operating assets and therefore a direct or indirect shareholder of the operating company, the bonds will have an equity claim on the assets only at the level of the company's operations, absent guarantees. Claims of creditors (eg, bank loans or trade creditors) of the operating company are superior to the claims of the bondholders to the extent of the value of the assets of such subsidiaries, even if the bonds are senior notes. The bond claims on the operating company in an insolvency are equity claims and therefore depend on there being value left for shareholders after payment of the operating subsidiary's creditors.

The position of the bonds in the corporate financing structure can be improved through guarantees and security. The original structure of high yield bonds in the United States assumes that all subsidiaries of the issuer will be guarantors of the bonds, which avoids the issue of structural subordination. New companies that are added to the group will also become subsidiary guarantors. For issuers located and operating outside the United States or US issuers with substantial non-US operations, the situation is more bespoke and is driven in part by the local rules regarding the ability of subsidiaries to provide guarantees. For example, many of the civil law jurisdictions in Europe limit the amount of a guarantee that a subsidiary can provide to its parent. In other parts of the world, there are structures where subsidiaries that are also public companies are limited in the ability to provide any upstream guarantees. The bond investor market has adjusted to situations where local laws limit or prohibit guarantees but such limitations will impact on the investor's appetite for the bond and therefore its interest rate.

Bonds can also be secured; again this ability to provide security is driven by local laws and regulations as well as the number of existing creditors and anticipated future financing needs. High yield bonds are often paired with bank financings in corporate structures and high yield investors are used to evaluating the security package and position of the bonds in an insolvency in relation to other debt.

Subordinated notes are subordinated contractually pursuant to the subordination provisions of the indenture. These provisions will prohibit the issuer from making payments of interest or principal to bondholders in certain circumstances. If the notes are subordinated there will be payment standstill provisions which provide that the issuer will be prohibited from making payments on the bonds if there is a payment default with respect to senior indebtedness (eg, a bank facility). A payment default generally includes both failure to pay the senior indebtedness and any acceleration of the senior indebtedness. The senior creditors are able to block payments on the bonds for a specified period, usually 179 days. The timing and number of times that the payment blockage can be exercised are negotiated and market practice has developed around the rights and abilities of the various parties.

2.3 Interest periods and call periods

In addition to the covenants typical for a high yield issuer, the nature of bond financing provides for differences in structure from bank financing. Generally, high yield bonds are not amortising, instead providing for a bullet maturity pursuant to which the entire principal amount of the bonds is repaid at maturity. Bonds will have a limited number of optional or mandatory redemption terms. Most high yield bonds are fixed rate and interest is paid semiannually. Some floating-rate bonds have quarterly interest payment dates. In either case, by market convention interest payment dates are typically the first or fifteenth of a month although this convention has evolved in some markets and is linked to the issuance date. High yield bonds can also be issued in the form of payment-in-kind (PIK) bonds, in which the semiannual payments of interest are made through the issuance of additional notes. Further variations include pay if you can (PIYC), or PIK toggle, which alternate between cash pay and PIK in certain circumstances.

Most bonds have a no-call period which prohibits optional redemptions during a certain period enabling the bondholder to lock in the yield for this period, thus reducing the risk that the bondholder will have to consider how to reinvest its monies too soon. Starting at the end of the no-call period, the bonds can be called (eg, redeemed) at a premium based on a percentage of the coupon. The call premium declines each year until there is no premium in the last year or two of the duration of the bonds depending on the overall tenor of the bonds.

There are several market conventions that have evolved to allow an issuer to call its bonds during the no-call period. One is the equity claw and another is a make whole. Typically, the equity claw is available for the first three years of the bonds. The rationale is that an issuer can redeem a portion (typically 35% although the percentage has evolved in certain markets) of the outstanding bonds if it has raised cash proceeds from the issuance of common equity and thereby increased the equity buffer in the company. The redemption price is usually par plus the coupon (eg, 107% for a 7% bond). Originally the equity claw required a public offering of equity so that bondholders would benefit from the increase in equity and have the added comfort of a public offering process and corresponding market-driven pricing for the equity but that requirement has eroded over time.

2.4 Documentation

The legal contract governing the bonds under New York law is referred to as an indenture and is signed on the day the bonds are issued, the closing date of the transaction. New York law governs most high yield bonds although there are regions where high yield covenants are contained in English law or local law documentation. Given the origins of high yield bonds as a US financing product, US courts have tended to have more familiarity with covenants and how they function. If English law governs the bonds, the operative documents are the trust deed governing the terms and conditions of the bonds and the paying agency agreement governing the relationship with the paying agent that makes interest payments on the bonds on behalf of the issuer. Under New York law, the indenture governs both those functions. The bonds themselves are evidenced in a global note that is held by a depository on behalf of the clearing systems. There is also a purchase agreement signed at the pricing date in which the initial purchasers agree to buy the bonds that will be issued on the closing date. In a Rule 144A or Regulation S offering, the underwriters for the transaction will generally also be the initial purchasers and they will onsell the bonds to investors. The closing date usually occurs between three and five business days after the signing of the purchase agreement.

3. Covenants

High yield covenants are designed to protect investors from specific corporate actions that could deteriorate credit quality but to allow the company to carry on its business as normal. There are a number of covenants including a restriction on incurring additional indebtedness or paying cash to equity holders before creditors. The major covenants and related defaults or amendment and waiver provisions are discussed below. One of the challenges in looking at a high yield bond for the first time is in the drafting. Conceptually, the covenants are drafted so that the beginning of the covenant prohibits taking the specified actions, for example incurring debt or making a restricted payment. Major covenants then include a provision that would allow those actions subject to some kind of test of financial health or ongoing suitability, for example the ratio test described later in this chapter. The final part of the covenant is dedicated to what actions are permitted in any situation, commonly referred to as 'carve outs' (eg, permitted debt). Due to this drafting convention, many first-time issuers looking at the covenant package are, quite rightly, perplexed by what is allowed and what is prohibited.

The covenants are referred to as incurrence-based covenants and are designed to function in light of the bond's nature as a capital markets instrument. Due to that nature, the bond can be traded and sold by bondholders on an ongoing basis during the duration of the bond to other bondholders. Most bonds are held through a clearing system and the holders of the bonds are recorded in the clearing system accounts as well as in brokerage houses. The practical implication of this process is that it is rather difficult for the issuer to know the current bondholders at any given time. Bonds can be traded at whatever level the market will bear. Therefore, a company's bonds can trade up in value, in which case they would be purchased by investors at a price higher than the par value of the bond, or trade down in value, in which case they would be purchased at a price lower than par. The trading price of bonds can reflect a number of different factors including:

- current interest rates;
- the maturity date of the bonds;
- the performance of the issuer; and
- the market's view of the industry in general.

The covenants therefore need to operate in a way that permits the issuer to run its business without having to have ongoing dialogue with its creditors.

With incurrence-based covenants, an issuer will test compliance with the covenants if it proactively intends to take an action, such as incurring debt, paying dividends or selling assets. Since there are generally no maintenance covenants to be tested, events beyond the company's control, like movements in the price of oil, do not necessarily cause the company to breach the covenants. The covenants create a credit value box around the company and its subsidiaries through the designation of a restricted group comprising the issuer, subsidiaries designated as restricted subsidiaries, and in some cases depending on the structure, the parent guarantor. Conceptually, actions within the restricted group are permitted (eg, intercompany loans, dividends, reorganisations) while an action with any subsidiaries outside the restricted group requires the company to test the action for compliance with the covenants. Subsidiaries within the corporate organisational structure can be designated as restricted or unrestricted, subject to certain tests. The default approach in structuring a transaction is for all subsidiaries to be restricted to facilitate actions between and among the group companies unless there is a specific reason to exclude them, for example the unrestricted subsidiary can function on a stand-alone basis with access to better funding on a non-recourse basis than it would have if it were a member of the restricted group.

3.1 Indebtedness

The limitation on the incurrence of indebtedness is designed to prohibit the issuer and its restricted subsidiaries incurring additional debt unless the issuer has the capacity (usually tested through a fixed charge coverage ratio) to service all its debt on a pro-forma basis, including the proposed new debt. This test is called 'the ratio test' or 'debt incurrence test'. In certain structures that have parent guarantors, this test includes the parent guarantors as well as the issuer and all the restricted subsidiaries. Even if the issuer cannot incur ratio debt, the covenants include certain specified exceptions known as 'permitted debt' or 'permitted indebtedness'.

Indebtedness under the bonds includes indebtedness for borrowed money, bonds, notes, letters of credit (to the extent drawn), capital lease obligations, hedging obligations, debt that has been secured by a lien on any assets of the group and guarantees. A key consideration in the indebtedness test is which entities within the group are able to incur the different types of indebtedness; again this is a result in part of market practice and in part of what the company anticipates needing to do over the life of the bond. To the extent that subsidiaries other than subsidiary guarantors can incur debt, that debt would be structurally senior to the claims under the bonds and therefore that aspect of the incurrence test is a point to focus on in understanding the covenants.

The key to the high yield covenant package and one of its major strengths for companies that operate in volatile times is that the debt test is not invoked on an ongoing basis. So long as, at the time of incurrence, the company is able to incur the debt under the covenants, that debt is permitted to remain even if the company's EBITDA or debt servicing ability deteriorates at a later point in time. This is a critical difference in the high yield covenant package versus a traditional bank financing. If the issuer's situation deteriorates so much as to cause it to fail to pay its interest payments on the bonds, that would constitute a default, as discussed below.

The ratio test will require the issuer to test a fixed charge coverage ratio (EBITDA/cashflow to fixed charges including cash and non-cash charges) or in certain situations a leverage ratio (debt to EBITDA/cashflow) in order to assess whether it can incur additional ratio debt. The ratio test, whether it be a fixed charge coverage ratio or a leverage ratio, requires the company to have been able to service the debt on a last four quarters basis, that is, as if the proposed new indebtedness had existed for the last four quarters of the company's actual performance. This pro-forma calculation takes into consideration actual performance and makes a pro-forma adjustment for any incurrences or repayments of indebtedness and acquisitions or dispositions as if they had occurred at the beginning of the period rather than a hypothetical period. The four-quarter period is similar to a bank financing and also enables the issuer to account for seasonality in earnings which is helpful for energy companies that have variations in their production due to weather conditions such as rainy seasons that reduce extraction or alter wind and hydro production patterns.

Even if the ratio test is not met, the covenants permit the group to incur certain types of permitted debt. Permitted debt can be considered as debt that the investors have accepted to be added to the group and debt that the group needs to function normally. Debt that is generally accepted includes bank facility debt, limited to a specified total amount or a limited percentage of total assets or borrowing base, a general basket of unspecified debt (referred to as the general basket) and purchase money or capitalised lease obligation debt, also generally limited to a certain percentage of total assets. There are also a number of types of debt that are permitted within the group in order to allow for the company to operate and function normally. Intercompany loans within the restricted group are permitted as long as they stay within the group. If the debt is held by a company that moves outside of the restricted group or is transferred to a company outside the restricted group or a third party, it ceases to qualify as intercompany debt under the indenture and is no longer permitted debt. Other operational types of debt are also permitted, such as debt created in respect of performance and surety bonds in the ordinary course of business and honouring bank overdrafts inadvertently drawn as long as they are repaid in a certain short period (eg, five days). The indenture will also permit the group to refinance its indebtedness, the requirements for refinancing depending in part on what type of debt is being refinanced. The group is usually able to replace certain existing indebtedness so long as the replacement financing is limited to the same principal amount, has a final maturity later than the debt being replaced and a weighted average life to maturity equal to or greater than the indebtedness being refinanced. The issuer is not permitted to refinance subordinated indebtedness with senior indebtedness. Most indentures will allow the company to classify debt between the different baskets, making the covenant package more flexible.

Issuers need to pay close attention to the definitions in the indenture, in particular consolidated EBITDA/consolidated cash flow and fixed charges in order to assess the impact and suitability of the bonds for their financing needs.

3.2 Restricted payments

The general principle of the restricted payment covenant is that the bondholders want the company to focus on building the assets and EBITDA-generating capabilities of the group and only allow cash to exit the credit value box created around the restricted group in limited circumstances. The term 'restricted payments' includes:

- dividends on capital stock;
- the purchase of capital stock;
- the early purchase or redemption of subordinated debt; and
- the making of investments (a term that is defined quite broadly to be investments in the form of equity or debt as well as guarantees of another entity's debt).

The purpose of the covenant is to control what an issuer can do with its cash and to govern payments to:

- shareholders;
- creditors subordinate to the bonds; or
- entities the group does not control.

The restricted payments provision classifies these types of things as restricted payments which are prohibited unless the issuer has earned enough restricted payment capacity through its basket build up. The build-up mechanism is structured so that the issuer gets credit for 50% of its consolidated net income but the basket is decreased by 100% of loss if consolidated net income is not positive. If the issuer issues and sells additional equity to non-affiliates, it gets a one for one increase in the basket from such issuance. For example, if the equity issuance results in $/€80 million of proceeds, the basket is increased by $/€80 million. In order to qualify for credit in the restricted payments covenant the equity issued cannot have any attributes of debt. Similarly, repayment of investments and redesignation of an unrestricted subsidiary as a restricted subsidiary will also build the basket on the theory that the issuer is bringing assets back into the restricted group. If an issuer wants to make a restricted payment, it must calculate the size of its basket, which typically runs from the first quarter that the bonds were issued (although some start in the quarter after issuance or from an earlier date if the issuer has multiple bonds already in existence), and then subtract all the restricted payments it has made in such a period to determine whether there is additional room in the basket to incur further restricted payments. In order to be able to use the basket, the issuer must also fulfil two further requirements:

- no default under the indenture and ratio capacity, and
- the ability to incur one additional unit of currency, dollar or euro, under the ratio test.

This additional dollar/euro test acts as a health check of the restricted group.

As always, there are exceptions (carve outs) to the restrictions. One common carve out is the replacement of equity or subordinated debt, respectively, with a substantially concurrent issuance of equity or subordinated debt. The covenants will also generally allow replacement of subordinated debt with equity. Another carve out is the payment of dividends which were permitted at the time of declaration even if they would not be permitted on the date of payment. This is to ensure that the issuer can comply with its corporate obligations to honour the declaration of the dividend. Important carve outs to the restricted payments provision are contained in the definition of permitted investments. This includes certain standard investments which will enable the group to carry on its business as usual but can also include specific items based on the types of investment and activities the issuer anticipates investing in over the life of the bond, such as joint ventures and any particular structures of investment typical to its industry.

3.3 Restrictions on distributions from restricted subsidiaries

The restriction on distributions from the restricted subsidiaries covenant prevents the restricted group from agreeing to any contractual limitations on the ability of the subsidiaries to distribute cash or other assets up to the issuer since the issuer of the bonds will be reliant on cash from the subsidiaries to service the bonds in many high yield structures. The distribution can be in any form including dividends, loans or other transfers.

As with the other covenants, the blanket prohibition does allow for certain exceptions. Key exemptions include restrictions that are contained in agreements in effect on the date the bonds are issued and in any refinancing of those pre-existing agreements so long as the refinancing restrictions are no more restrictive than those in the original agreement.

3.4 Sales of assets

The covenant governing the sales of assets is more permissive than a typical bank covenant, reflecting the nature of the instrument as one that permits the company to run itself during a longer period without the intervention of an agent or communications with the bondholders. The covenant does not prohibit an issuer from selling assets. It merely requires the issuer to comply with certain conditions including that the sales of assets be made at fair market value and a large portion, typically 75%, of the consideration be received in cash. The issuer must use the proceeds to pay down senior debt or replace the assets with assets in a business that is a permitted business. From the bondholders' perspective, the key consideration is that the group can generate income to pay down debt or, if there are less assets, that the issuer has in fact reduced the amount of leverage in the corporate structure. The covenant provides the issuer with a long period (typically 360 or 365 days) for acquisitions of replacement assets and in some cases an even more extended period provided acquisitions agreements have been entered into by the issuer. If the issuer does not pay down debt or buy replacement assets in that period, it is required to offer to repurchase the bonds. Bondholders can choose whether to be redeemed.

As added flexibility, certain small or ordinary course assets sales (eg, worn out or obsolete assets) or sales of minor amounts are exempted.

3.5 Transactions with affiliates

The transactions with affiliates covenant is intended to prohibit value from leaking out of the restricted group to an affiliate (an entity under common control within the group). Accordingly, the covenant requires transactions with affiliates to be on terms that are similar to those that would be obtained with unrelated third parties. The size of the transaction triggers heightened controls with a lower level requiring approval by a majority of disinterested directors and/or a higher threshold requiring a fairness opinion from an independent valuation firm or investment bank.

The thresholds are calculated on the size and nature of the restricted group as well as market expectations. Most public companies are subject to restrictions on affiliate transactions pursuant to the relevant listing rules and usually this covenant does not significantly increase its obligations. As with all high yield covenants there are exemptions, although these are kept to a minimum.

3.6 Liens

The lien covenant plays a critical role in the covenant package and is crucial in determining the position of the creditors in an insolvency. The provision restricts the group from providing liens (eg, security interests or mortgages) over its assets other than permitted liens, unless the issuer is willing to grant at the same time an equal and ratable lien for the benefit of the bondholders. When negotiating the covenant package, the parties will pay particular attention to the list of permitted liens. As with the other covenants, there will be a list of customary liens that are necessary for the day-to-day operations of the group. These would include workers' compensation, statutory liens and liens arising through operation of law. More attention will be paid to the particular liens needed for the company in response to any particular aspects of the company's business and the amount of indebtedness other than bonds that is allowed to benefit from a lien. To the extent the indenture allows the company to incur purchase money debt or capitalised lease obligations, the permitted liens will include a lien in relation to those assets but such a lien will be limited to the actual asset being financed through such purchase money or capitalised lease. Similarly, the indenture will permit liens in connection with bank facilities to the extent that bank financing is permitted under a credit facility permitted debt basket. These two areas enable the company to get financings for these types of debt but since the debt itself is capped, the noteholders will also be able to assess how such secured debt will exist in the structure in the case of any insolvency or restructuring. In a senior subordinated note offering, the covenant package includes an anti-layering provision prohibiting the issuer from granting liens to secure other subordinated debt.

Permitted liens usually include a number of ordinary course liens necessary for the company to carry on business as well as important exceptions for financings including:

- purchase money on capital lease;
- certain permitted debt;
- preexisting or acquired liens; and
- refinancings of debt that is already secured.

The type of liens and assets that are permitted to be subject to the liens is limited but designed to reflect the commercial reality of typical financings.

3.7 Mergers and consolidations

The merger covenant applies to a merger or consolidation of the issuer and generally the guarantors. It seeks to ensure that any successor of all or substantially all the assets of the issuer results in an entity that is able to service the debt of the bonds. There are a number of requirements in the merger covenant including requirements regarding the jurisdiction of incorporation of any successor company, assumption by the successor entity of the obligations under the indenture and application of the ratio test. The ratio test again serves as a health check of the new entity providing the bondholders with the reassurance that the group, once it merges, will still be in good shape and is not merging into an entity that would strain the ability of the combined group to service the bonds together with any other indebtedness at the other company.

3.8 Reporting

The reporting covenant provides ongoing information to the bondholders. If the issuer is a publicly listed company, the reporting covenant will be fulfilled by providing the reports required by the relevant exchange. If the company delists or is not publicly listed, the covenant generally requires audited annual financial statements, and reviewed quarterly and semiannual reports. Certain indentures also require management discussions of results similar to disclosure in the original offering memorandum and may include additional items, such as updated reserve reports or summary reports.

In a US registered deal, the issuer will be subject to SEC reporting requirements, unless certain exemptions are met.

3.9 Other covenants

Other covenants which may be included are those limiting the issuer's ability to enter into sale and leaseback transactions, and issuance and sale of the capital stock of restricted subsidiaries. These covenants depend in part on the market and region of the credit.

3.10 Defaults

Default provisions for a bond are slightly different from a typical bank financing. Non-payment of principal is an immediate default with no grace period. Non-payment of interest will generally have a cure or grace period of 30 days. The failure to comply with the covenants will also constitute default and there are various cure or grace periods depending on the importance of the action. A key event of default and an instance where bank refinancing and bond financings differ is the cross acceleration default present in bond indentures. A cross acceleration is a default provision that provides the bondholders with the right to declare an event of default if the issuer fails to comply with its obligations under other debt instruments (eg, bank credit agreements), but the default is triggered only upon the actual payment default or acceleration of indebtedness by the other lender. Traditional bank financings will instead have a cross-default provision triggered when the other lender has a right to accelerate even if it has not exercised that right.

3.11 Amendments/waivers

Changing or waiving the provisions of a high yield bond can be more challenging than obtaining consents under a bank facility. In general, most covenants can be amended or waived with the consent of a majority in principal amount of the outstanding bonds. To the extent that the issuer seeks the consent of holders and offers to pay them for their consent, many indentures require the issuer to offer to pay a consent fee to every holder that is willing to provide its consent in the prescribed time period. Fundamental changes such as changes to principal, interest rate and maturity require unanimous consent of the holders or, in some markets, 90% consent. Minor changes or changes that are not adverse to the bondholders (eg, adding guarantors) do not require holders' consent.

3.12 Defeasance

The indenture governing the bonds will allow the issuer to defease the bonds at any time. Defeasance is a process whereby the issuer will not have to comply with the restrictions in the covenants. The issuer must deposit cash or government securities in trust with the bond trustee in an amount sufficient to pay all the interest, principal and premium, if any, of the bonds when they are due on their first call date, depending on whether the notes are callable. Once the defeasance trust is established, the substantive covenants are effectively rendered inoperative together with the related events of default and definitions.

However, defeasance is expensive and issuers may get a similar result at a better price by offering to buy the bonds in a tender offer and consent solicitation that removes most of the restrictive covenants (known as an 'exit consent' or a 'covenant-strip').

3.13 Change of control

The bonds include a change of control provision that provides the bondholder with a put right upon a change of control, as defined in the indenture. This put right gives the bondholders the right to reevaluate their investment decision in the issuer in light of a change of control. In a high yield offering, investors will consider the person or persons who control the group as an important aspect of the overall transaction. Any change to that person or group, frequently referred to as the 'permitted holders', either through a change in the shareholdings such that the permitted holders discussed in the offering memorandum would no longer control the issuer or through the sale of all or substantially all of the assets of the group, may cause the bondholder to want to exit the investment. The issuer in such cases is required to buy the bonds at a purchase price of 101% of the principal amount of the bonds. The percentages for the permitted holders' definitions depend in part on whether the issuer is a public company. There are several other prongs in the change of control definition including those covering liquidation of the issuer and certain types of mergers. Additionally, in certain regions the change of control is subject to a change of control triggering event in the form of a ratings decline.

4. Points for consideration

In light of the nature of bond financing and, in particular, the incurrence-based nature of high yield covenants, issuers should consider whether bonds can play a role in their financing structures. The structure of bonds with bullet repayment and semiannual interest rates at a fixed rate can also provide some benefits to complement traditional bank financing. The energy sector is not new to high yield investors and, although affected by the markets, bond financing continues to grow and evolve year on year providing a viable financing component for consideration.

Norwegian high yield bonds

Erlend B Bakken
Geir Evenshaug
Michelet & Co
Hege Dahl
Arntzen de Besche Advokatfirma AS

1. Introduction to the Norwegian high yield market

1.1 The size and scope of the Norwegian high yield bond market

This chapter addresses some features and characteristics of the Norwegian high yield bond market. By 'high yield bonds' we mean bonds issued by companies which have a credit rating of BB/Ba (from S&P/Moody's, respectively) or below.

A Norwegian high yield bond issue will typically be in the amount of $100–200 million, but can be as large as $300 million (or a corresponding amount in another currency). It will typically have a tenor of three to five years, but seven years can also be available. The bonds can be secured or unsecured, and will be issued pursuant to a loan agreement which is based on a standard agreement governed by Norwegian law. Norwegian bonds are issued with no underwriting by the issuer's manager, and any manager will operate on a best efforts basis only.

Even on a European or global scale, the Norwegian high yield market is, relatively speaking, large. For example, in 2007 the market saw primary issuances in the amount of approximately 50 billion Norwegian krone (NOK).[1] Due to the global financial crisis, the market receded somewhat in 2008 and 2009. In 2010, primary issuances were in the amount of approximately NOK 30 billion. The market has increased steadily since 2011, and in 2014 the amount of primary issuances reached almost NOK 60 billion, representing a new record. Issuances in 2015 have so far been very few, with the market more or less being closed during Q1 2015. This is mainly attributed to the substantial reduction in the Brent oil price, and the uncertainties this has created for the Norwegian economy in general and businesses linked to the oil and offshore sector in particular. It is common for the market to close and open for periods of various durations, and it is expected that the market will open again during the course of 2015.

The Norwegian market has traditionally been utilised by Norwegian issuers, or at least issuers with a direct link to Norway (eg, overseas companies being controlled by Norwegian investors). In recent years, the issuer world has expanded and foreign issuers with only a weak link or no link at all to Norway have tapped into the market. Consequently, we now see issuers, or prospective issuers, from all parts of the world. See also section 2 below.

The sectors in which issuers operate have also expanded in recent years. While

1 $1 = approximately NOK8.

the Norwegian high yield bond market was traditionally utilised by issuers within the rig, offshore and oil services sectors, issuers are now from a variety of business segments, many of which have nothing to do with oil, offshore or energy. Looking only at the second half of 2014, the Norwegian bond market experienced bond issues from issuers within the pharmacy and life science industries, the fishery and marine sectors, the consultancy sector, real estate, and the aviation business.

During the same period, Norwegian banks and other advisers have been able to push the advantages of the Norwegian bond market compared with, for example, the New York market, and as such have created much more interest from new types of issuers, both from a geographical and business sector point of view.

1.2 Competitive advantages for Norwegian high yield bonds

The advantages mentioned under section 1.1 above, and the reasons for the development of the Norwegian high yield bond market into one of the largest bond markets in the world outside of the United States and the United Kingdom, can be explained by at least six main factors.

First, Norwegian investment banks have been extremely good at marketing the product to potential issuers and in placing high yield bonds with investors. The expansion of the issuer world and geographical scope of the Norwegian bond market has coincided with Norwegian investment banks moving into new geographical territories and thereby making the Norwegian market more known and accessible to foreign issuers. During the same period, traditional bank lending has become less available for certain types of borrowers, paving the way for Norwegian bonds as an alternative, and often more accessible, source of funding for those borrowers.

Secondly, the process of marketing and having issued Norwegian bonds is considerably less time- and cost-consuming than tapping into the New York or London high yield bond markets. Norwegian bonds are often issued and settled within five to six weeks from the internal start-up of the process. Importantly, from both a time and cost perspective, there is no need to do anything close to a traditional 10b-5 opinion due diligence, which is a pivotal part of any high yield bond issues in the New York market. The loan documentation is rather standardised and, partly due to a civil law tradition as opposed to a common law tradition, the loan documentation is much less detailed than is common under New York or English law. Also, there is no requirement for a formal credit rating. (See sections 3 and 4 below for a more detailed description of the process and the loan documentation.)

Thirdly, companies within the traditional Norwegian industries linked to the offshore and oil service sectors have been, and still are, often first-line users of bonds as a source of financing. In brief, bonds have over the years become much more part of the debt financial structure of Norwegian companies than in many other jurisdictions. This has, in turn, led to substantial experience and expertise among Norwegian banks, lawyers and advisers, as well as issuers, as to bond loans as a financial instrument. This experience and expertise has likely been an important driver for the success of the Norwegian investment banks' export of the concept of Norwegian high yield bonds.

Fourthly, the identity of bondholders is not public information and is only known by the trustee for the bond loan (save that the investment bank(s) involved will also have a list of the initial investors in the bond loan available to them). While such confidential treatment of the identity of bondholders is similar to the situation in many other jurisdictions, it is fair to assume that the Norwegian high yield bond market would be considerably smaller if, as one out of few jurisdictions, the identity of bondholders was public information.

Fifth, whereas the traditional argument against high yield bonds has been the pricing, we now see that the coupon on Norwegian bonds generally has come down and is to a larger extent competing with New York bonds and even, in some instances, bank lending. In addition, Norwegian bonds normally will have a more relaxed covenant structure, and more issuers have found that the Norwegian high yield bond market is competitive from a number of perspectives.

Finally, Norwegian bonds can be more flexible in terms of covenants, denomination and other commercial conditions. A Norwegian bond can be denominated in whatever currency, although the most common are the Norwegian krone, US dollar and the euro. Section 4 below gives a summary of typical covenants and other main terms.

2. The players in the market

The main players in the Norwegian high yield bond market include the issuers, the investment banks, the investors/bondholders and the trustee. We have given a short introduction to the issuers in section 1.1 above, including how they have become a more diverse group compared with a few years ago. For the other players, we will give a brief introduction to each of them below.

We have already mentioned that the Norwegian investment banks have been a driving force in increasing the size and scope of the Norwegian bond market. Norwegian investment banks of any size in the high yield bond market are few in number and they operate without any particular fear of competition from the major international investment banks. The reason is quite simply that the structure, fast-track process, lack of due diligence and documentation would make it nigh on impossible for international banks to operate as managers in a Norwegian high yield bond issue – their internal compliance departments would most likely not allow it.

The investors are mostly institutional investors and can be Norwegian, from other Nordic or European countries, or from North America. In 2014, non-Nordic investors accounted for approximately 37% of the total investments into Norwegian high yield bonds, and in bonds issued to non-Nordic issuers, the international (non-Norwegian) investors represented 75% of the total. Compare this with the situation in 2009 where non-Nordic investors represented only 3% of the total and it is evident that the investor world (with the change in the issuer world through the same period of time) has changed substantially.

Further distinctions include that unsecured bonds in Norwegian krone are dominated by Norwegian/Scandinavian investors, whereas secured bonds in US dollars and with a higher yield (higher risk) are dominated by international investors. Also, in general, the weaker the credit rating of a bond, the higher the share of foreign high yield funds and foreign distressed value investors that will normally participate.

Particular mention must be made of the trustee for the bonds. Unlike bonds issued under certain other jurisdictions, Norwegian bonds are almost always structured with a trustee that acts as the agent for the bondholders. This creates a legal situation where there is no direct interaction between the issuer and the individual bondholders and the bondholders' rights are exercised by and through the trustee.

In Norway, the market is completely dominated by Nordic Trustee ASA (formerly Norsk Tillitsmann ASA), which acts as trustee for approximately 95% of all Norwegian bonds, both high yield and investment grade (but excluding government bonds). Nordic Trustee ASA was established in 1993 in response to the then banking crisis in Norway and in order to facilitate the issue of bonds and thereby a source of financing. It is owned by several of the market participants (mostly Norwegian banks and financial institutions). The fact that the owners of the trustee are often also managers or stakeholders in bonds issued has in our experience not created any substantial conflict of interest issues. (See section 5 below for a summary of the trustee's legal position, especially in distressed situations.)

3. Structuring and timeline for a Norwegian high yield bond

As mentioned under section 1.2 above, one of the key advantages with Norwegian high yield bonds compared with, for example, bonds under New York law, is the short time and low cost from commencement of the process to settlement. A typical Norwegian bond can be issued within two weeks, although the more common time frame would be five to six weeks.

3.1 The mandate agreement

The more formal process will typically start with engagement of a manager/investment bank by virtue of a mandate agreement. Typically, the manager will require a fee in the region of 2.5–3.5% of the issued amount, but this varies to some extent based on, among other things, the market conditions and issuer quality.

3.2 Term sheet and investor presentation – pre-sounding of selected investors

The manager will normally have a clear view on what terms investors may accept for the bond loan, and will together with the issuer and legal counsel discuss and draft a term sheet containing:

- a range for issue amount and interest/coupon;
- a suggested tenor;
- any offered security;
- a brief summary of covenants and warranties to be given by the issuer; and
- any other particular issues of substantial importance.

In addition to the term sheet, the issuer and manager will prepare marketing material typically consisting of an investor presentation or an offering memorandum. Such marketing material will typically contain a summary of publicly available information (or, at least, information which will be made public before any subscriptions of bonds are accepted). As part of the material prepared, the manager will often have its own credit analysts prepare an in-house shadow rating of the bond issue. There is typically no formal credit rating, which is also an element that contributes to both cost and time savings.

Based on the initial term sheet and the manager's assessment of the market conditions and the likelihood of success, the issuer will then make a decision on whether the manager should do a pre-sounding of a limited number of investors. Such a pre-sounding may represent inside information[2] with respect to the issuer's listed shares or other listed securities (most issuers will be listed entities, but not necessarily). Thus, the manager will normally wall-cross pre-sounded investors, meaning that such investors will have to accept being placed in an inside position with respect to the issuer.

During pre-sounding, the manager will receive feedback from the pre-sounded investors. Such feedback could relate to all the commercial terms for the loan, but will typically concern the coupon, tenor, security package and, for example, lenders' right to a premium in case of prepayments of the loan. Based on feedback from the pre-sounding, the issuer and the manager will, together with legal counsel, make amendments to, and finalise, the term sheet. It is important to note that in this period the role of the manager starts to change. From the outset, the manager will be very much on the issuer's side looking to convince the issuer to engage the manager and proceed with the bond issue. The manager will put a lot of effort into helping investors in their considerations, partly because the more friendly the terms are for the investors, the easier the marketing of the bond issue will be, but also because the investors will often be regular clients of the manager.

We describe in some more detail in section 4 below the importance of the term sheet as part of the finance documentation, but emphasise also here that the term sheet needs to contain all major commercial terms for the loan. The term sheet is used in the marketing of the bond loan and investors will subscribe and commit to the loan based on the terms and conditions as set out in the term sheet. Thus, changes to the commercial terms after subscriptions have been made will typically require that all investors are released from their obligations and asked to renew their commitments.

3.3 Pre-commitments, launch of transaction and subscription period

As part of the pre-sounding, investors may pre-commit to the bond issue. This may take the form of an unconditional pre-commitment, or a commitment which is subject to certain conditions.

After the end of the pre-sounding period, the manager will make its recommendation to the issuer on whether a bond issue based on the terms set out in the term sheet (often adjusted based on investor feedback during the pre-sounding

---

2 Inside information is defined in the Norwegian Securities Trading Act as non-public and precise information about the issuer or its financial instruments which is likely to have a significant effect on the price of such financial instruments. When the term is used herein, the same definition will hereinafter be applied.

period) will be successful. If the issuer decides to go ahead, the transaction will be launched by the manager contacting a larger, but still limited, number of investors. Due to applicable exemptions and as described in section 7 below, the transaction does not require an offer prospectus, but the launch may have to be made public by the issuer.

Typically, the subscription period could be over within a few hours. If a roadshow is deemed necessary, the subscription period will normally be set at one or two weeks, and this will consequently have a considerable impact on the overall timeline.

Roadshows are normally deemed necessary only if the issuer is new to the Norwegian bond market and/or the sales process for any reason is deemed to be challenging by the manager.

3.4 Subscriptions and bond loan agreement

Once the subscription period is over, the manager and the issuer will confirm allocation of subscriptions and notify the bondholders/investors. Then, the trustee comes into play by negotiating the loan agreement on behalf of all bondholders/investors. As already mentioned, the loan agreement cannot deviate from the term sheet and will be based on the Nordic Trustee's standard bond loan agreement. If the term sheet has been carefully drafted, negotiations regarding the loan agreement should not take more than a few days to complete. If the bond loan is secured, all security documents must also be finalised and this may take longer, especially if the security documents are not governed by Norwegian law. In some jurisdictions, formalisation of such security arrangements may take several weeks or even months to achieve. However, unless such security arrangements represent the sole or substantial security for the bond loan, it would normally be possible to have the formalisation as a condition subsequent and as such avoid a severe delay in the settlement and closing of the bond loan.

The Nordic Trustee will not normally require any formal legal opinions if there is a Norwegian issuer and all documents are governed by Norwegian law. However, if security documents are not governed by Norwegian law, or if the issuer is a non-Norwegian entity, the trustee may require legal opinions from local counsel with respect to the security documents and the issuer's capacity and legal authority to enter into the bond loan agreement.

3.5 Closing and settlement

Once all documents have been finalised and other conditions precedent have been satisfied, closing will occur and the loan proceeds will be released to the issuer. In some bond issues, the loan proceeds will only be placed into an escrow account from which the issuer is allowed to draw subject to certain further conditions being satisfied.

3.6 Listing of bond loan

As most investors will require a tradable instrument, Norwegian high yield bonds are typically listed on Oslo Børs, which represents a regulated market for EU purposes. An alternative is the Nordic ABM which, however, is not a regulated market.

Listing on Oslo Børs will require a listing prospectus in accordance with ordinary EU rules on prospectus requirements, and a listing application to Oslo Børs. The process is fairly straightforward and will not delay closing or settlement of the bond loan since the listing process will be undertaken after closing.

The process for a listing on Nordic ABM is simpler than on Oslo Børs, and the Nordic ABM is not a regulated market for EU purposes. There is, among other things, no requirement for financial reporting in accordance with International Financial Reporting Standards (IFRS). Listing on Nordic ABM will also require a listing document, but this is a simpler and less extensive document compared with the Oslo Børs listing prospectus. The information obligations and trading rules are, however, virtually the same in both market places.

3.7 What about disclosure and due diligence?

One notable feature of Norwegian high yield bond issues is the short time span from commencement of the process to settlement and the main reason for this is that no substantial due diligence is required. This is substantially different from bond issues in, for example, the US market, where there is an extreme focus on so-called 10b-5 opinions[3] and associated disclosure and due diligence requirements.

As mentioned above, the bond loan is marketed purely on the basis of the term sheet and some marketing material. The subscription materials will state that the investor is responsible for reviewing any public information about the issuer and that the investor acknowledges that a listing prospectus will be made public after subscription and settlement of the bond loan.

The manager will not conduct a full audit of financials and will normally rely on the issuer's audited accounts (or quarterly unaudited accounts if the issuer is listed on a regulated market). The manager will, however, as part of its preparations and drafting of the investor presentation, run a test on the financial estimates and assumptions of the issuer. There will typically be particular focus on future cash flows and liquidity and whether the issuer has sufficient cash – including proceeds from the bond loan – to cover its commitments for the following 12 months. If the purpose of the bond loan is to finance a particular project and to make that project fully funded, it is to be expected that the manager will have close scrutiny on whether such a statement is, in fact, fair and true.

Further, the legal counsel and manager will often arrange for some form of limited due diligence exercise. The scope of such exercise will vary with the issuer and the specific circumstances, but in latter years the trend has been towards limiting it to a Q&A session with the executive management of the issuer, covering material operational, legal and financial issues. Such sessions will be organised as telephone conferences and there is typically one call at the public launch of a bond issue and one bring-down confirmatory call just before the close of the bond issue. It is also common for the manager to require key executive management of the issuer to sign

3 In short, this will allow a safe harbour for the managers involved provided that the due diligence exercise has met certain criteria (ie, the managers cannot be held liable even if the issuer/bond issue later defaults and creates a loss for investors).

a so-called completeness and indemnification statement (C&I statement), whereafter the executives confirm to the manager that the marketing material for all practical purposes provides a fair summary of the issuer, its business and the risks involved and furthermore undertake to indemnify the manager should they be held liable in connection with disclosures related to the bond issue.

Provided that the investor presentation contains a fair summary of risks associated with the issuer, its business and financials, and provided further that the investor presentation and subscription materials do not omit to state material facts, it is generally assumed that this form of limited disclosure and due diligence is acceptable. Possible liability for the issuer and/or manager is further addressed in section 6 below.

4. Loan documentation

The Nordic Trustee has together with the Norwegian legal community and other interested parties prepared a standard bond loan agreement. The standard is to a great extent based on Loan Market Association (LMA) terms and conditions. While it has increased in scope in recent years, it is still only slightly in excess of 30 pages long. The actual bond loan agreement is entered into between the issuer and the Nordic Trustee typically based on a term sheet and the standard bond loan agreement. While the bond loan agreement will be governed by Norwegian law, the security documentation (if applicable) will typically be governed by the law of the relevant jurisdiction for the specific asset subject to the security. To the extent that an oil company with oil and gas assets on the UK Continental Shelf (UKCS) issues a secured bond, the security documents relating to the oil and gas assets on the UKCS would thus typically be governed by English law.

As already mentioned, the term sheet will set out the key commercial terms and covenants, and will be the document based on which bondholders commit to invest in the bond. The actual drafting and negotiation of the bond loan agreement is therefore often a straightforward process merging the standard loan agreement with the relevant term sheet.

The bond loan agreement will contain, among other things:

- provisions setting out the status of the bonds;
- provisions on requirements to list and register the bonds in VPS;
- a regulation of the transferability of the bonds and matters related to closing and disbursement of the proceeds (conditions precedent, escrow arrangements and representations and warranties);
- covenants applicable to the issuer (and/or other group companies and guarantors); and
- regulation of event of default situations.

The bond loan agreement will also regulate the role of the Nordic Trustee and the relationship between the Nordic Trustee and the bondholders.

In relation to covenants, these have traditionally been maintenance covenants requiring the issuer to maintain compliance with the covenants at all times. The trend in international bond loans has been to have so-called incurrence covenants, that is, covenants that are tested only in connection with the incurrence of specific events (eg, a transaction or taking on new debt). In recent years, we have seen some examples where incurrence covenants have also been introduced in Norwegian bond loan agreements. It is important to note, however, that the introduction of incurrence-based covenants will need to be specifically addressed in the term sheet and also in the marketing information.

The standard bond loan agreement vests certain authority in the Nordic Trustee to make amendments or modifications to the terms of the bond loan agreement, as well as providing waivers of certain provisions. The condition is that such amendments, waivers and/or modifications do not (in the opinion of the Nordic Trustee) materially and adversely affect the rights of the bondholders. The Trustee will typically act with caution when exercising its authority, and in most situations amendments, waivers and modifications are referred to a bondholders' meeting for decision. The standard bond loan agreement also sets out specific provisions relating to the procedure for calling a bondholders' meeting, a quorum and voting requirements.

5. Distress situations – restructurings and enforcement

Under the standard bond loan agreement, an individual bondholder will not have the right to take action or initiate legal proceedings against an issuer. Such action or legal proceedings will need to be taken by the Nordic Trustee on behalf of the bondholders. The legal capacity of the Nordic Trustee to act on behalf of the bondholders was the subject of rulings from the Norwegian High Court and the Norwegian High Court's Appeal Committee on two occasions in 2010, which concluded that the Nordic Trustee had such legal capacity to act on behalf of the bondholders, including acting as party to legal proceedings against an issuer and in connection with an issuer's bankruptcy.

The Norwegian high yield bond market has a relatively high default rate, which peaked in 2009 at 31%, resulting in a number of restructurings in recent years. In such situations, bondholders will often establish a bondholder committee to facilitate the dialogue with the Nordic Trustee as well as the issuer. As set out previously, the issuer will as a starting point not know (and will not have access to) who the bondholders are. The role of the bondholder committee will not be a formal role, and any restructuring proposal will need to be approved by a bondholders' meeting. Corporate approvals will typically also be required, for instance a restructuring proposal involving a debt to equity conversion will require a corporate resolution to issue the required equity. The objective of the issuer will often be to have some commitment from all involved stakeholders (typically bondholders and shareholders) to a restructuring proposal before the respective bondholder and shareholder meetings are called. In such a context, a bondholders' committee may facilitate obtaining such pre-commitments to support a restructuring proposal.

6. Liability

Even though the individual bondholders may not initiate legal proceedings against the issuer under the bond loan agreement, as described in section 5 above, legal proceedings may be brought against the company, managers, board members or the management in the civil courts and result in liability to pay compensation based on negligence.

On the basis of professional liability, managers may for instance be liable for misinformation and withholding of information in relation to the arranging and placing of the bond issue. There are very few examples of court cases in this category; however, this is probably not because losses and threats of proceedings do not occur but rather because such cases are conciliated and not published. Further, a scorned investor or others may inform the Norwegian Financial Services Authority which in serious cases has the power to revoke the manager's authorisation.

Each individual member of the board may be held liable as a company representative based on directors' liability and negligence. In recent years it seems as though board members are increasingly the preferred subject for proceedings. A contributing factor is probably that board members will often hold director liability insurance, thus increasing the chance of recovery should a claim be successful.

In serious circumstances, criminal proceedings can be initiated against the issuer, board, board members, management or a manager. Possible penalties include imprisonment and/or fines.

7. Securities law considerations

Before the bond loan is made public, the fact that the issuer is considering a bond loan issue may constitute inside information with respect to the issuer and its financial instruments. This assumes, of course, that the issuer is listed on a regulated market or that the issuer already has a bond loan listed on a regulated market, or on Nordic ABM which has adopted similar information obligations in case of disclosure of inside information even though it is an unregulated market.

As a rule of thumb, a possible issue by an Oslo Børs listed entity of a Norwegian high yield bond will be deemed as inside information when a decision has been made to start pre-sounding of a limited number of potential investors. However, pursuant to the rules of the Norwegian Securities Trading Act, the issuer may defer disclosure of the relevant facts, provided that:

- confidentiality of the matter is kept intact;
- the issuer drafts and keeps lists of individuals with knowledge of the matter; and
- immediate disclosure would harm the legitimate interests of the issuer, typically that ongoing negotiations would be affected by disclosure.

With respect to the final point, it is generally accepted that a standard and confidential pre-sounding of investors will meet the test. If the feedback from pre-sounding is negative and the issuer decides to terminate the process, no further public announcements will be made.

If the issuer is listed on Oslo Børs, the launch of the subscription period will normally have to be made public. As Norwegian high yield bond issues are not underwritten by the manager, making the process public obviously represents a risk for the issuer of having to notify the market of a failed book-building should the marketing of the bond not be successful. Usually, this is mitigated by obtaining pre-commitments from investors during the pre-sounding phase (see section 3.3 above), or quite simply by the manager's recommendation that the book-build will be successful; the issuer will typically have a rather high level of confidence of success before publicly launching a bond issue.

After the settlement and issue of the bonds, the issuer will be subject to disclosure obligations with respect to inside information concerning the bonds. The scope of what represents inside information with respect to bonds is usually narrower than the scope relating to shares. For bonds in isolation, inside information will typically concern facts and circumstances about the issuer's ability to service the bond and interest payments, as well as facts and circumstances about any secured assets. At the same time, inside information with respect to an issuer's bonds will normally also represent inside information with respect to such issuer's shares, if they are listed on a regulated market.[4]

As set out in section 1.2 above, the identity of the bondholder is not public information. Consequently, there is no obligation for bondholders to disclose ownership levels or when crossing certain ownership thresholds for bonds listed on Oslo Børs.

The offering is normally structured so that an offering prospectus is not required, for instance by applying available exemptions from the prospectus requirements so that the bonds are issued in individual amounts with a par value or claim for payment of at least €100,000 and/or offered only to professional investors.

4 For issuers listed on a regulated market other than Oslo Børs, there may be different assessments of what represents inside information pursuant to the local regulated market's rules and regulations with respect to such issuer's shares.

Hedging

Kerion Ball
Ashurst LLP

1. Types of hedge transactions commonly found in energy and natural resources financings

Hedging is a generic term for the management of risk covering a number of derivative products, such as foreign exchange swaps and options, interest rate swaps, and commodity swaps and options, which can be used in a particular business, industry or project. Specifically, in the case of energy financings, the risks which are most typically hedged are:

- interest rate and currency risk; and
- commodity price risk.

1.1 Interest rate and currency risk

(a) Why is it necessary to manage interest rate and currency risk?

Borrowers often raise finance at rates of interest which vary over the life of the financing, such as LIBOR or EURIBOR, reflecting the manner in which lenders fund themselves in the interbank market. This exposes borrowers to the risk of adverse movements in interest rates which can result in significantly increased payment obligations under their financings. Similarly, where a borrower's cash flows are linked to a particular currency which is different to the currency of the financing, the borrower is exposed to adverse movements in the exchange rate resulting from the cash flow currency depreciating against the currency of the financing, which makes it more expensive for the borrower to service its interest obligations. Both of these risks inhibit borrowers from conducting effective financial planning.

To mitigate these risks, it is common in energy and natural resources financings for borrowers to enter into hedging transactions. This is accepted practice in the market, although the lenders will wish to ensure that the process is closely monitored, particularly given the potential financial risk that derivatives trading can present. While under the terms of the relevant facility agreement the borrowing group may be permitted to enter into hedging transactions, the lenders and the borrower will agree a hedging policy which is typically given in a schedule to the facility agreement and which sets out the parameters within which the borrowing group must keep in pursuing the borrower's hedging strategy as well as any consultation or other requirements the lenders may have. In the context of energy and natural resources financings, it is also usually the case that the borrowing group will be subject to certain mandatory hedging requirements such that, for example, a minimum percentage of the borrower's term loans or the borrower's total annual oil production must be hedged for the duration of the financing to mitigate downside commodity price risk.

1.2 Interest rate hedging

There are various forms of hedges against interest rate movements. The most common in the context of loan financings is the fixed/floating interest rate swap. This is where the swap counterparty pays the borrower an amount calculated by reference to the floating rate of interest applicable to the borrower on the loan it is hedging in order to enable the borrower to service its interest obligations under that loan. The borrower then pays the swap counterparty an amount calculated by reference to an agreed fixed rate.

By entering into a fixed/floating interest rate swap, in economic terms, a borrower can convert a floating rate financial obligation into a fixed rate financial obligation. A borrower may prefer – and indeed lenders may insist upon – the obligation to pay a fixed rate of interest as this more closely corresponds to the income it receives from its business operations or, more simply, reduces uncertainty as to its financing costs. The trade-off, however, is the possible benefit the borrower forgoes where interest rates fall, which would otherwise reduce its interest payment obligations.

1.3 Currency risk hedging

Currency risk hedging is similar to interest rate hedging and there are also various forms of hedges against foreign exchange risk. A common form of foreign exchange hedging in the context of energy and resources and other loan financings is the cross-currency swap which involves the exchange of fixed or floating rate payments denominated in different currencies and the exchange of two notional principal amounts at the beginning and the end of the transaction.

Consider, for example, an oil and gas exploration and production company whose cash flows are principally denominated in dollars but who enters into a sterling denominated loan because it can attract a more favourable funding rate in sterling. At inception of the cross-currency swap, the borrower will pay to its swap counterparty the sterling proceeds of the loan in exchange for the dollar equivalent at the agreed rate of exchange. During the life of the transaction, the swap counterparty will pay to the borrower an amount equal to the sterling interest payments due on the loan in exchange for the borrower paying to the swap counterparty an amount in dollars equal to the sterling interest payment converted at the agreed exchange rate. On maturity, assuming a hard bullet repayment, the swap counterparty will pay to the borrower the sterling principal amount of the loan and the borrower will pay the dollar equivalent it received at inception. If the loan amortises, there will be interim exchanges of sterling principal amounts and dollar equivalents. By entering into the cross-currency swap, the borrower is able to protect itself against adverse movements in the dollar/sterling exchange rate by fixing the rate between its dollar cash flows and its sterling liabilities under the loan.

1.4 Commodity price risk

(a) *Why is it necessary to manage commodity price risk?*

Commodity price risk is particularly relevant in the context of energy and natural resources financings. Given the nature of the borrower's business, its cash flow and, therefore, its ability to repay the loan is linked to the future price of one or more commodities. For example, an oil and gas exploration and production company's income will be linked to the price of oil and gas, therefore exposing the company to falls in the price of such commodities. The lenders may, therefore, require the borrower to protect itself from the risk of downward movement in the price of the relevant commodity. The permitted transaction types, term, and maximum and minimum limits of the borrower's hedging activities will be prescribed by the hedging policy.

1.5 Commodity price hedging

The simplest and most common form of commodity price is the cash-settled pre-paid put option as it locks in a certain price for a certain period in respect of a certain quantity of reserves and the borrower pays the premium up front. Under this arrangement, in exchange for the payment of a premium – or fee – the borrower would, typically at the end of each quarter, have the right to sell to its counterparty a pre-agreed amount of the commodity at an agreed strike price. If at the end of the quarter the price of the commodity has fallen to a level which is below the strike price, the borrower will exercise the put option and its counterparty will pay it the difference between the agreed strike price and the then market price, multiplied by the amount of the commodity in respect of which the option has been entered into.

Other commodity price hedging by way of deferred premium put options, swaps and collars (including credit contingent hedging where the payout is contingent on a credit-related event as well as asset-related price movements) may also be permitted subject to limitations.

1.6 Reasons for entering into commodity hedging in an energy and resources financing transaction

In the context of reserve-based lending (RBL) facilities, where the amount of financing made available (the borrowing base amount) is determined by reference to the value of the borrower's oil and gas reserves, a key input to the calculation of the borrowing base amount is the economic assumption adopted as to future petroleum prices given that future petroleum prices will have a material impact on the borrower's available cash flow.

If there is a long-term offtake contract with a dependable offtaker at non-market pricing, which is more often the case with gas rather than oil, the lenders under the RBL facility are likely to use that pricing in the commodity price assumption. Otherwise the lenders will use a price somewhere below standard market forward curves, such price deck being set at a level designed to absorb any short-term volatility in commodity prices.

When used properly, commodity price hedging can further mitigate the risks to borrowers, and so indirectly lenders, of movements in commodity prices by locking in a certain price for a certain period in respect of a certain quantity of reserves by way of swaps, call options or put options.

If the hedging is undertaken with an acceptable hedge counterparty (the criteria for which will typically include an acceptable credit-rating), such hedging should be taken into account in the calculation of the borrowing base amount. Given that the hedging will in all probability be undertaken at a price level above the price deck, hedging should increase the Borrowing Base Amount. This is particularly useful:

- where borrowers need to maximise availability under the RBL facility, for instance in the context of a competitive bid for the acquisition of assets; or
- where letters of credit to secure decommissioning liabilities need to be posted, and which may reduce the amount available to be drawn as cash advances under the RBL facility.

2. Documentation

The documentation used in relation to hedge transactions will typically employ industry standard forms and sets of definitions which have been developed over time by industry specific bodies, allowing market participants to minimise negotiation time while securing a degree of certainty as to their terms. Under English law, the hedge documentation will most commonly consist of the ISDA Master Agreement, either in its 1992 or 2002 form depending on the requirements of the relevant financing documents, the related schedule of elections and bespoke terms and the trade Confirmation containing the commercial terms of the transactions. The 2006 ISDA Definitions, the 2005 ISDA Commodity Definitions and/or the 1998 ISDA FX and Currency Option Definitions may also be incorporated in the hedge documentation depending on whether commodity and FX hedging is contemplated in addition to interest rate hedging. These documents form part of the industry standard ISDA architecture of documents, all as published by the International Swaps and Derivatives Association Inc (ISDA®).

The hedge documentation will be regulated by the terms of the facility agreement and, where one is used, the intercreditor agreement. These documents will typically contain undertakings requiring any hedge documentation to be in a prescribed form and regulating the making of payments to and from the hedge providers.

As with hedge documentation for other loan types, early termination events will be substantially aligned with prepayment events under the facility agreement but the hedge counterparty's right to exercise an early termination will be limited to circumstances that are considered so fundamental to the hedge counterparty's interests that it should not be required to continue the hedge transactions. The circumstances in which a hedge counterparty can terminate early are increasingly the subject of negotiation and can range from being limited to failure to pay under the ISDA Master Agreement and acceleration or full repayment or discharge of the facility agreement, to insolvency, illegality, tax and even misrepresentation default or termination events. These limitations are commonly found in the intercreditor agreement, where one is employed, or the facility agreement itself in the absence of an intercreditor arrangement.

Typical hedging-related provisions found in the financing documents include:

- restrictions set out in an agreed hedging policy on the borrower entering into hedge transactions;
- rights of lenders under the facility agreement to quote for hedging;
- requirements as to the form of hedging documentation;
- ranking of claims of hedge providers as regards security (typically equality with the senior lenders if the hedging is entered into with a senior lender under the facility agreement);
- cash flow waterfall in respect of project revenues including allocation of project cash flows to hedging payments (typically equality with the facility agreement debt service if the hedging is entered into with a lender under the facility agreement);
- restriction on exercise of termination rights by hedge providers (typically more restrictive than those found in a leveraged financing). The principle here is that the lenders should be afforded some room for manoeuvre to deal with any potential default under the facility agreement without their hands being forced by a pre-emptive termination by hedge providers;
- restrictions on hedge counterparties exercising their rights of set-off other than in accordance with the financing documentation;
- restrictions on hedge counterparties' rights to amend or transfer the hedge agreements other than in accordance with the financing documentation;
- rights of hedge counterparties to receive information; and
- voting rights of hedge counterparties.

2.1 Drafting the hedge documentation

The hedge documentation will either be drafted by the hedging desks of the hedge counterparties, by their legal counsel or by lenders' legal counsel. Hedge counterparties will often have a standard form of ISDA schedule containing their preferred set of terms, although as noted above, to the extent these terms conflict with the requirements of the hedge documentation set by the financing documents, they may not be acceptable to the borrower or the lenders. Where there are multiple hedge counterparties, borrowers will often push for all of their hedge documentation to be as close to identical as possible to provide them with greater certainty and to reduce the time taken to negotiate such documentation and, therefore, reduce legal costs.

The hedge counterparties will be party to the intercreditor agreement, where one is used, but it may also be appropriate for them to be party to the facility agreement depending on the circumstances of the transaction.

The borrower's rights under the hedge documentation (principally its right to any close-out amount) are usually subject to the finance parties' security package and a notice of assignment or charge will need to be delivered to the hedge counterparties to give effect to this.

3. Common issues arising in the context of energy and resources finance hedging

There is a natural tension between the lending group, who as a body generally wish to avoid a situation where the debt they have extended is unhedged (particularly at a time when the borrower is not actually in default under the facility agreement but is perhaps in financial difficulty), and the hedge counterparties who will want to be able to close out the hedge transactions in the broadest range of circumstances. The borrower's and the hedge counterparty's interests will also often not be aligned. These tensions give rise to a number of important issues that must be considered in the course of negotiation between the parties.

3.1 Identity of hedge counterparty

It makes sense for borrowers to hold a competition in respect of the hedging in order to ensure the most competitive rates. However, it is relatively common for the facility agreement to include the requirement that the hedge counterparties must be lenders or affiliates of a lender. While borrowers might push for a wider group of hedge counterparties, the margins to be made on the hedge transactions can be significant in the context of tight margins on arrangement fees, so the arranging banks may be able to reduce their arrangement fees if the hedge transactions are done by them or be able to bid lower than independent third parties in a competition, because they receive the arrangement fees in addition. Thus the hedge counterparties will often also be lenders.

3.2 Ranking and security

(a) Ranking

Liabilities owed by an obligor to a hedge counterparty under the hedge documentation will typically constitute and be treated as senior debt.

A hedge counterparty's exposure will, therefore, have senior status for the purposes of the financing documents, ranking equally with the lender's liabilities under the facility agreement as to right of payment and sharing in the security package. Although the size of exposures under the hedge transactions (and therefore the hedging liabilities) can dramatically increase, thus reducing potential recoveries by the lenders where the transaction security is enforced, such equality is rarely challenged by the lending group and is representative of market practice.

The extent to which payments between the relevant obligor and hedge counterparty are permitted to be made will also be regulated by the financing documents. Prior to acceleration of the facility agreement, only the following types of payments between the parties are likely to be permitted:

- scheduled payments due under the hedge documentation; and
- early termination payments in connection with the close-out of any hedge transactions which is permitted by the financing documents.

Following acceleration of the facility agreement, any payments under the hedge documentation will be required to be made to the facility or security agent for application in accordance with the payment waterfall provided in the financing documents.

The financing documents may also permit the obligors to enter into unsecured hedging transactions for the purposes of the borrowing group's general corporate purposes. The relevant obligor's rights under such unsecured hedging arrangements will not form part of the security package in relation to the financing made available under the financing documents.

(b) ***Rights to transaction security***

A hedge counterparty will want to ensure that it takes whatever steps are necessary under the financing documents to become a secured creditor and get the benefit of the guarantees and security provided by the borrowing group. This typically will include acceding to the facility agreement and, where one is used, the intercreditor agreement.

The security agent will act in relation to enforcing the transaction security in accordance with the decisions of the instructing group (of which the hedge counterparties will form part). The hedge counterparties have no separate rights in relation to security. Prior to the date on which all of the senior liabilities are discharged, this will typically mean the majority senior creditors which includes the hedge counterparties – but only by reference to their participation (see 3.4 below).

3.3 Enforcement rights

It is standard practice for hedge counterparties' termination rights under the hedging documentation to be limited. In the context of energy and resources financings these will be limited to a greater degree than would otherwise be the case on a typical leveraged financing. This is largely a reflection of market practice in this area but also because of the tighter regulation of borrower cash flows given the nature of the financing. The aim of the lending group is to restrict the hedge counterparties' close-out rights at a time when the borrower's financial situation is rocky (so that hedging would be difficult to replace, presenting the obvious risk of leaving the borrower with an unhedged debt) but not at the point of no return. The lenders may need the hedging to remain in place in order to more easily facilitate a group restructuring and to ensure continuation of stable cash flows. From the perspective of a hedge counterparty, this is far from satisfactory. In these circumstances, a hedge counterparty will most likely want to close-out its hedge transactions, thereby crystallising its position and recovering any amounts due to it. If a hedge counterparty's position is out of the money, the risk to it of not crystallising its position when the borrower is not performing is that a restructuring or adverse movement in the price of the underlying reference rate or commodity price could lead to it being even further out of the money.

The typical negotiated position on an energy and resources financing is to restrict a hedge counterparty's rights to terminate any hedge transactions to the following list.

- A failure to pay event of default under the ISDA Master Agreement with a grace period (often 10 to 15 business days) following notice of default being given to the security agent: Allowing termination following a failure to pay is market practice. The length of the grace period is naturally a common point of negotiation. Hedge counterparties will clearly prefer this to be as short as possible with the lenders typically reluctant to accept anything less than 10 business days.

- Insolvency of the obligor party to the hedge agreement: Rather than allowing the hedge counterparties to rely on the ISDA Master Agreement standard bankruptcy event of default or its equivalent, a description of the insolvency event itself will be set out in the relevant financing document. Typically, the event will only be triggered following an end-stage insolvency event with a grace period included for frivolous or vexatious claims. The standard ISDA bankruptcy event is broader than the insolvency event typically found in the financing documents, making it a more sensitive trigger. Given the equal ranking of lenders and hedge counterparties under the security, it can be viewed as being in the interests of the lending group for a hedge counterparty to have the ability to terminate in the case of an insolvency event. This is because a subsequent adverse movement in the mark-to-market value of the hedge transactions increases the risk of loss to the lenders.
- An illegality, *force majeure*, tax event or tax event upon merger termination under the ISDA Master Agreement or their respective equivalent: These termination events are triggered by circumstances which fundamentally change the nature of the transaction for the hedge counterparty. Lenders are accepting of this and their inclusion is rarely challenged.
- Acceleration of the loans: This is generally favourable to both the lenders and the hedge counterparties.
- Discharge of the senior liabilities: Clearly, the hedge counterparties should be entitled to terminate in these circumstances.
- Termination for overhedging: Where loans are prepaid, it is accepted that hedge counterparties should be entitled to close-out (indeed, in many cases, they would also be required to close-out) the excess portion of any hedge transactions to avoid the costs and increased exposure of the borrower being overhedged. Some financings may include a certain tolerance for overhedging up to a designated threshold to avoid the operational burden or unwinding small notional amounts of overhedging.
- Direction of the facility or security agent: The facility or security agent may be able to direct the hedge counterparty to terminate the hedge transactions in certain circumstances agreed in the intercreditor terms.

(a) Application of termination payments

Following acceleration of the facility agreement, any termination payments due from an obligor under the hedge documentation will generally be required to be made to the facility or security agent for application in accordance with the payment waterfall provided in the financing documents. Equally, any termination amounts due from a hedge counterparty will be paid over to the agent and applied down the waterfall following acceleration.

3.4 Voting and information

(a) *Voting*

The hedging liabilities are treated differently to the liabilities of the lending group with respect to voting since a hedge counterparty's exposure can be subject to significant fluctuations. Voting entitlement will be determined according to the participation of the relevant finance party with regard to the borrower's liabilities. In a typical energy and resources financing, the senior lenders will vote according to their aggregate commitments (ie, including undrawn commitments) whereas a hedge counterparty's participation will be determined on the basis of the close-out amount payable to that hedge counterparty under any hedge agreement which has actually been closed-out at that time but which remains unpaid.

In other words, the hedge counterparties are without a vote in the normal course of decision making. Only when they close-out do they get a vote. There is some tension here in that, historically, hedge counterparties were invariably the same institution as – or an affiliate of – a lender and the lender was therefore (notionally) expected to look after the interests of its related hedge counterparty. While the lender/hedge counterparty overlap is still likely (for the reasons set out in 3.1 above), it is more common even for related hedge counterparties to operate as independent stakeholders in the financing, though in practice they may not wish to participate in decision making while matters are running smoothly.

As a consequence, market practice in respect of voting rights of hedge counterparties varies. Some hedge counterparties are able to negotiate more significant voting rights enabling them to vote according to the mark-to-market value of outstanding hedge transactions. However, determining the extent of this vote presents difficulties as the mark-to-market of the hedge transactions is naturally subject to fluctuation and, despite seemingly identical economic terms, one hedge counterparty's determination of the close-out amount of its hedge transaction may be different from the same determination made by another hedge counterparty, thus resulting in its participation for voting purposes being greater than that of its fellow hedge counterparty.

(b) *Information*

A corollary of the increasing focus on greater voting rights for hedge counterparties is the need for them to remain as far as possible in the information flow under the financing documentation. Hedge counterparties should be cognisant of the importance of being notified of key events during the life of the financing, such as:

- the occurrence of events of default and any subsequent acceleration of the facilities;
- enforcement of the transaction security; and
- notifications of prepayment in relation to any outstanding loans.

Hedge counterparties in strong bargaining positions are often able to negotiate a much better position in this respect where, for example, any notices to the lending group must by default also go to the hedge counterparties. As a group, the lenders should not be averse to this, yet it is an area which is sometimes overlooked by hedge counterparties.

3.5 Amendments to the financing documents

It is generally accepted that amendments to the financing documents which affect the rights and obligations of a hedge counterparty should not be made without the consent of that hedge counterparty. While this is typically not contested by the lending group, occasionally the requirement is that such a restriction applies only to the extent that the amendment or waiver would adversely affect the hedge counterparty or its interests. This is clearly a less favourable position from the hedge counterparties' perspective as it puts the decision on a more objective footing, increasing the likelihood of dispute in such circumstances.

Hedge counterparties will also generally have an effective veto right in relation to certain key areas such as amendments or waivers of the financing documents which relate to guarantees given by the borrowing group in favour of the finance parties. Amendments to the ranking or subordination provisions of the financing documents are also generally not permitted without the consent of the hedge counterparties.

3.6 Refinancings

Ideally, hedge transactions should be sufficiently independent of the underlying financing to allow the facilities to be refinanced without incurring unnecessary break costs. This is easier in theory than in practice as the hedge counterparties will generally expect to be secured on substantially the same terms as they enjoy under the original financing, so may not be willing to agree to the terms of the new finance documents. As a result, hedge counterparties will often request a right to terminate on a refinancing occurring. This right may be tempered by a discretion or obligation to negotiate the terms of the new finance documents to enable the hedge transaction to remain in place.

Where the hedge documentation is silent on refinancing, there is the possibility of novating the swaps to a new lender of the refinanced debt but this is a solution that needs to be agreed by the parties at the time of refinancing and is not documented at financial close. ISDA has published standard form novation documentation and, where the hedge transactions are documented under an ISDA Master Agreement, this can be used to document novations.

3.7 Transfer rights

A hedge counterparty's ability to transfer its rights or obligations under the hedge agreement and any hedge transactions will also be restricted. Generally, transfers without the consent of the lending group (although typically the consent of the borrower must still be obtained as required under Section 7 of the ISDA Master Agreement) are permitted to other lenders or their affiliates. Transfers to lenders' affiliates may also be subject to additional restrictions to ensure, for example, that no withholding tax would apply in respect of swap payments and that close-out netting is enforceable in the jurisdiction of incorporation of the proposed transferee.

3.8 Linking the hedge documentation to the financing documents

Although the financing documents themselves will generally be particularly prescriptive with respect to the circumstances in which a hedge counterparty can terminate any hedge transactions, it is nevertheless important, particularly from the borrower's perspective, to ensure that the hedge documentation is appropriately linked to the financing documents.

One assumption to be avoided is that the extensiveness of the representations, covenants and events of default under the hedge documentation is irrelevant given the restrictions which the hedge counterparty is subject to under the financing documents. The hedge agreements will invariably be finance documents for, among other matters, the events of default under the facility agreement and breaches of representation or obligation under any finance document will trigger the relevant event of default under the facility agreement. Consequently, a prudent borrower should ensure that these provisions are no wider or more extensive than those in the facility agreement, thus avoiding hair trigger defaults under the hedge documentation, which would undermine the main negotiated position under the facility agreement. While this is primarily a borrower point, lenders should also be alive to the issue so as to avoid the situation where waivers of default are required with respect to such hair-trigger defaults.

By contrast, a hedge counterparty will want to avoid the situation where there is a serious default or acceleration under the facility agreement and there is no way to terminate the hedging. As mentioned in 3.3 above, acceleration under the loan will typically give the hedge counterparty a termination right.

The hedge documentation may also include a financing document override so that conflicts between the two documents are resolved by reference to the relevant financing document rather than the hedge documentation. Hedge counterparty termination rights are limited to circumstances contemplated in the financing documents.

(a) Approaches to ensure coherence between the hedge documentation and the financing documents

There are a number of different ways in which the desired outcome can be achieved. It is important to remember that the hedge documentation applies mutually to both the hedge counterparty (usually Party A) and the relevant obligor (usually Party B), so when events of default – or other terms – are amended to match the Party B position agreed in the financing documents, it must be made clear that these changes apply in respect of Party B only.

A common approach is to disapply (at least until the date on which the senior liabilities have been discharged) all events of default and termination events under the hedge documentation against Party B, other than those which represent a permitted termination right for the hedge counterparty (eg, failure to pay) which are appropriately amended to conform to the negotiated position in the financing documents. Additional termination rights for the hedge counterparty are then included either as additional events of default or additional termination events with respect to Party B under the hedge documentation. This approach ensures the hedge documentation dovetails as closely as possible with the hedging provisions of the financing documents.

4. Issues specific to energy financings

4.1 Pre-hedging

In some transactions relating to energy infrastructure, particularly those which involve a public authority sponsoring the project, it may be necessary to undertake pre-hedging in order to retain some secrecy surrounding the date of execution of the hedge transactions so as to prevent a spike in the market resulting in a less economically advantageous price for the borrower (or, in the case of a concession-type project, the sponsor which ultimately pays for the hedging by way of the payment it makes to the borrower in consideration of its agreement to undertake the project). Pre-hedging is also used if a particular market is illiquid (eg, where the financing is denominated in a less widely traded currency), which means that the hedging may need to be transacted in tranches over a period of days before financial close.

Pre-hedging is usually undertaken in the days before financial close of a transaction (ie, the date on which the funding is extended to the borrower) by one or a small number of execution banks which will make the initial swap transactions that are then novated in the relevant proportions to the other hedge counterparties at financial close.

There is always the risk with pre-hedging that financial close will not occur, leaving the borrower and the execution banks with swap transactions that are no longer required. Failure to reach financial close will usually be an additional termination event under the hedge documentation entitling the parties to terminate the transactions. This may give rise to a liability for the borrower to make a payment to the execution banks if the swap transaction is out of the money for the borrower, which is problematic as the borrower will have no assets from which to make the payment. The execution banks may therefore require an indemnity for payment of any such amounts from an entity of substance (eg, the sponsor) to insure against this risk.

5. Key regulatory issues

5.1 EMIR

Regulation 648/2012 of the European Parliament and of the Council of July 4 2012 on over-the-counter (OTC) derivatives, central counterparties and trade repositories, otherwise known as EMIR, represents the European Union's response to the international effort to more closely regulate the OTC derivatives market in the wake of the financial crisis of 2008. As an EU regulation, EMIR is directly applicable in member states' national law without the need for domestic implementation. Many of the detailed requirements of EMIR are contained in delegated regulations – Regulatory Technical Standards (RTS) and Implementing Technical Standards (ITS) – laid down by the European Commission.

The key requirements imposed by EMIR that are relevant to hedge transactions are:

- the reporting of the transactions to a trade repository;
- the risk mitigation techniques for uncleared derivatives;
- the requirement to clear certain categories of derivatives through a central counterparty; and
- the requirement to exchange collateral with respect to non-cleared derivatives.

These requirements apply equally to all EU derivative market participants, and the risk mitigation requirements may also apply indirectly to entities established outside of the European Union that enter into derivative transactions with an EU market participant subject to those requirements. The clearing requirement (which has now been finalised with respect to certain interest rate derivatives but remains in draft form with respect to credit derivatives) will also apply to non-EU entities that would be subject to the obligation if they were established in the European Union and the margining requirement (currently in draft form) will apply to all counterparties of EU market participants to whom such requirements apply unless certain opt-outs are applicable.

Whether the requirement to clear certain derivative transactions applies will depend on the class of the derivatives being traded and the categorisation of the borrower. Although the final RTS on the initial classes of derivatives to be subject to mandatory clearing is yet to be published, standardised interest rate swaps, basis swaps, forward rate agreements and overnight index swaps denominated in euros, pounds sterling, Japanese yen or US dollars will be first among them and could take effect as early as April 2016. In contrast, foreign exchange and commodities derivatives are not likely to be subject to mandatory clearing in the foreseeable future.

Most borrowers in energy and natural resource financings will be non-financial counterparties for the purposes of EMIR (or non-EU equivalents thereof) which means that the clearing obligation will apply only if the aggregate derivative exposures of all non-financial counterparties in the same group, other than hedging exposures, exceed specified thresholds (€3 billion for each of interest rate and foreign exchange, €1 billion for each of the equities and credit and €1 billion in aggregate for commodities and all other classes).

It is also important to note that where the clearing threshold is exceeded by a borrower with respect to any class of derivative, the clearing obligation will apply to all future OTC derivatives concluded by that borrower, including hedging transactions that are of any other class of derivative subject to mandatory clearing.

Once the margining obligation under EMIR takes effect (the timing of which is uncertain), borrowers entering derivatives transactions with EU financial institution counterparties will be required to exchange initial and variation margin with respect to their derivatives exposures with such counterparties unless an opt-out is available. The opt-outs that borrowers in energy and natural resource financings are most likely to seek to avail themselves of are:

- being a non-financial counterparty below the clearing thresholds referred to above or a non-EU equivalent thereof, which enables an opt-out of both initial and variation margin exchange; and
- with respect to initial margin only, belonging to a group whose aggregate notional amount of non-cleared derivatives is below the specified threshold currently proposed as €3 trillion as of December 2015, reducing to €8 billion by December 2019.

ISDA has published the following EMIR-specific protocols which parties can include in the terms of their ISDA Master Agreement, either by both parties adhering to the relevant protocol or by incorporating by reference the terms of the protocol into the ISDA Master Agreement:

- The ISDA 2013 EMIR Portfolio Reconciliation, Dispute Resolution and Disclosure Protocol enables parties to meet their obligations in respect of the portfolio reconciliation, compensation and dispute resolution requirements imposed by EMIR (part of the risk mitigation techniques referred to above) and includes a disclosure waiver to help ensure parties can meet the various reporting and record-keeping requirements under EMIR without breaching contractual confidentiality restrictions that they may be subject to.
- The ISDA 2013 EMIR NFC Representation Protocol, enabling parties to classify the status of their counterparties for EMIR purposes to determine whether or not certain of the risk mitigation techniques, and in future the clearing and margining requirements, apply.

It is common for borrowers to delegate their obligation under EMIR to report hedge transactions to a trade repository to their hedge counterparty pursuant to a delegated reporting agreement. Bank counterparties will typically have their own standard preferred form of delegated reporting agreement which is usually based on the form of agreement published by ISDA and the Futures and Options Association – now known as FIA Europe – and which borrowers are usually requested to enter into with little or no negotiation. Although the terms of the agreement are favourable to the bank counterparty, the trade-off is generally accepted by borrowers given the operational burden that EMIR trade reporting may otherwise place on self-reporting borrowers.

(a) *Other relevant regulation*

Reporting requirements similar to those under EMIR are imposed by certain other EU regulations, including Regulation 1227/2011 on Energy Market Integrity and Transparency (REMIT) and Directive 2014/65/EU and Regulation 600/2014 which, together, comprise what is known as MiFID II which will repeal and recast Directive 2004/39/EC, otherwise known as MiFID.

Under REMIT, the entry into certain wholesale energy products – both OTC and those transacted on an exchange – is required to be reported to the newly established EU energy regulator, the Agency for the Cooperation of Energy Regulators (ACER). The interplay between these reporting requirements and those imposed by EMIR is the subject of discussion although the regulators acknowledge that such regulations are not intended to impose double reporting obligations. In addition to reporting requirements, REMIT also introduces a market abuse regime for wholesale energy markets. The regime is based on that imposed under the more widely known Market Abuse Directive (2003/6/EC) (MAD) but tailored to the gas and electricity markets. Its purpose is to prohibit market abuse (ie, insider dealing and market manipulation) in relation to wholesale energy products. MAD is also under revision and will be replaced by the MAD II legislative package, comprising the Market Abuse Regulation (Regulation 596/2014) and the Directive on Criminal Sanctions for Market Abuse (2014/57/EU) from July 3 2016.

Under MiFID II, which is yet to be fully implemented, certain transactions, including commodity derivative transactions, will also need to be reported. Reporting to a trade repository under EMIR will also satisfy the MiFID II reporting obligation, provided that the EMIR report contains at least the same information as the report required by MiFID II.

In addition, similar requirements to those imposed by EMIR are imposed under the Dodd-Frank Wall Street Reform and Consumer Protection Act of 2010, otherwise known as Dodd-Frank. Dodd-Frank is the US equivalent of EMIR and is likely to apply where the hedge counterparty is a major swap dealer even if it is established in the European Union. Similar legislation exists or is in the process of implementation in most other developed jurisdictions. However, as progress on effective reciprocal recognition of the new derivatives regulation being implemented across the globe is slow, advice should always be sought to determine the relevance of Dodd-Frank or other similar legislation to any derivative transactions which are being entered into and whether there are conflicting or duplicative rules that may apply to either party to such transactions.

The author would like to thank Oliver Attinger, associate in the securities and derivatives group of Ashurst LLP, London for his assistance with this chapter.

Private equity

Anthony Martinez
Clifford Chance LLP

1. Introduction

Over the past several years, private equity (PE) firms have invested heavily in the oil and gas sector, most notably helping to drive the boom in shale and other unconventional oil and gas projects in North America. The excitement that many PE firms feel about the opportunities in the oil and gas sector was summed up by Blackstone's chairman and CEO Stephen Schwarzman, who claimed at the 2015 World Economic Forum in Davos, Switzerland, that: "Oil is the biggest investment opportunity in the world." Underlying this excitement is the view, common in the PE industry, that energy prices will recover. As Blackstone president Tony James told analysts on January 29 2015: "We believe the recent free-fall in energy prices will prove to be relatively short term, so we view this as a good buying opportunity." Accordingly, Blackstone announced that it was "scrambling" to raise more than $10 billion for investment into energy companies.[1] In support of this strategic view, Blackstone raised its second energy-focused fund, announcing the closing of that fund in February 2015 at $4.5 billion, the first energy fund having closed at $2.4 billion in September 2012.[2] Blackstone has not been alone in raising a huge war chest to take advantage of opportunities in the oil and gas sector. In October 2014, Warburg Pincus launched a $4 billion energy fund, $1 billion more than it had originally sought.[3] In December 2014, Carlyle co-founder, David Rubenstein, said his firm had around $9 billion to invest in energy, including its first-ever international energy fund, which raised $2.5 billion, surpassing its $1.5 billion fundraising target.[4] Likewise, Riverstone Holdings' natural resources fund is targeting $8 billion and held a first close in February 2015 on $1.5 billion.[5]

In 2014, a total of $17.5 billion was raised by PE funds for investment into natural resources.[6] According to Preqin, an alternative asset industry data provider, 52 PE funds closed in 2014 that targeted investments in the oil and gas industry,

1 Dana Mattiolo, "Blackstone's CEO: oil is 'biggest investment opportunity in the world'", *The Wall Street Journal*, January 22 2015; Devin Banerjee, "Blackstone 'scrambling' to invest in energy, James says", *Bloomberg*, January 29 2015.

2 Kanchan Kumar, "Growing opportunities for private equity in oil and gas", *HedgeThink*, April 1 2015; Blackstone Press Release, "Blackstone Energy Partners II is oversubscribed at $4.5 billion", February 23 2015.

3 Cripps Sears and Partners, "Is private equity funding the answer for the cash-strapped oil sector?", April 1, 2015.

4 Kanchan Kumar, "Growing opportunities for private equity in oil and gas", *HedgeThink*, April 1, 2015.

5 Preqin, *Private Equity Spotlight*, March 2015.

6 "Private equity reaches oil price nirvana", *Wall Street Daily*, February 18 2015.

either exclusively or as part of a wider industry focus. That year also saw the largest amount of capital ($39.2 billion) raised in the period from 2008 to 2014, surpassing the totals raised in 2013 by $6.2 billion.[7] PE investors' interest in energy is demonstrated not only by the amount of funds raised, but also by the fact that energy-focused funds reduced their average time spent on the road raising funds from 16 months in 2013 to 13 months in 2014.[8]

Figure 1: Private equity funds closed that include oil & gas investments as part of a wider industry focus. 2008–2014.

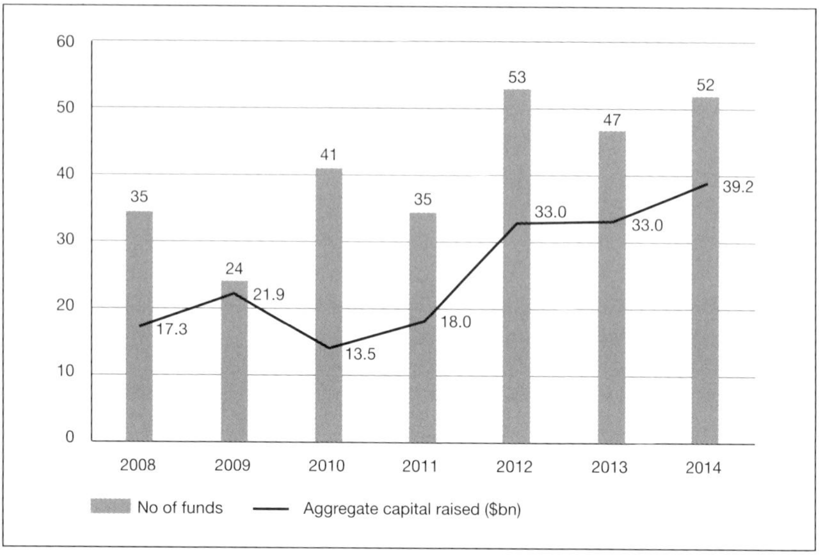

Source: Prequin funds in market

Of the total number of energy-focused funds, 76% were raised by specialist GPs, although non-specialist fund managers tended to close with larger fund sizes.[9]

While these figures are already impressive, many believe this is just the beginning. According to Bill Macaulay, co-founder, chairman and CEO of First Reserve: "There's been a big increase in private equity coming into the business, but energy is still the most under-represented business in the world in terms of private equity."[10] The size of these war chests and the important role PE has already played in the oil and gas industry is all the more remarkable when one considers that PE was hardly involved in oil and gas as recently as a few years ago.

7 Greg Roumeliotis, "Exclusive: Blackstone sets up new credit fund to seek undervalued oil and gas assets", *Reuters*, January 27 2015.
8 Preqin, "Outlook for energy-focused private equity fundraising – March 2015", March 24 2015.
9 Preqin, *ibid*; Preqin, *Private Equity Spotlight*, Volume 11: Issue 3, March 2015.
10 BerchWood Partners, "Global energy: the private equity opportunity of the century", 2013.

Figure 2: Historical fundraising by specialist and non-specialist fund managers.

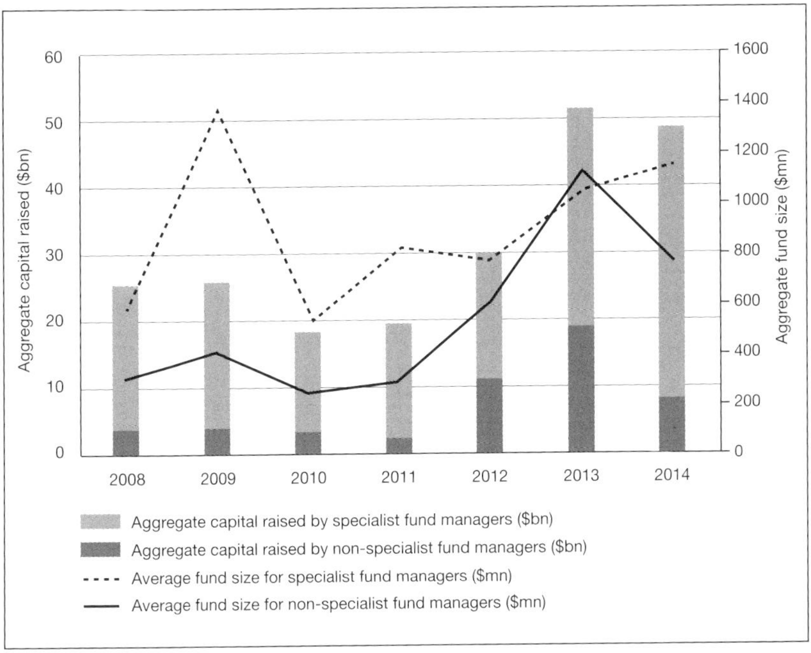

Source: Prequin secondary market monitor

2. The PE model

PE refers to medium-to-long-term finance provided in return for an equity stake in potentially high-growth unquoted companies.[11] However, usage of the term 'PE' varies. PE may be considered to be a generic term used to identify an asset class that encompasses a variety of investment strategies, including leveraged buyout (LBO) funds, venture capital (VC) funds and growth equity funds (see section 3 below). In Europe, PE typically refers only to LBO funds as well as VC funds investing at various stages of the portfolio company's development, whereas in the United States VC is typically treated as a category separate from PE and refers only to investments in early stage and expanding companies. Regardless of the stage at which PE funds invest, they generate returns for investors by increasing the value of their portfolio companies. In return, PE firms receive a fee together with a portion of the upside from the returns they generate for investors if they have been successful.

To complicate matters further, many of the largest firms typically described in the media as 'PE firms' now describe themselves as 'alternative asset managers'. Alternative assets are loosely defined as asset classes other than stocks, bonds and cash. Alternative asset classes include PE funds, real estate funds, hedge funds, solution funds, credit-oriented funds and publicly traded closed-end mutual funds, among others. This evolution of PE firms into alternative asset managers is a

11 BVCA, "A guide to private equity", February 2010.

reflection of the fact that the lines between various asset classes are becoming increasingly blurred.

For example, PE is generally considered to be a separate asset class from infrastructure funds, which are considered 'real assets' (ie, assets, which derive their value from their intrinsic characteristics, unlike financial assets, which derive their value from a contractual claim on an underlying asset). However, because of the growing demand by institutional investors for real assets, given their high correlation with inflation and low correlation with traditional asset classes such as stocks and bonds, it is becoming more and more common to see PE funds making infrastructure investments, and many such funds refer to themselves as 'private equity infrastructure funds'. For example, in June 2014, First Reserve, a firm often described as a PE firm, but which describes itself as a 'private equity and infrastructure investment firm', closed its second energy infrastructure fund, which was oversubscribed beyond its initial target of $2 billion, ultimately closing at its $2.5 billion hard cap, bringing the total amount of funds which First Reserve has dedicated to investing in energy infrastructure opportunities to over $4 billion.

In view of the growing convergence of investment activities across asset classes, in this chapter, the term 'PE' is used in its broadest sense to refer to any fund that makes an equity investment in an unquoted company, including:

- LBO funds;
- VC funds;
- growth equity funds;
- infrastructure funds; and
- distressed securities funds and other types of special situations funds.

2.1 Capital structure

PE funds have historically raised capital from institutional investors, such as pension funds and insurance companies. However, in recent years, PE funds have also raised capital from other sources, including public capital markets. For example, in 2007, Blackstone listed shares in its management company on the New York Stock Exchange in a $4 billion initial public offering. Regardless of the source of their capital, the fact that the largest PE funds have access to significant amounts of capital makes them one of the few types of investors capable of investing in capital intensive industries such as the oil and gas industry. Moreover, PE funds typically raise funds in the form of committed capital through a closed structure, which means that investors cannot withdraw capital easily, if at all.

2.2 Deployment of capital

The fact that PE funds have access to long-term, committed capital allows fund managers to make medium- to long-term investments through market cycles and to support the long-term strategies of their portfolio companies. Historically, PE firms typically held investments for between three and five years. More recently, however,

---

12 Jennifer Bollen, "Average private equity fund life span exceeds 13 years", *The Wall Street Journal*, March 31 2015.

PE firms have expanded their investment horizons, with Palico SAS reporting that the median investment period of a PE fund – across all regions and sectors – had reached 13.2 years.[12]

Each PE fund will raise capital from investors based on the investment criteria set out in the fund documentation. These criteria will establish the geography, sector, scale and diversification required of the fund. Given the sophistication of the PE market, there are a broad range of funds, from global funds with wide-ranging sector coverage to much more narrowly focused funds. Even in the oil and gas sector, funds may be global or local and can focus narrowly, such as Epi-V, a specialist growth capital firm targeting technology-driven upstream oil and gas services.[13]

The PE fund cycle will see capital invested during the initial period of the fund, after which the assets will be managed through to their exit. PE funds typically invest in private companies, taking controlling stakes that allow them to work with management to develop the business. The committed capital nature of the funds allows them to move quickly, calling upon the investors (typically, but not always, structured as a limited partnership) to provide funding on short notice towards the end of the deal process. Often, funds will be 'blind pools', in which investors make a binding capital commitment to the fund at the outset, and the fund manager is given discretion to call on this capital to make investments when attractive opportunities are identified without having to obtain approval from investors, provided the investments comply with the fund's investment strategy and any restrictions contained in the fund documentation.

A traditional PE fund will deploy its capital as equity into the portfolio company, although this will be through an efficient acquisition structure which may involve a number of different equity, debt and quasi-equity securities. As noted above, it is standard for a PE fund in a developed market to use acquisition finance alongside its own equity commitment to fund investments – the leveraged buy-out model. However, where debt is not available, particularly in emerging markets, the growth capital model will be used.

2.3 Returns

As with any other equity investment, the value which a PE fund derives from ownership of an asset can be broken down into two components. First, the cash flow that the asset generates during the period of ownership (eg, in the form of dividends); secondly, the capital gain realised upon exiting the investment.

For infrastructure funds, for example, the yield generated during the period of ownership will be the primary objective, with capital growth representing a relatively small component of the fund's overall return. In the oil and gas sector, infrastructure funds typically seek to earn steady, long-term returns from largely de-risked assets such as pipelines, which generate revenues from fee-based, long-term and, often, inflation-adjusted contracts. Producers with long-term offtake contracts may similarly generate such stable, long-term returns. These types of assets are attractive to infrastructure funds' typical investors such as pension funds and insurance funds,

13 See www.epi-v.com/about/ (accessed July 20 2015).

which seek stable revenue streams to match their long-term liabilities. In contrast, for the types of funds most commonly associated with PE, namely LBO funds and VC funds, capital appreciation usually generates the lion's share of returns.

2.4 Management

The PE fund will oversee its asset, but very few funds carry people with the relevant expertise to manage the day-to-day operations of a business. As such, they rely on management, and finding the right management team is, therefore, vital to the PE fund's investment. Regardless of whether the PE fund is using the company's existing management team or importing its own team, it is crucial to create the right incentives to ensure that the management team's interests are aligned with the PE fund's strategy. PE funds will look to develop relationships with the management team from the beginning of the investment process, and may strengthen existing management by bringing in someone well-known to them, perhaps as a result of having worked together in a previous transaction. Alignment of the management team's interests with the PE fund's strategy is almost invariably created by giving senior members of the management team an equity interest in the portfolio company together with other equity incentives, such as a ratchet or leaver provisions. These allow the management team to share in the upside of a successful investment and, conversely, to lose out if they are unsuccessful. The incentives will be linked to the business plan of the portfolio company, which will be prepared by the management team.

If, as is often the case in LBOs, the PE fund takes a controlling equity stake in a portfolio company, the PE fund will have considerable leverage over management. However, PE funds often take a minority stake, particularly in the case of VC and growth equity funds. In these circumstances, PE funds will have to rely primarily on their due diligence to ensure they have a good management team in place. PE funds' relationship with management may also be reduced in emerging markets, where the PE funds may be more reliant on the management team's familiarity with the assets and knowledge of the intricacies of doing business in that country or where the management team has established strong local relationships. This issue is particularly acute if local laws require a certain level of local ownership.

2.5 Exits

A fundamental consideration for the PE fund's investment decision is identifying the exit strategy and assessing its risks. Options include:

- public flotation (eg, an initial public offering) – in which the portfolio company's shares are listed on a stock exchange. This consists of a primary offering of the portfolio company's shares to new investors, typically accompanied by a secondary offering of existing shares of the portfolio company held by the PE fund and/or management;
- trade sale – in which the entire share capital of the portfolio company is sold to a strategic trade (ie, non-fund) entity;
- secondary buyout – in which the portfolio company is acquired by its existing management team backed by equity finance from a new PE fund and

often new replacement debt finance from new lenders in a further buyout transaction;

- break-up and distribution of proceeds – in which a portfolio company, typically the holding company for a group of diverse businesses (often non-core assets acquired from a corporate seller in a buyout transaction) is restructured, developed and then broken up by selling each business separately;
- portfolio sale – in which a PE fund divests an entire portfolio comprising a number of investments by transferring its shares in several portfolio companies simultaneously; and
- master limited partnerships (MLPs) – in the United States, federal law allows limited partnerships to be publicly traded on an exchange as MLPs, combining the pass-through tax benefits of a limited partnership with the liquidity of publicly traded securities. MLPs are limited by US federal law to enterprises that generate at least 90% of their income from certain qualified businesses, mostly relating to natural resources. Although MLPs are not a new structure (the first MLP was formed by Apache Oil Company in 1981), their popularity has grown in recent years, particularly for midstream assets. The cumulative market capitalisation of MLPs increased from $50 billion in 2003 to more than $450 billion by 2014.[14] MLPs are an attractive option for exiting portfolio companies that might be considered to be too small for an effective public listing and may allow the PE fund to exit at higher multiples of EBITDA (earnings before interest, tax, depreciation and amortisation) as compared with exiting through a public listing.[15]

Entering an investment with the exit in mind allows PE funds to adopt the best strategy for enhancing the value of their portfolio companies. For example, if a PE fund plans to exit by means of an initial public offering (IPO), then the portfolio company should be developed so as to maximise the value of the portfolio company as a publicly traded company. Conversely, if a PE fund contemplates the exit being by means of a trade sale, the PE fund will often have identified a set of potential acquirers and will develop the portfolio company in large part so as to maximise the value of the portfolio company to such acquirers. Understanding the likely exit route, therefore, helps shape the strategy for developing the portfolio company and allows the PE fund to maintain a disciplined approach to implementing that strategy.

2.6 Entry

While entering investments with the exit in mind is a defining characteristic of the PE model, the other key element in maximising the value of the investment is obviously entry, as overpaying for an asset will necessarily limit the potential returns it can generate regardless of how well the asset performs. Ensuring that the PE fund does not overpay also requires discipline and can be made more difficult if, for

14 Jared E David, "Investors flock to energy partnerships in new shale play", *CNBC*, April 3 2014.

15 Andrew Hawkins, "Creative exits: private equity in troubled times", *FINalternatives*, March 15 2013.

example, the asset is being sold by means of a competitive auction process or where there is a gap between the value which the seller and the PE fund attribute to the asset. This was the case, for example, in the oil and gas industry in 2013, when deals slowed because owners of North American gas assets did not want to sell at what they saw as temporarily depressed prices.[16] The same phenomenon has been occurring as a result of the oil price decline which began in June 2014, given uncertainty about whether the lower oil price is a new normal.

While at the time of writing there is an abundance of assets available for investment in the oil and gas sector, the number of good assets at attractive prices is more limited. In particular, although PE funds tend to prefer mature, producing assets because they are relatively de-risked as compared with pure exploration plays, which entail exploration and project development risk, the high demand for mature assets means they are likely to sell at a premium. PE funds may, therefore, prefer to acquire assets at an earlier stage of development if they wish to pay a lower price on entry. In circumstances where the PE fund feels that it has a competitive advantage such as a top management team with familiarity with the target asset or similar assets, the fund may be willing to tolerate a higher level of risk if this allows it to enter the investment at a more favourable price. For example, this is the strategy employed by Warburg Pincus' and Blackstone's portfolio company Kosmos Energy Ltd, which aims to create value 'at the drill bit' (see section 5.5(c) below).

3. Types of PE firms

PE funds use a variety of strategies to maximise the value of their portfolio companies. In addition to providing capital, they can contribute operational and strategic expertise, provide restructuring advice and use their network of industry contacts to find new customers, suppliers, partners or executives for their portfolio companies. Beyond these commonalities, however, the strategy employed by a particular fund will vary depending on its nature.

3.1 Leveraged buyout funds

An LBO fund will acquire an equity stake in a portfolio company using a combination of equity capital (from the firm's general partners and limited partners) and debt (in the form of acquisition finance).

Unlike VC or growth capital, both of which often involve minority investments in early-stage or growing companies, an LBO fund typically acquires controlling stakes, either alone or in partnership with other PE firms, in mature companies capable of generating stable cash flows. Generating cash flow is crucial to LBO funds' strategy, as it is required in order to be able to make interest and principal payments on the debt used to acquire the portfolio company. The LBO fund generates returns through a combination of financial leverage and enhancing the value of the portfolio company, usually by employing a combination of techniques, including improved cost management, streamlining working capital, facilitating new

16 Henny Sender and Ed Crooks, "Pain of private equity's TXU disaster fades amid renewed interest", *Financial Times*, May 15 2014.

partnerships, acquiring related companies or assets and combining them with the portfolio company and disposing of non-core or otherwise underproductive assets.

3.2 Venture capital funds

VC funds usually take minority stakes in potentially high-growth start-up companies. While the role of VC in the internet and technology sectors has been well documented, as the oil and gas sector has become increasingly disaggregated and specialised in recent years (see section 4.2 below), VC funds have played an increasingly key role in supporting niche market participants, a trend that seems only likely to accelerate as oil and gas producers focus on increasingly hard-to-find and hard-to-produce resources.

VC firms generally seek to maximise the growth potential of their portfolio companies by providing funding to support development of an untried idea such as a new technology or frontier exploration. They may also facilitate expansion of an early-stage business by introducing it to new partners, helping it recruit technical specialists or improving management. Because of the nature of VC investment, it necessarily entails a high risk of failure accompanied by potentially high returns. As new specialist firms have emerged in the oil and gas industry, the opportunities for VC funds are likely to increase over the coming years. For example, VC funds may play an important role in supporting new players in the enhanced oil recovery sector (see section 5.5(b) below). VC funds are also benefiting from the low interest rate environment of recent years, which is driving more capital to seek higher yields, even if this entails higher risk.

3.3 Growth equity funds

Like VC funds, growth equity funds generally make minority investments in developing businesses. However, the businesses are more mature than those targeted by VC funds. Typically, these portfolio companies will have proven business models and will often have begun generating positive cash flow. These companies often seek PE investment and expertise in order to help them scale up their operations and become more efficient. In addition, growth equity funds are often active in markets in which access to capital is relatively limited, such as emerging markets (where capital markets and banking systems are less developed) or certain niche industries (which may not receive adequate capital provision because lenders sometimes lack the specialist knowledge necessary to understand their business models).

3.4 Infrastructure funds

As their name suggests, infrastructure funds invest in public infrastructure projects, for example:

- pipelines and related infrastructure;
- oil and gas transmission;
- distribution;
- processing and storage; and
- electricity generation, transmission and distribution.

Infrastructure funds are by far the largest energy PE subsector, with over $240 billion raised since 2006, only a fraction of which has been invested.[17]

Infrastructure funds aim to generate steady returns from assets that have limited downside risk, for example because of limited demand elasticity, regulated income streams or high barriers to entry. While limiting downside risk is crucial to these investments, infrastructure funds can create upside potential through improved sourcing and by enhanced operational efficiency. Nevertheless, as compared with other PE investment, the upside potential is relatively limited. Infrastructure funds are, therefore, generally a low-risk, low-return investment. In this regard, it is important to distinguish between investments in existing infrastructure and those in new infrastructure projects. The latter entail project development risk, but may also provide greater upside potential.

Investment in new infrastructure has grown in recent years in response to the growing demand for energy infrastructure necessitated by increased production. For example, infrastructure funds have been heavily involved in financing the boom in North American energy infrastructure projects required as a result of the emergence of North American unconventionals. Analysis by IHS indicates that direct capital investment in US oil and gas infrastructure increased by 60% between 2010 and 2013, from $56.3 billion to $89.6 billion,[18] with infrastructure funds having provided a great deal of this financing. Moreover, demand for energy infrastructure is projected to continue to grow in order to support expanding North American production. KKR has estimated that $250 billion in capital expenditures will be required between 2011 and 2035 for gas infrastructure to service North American production growth.[19]

Demand for energy infrastructure is also likely to grow outside of North America in order to service the increased production required to meet growing global energy demand. The IEA estimates that, in a favourable scenario, the cumulative investment in gas supply infrastructure could amount to $9.7 trillion between 2012 and 2035.[20] Infrastructure funds are already particularly active in emerging markets, where the demand for new infrastructure is high, and this trend is likely to continue. For example, Blackstone and First Reserve recently announced that they had agreed with PMI, a subsidiary of the state-owned oil company Petroleos Mexicanos, to take an equity interest of approximately 45% in projects to build two new gas pipelines, known as the Los Ramones II Projects, to carry US shale gas through 744 kilometres of pipelines from Texas to central Mexico. These will be the first infrastructure assets to be built with a foreign stake since the energy reform law of 2013, which allowed foreign participation in the Mexican oil and gas industry.[21]

17 "Private equity in the energy sector", *Financier Worldwide*, June 2014.

18 IHS, "Oil and natural gas transportation and storage infrastructure: status, trends, and economic benefits", report for the American Petroleum Institute, December 2013.

19 Marc S Lipschultz, *Historic Opportunities from the Shale Gas Revolution*, KKR Report, Kohlberg Kravis Roberts & Co LP, November 2012, p5.

20 *Golden Rules for a Golden Age of Gas*, World Energy Outlook Special Report on Unconventional Gas, International Energy Agency, 2013, p88.

21 Cripps Sears and Partners, "Is private equity funding the answer for the cash-strapped oil sector?", April 1 2015.

While the midstream sector has historically meant pipelines, in recent years the emergence of liquefied natural gas has begun to create a global gas market, which is generating opportunities for price arbitrage as a result of the different prices for natural gas in various regions of the world that had previously been segregated and also the low cost of natural gas as compared with crude oil. As Blackstone's David Foley notes: "In commodity businesses where there's usually easy substitution, [it's] amazing to have that kind of difference in price per Btu." This opportunity is increasingly attracting PE investment. For example, in 2012 Blackstone invested $1.5 billion in Cheniere Energy Partners to help it build the first natural gas liquefaction export facility in the continental United States. The project is one of the first attempts to link expanded US gas reserves with overseas gas markets.[22]

4. Evolution of PE

The types of PE funds described above first appeared as a result of various market and/or legislative changes that brought about financing requirements that were not able to be met using the types of finance available at the time. However, although PE can trace its roots to the late 18th century in the United Kingdom and to the 1930s and 1940s in the United States when wealthy individuals or families such as the Vanderbilts and Rockefellers began providing angel investment to entrepreneurs to back their projects on an informal basis,[23] for the majority of its existence, PE has had almost no role in the oil and gas sector. The rapidly expanding role played by PE in the oil and gas sector in recent years is explained in part by the evolution of PE firms into alternative asset managers undertaking a wider array of activities, but more importantly, by the increasing disaggregation of the oil and gas industry and the corresponding demand for alternative capital to finance new industry participants.

4.1 Beginning of PE involvement in oil and gas

PE only began seriously focusing on the energy sector in the 1980s. First Reserve, founded in 1984, was the first, and is currently the largest, global PE firm exclusively focused on energy. Another pioneer in this sector was Riverstone, a buyout and growth capital firm founded in 2000, specialising in the energy sector, with investments in exploration and production (E&P), midstream, oilfield services, power and renewables. Warburg Pincus, a generalist PE firm which invests in several sectors including energy, was also one of the first PE firms to invest in the energy sector.

Other large PE firms, such as KKR, Blackstone, Carlyle and Apollo Global Management, entered the energy space relatively recently. However, once these firms decided to establish dedicated energy-focused funds, they quickly built up their own specialist teams and began raising substantial amounts of capital.

4.2 The new oil and gas landscape

The expansion of PE into the oil and gas sector in recent years has been largely driven

22 Lawrence Delevigne, "Private equity bets on energy 'revolution' – in oil and gas", *CNBC*, November 17 2014.

23 BVCA, "A guide to private equity", February 2010.

by fundamental changes to the structure of the global oil and gas industry. One of the key drivers in this transformation has been the emergence of national oil and gas companies (NOCs) as major players in the oil and gas industry. Until relatively recently, the Seven Sisters, a group of seven international oil companies (IOCs), controlled 85% of global reserves,[24] whereas NOCs controlled less than 10% of the world's oil and gas reserves.[25] In contrast, today approximately 86% of the world's known proved reserves are owned and controlled by the state or state companies of the countries in which they are located.[26] The corollary of the expanded role of NOCs has been the reduced availability of easily accessible conventionals (ie, on land or in shallow water) to IOCs and independents. According to IHS Energy, 90% of all known conventional reserves are now in production.[27] Moreover, of the 40 major discoveries worldwide between 2006 and 2011 with resource estimates greater than 500 million barrels of oil equivalent, 28 are in countries with active NOCs.

The growth of NOCs, together with the emergence of unconventional resources and rapid technological improvements across the oil and gas industry, has in turn helped drive disaggregation of the oil and gas industry. As NOCs have become increasingly capable of working either autonomously or in collaboration with IOCs (although on improved terms for the NOCs) or oilfield service companies (OSCs), IOCs and smaller private oil and gas companies, or independents, have been forced to focus on increasingly difficult-to-produce, more capital-intensive barrels, often with lower margins (eg, deep-water and unconventional plays). In addition, the larger OSCs have responded to the changing landscape by growing and beginning to perform functions which were historically performed by IOCs. For example, whereas OSCs traditionally provided technology services to oil operators, which managed the projects and selected the technology to be used, the largest OSCs now provide integrated project management services and offer contracts whereby the OSC takes on capital risks by receiving remuneration linked to a project's success rather than a fixed remuneration. In contrast, smaller OSCs are increasingly becoming specialists in providing technical services for certain types of reservoirs or for certain types of petroleum, such as shale. Finally, in many countries, national OSCs, which have so far focused on providing services to their respective NOCs, are likely to grow alongside their NOCs and may eventually expand their activities abroad, competing with other OSCs.[28]

As this evolution continues, private companies, which had already been differentiated by scale, are increasingly differentiating themselves by specialisation as well. Today, the oil and gas industry consists of NOCs, together with the following private sector participants:

- Supermajors – fully integrated, global players increasingly focused on large-scale, complicated projects in which they continue to have a competitive advantage;

---

24 Aaron Menenberg, "The death of the independent oil company is on the horizon", *EconoMonitor*, September 4 2013.

25 Jorge Leis, John McCreery and Juan Carlos Gay, "National oil companies reshape the playing field", Bain & Co, October 10 2012.

26 *Ibid.*

27 *Ibid.*

28 *Ibid.*

- Majors – fully-integrated companies that are often willing to invest in smaller projects;
- Midcaps and independents – non-integrated E&P companies with relatively few or no downstream assets, which focus on opportunities which are too small for, or otherwise unappealing to, bigger companies; and
- OSCs – service companies of various types, working with a variety of private and state-owned explorers and producers.

Moreover, the independents that have emerged in recent years can themselves be broken down into different categories. John Mitchell, Valérie Marcel and Beth Mitchell of Chatham House have identified three types of independents:[29]

- Lower-risk exploration companies (gleaners) – which acquire depleted fields from large companies and try to squeeze out some extra production with lower cost;
- Frontier exploration companies – which look for exploration licences in areas where the probability of large discoveries seems low or the fiscal and regulatory regime is uncertain owing to a lack of previous oil industry development; and
- Technology independents – a newer breed of oil industry player that develops technological expertise in selective spheres (eg, US shale gas specialists).

This new energy landscape rewards specialist companies and smaller, more dynamic companies of the type in which PE specialises in investing. As W Greg Dunlevy, a founding partner of PE-backed firm Kosmos Energy, explains:

> *Because major oil & gas companies and large independent E&Ps have reduced their exploration efforts during the last decade or two, small-to-mid-size independent E&P companies have a more important stake in the industry's future. They are free from the constraints that often hinder progress at larger corporations, have lean, flexible processes for getting the job done and are dedicated to value creation. We do not take it for granted that making acquisitions is the most expeditious and economical way to achieve growth in the energy business. It would appear that many companies, especially larger firms, take this view, which has become the norm.*[30]

The new oil and gas industry landscape, therefore, is composed of a broad range of businesses requiring investment across the entire value chain, thereby creating a wide array of investment opportunities for PE and other investors. As PwC observes, these opportunities are particularly appealing to PE as they cater to practically all risk profiles and strategies, from relatively low-risk, low-return infrastructure deals and mature companies with producing assets; to companies with diversified portfolios of producing and exploration assets requiring growth capital; to higher-risk, higher-return start-ups and pure exploration plays.[31]

---

29 John Mitchell, Valérie Marcel and Beth Mitchell, *What Next for the Oil and Gas Industry?*, Chatham House, October 2012.

30 W Greg Dunlevy, "Private equity funding empowers Kosmos energy", *Oil & Gas Financial Journal*, September 2008.

31 PwC, "The US Energy Revolution: The role of private equity in oil and gas", February 2013.

Figure 3: Private Equity risk continuum

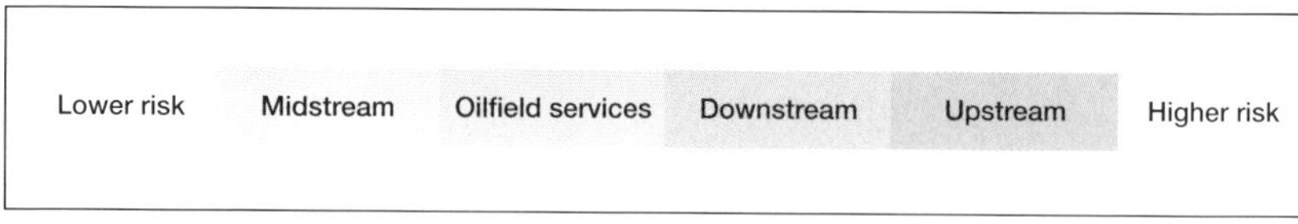

Source: PwC.

Each of these segments can, in turn, be broken down into activities entailing greater or lesser degrees of risk. For example, PwC argues that within the oilfield service segment, companies where service offerings are tied more to production than drilling face lower risk as they are less leveraged to commodity price swings, which directly affect capital expenditure budgets.[32]

Figure 4: Oilfield services risk profile

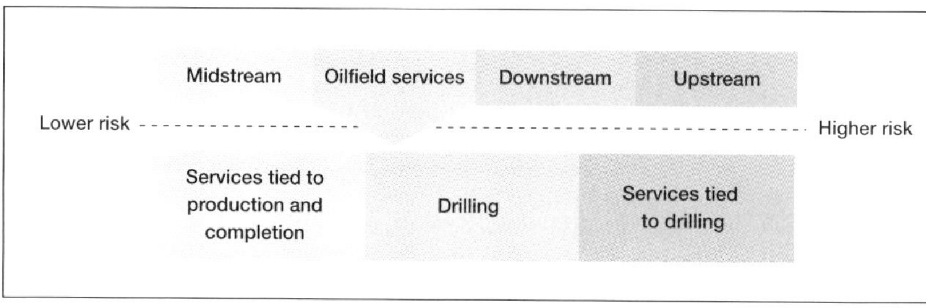

Source: PwC.

Moreover, the capital intensive nature of the industry and the inability of traditional sources of finance to meet the financing needs of new market participants has created a demand for alternative capital provision in general, and for PE in particular. Finally, the specialised, technical nature of the oil and gas industry fits well with the PE model, relying as it does on using sector expertise and top management teams to generate returns.

While the transformation of the oil and gas industry landscape has already created opportunities for PE investment, these opportunities seem only likely to increase as disaggregation continues. For example, in the short term, although even the largest OSCs are likely to continue to work on smaller-scale fields that are too marginal for the oil majors or beyond the financial or technical capabilities of other producers, in the longer term it is possible that OSCs could partner with PE or other alternative capital providers to expand their reach into assets requiring large-scale capital, thereby competing more directly with IOCs and NOCs.

5. Evolution of PE investment in oil and gas

The recent increase in PE involvement in the energy sector has been driven by the

32 *Ibid.*

growth of interest in upstream assets, and much of this investment has focused on OSCs. Until 2008, utilities accounted for the great majority of PE investment in energy. For example, they represented approximately 80% of the total in 2004.[33] However, by the first four months of 2014, upstream investments accounted for 65% of all PE investment in energy. The vast majority of this investment has been related to the North American unconventionals boom. This boom also drove considerable PE investment in infrastructure projects, which were required in connection with the growth of unconventionals production.

5.1 The land grab era

In the 2000s, during the early stages of the North American unconventional boom, PE firms made billions simply by acquiring exploration rights for gas fields, drilling a few wells and then selling them on to IOCs. Two investments by KKR were typical of this era.[34] In June 2009, KKR paid $350 million to acquire a roughly one-third stake in East Resources, a company buying up land in the Marcellus shale formation. Just 11 months later, East Resources was sold to Royal Dutch Shell for $4.7 billion. Similarly, in 2010, KKR paid about $400 million for a 40% stake in Hilcorp Resources, which owned roughly 100,000 acres in the Eagle Ford shale formation in south Texas. Less than a year later, Hilcorp Resources was sold to Marathon Oil for $3.5 billion.

However, within a few years, many PE firms suffered large losses, partly victims of their own success as the natural gas boom that they had helped propel drove down prices. To make matters worse, this price decline came as the United States entered into recession at the end of 2007. Gas prices, which had been over $15 per MMBtu[35] in 2005, began gradually declining and then crashed from $4.98 per MMBtu in 2011 to just $1.90 in 2012. While some PE portfolio companies were able to pivot from exploring for dry gas to producing oil and gas liquids before gas prices began falling, others were caught out by the timing and severity of the price decline as the gas that they were producing was often uneconomical to produce at these lower prices and generated insufficient cash flow to cover capital costs and debt repayments.

As Blackstone's David Foley observed at the time: "The land grab phase of the gold rush, where you could flip acreage early on, has largely passed. There will be more development drilling that will require more capital, and it will take longer."[36] Many of these investments were not particularly representative of the traditional PE model, which consists of medium to long-term investments and using successful management to create value. Rather, they were examples of opportunistic investments in assets that were appreciating as a result of rapid changes to the industry brought about by a technological shock. If PE firms were successful during this period, it was perhaps as a result of their ability to identify investment

33 Henny Sender and Ed Crooks, "Pain of private equity's TXU disaster fades amid renewed interest", *Financial Times*, May 15 2014.
34 Peter Lattman, "K.K.R.'s energy billionaires club", *New York Times*, November 25 2011.
35 Million British thermal units.
36 David Carey, "Private equity shifts shale strategy as land grab ends", *FuelFix* (posted by Bloomberg), March 21 2014.

opportunities more quickly than many of their less nimble rivals and, later, from the specialist industry knowledge they had acquired from being first movers.

5.2 The success of the PE model in North American unconventionals

While some of the most spectacular successes and failures of PE investment during the land grab era may not have been particularly representative of the PE model, many investments were successful and, particularly after natural gas prices collapsed and investors were forced to focus on fundamentals, many PE firms showed why the PE model could be such a good fit for the needs of unconventional producers.

First, as with production of conventionals, production of unconventionals is capital intensive. PE was quicker than many other sources of finance in spotting a huge new investment opportunity. Secondly, because production of unconventionals requires significant mechanical stimulation of the reservoir in order to allow petroleum to flow to the wellbore, it depends on technological innovation led by entrepreneurs, such as new drilling and well completion technologies. PE firms were able to play a leading role in identifying and financing these technological entrepreneurs. Thirdly, because knowledge of unconventional resources increases as more wells are drilled, thereby reducing exploration risk, PE firms were able to leverage the operational capabilities and experience of their management teams to increase efficiency and further reduce risk over time.

In turn, there were several reasons why unconventionals were an attractive investment opportunity for PE. First, the production profile of unconventionals typically entails less upfront capital expenditure, shorter lead times (although steeper decline rates) and quicker cost recovery (because exploration and production can occur simultaneously and because of the shorter lead times) than for conventionals projects, where significant capital expenditure is front-loaded in long exploration phases, but costs can only begin to be recovered during the production phase. Secondly, investment opportunities in unconventionals fall along a continuum from start-ups to growth capital to more mature businesses generating cash flow. Finally, as interest in unconventionals increased, a liquid market in these companies emerged, providing a wide array of exit options.

5.3 PE investments in conventionals

One effect of the growing interest in North American unconventionals was that North American conventionals began receiving comparatively less attention. The resulting availability of undervalued assets, particularly producing assets, created opportunities for LBO, VC and growth capital funds to enter investments at favourable prices. For example, in 2013, Ridgemont Equity Partners, a middle-market buyout and growth equity firm which had been spun out of Bank of America Merrill Lynch in August 2010, formed a partnership with Unitex Oil & Gas's management team and closed the partnership's first acquisition of conventional oil assets in Scurry County, Texas.[37] Unitex had been formed in 2003 to improve production from conventional oil assets in the Permian Basin by optimising wellhead operations,

37 See www.pintailoil.com/strategy/ (accessed July 20 2015).

increasing production by way of workovers and generally 'through the drill bit'. In 2014, Ridgemont also formed a new partnership with Pintail Oil & Gas's management team to focus on the acquisition and enhancement of onshore producing properties along the US Gulf Coast. As the company explained: "As many larger companies have moved toward unconventional plays, they are divesting Gulf Coast properties at attractive values."[38]

Similarly, in December 2012, Quantum Energy Partners and Global Reserve Group made a $125 million equity commitment to grow Gulf Coast Energy Resources LLC (GCER), a Texas E&P company, managed by an experienced management team, which aimed to use technologically innovative exploration techniques in order to increase the value of conventional geological plays along the Texas and Louisiana coastlines and offshore Gulf of Mexico. The $125 million commitment, together with the approximately $250 million of equity from the original investors (Warburg Pincus and GCER's management team), brought the total equity investment up to $375 million.[39] The funds were used by CGER to continue its acquisition, exploration and production activity along the Gulf Coast and offshore Gulf of Mexico and to develop three discoveries that had been made by the company. As GCER noted, its focus on conventionals was part of a contrarian strategy offering a window of opportunity for less competition and lower costs than the unconventional arena. By acquiring undervalued assets using the experience and industry relations of its management team and their knowledge of the Gulf of Mexico and applying seismic technology more innovatively (eg, by bringing offshore techniques onshore), the company hoped to create high-margin value through exploration and build scale through acquisitions of producing properties with viable, non-exploited upside and improve operational efficiency. This strategy of acquiring assets with a limited downside but potentially high upside was typical of many PE investments.

Often, conventional assets were acquired and folded into a company holding both conventional and unconventional plays. For example, in 2010 Riverstone Holdings and the Carlyle Group bought Three Rivers Natural Resource Holdings LLC, a Texas-based company that focuses on developing oil and gas in the Permian Basin in West Texas and eastern New Mexico.[40] The company, which was led by Michael Wichterich, the former CFO of Riverstone's former portfolio company Mariner Energy Inc.,[41] had grown rapidly by acquiring a number of energy assets from the Chesapeake Energy Corporation for $203 million in 2010 and Samson Resources for $344 million in 2011. In 2012, the PE firms filed paperwork for a planned $1 billion initial public offering, although this was scrapped when Three Rivers was instead sold to Concho Resources later that year for approximately the same amount.[42] The parent company of Three Rivers, a joint venture controlled by the PE funds, had

---

38 *Business Wire*, "Ridgemont equity partners and management form Pintail Oil and Gas", February 4 2014.

39 Quantum Energy Partners press release, "Gulf Coast Energy Resources, LLC announces additional equity financing", December 2010.

40 Mark Scott, "Concho resources to buy Three Rivers for $1 billion", *New York Times*, May 14 2012; Three Rivers Operating Co Inc registration statement (Form S-1) filed with the Securities and Exchange Commission on January 27 2012.

41 Claire Poole, "Concho buys assets of PE-backed Three Rivers", *The Deal Pipeline*, May 14 2012.

42 Mark Scott, "Concho resources to buy Three Rivers for $1 billion", *New York Times*, May 14 2012.

injected $270.7 million in capital into the company from inception to the end of September and had already received $60.1 million in distributions.[43]

The fact that so many conventional assets acquired by PE investors were situated in the Permian Basin is not coincidental and reveals a great deal about PE firms' strategy. In addition to being one of the largest producing oil and gas regions in the United States, containing generally long-lived reserves with shallow decline profiles, it benefits from having in place a fully developed infrastructure, and a large, mature group of oilfield service providers. This combination of factors means that the assets could be relatively de-risked as compared with other regions, particularly when a significant portion of future oil and natural gas production could be hedged against commodity price fluctuations, as was the case with Three Rivers.[44] However, these assets could also provide strong upside potential by leveraging technology and management experience.

5.4 Distressed assets

As with the crash of natural gas prices in North America beginning in 2011, the financial crisis and the decline of oil prices beginning in 2014 caused losses for many PE portfolio companies. However, it has also created opportunities for PE firms and forced them to focus on efficient asset management. According to Blackstone CEO, Steve Schwartzman: "I think this [oil prices falling] is going to be a wonderful, wonderful opportunity for us. It's going to be one of the best opportunities we've had in many-many years."[45]

The growth of independents and small specialist companies in recent years was due in large part to the change in the oil and gas landscape described above, but also to the availability of cheap capital and high oil and gas prices. As prices have declined, many of these companies' finances have been placed under stress, with the decline in value of their reserves often triggering covenant defaults under their loans. At the same time, these companies experienced reduced access to bank lending and capital markets as traditional sources of financing dried up as a result of the financial crisis and the more stringent capital adequacy requirements put in place in its aftermath. The need for these independents to be able to raise capital quickly means that they have begun looking to farm out stakes or bring in equity investors, many effectively putting themselves up for sale.

Some of these companies received investment from distressed securities funds, also sometimes referred to as vulture funds, which invest in firms with a fundamentally sound business model but which are undergoing difficulties for other reasons such as an unsustainable capital structure or reduced access to capital because of exogenous factors such as lower oil and gas prices or reduced bank lending in the wake of the global financial crisis. An example of this type of fund is the RAB

43 Greg Roumeliotis, "Concho resources to buy Riverstone assets for $1 billion", *Reuters*, May 13 2012.
44 Three Rivers Operating Co Inc registration statement (Form S-1) filed with the Securities and Exchange Commission on January 27 2012.
45 Deal Book Conference in Manhattan on December 11 2014.
46 *MercoPress*, "Hedge funds quietly investing in Falklands' oil exploration companies", November 1 2012. As at July 2015, RAB Special Situations Co Ltd had 34.2% of gross assets invested in the company. RAB Special Situations Co Ltd, RNS announcement, June 18 2015.

Special Situations fund, which owned more than 10% of Falkland Oil & Gas and which had 28% of its portfolio invested in the company.[46]

However, distressed companies also provide attractive investment opportunities for PE firms of all types. The urgent funding needs of distressed companies have served to underscore the advantages that PE has always enjoyed over alternative sources of funding available to companies, including bank loans and tapping public capital markets.

PE offers several advantages to companies as compared with bank loans. First, loan finance is subject to interest payments, whereas with an equity investment the portfolio company's cost of capital can be deferred until the asset starts generating sufficient revenue. Secondly, banks will typically demand security over the company's assets and guarantees from the company and/or its shareholders. Certain private companies, such as the smaller independents that proliferated during the years of high oil prices and widespread availability of capital, may have few or no assets over which to give security, and management teams are generally unable to provide sufficient guarantees. In many cases, the relative advantages and disadvantages of bank lending are academic, as bank lending may not be available at all since banks curtailed lending following the financial crisis because of higher capital adequacy requirements and a reduced appetite for risk, and as credit committees began to take a more cautious approach. Moreover, even if banks were willing to lend, the increasingly specialised and differentiated nature of the oil and gas industry has made the process of assessing and pricing project risk more difficult. Because there is a limited pool of banks with specialist oil and gas teams with the technical expertise and resources necessary to assess and price these risks, bank financing may be unable even to fund good projects.

Another alternative source of capital for companies is a listing of their existing shares and issuing new shares on public stock exchanges and/or tapping debt capital markets by issuing bonds. However, many of the companies that proliferated during the years of high oil prices have not yet reached a sufficient level of activity or do not otherwise meet the requirements necessary to allow them to list. Moreover, even if a company were technically able to list, the financial crisis brought about a slump in equity capital market activity in recent years and has particularly lessened investor appetite for companies with exploration risk. Finally, by going public, a company will be subject to greater regulatory requirements, making this a comparatively expensive and burdensome means of raising finance. A public listing also means that the company will be under greater pressure from shareholders to meet targets such as achieving production milestones in order to maintain their share price. These pressures may make it difficult for companies to pursue the type of long-term, disciplined or contrarian strategies that are often necessary to generate value, particularly in the oil and gas industry with its characteristically long lead times. In contrast, PE firms are able to invest for the long term. As Blackstone's Mustafa Siddiqui points out: "We are patient. We are not focused on quarterly metrics."[47]

47 Guy Chazan and Anne-Sylvaine Chassany, "Private equity seizes chance to expand oil interests", *Financial Times*, August 31 2014.

In these circumstances, PE is often not just a better alternative to bank lending and public capital markets, it is sometimes the only alternative. As Carlyle chief operating officer Glenn Youngkin explained: "The constraint used to be finding energy. Today, capital is the main constraint."[48] As in past downturns, the initial response of many companies has been to seek short-term solutions such as agreeing loan resets with their lenders and otherwise restructuring their debt in the hope that they can weather the storm and avoid fire sales until oil prices recover. So far, this approach has meant that PE investment has remained below the level one might otherwise expect given declining asset values. However, as prices continue to remain depressed and the need to raise capital becomes more acute, PE is increasingly likely to play the role of 'buyer of last resort'.

5.5 Investment in mature producing assets

In addition to acquisitions relating to distressed companies, PE is likely to expand its investment in mature producing assets as a result of a wave of disposals by IOCs of their mature assets. In addition, PE is likely to become increasingly involved in financing companies undertaking enhanced oil recovery. Both of these cases could potentially fit well with the PE model as they entail the application of efficient management and technology to try to enhance the value of under-producing assets.

(a) Acquisitions from IOCs

As with acquisitions from distressed companies, the projected sell-off of non-core assets by IOCs is likely to provide PE investors with a good opportunity to enter investments at a favourable price. Even before the decline in oil prices, IOCs were coming under pressure from shareholders to increase their focus, reduce diversification and cut spending in order to maintain their dividends. This pressure has only increased as a result of the oil price decline, as companies that had acquired assets during the boom years are focusing on their highest-return assets and looking to sell off non-core assets. IOCs are, therefore, expected to try to divest more than $300 billion of oil and gas assets in the coming years.[49] PE firms are already raising funds to take advantage of these opportunities. For example, in 2012 KKR raised a $1.25 billion fund to buy mature, fully drilled acreage that large companies no longer want to own.[50]

One area where IOCs are looking to sell assets, and where PE firms have been mentioned as potential buyers, is the North Sea. As a mature basin with declining production, the North Sea may offer a potentially attractive high-risk, high-return investment for PE funds that back the right projects.[51] "Look at the inventory of what's for sale in the North Sea," First Reserve's Will Honeybourne told the *Financial Times*. "It's massive."[52] The oil and gas consultancy, 1 Derrick, reports that more than

---

48 Henny Sender and Ed Crooks, "Pain of private equity's TXU disaster fades amid renewed interest", *Financial Times*, May 15 2014.

49 "Private equity in the energy sector", *Financier Worldwide*, June 2014.

50 David Carey, "Private equity shifts shale strategy as land grab ends", *FuelFix* (posted by Bloomberg), March 21 2014.

51 "Private equity in the energy sector", *Financier Worldwide*, June 2014.

52 Guy Chazan and Anne-Sylvaine Chassany, "Private equity seizes chance to expand oil interests", *Financial Times*, August 31 2014.

£6 billion worth of North Sea assets are already up for sale, with majors including Total, ConocoPhillips, BP and Shell already working on plans to exit their investments.[53]

One of the PE-backed firms operating in this area is Siccar Point Energy, a UK E&P company established to build a full-cycle, operated North Sea exploration, development and production business through acquisitions, farm-ins and the licensing of new acreage. Siccar Point is backed by Blackstone and Blue Water Energy, a London-based PE firm founded in 2011, and is led by Jonathan Roger, Centrica Energy's former head of upstream, and includes a management team with years of experience working in the North Sea. Other recent PE investments in the North Sea in recent years include Warburg Pincus' and Riverstone's investment in Fairfield Energy[54] and the acquisition of Bridge Energy UK by Spike Exploration, backed by PE firm HitecVision.[55]

Another PE firm that has expressed interest in North Sea assets is Carlyle. Carlyle International Energy Partners (CIEP) was launched in May 2013 as Carlyle's first international energy fund focusing on the oil and gas sector. The fund raised $2.5 billion from 160 investors, surpassing its $1.5 billion fundraising target. The fundraising represented the largest amount ever from a first-time fund in Carlyle's 28-year history and increased Carlyle's war chest for energy deals to over $10 billion.[56] CIEP is reported to be looking to take operating stakes in assets that have many years of production left, and is said to be particularly interested in assets in Europe and Africa.[57] As CIEP's managing director, Marcel van Poecke, told *The Wall Street Journal*:

> *We're really talking about mature oil & gas fields. The major European companies and the utilities are on the sell side [and] through operational improvements you can get to good returns.*

However, it may be telling that CIEP's first investment was not in the North Sea, but in Discover Exploration Ltd, an exploration company specialising in deepwater with assets in offshore New Zealand and the Union of the Comoros.

Although the UK government recently introduced a more favourable fiscal regime for the North Sea, including reduced windfall profit taxes and the introduction of an investment allowance, interest in North Sea assets has been diminished by uncertainties concerning access to infrastructure as well as massive decommissioning liabilities. When combined with uncertainty about the future of the oil price, these factors may make it difficult to price assets and to finalise deals.

(b) Enhanced oil recovery

Another possible area of focus for PE investment is in companies specialising in

53 Ashley Armstrong, "The flight from the North Sea continues: German outfit E.ON is selling off its North Sea assets as the oil price continues to slump", *The Telegraph*, March 21 2015.
54 See www.fairfield-energy.com/pages/view/about-us (accessed July 20 2015).
55 "Bridge Energy agrees £103m takeover deal", *Herald Scotland*, September 17 2013.
56 Will Kennedy, "Carlyle Group raises $2.5 billion for international energy deals", *Bloomberg Business*, March 19 2015.
57 "Private equity firms scouting North Sea oil and gas assets", *DealMarket Blog* (posted by alexander@dealmarket.com), March 23 2015.

enhanced oil recovery (EOR). Production of conventionals can be broken down into three phases: primary, secondary and tertiary (or EOR). Primary recovery, which uses the natural pressure of the reservoir or gravity to drive oil into the wellbore, combined with artificial lift techniques – such as pumps – to bring the oil to the surface, accounts for only about 10% of the production from a reservoir's original oil in place. As fields are depleted as a result of production, the natural well pressure decreases and secondary recovery techniques, such as water and gas injection, must be used to maintain well pressure and drive the oil to the wellbore, resulting in the recovery of 20 to 40% of the original oil in place. However, with much of the oil capable of being produced through primary and secondary recovery having already been produced, producers are increasingly seeking to use EOR to recover the oil remaining in place. EOR techniques include:

- thermal recovery – the introduction of heat such as the injection of steam to lower the viscosity, or thin, the heavy viscous oil, and improve its ability to flow through the reservoir;
- gas injection – the injection of gases such as natural gas, nitrogen, or carbon dioxide (CO2) or other gases that dissolve in the oil to lower its viscosity and improve its flow rate; and
- chemical injection – the injection of long-chained molecules called polymers to increase the effectiveness of waterfloods, or the use of detergent-like surfactants to help lower the surface tension that often prevents oil droplets from moving through a reservoir.[58]

PE firms have already begun investing in EOR. For example, Blackstone made a $700 million investment in Windy Cove Energy, a company formed for the purpose of acquiring and developing CO2 EOR assets in the United States with the aim of becoming a leading producer of oil generated from CO2 EOR from mature oil fields.[59] Another example is the $130 million acquisition by Morgan Stanley Global Private Equity's portfolio company Trinity CO2 Investments LLC of SandRidge Tertiary LLC, an EOR company with projects in the Permian Basin. The acquisition by Trinity, a Texas-based CO2 pipeline and supply company, is intended to combine Trinity CO2's strategically located CO2 pipeline and supply assets with SandRidge Tertiary's EOR operations to create a leading CO2-based EOR company.[60] Finally, KKR and Fleur de Lis Energy recently acquired CO2 EOR assets in the Powder River and Green River Basins of Wyoming from Anadarko Petroleum Corporation. The acquisition was the third as part of a 2014 partnership between KKR and Fleur de Lis for investments in producing oil and gas properties in North America.

The production potential of applying new technologies to known resource deposits was demonstrated not only by the explosion of North American unconventionals production, but also by TNK-BP and other companies operating in

---

58 US Department of Energy, "Enhanced oil recovery".

59 Blackstone press release, "Windy Cove Energy receives up to $700 million from Blackstone to acquire and develop CO2 enhanced oil recovery assets in the United States", October 8 2014.

60 Morgan Stanley Private Equity press release, "Morgan Stanley global private equity portfolio company Trinity CO2 Investments acquires SandRidge Tertiary for $130 Million", June 4 2012.

Russia during the 1990s. These companies were able to considerably boost production by applying western production techniques to brownfields that had been in production for decades. The possibility of applying EOR to boost production of known reserves could be particularly appealing to PE firms as this type of production would entail no exploration risk, but could have a considerable upside if the EOR techniques prove successful and if their costs can be reduced.

(c) *Pure exploration plays*

If the independents described in the previous section are the types of company which Chatham House refers to as 'gleaners', then one of the PE portfolio companies that has garnered the most attention in recent years, Kosmos Energy Ltd, typifies another of the categories in Chatham House's typology: the frontier exploration company.

Kosmos, a Texas-based international oil E&P company with a focus on emerging and frontier basins is backed by Warburg Pincus and Blackstone. The company was founded in 2003 by members of the management team of another Dallas-based international E&P company, Triton Energy Ltd.[61] This team included Kosmos' then-Chairman and CEO James C Musselman and chief exploration officer Brian Maxted, who had discovered La Ceiba oilfield in offshore Equatorial Guinea in the early 2000s.[62] After selling Triton to Hess in 2001, Musselman and Maxted formed Kosmos with backing from Warburg Pincus and Blackstone, initially with a sole focus on offshore Africa.

The Kosmos management team quickly went on to repeat the success they had enjoyed at Triton when Kosmos, together with its partners Anadarko Petroleum Corporation and Tullow Oil Plc, discovered the Jubilee field, the first commercial discovery in Ghana and the second-largest discovery worldwide in 2007.[63] Today, Jubilee is Kosmos' cash-flow generator in a more diversified asset portfolio, which includes existing production (the Jubilee field), major discoveries and exploration prospects for offshore Ghana, as well as exploration licences for offshore Ireland, Mauritania, Morocco, Portugal, Senegal, Suriname and Western Sahara.[64] Kosmos now combines primary exploration plays in frontier, emerging and established basins in deep water with secondary exploration of new plays in developing and mature basins.[65]

Like many frontier exploration companies, Kosmos' business plan is to use its experienced management team to develop a contrarian perspective, allowing it to sign up deals while governments are keen to license blocks and there is relatively low demand from other E&P companies. That first mover advantage allows Kosmos to acquire very large acreage positions with high working interests at low or no-cost entry with a long contract period, and favourable fiscal terms. In sum, W Greg Dunlevy, a founding partner of Kosmos Energy, told *Oil & Gas Financial Journal*: "Our

61 Interview of Brian F Maxted by Leslie Haines, "Kosmos' Cosmos", *Oil and Gas Investor*, December 2012.
62 See www.kosmosenergy.com/about-leadership.php (accessed July 20 2015).
63 See www.warburgpincus.com/investments/kosmos-energy-ltd/ (accessed July 20 2015).
64 See http://investors.kosmosenergy.com/phoenix.zhtml?c=238878&p=irol-IRHome (accessed July 20 2015).
65 W Greg Dunlevy, "Private equity funding empowers Kosmos Energy", *Oil & Gas Financial Journal*, September 2008.

strategy was straightforward: aggressively pursue success through the drill bit rather than by acquiring oil & gas assets."[66]

The decision by Kosmos' management team to partner with PE was one of several options which it had considered, and was based on the team's positive experience working with PE in the past. In particular, Kosmos' former chairman and CEO, James C Musselman, had arranged a $350 million infusion for Triton as well as follow-up investments from PE firm Hicks Muse Tate & Furst. According to Musselman, this partnership allowed Triton to sharpen its exploration focus, reduce expenses and restore relations with investors, eventually leading to Triton's sale to Amerada Hess Corporation for $3.2 billon, a 50% market premium.[67]

Given that Kosmos' exploration periods are from six to eight years, the firm's founders were seeking patient capital willing to look through the commodity price cycle. As Dunlevy explained:

> *A principal reason that E&P companies fail as start-ups is that funding and business strategies are inadequately matched, so we had to think through this aspect carefully. We investigated the public-company route, looking at London's Alternative Investment Market (AIM), which is targeted at companies with less than $100 million in market capitalization, but concluded it would not provide the long-term depth and breadth of liquidity that we required. We also believed it was premature to travel the public company route. Capital markets are often risky, but especially for an E&P start-up that must consider the fluctuating price of crude oil as an element critical to its success. When Kosmos was formed, crude oil was selling for about $30 a barrel. Because most of us had been management team members at Triton Energy, a public company whose exploration program was partially funded by the private equity firm of Hicks Muse Tate & Furst, we were familiar with the advantages of dealing with notable private equity organizations.*[68]

Warburg Pincus and Blackstone made an initial equity investment in Kosmos of $300 million in March 2004 followed by three follow-on financings totalling $1.05 billion, including an additional $500 million in equity funding in June 2008, making the company the first and largest private equity-backed oil and gas venture focused on Africa.[69] In May 2011, Kosmos completed an IPO on the New York Stock Exchange.[70] Prior to the IPO, all of Kosmos' equity had been provided by funds affiliated with either Warburg Pincus or Blackstone, as well as the management group and certain accredited employee investors and directors. Following the IPO, Warburg Pincus and Blackstone remained the largest shareholders in Kosmos, with funds affiliated with Warburg Pincus holding approximately 31% of Kosmos' outstanding common shares and funds affiliated with Blackstone holding 25% as at December 31 2014.

---

66 *Ibid.*

67 Kosmos Energy Press Release, "James C. Musselman retires as Kosmos Energy Chairman and CEO", January 3 2011.

68 W Greg Dunlevy, "Private equity funding empowers Kosmos Energy", *Oil & Gas Financial Journal*, September 2008.

69 *Ibid.*

70 Kosmos Energy Ltd registration statement (Form S-1) filed with the Securities and Exchange Commission on April 25 2011.

Notwithstanding Kosmos' success, PE investment in pure exploration plays, particularly outside of North America, has been relatively rare for the simple reason that even with experienced management teams and prospective assets, oil and gas exploration remains a high risk business. Instead, most PE firms have taken an approach more in line with the traditional PE model by acquiring assets which are already producing cash flow to minimise risk and aiming to enhance their value through better management.

Nevertheless, in recent years, as prices for assets generating significant cash flow, including producing upstream assets and midstream assets such as pipelines, have been driven higher as a result of low interest rates and competition from other potential acquirers such as NOCs and other PE firms, many PE investors have become more willing to accept greater exploration and development risk in order to have the chance of achieving higher returns. Demand for higher yielding assets helps explain much of the recent growth of PE activity in commodities in general and also in emerging markets, which often have considerable political risk, underdeveloped infrastructure and small national markets, all of which make achieving high, de-risked returns a major challenge.

Other PE firms are more sceptical. As Carlyle chief operating officer Glenn Youngkin explains: "We increase and improve production. We don't want to play a price game. That is speculating."[71] Indeed, there is anecdotal evidence to suggest that at least some of this riskier PE activity may generate losses in future years. With the long lead times associated with oil and gas and other commodities projects, it will still be several years before it becomes clear whether PE's sudden interest in higher risk assets was justified, or whether it will turn out to be nothing more than an expensive bet on commodity prices.

5.6 PE investment outside of North America

The United States still accounts for the vast majority of PE investment in the oil and gas industry. According to Preqin, between 2006 and 2014 there were 510 PE deals in the United States in the oil and gas industry, with an aggregate value of $102 billion, accounting for 57% of the deal volume and 65% of the aggregate deal value. The US share of the global deals by number has remained fairly constant, while its share by aggregate deal value has oscillated from as high as 88% in 2006 to as low as 28% in 2008. After the United States, the most active regions for PE investment in the oil and gas industry have been the United Kingdom and Canada, with 9% and 7% of deals between 2006 and 2014, respectively.[72]

However, there are good reasons to believe that PE oil and gas investment outside North America is likely to increase over the coming years. First, 86.3% of the world's total proved oil reserves and 93.5% of the world's total proved natural gas reserves are located outside of North America.[73] Similarly, while North America has accounted

---

71 Henny Sender and Ed Crooks, "Pain of private equity's TXU disaster fades amid renewed interest", *Financial Times*, May 15 2014.

72 Preqin, "Increase in oil and gas private equity-backed deals in the US 2006–2014 YTD" (blog post by Emily Forbes, September 26 2014).

73 *BP Statistical Review of World Energy*, June 2015.

for 99.9% of global shale production to date, and is projected to still account for 70% of production in 2035,[74] 84% of technically recoverable shale gas reserves are outside the United States and Canada.[75] Secondly, most of the world's projected energy demand growth is likewise outside of North America. Between 2013 and 2014, OECD energy consumption fell by 0.9%, reflecting EU and Japanese consumption decreases of 3.9% and 3.0%, respectively, which offset the US energy consumption increase of 1.2%. In contrast, energy consumption in emerging markets increased by 2.4%, which included consumption increases by China and India of 2.6% and 7.1%, respectively. Although emerging market consumption growth between 2013 and 2014 was well below its 10-year average of 4.2%, it remains clear that emerging markets will continue to account for the bulk of energy demand growth. Thirdly, although there are many good assets available in North America, competition from other PE firms and other sources of capital mean that North American assets may be comparatively more expensive than those in emerging markets, where there is often a larger amount of attractive assets with thinner competition, allowing investors to enter at lower prices and, therefore, achieve higher potential returns.

In emerging markets, there are also other demand-side factors that are likely to lead to increased PE investment. Given their comparatively underdeveloped capital markets and weaker banking systems, many emerging markets have a higher demand for PE investment and other forms of alternative capital than more mature markets. In part for this reason, many countries are starting to introduce legislation to make it easier for PE firms to invest. For example, some governments, including China and India, are introducing legislation that is likely to facilitate PE investment, such as changing rules on distressed investments. In other countries, both in emerging and mature economies, governments are making changes that may have the indirect, but no less significant, effect of incentivising PE investment. For example, the United Kingdom has changed its decommissioning rules to allow for easier access to finance and support increased levels of investment into the North Sea, although challenges remain.[76] In addition, returns on invested capital are generally higher in emerging markets than an equivalent project in North America or Western Europe to compensate for added risk.[77] Finally, the need for energy production and infrastructure to accommodate emerging markets' growing demand is huge, particularly in Africa. The World Bank estimates that African nations need an extra $50 billion per year to ease energy shortages and transportation bottlenecks. In part for this reason, Carlyle Group LP co-chief executive officer David Rubenstein believes that:

> *opportunities there are far greater than people thought years ago and the great explosion in private equity, if it's going to occur anywhere around the world in the next couple of years, is probably going to be in Africa.*[78]

Nevertheless, despite these advantages, PE investment in emerging markets has

74 Lawrence Delevigne, "Private equity bets on energy 'revolution' – in oil and gas", *CNBC*, November 17 2014.
75 BerchWood Partners, "Global energy: the private equity opportunity of the century", 2013.
76 "Private equity in the energy sector", *Financier Worldwide*, June 2014.
77 *Ibid.*
78 Jeff Kearns, Elizabeth Dexheimer and Devin Banerjee, "Carlyle Co-CEO sees Africa private equity 'explosion'", *Bloomberg Business*, August 6 2014.

not yet taken off. For example, PE investment in energy and natural resources in sub-Saharan Africa totalled just $747 million in 2013, the majority of which was Warburg Pincus' $600 million investment in Delonex Energy Ltd, a newly formed E&P company with a focus on Central and East Africa.[79] Between 2010 and 2013, there were just 27 PE energy and natural resources transactions in sub-Saharan Africa with an aggregate value of $1.2 billion.[80] The comparative paucity of PE investment in sub-Saharan Africa despite the numerous advantages the region offers points to the considerable challenges the region still faces, most notably political risk and problematic enforcement of contracts. As Dan Revers, co-founder of ArcLight Capital explains: "I can hedge interest rates. I can hedge commodity risk. But I can't hedge politics."[81] Moreover, this political risk means that PE investors will have to rely on local management teams, which not only have the requisite technical experience but also understanding of the practicalities of doing business in that jurisdiction. In these circumstances, the balance of power between PE firms and the management teams of their portfolio companies may be more skewed in favour of the management teams than would typically be the case in a traditional PE deal.

In other regions, the outlook for PE investment appears more hopeful. In Asia, in particular, there are a large number of small- to mid-sized 'junior' oil and gas companies run by skilled, entrepreneurial management teams staffed by oil industry veterans with experience working in the regional offices of major or large independent oil and gas companies. The demand for capital and partners willing to back long-term strategies means that PE firms may be able to enter these investments at favourable prices. A good example is Blackstone's portfolio company, Tamarind Energy. In July 2014, this South East Asian focused company with headquarters in Kuala Lumpur was formed with an $800 million investment from Blackstone. The company's management team comprises senior executives with experience across a range of basins in South East Asia. Tamarind aims to grow production and reserves from producing oil and gas fields, efficiently developing discoveries and capturing exploration potential in and around proven plays to build a high-quality portfolio and to build strategic relationships with host governments, South East Asian NOCs and key regional stakeholders.[82] Moreover, because many Asian NOCs have shown a preference for increasing their reserves through acquisitions rather than developing them themselves, particularly where reserves are located in Asia near the region's demand centres, PE firms are likely to have ample choice to exit their investments on favourable terms.[83] The emergence of smaller, more nimble companies in the region seeking to partner with PE firms has accelerated in recent years as IOCs have begun disposing of oil and gas assets across the region.

Similarly, Mexico may be a bright spot for PE investment as a result of the

79 Delonex Energy press release, "Delonex Energy announces $600 million investment led by Warburg Pincus to fund oil and gas exploration in central and east Africa", June 17 2013.

80 EY, *Private Equity Roundup: Africa*, 2014.

81 BerchWood Partners, "Global energy: the private equity opportunity of the century", 2013.

82 Blackstone press release, "Tamarind Energy and Blackstone Energy partners to form $800 million partnership with a focus on South East Asia oil and gas development", July 30 2014.

83 Jason Cheng, "A new leaf in Asia private equity", *Hong Kong Venture Capital and Private Equity Association Journal*, autumn 2014, p17.

sweeping energy reforms introduced by the government in 2013 to allow for private participation in the oil and gas industry for the first time since 1938. As noted above, Blackstone and First Reserve's investment in the Los Ramones II Projects to carry US shale gas from Texas to central Mexico will see the first infrastructure assets to be built with a foreign stake since the enactment of the energy reforms. Other PE firms are already taking advantage of the reforms to make upstream investments. For example, in September 2014, Riverstone announced a $225 million commitment to Mexican start-up Sierra Oil, which plans to bring new technology, such as horizontal drilling, to Mexico to access and develop low- to medium-risk oil and gas opportunities.[84] Mexico may be particularly attractive to PE because its oil and gas assets have similar geological properties to assets operated in the United States by PE-backed portfolio companies. In addition to reserves located offshore in the Gulf of Mexico, Mexico ranks sixth on the list of technically recoverable shale gas resources with 545 Tcf compared to first place China (1,115 Tcf) and fourth place United States (665 Tcf).[85] Mexico's shale gas assets include 343 Tcf in the Burgos basin, which is the extension of the Eagle Ford shale formation which has been so prolific in Texas. However, whereas Eagle Ford shale has been producing at high rates for years, it was not until April 2013 that Pemex announced Mexico's first ever production of shale gas from a test well.[86] The need to further develop these resources, together with associated infrastructure, should provide a good opportunity for PE to apply strategies that have already proven successful in the United States.

6. The expansion of the PE landscape

Over recent years, other private investment vehicles have emerged that perform functions similar to those performed by PE firms. In addition, as PE firms invest in increasingly larger and riskier investments, including those in the oil and gas industry, they are often partnering with other PE firms, other private investment vehicles and their own limited partners in order to reduce their equity commitment and exposure to particular assets. Finally, PE firms are increasingly expanding the activities they engage in, sometimes blurring the line between PE and other forms of investment.

6.1 Other private investment vehicles

An important trend that has emerged in recent years is the appearance of new types of investment vehicles that perform functions similar to PE firms. Examples include L1 Energy, an oil and gas investment company established by Russian billionaire Mikhail Fridman's Alfa Group to invest the bulk of Alfa's proceeds from the sale of TNK-BP. The fund, which is chaired by former BP CEO and Riverstone partner, Lord John Browne, and has an advisory team comprising experienced oil and gas industry executives, will be an active financial investor, but will not act as an operator. If PE is defined as medium- to long-term finance provided in return for an equity stake in

84 See www.riverstonerel.com/portfolio/sierra-oil-and-gas/ (accessed July 20 2015).

85 EIA, "Technically recoverable shale oil and shale gas resources: an assessment of 137 shale formations in 41 countries outside the United States", June 10 2013.

86 David Alire Garcia, "Mexico still far from tapping shale potential, minister says", *Reuters*, May 8 2013.

potentially high-growth unquoted companies, then L1 Energy is, in a sense, a PE firm. However, it is rarely described as such, most likely because it is an investment vehicle for a small group of investors rather than a firm which raises capital from large institutional and other investors through various funds.

6.2 Partnering with other private investors

It is common to see PE firms partnering with other PE firms to reduce their equity commitment or exposure to a particular asset or class of assets. Examples include the partnership between Warburg Pincus and Blackstone in respect of Kosmos Energy and between Blackstone and First Reserve in respect of the Los Ramones II project.

In other cases, PE firms may partner with other private investment vehicles. For example, when Apache Corporation sold its Australian subsidiary Apache Energy Ltd to a consortium of PE funds managed by Macquarie Capital Group Ltd and Brookfield Asset Management Inc. for $2.1 billion in April 2015, it emerged that Macquarie participated in the acquisition alongside AMB Holdings, the family investment company of mining heiress Angela Bennett, which took a 20% stake in the Macquarie investment vehicle, thereby reducing Macquarie's equity commitment.[87]

6.3 Co-investment

Often, PE funds' limited partners may wish to make an equity co-investment directly into the portfolio company alongside the PE fund. From the investors' perspective, the co-investment opportunity may be a convenient way of sourcing transactions, particularly in competitive mergers and acquisitions (M&A) markets where demand for good assets will be high. The direct co-investment may also improve returns and allow investors to manage their asset allocation more specifically, as well as allowing the investor to develop its relationship with the manager of the PE fund. However, in some cases, the PE fund may limit co-investment opportunities to those limited partners which have made minimum capital commitments to the fund. Co-investment has become particularly widespread in infrastructure, as many institutional investors in this asset class have direct investment programmes and increasingly expect co-investment opportunities. Nevertheless, as Brian DeFee of Capstone Partners observes, funds "need to bear in mind that [limited partners] are often overconfident of their ability to execute on co-investments in an efficient and expedited manner."[88]

A co-investment also has numerous advantages for the PE fund and the portfolio company.[89] From the PE fund's perspective, a co-investment may be an attractive means of raising strategic capital for a portfolio company because the PE fund does not need to cede control over the governance of the company to new investors and a co-investment may be a cheaper way of raising capital as compared with raising it

---

87 Joyce Moullakis, "Macquarie partners with AMB, Brookfield for Apache buy", *Financial Review*, April 10 2015.

88 Brian DeFee, "Fundraising in focus", The 2015 Preqin Global Infrastructure Report, 2015.

89 C Spencer Johnson III and Archie Fallon, "Private equity options during oil price downturn", *Oil & Gas Journal: Unconventional Gas Report*, March 31 2015.

from third parties. A co-investment may be particularly useful if rescue capital or growth capital are required. In addition, a co-investment may be appealing to PE funds in circumstances where a further investment from the PE fund would cause it to exceed its capital commitments or breach geographic concentration limits.

From the portfolio company's perspective, a co-investment may provide a broader shareholder base and access to additional capital. This may be important for portfolio companies with high future capital expenditure needs, as the investor will already be familiar with the portfolio company's assets and strategy. Accessing existing investors may also be quicker than raising capital in the market, which can often be important for companies undertaking exploration and production, as they will be operating under time constraints imposed by their licence. In addition, a co-investment may allow the portfolio company to avoid triggering change of control provisions in its licences, joint operating agreements and financing documents, although this will depend on the specific drafting of the relevant documents.

6.4 Direct investment by institutional investors

It is also becoming increasingly common to see large pension funds and other institutional investors of the type that traditionally would have made investments through PE funds investing directly into companies rather than through a fund. As many have observed, direct investment is a logical extension of co-investing, as large institutional investors make use of the in-house capabilities they have developed through co-investments. For investors with sufficient in-house resources, direct investment offers greater control over investments, reduced transaction costs and no external fees as compared with an investment through a fund. Although institutional investors may find it more difficult than PE funds to attract top talent, their lower costs mean that they are often able to compete with PE funds.

It has been argued that this trend accelerated following the financial crisis, as many large institutional investors came to realise that they had little understanding of their own portfolios, were overpaying middlemen and were working to different schedules, as the investment horizons of pension funds and other institutional investors are longer than those of PE funds.[90] For these reasons, a direct investment may be an attractive alternative to investing through an infrastructure fund, particularly in the case of long-term investments which do not require active management.

6.5 Sovereign wealth funds and other state-backed entities

Sovereign countries are very active in the oil and gas sector and are deploying their financial resources in numerous ways, both at home and abroad, often in cooperation with PE firms, but at other times in competition with them. Investments are not just made through designated sovereign wealth funds but in a variety of ways. This can be illustrated through examples of the ways in which the Emirate of Abu Dhabi participates in the oil and gas sector.

---

90 "In-house revolt: big pension and sovereign-wealth funds are cutting out the middleman", *The Economist*, November 1 2014.

In some cases, state-backed entities have invested in PE funds as limited partners or in PE firms as shareholders. For example, Mubadala, an investment vehicle wholly owned by the government of Abu Dhabi, has invested in the Carlyle Group,[91] and the Abu Dhabi Investment Authority (ADIA) has invested in Apollo.[92] As noted above, such investments may also give rise to co-investment. For example, one of the stated aims of the private equity department of the Abu Dhabi Investment Council (ADIC) is: "to establish a close and long-term relationship with a few truly outstanding [PE] managers and leverage these relationships to generate direct and co-investment opportunities."[93]

In other cases, states will adopt a more standard corporate model for developing business – often referred to as 'state-owned enterprises'. For example, the government of Abu Dhabi formed the International Petroleum Investment Company (IPIC) in 1984 to invest in the energy and related sectors around the world. In 2011, IPIC acquired 100% of the Spanish integrated energy company Compañia Española de Petróleos (CEPSA) and de-listed the company. IPIC now operates a group of more than 18 companies and investments across the hydrocarbon value chain, including exploration and production, shipping and pipelines, downstream retail and marketing, petrochemicals, power and utilities as well as industrial services.[94]

Finally, as noted above, NOCs such as the Abu Dhabi National Oil Company (ADNOC), which was established in 1971, play an increasingly important role in the global oil and gas industry. As NOCs expand their activities beyond their own borders, they will increasingly compete with PE portfolio companies.

6.6 Expansion of PE activities

In addition to new private equity investors coming onto the scene, the PE landscape has expanded insofar as traditional PE firms are now undertaking activities outside of the traditional PE model. For example, many PE firms have already expanded their investment horizons to fit the requirements of oil and gas production. As Andy Brogan, head of global oil and gas transaction advisory services at EY observes:

> *One of the things that's changed about private equity investors in oil is that they seem to be willing to hold things for longer – say for seven to eight years rather than two to three. Specialist PE investors seem to be more willing to take on exploration risk.*[95]

As was noted above, as good quality producing assets become relatively expensive in response to high demand from PE and other investors, PE is increasingly making earlier stage investments to create value 'at the drill bit'. However, while Kosmos Energy is a notable example of this type of investment, PE has generally taken a conservative approach to investment in the oil and gas industry, preferring investments in producing assets capable of generating cash flow with several possible means of exiting their investment. Nevertheless, as KPMG has

91 See www.mubadala.com/en/what-we-do/capital-investments/carlyle-group (accessed July 20 2015).
92 Michael Flaherty, "Apollo chief says sold nine percent of firm to Abu Dhabi", *Reuters*, November 7 2007.
93 See www.adcouncil.ae/BusinessFunctions/PrivateEquity/tabid/66/Default.aspx (accessed July 20 2015).
94 See www.ipic.ae/english/about-ipic/who-we-are (accessed July 20 2015).
95 Guy Chazan and Anne-Sylvaine Chassany, "Private equity seizes chance to expand oil interests", *Financial Times*, August 31 2014.

observed, if PE investment in oil and gas is to continue to expand with funding for earlier stage projects:

> *the requirement is for a reinvention by at least part of private equity into something more akin to venture capital with the potential to sell to other private equity funds as the projects mature. Whether this will happen and over what time period is unclear.*[96]

In the meantime, PE is already making investments that fall outside the traditional PE model. This includes making quasi-equity investments or using their credit arms to acquire distressed debt issued by energy companies and enter the debt refinancing space. For example, GSO Capital Partners LP, the credit arm of Blackstone, agreed in January to commit up to $500 million with five-year availability to fund drilling programmes on locations provided by LINN Energy LLC.[97] Under the arrangement, sometimes referred to as a 'project equity structure',[98] GSO will receive an 85% working interest in newly drilled wells, decreasing to 5% once the wells achieve a 15% internal rate of return.[99] Similarly, in July 2014, KKR's special situations fund provided Preferred Sands LLC, a producer of sand used to frack oil and gas wells which was 40 days away from a potential bankruptcy, a $350 million first-lien loan that pays a minimum 6.75%, a $300 million loan paying 15% (almost 6% more than the average at the time for the riskiest junk bonds)[100] and a $50 million asset-based credit line. Under the terms of the transaction, KKR also took a 40% ownership stake in the company.[101] The loans were underwritten by KKR's capital markets arm and investment bank Jefferies Group LLC.[102]

In addition, PE firms are now making quasi-equity investments through mezzanine debt funds, particularly in relation to North American shale plays. These investments typically take the form of either unsecured or subordinated debt with warrant or cash-flow participation or preferred equity investments. This type of investment has been increasing as oil prices have declined, although demand for this type of financing has not been as high as might be expected because many banks have been willing to make second-lien loans and some PE firms have been willing to do smaller deals.[103]

From the oil company's perspective, both project equity structures and mezzanine financing may be attractive in circumstances where the company lacks access to bank loans, but where the owners do not want to sell assets prematurely or raise equity capital at distressed prices.

7. Conclusion

There is no doubt that the transformation of the oil and gas industry in recent years has created exciting new opportunities for PE. However, several challenges remain.

---

96 Beth Mitchell and Anthony Lobo, "Oil: new rules, new game", KPMG, February 2015, p15.
97 "Linn Energy reduces 2015 oil and gas capital budget", *Oil & Gas Financial Journal*, January 5 2015.
98 Mark Druskoff and Hana Askren, "Room to maneuver: oil and gas M&A chatter abounds, but producers have plenty of options", *Forbes*, February 25 2015.
99 David Michael Cohen, "Lots of talk but little action except for private equity and Canada", *Oil & Gas Financial Journal*, April 10 2015.
100 Nabila Ahmed, "KKR seizing on banks' withdrawal amid leveraged-loan risk", *Bloomberg Business*, February 2 2015.
101 Nick Cunningham, "Rise of the vulture investing class", 'oilprice.com', posted on February 3 2015.
102 Greg Roumeliotis, "KKR to invest in troubled sand maker Preferred Sands", *Reuters*, July 25 2014.
103 Chris Sheehan, "Mezzanine moves", *Oil and Gas Investor*, February 1 2013.

First, even in emerging markets, where there may be less competition for good assets than in mature markets, PE may increasingly find itself competing for assets with other PE firms or other private investment vehicles, as well as NOCs, which are expanding their activities outside of their own jurisdictions, effectively becoming 'INOCs'. Many of these NOCs have a lower cost of capital and appear willing to accept lower returns than PE funds. Likewise, as state-owned OSCs begin acquiring greater experience, they may also start competing beyond their national borders. In these circumstances, the challenge will be finding good investments at attractive prices.

Secondly, in many emerging markets political uncertainties, difficulties with contract enforcement and underdeveloped infrastructure may make it a challenge to achieve attractive risk-weighted returns. This challenge may be exacerbated if interest rates rise, thereby necessitating even greater multiples to make these deals attractive.

Finally, in many regions, both in emerging markets and more mature markets, unattractive fiscal terms or other legislative impediments to investment may need to be addressed in order to generate sufficient certainty to attract PE investment. For example, uncertainty regarding decommissioning liabilities and the fiscal regime for North Sea assets may make it difficult to price and, therefore, finalise deals.

If these challenges can be met, however, there is good reason to believe that PE investment should only continue to grow in the coming years as the oil and gas industry continues to transform itself.

Export credit agencies

Clive Ransome
Milbank, Tweed, Hadley & McCloy LLP

1. Introduction

Export credit agencies (ECAs) are governmental and/or multinational agencies whose primary function is to facilitate cross-border credit (and therefore trade finance and, in particular, supplier and buyer credits). These institutions are most active in regions where commercial and political risks are relatively high and, as a result, commercial credit providers are unable or unwilling to make loans without political or country risk mitigation. Other institutions active in traditionally challenged markets are development finance institutions and multinational development agencies – these are briefly discussed below.

The primary goal of ECAs and multilateral institutions is providing credit to support exporters in the home country of the relevant export credit agency and, in the case of multilateral and development financial institutions, to support economic and social development goals in the country or region targeted for investment.

The credit crunch of 2008 thrust ECAs and multilateral institutions onto the global centre stage in relation to energy, infrastructure and project financing; the continuing slow emergence of developing economies at a time when commercial cross-border debt finance remains scarce results in these institutions remaining pivotal to major projects of all types in many jurisdictions and markets.

The Export-Import Bank of the United States (US Exim Bank) extended loans of more than $27 billion in 2013. Japan Bank for International Cooperation (JBIC) made loans, guarantees and undertook equity participations in the same year of Y4,240.9 billion – an all-time high. Commercial bank funding also suffered from the impact of Basel III on the capital adequacy regimes of many European lenders, reducing – for a period at least – their ability and willingness to extend limits and cover recourse credit. The post-2008 lending climate stands in stark contrast to that of pre-credit crunch years. During what has become known as the 'covenant-lite' era of 2005–2007 cross-border commercial bank funding was readily available; as a result sponsors of major projects in many jurisdictions went to great lengths to avoid involving ECAs and multilaterals in their financings. Sponsors' concerns most often were that ECAs brought an excessive emphasis on due diligence, environmental and regulatory compliance to projects, and that it took longer than commercial banks to obtain credit approvals.

On the other hand, ECAs are often perceived to be able to offer more competitive cost of funds and longer tenors than might be available in the commercial bank market for projects being developed in challenging markets. In times of high debt finance availability, sponsors often argue that ECA funding results in increased documentary and sourcing requirements, and stricter covenant packages, especially in the realms of coverage ratios, environmental and social issues, and bribery and corruption practices.

However, at present ECAs and multilaterals continue to be central to the financing of major projects across the emerging and semi-developed world.

2. What is an ECA?

An ECA is an arm or agency of a national government, created for the purpose of promoting or facilitating exports from that nation to other countries. ECAs are intended to promote employment and overall national economic well-being in the ECA's home country. By way of example, US Exim Bank was established by means of the Export-Import Bank Act of 1945; Section 2 of that Act states that:

> *The objects and purposes of the Bank shall be to aid in financing and to facilitate exports of goods and services, imports, and the exchange of commodities and in so doing to contribute to the employment of United States workers. The Bank's objective in authorizing loans, guarantees, insurance, and credits shall be to contribute to maintaining or increasing employment of United States workers.*

Similar provisions appear in the primary legislation establishing other major ECAs including UK Export Finance (UKEF), JBIC and Export-Import Bank of Korea (KExim).

An ECA might also be empowered to promote or facilitate national investment overseas and/or the exchange of commodities between its home country and other nations. ECAs are generally funded by the national treasury of their home nation. Virtually every nation in the world that is active in the global economy has its own ECA. In recent years, there has also been significant growth in the number of new ECAs – such as the Export Insurance Agency of Russia (EXIAR), which was established in 2011 – as well as the expansion of ECA activity into new areas of trade, such as investment in developed or OECD economies (historically outside the mandate of most ECAs). Examples of these developed market initiatives include UKEF's direct lending programme, Denmark's Eksport Kredit Fonden's (EKF) recent loan guarantee for debt to be advanced for the construction of the first offshore wind farm in the United States (Cape Wind) and JBIC's support of multiple projects in the United States in major oil and gas/LNG projects including Cameron LNG and Freeport LNG. In addition to expanding their geographic reach, ECAs are also increasing the suite of financial products on offer to include equity investments and project bond guarantees. Appendix 1 below sets out a full list of ECAs currently active across the globe. This growth in the number of, and offerings from, ECAs reflects their critical importance to markets and the robust manner in which ECAs have responded to the needs of investors and exporters worldwide.

3. Multilaterals and development finance institutions

Multilateral agencies and development finance institutions (DFIs) have some common features with ECAs; there are also key differences in their nature and primary functions.

Multilateral development banks are generally bodies or agencies created by international agreement or treaty among multiple nations whose purpose is to promote development among all, or specifically targeted, member states. These development goals normally target economic and social advancement coupled with protection of the environment and sustainability. For example, section 1 of Article 1 of the Agreement Establishing the Inter-American Development Bank states as follows:

The purpose of the Bank shall be to contribute to the acceleration of the process of economic and social development of the regional developing member countries, individually and collectively.

Unlike ECAs, multilaterals are generally funded or financed by contributions from member states through the multilateral agreement or other arrangement establishing the relevant multilateral.

Some multilaterals function globally, others have a regional focus. The World Bank Group is the principal globally active multilateral. The World Bank Group comprises:

- the International Bank for Reconstruction and Development (IBRD), an entity created in 1944 to help Europe rebuild after World War II. IBRD is the original World Bank institution and is owned by the governments of its 188 member countries;
- the International Development Association (IDA), a fund which targets the world's poorest 77 countries (39 of which are in Africa). IDA lends on concessionary terms, for long tenors at low (or no) interest;
- the International Finance Corporation (IFC), which provides finance (and financial advisory services) for public and private enterprises and was established in 1956; and
- the Multilateral Investment Guarantee Agency (MIGA), which aims to provide foreign direct investment into developing countries primarily by providing partial risk insured guarantees.

Other multilaterals function on a more regional basis. Examples of regional multilaterals include the European Investment Bank (EIB), the European Bank for Reconstruction and Development (EBRD), the African Development Bank (AfDB), the Inter-American Development Bank (IADB) and the Asian Development Bank (ADB). Common among each of these multilaterals is a desire to leverage their capital alongside that of the private sector, through co-financings or otherwise, while at the same time taking care not to displace or disincentivise private capital which might be available for a given use or project in the absence of multilateral participation.

While significant overlap exists, the range of ECA mandates differs widely depending on the home country and the policy objectives the applicable ECA was created to further or promote. By way of example, the US Exim Bank focuses primarily on the promotion of US exports, with each of its primary credit products being strictly tied to the US content of the goods being acquired. By contrast, Export Development Canada (EDC) provides funding that is not strictly tied to exports, with a focus that is more related to the potential benefit of the applicable investment to Canada (as measured by research and development potential, market share maintenance or growth, and the number of primary/lead contractor designations for projects). This broad mandate has allowed EDC to play a role in the financing of domestic infrastructure projects as well as overseas projects. Similarly, the Export Finance and Insurance Corporation (EFIC) of Australia has provided finance for domestic mining and infrastructure projects. Other ECAs have a dual mandate – to serve the home economy through the promotion and facilitation of trade and investment (the pure ECA purpose) while at the same time also having a developmental mission more akin to that of a multilateral (even if such a developmental mission is ultimately tied to fostering a trade environment that is intended to support the domestic economy). An example of this is JBIC, which in 2012 was spun off from Japan Finance Corporation and established as a stand-alone entity with robust backing from the Japanese government. Covering both policy goals, JBIC has the purpose of "contributing to the sound development of Japan and the international economy and society", and its credit products may either be tied to exports (to support Japanese industry) or imports (to obtain commitments of strategically important materials to Japan), or be altogether untied (to support overseas business environments to facilitate Japanese trade).[1] Through this broad mandate, JBIC has recently begun to offer untied financing and equity investments for the development of renewable and energy-efficient power projects around the globe.

There is a range of other official funding sources that cannot clearly be categorised as ECAs or multilaterals. An example is the Overseas Private Investment Corporation (OPIC), a development finance institution which is an agency of the US government. OPIC's purpose is to promote economic development in new and emerging markets through US private sector investment in a manner that is complementary to US foreign policy objectives. OPIC was established in 1961 by the Foreign Assistance Act of 1961; its purpose is to "mobilize and facilitate the participation of United States private capital and skills in the economic and social development of less developed countries and areas thereby complementing the development assistance objectives of the United States". Its authorising statute limits OPIC to participating in projects that meet specific eligibility criteria, including substantial US-person participation in the relevant project. Much like an ECA, OPIC provides two primary forms of support to projects: financing support, where OPIC provides either a loan guaranty or a direct loan; and political risk insurance.

In France, the mission of Promotion et Participation pour la Coopération Économique (PROPARCO) is intended as a catalyst for private investment in developing countries which targets growth and sustainable development. PROPARCO is a bilateral agency owned by Agence Française de Développement (AFD) and private shareholders. It finances operations which are economically

---

1 See JBIC's Profile: Role and Function, available at www.jbic.go.jp/wp-content/uploads/page/2013/08/35019/jbic-brochure-english.pdf ("JBIC has the purpose of contributing to the sound development of Japan and the international economy and society by conducting its operation in the following fields: (i) promoting the overseas development and securement of resources which are important for Japan, (ii) maintaining and improving the international competitiveness of Japanese industries, (iii) promoting the overseas business having the purpose of preserving the global environment, such as preventing global warming, and (iv) preventing disruptions to international financial order or taking appropriate measures with respect to damages caused by such disruption.")

viable, socially equitable, environmentally sustainable and financially profitable, and it tailors its operations to the level of a country's development, focusing on infrastructure and equity investments. PROPARCO's products include a range of financial instruments for private investors in developing countries, including direct loans and equity guarantees.

Another example of a development finance institution is the Millennium Challenge Corporation (MCC), an entity created in 2003 whose purpose is to provide large-scale grants to less developed countries to fund projects aimed at reducing poverty. Grants given by MCC fall into two categories: 'compacts', which are five-year grants for countries meeting MCC's eligibility requirements, and 'threshold programs', which are generally smaller sized grants awarded to countries that substantially meet MCC eligibility requirements (and undertake to fully meet those requirements). A final example is Clifford Capital of Singapore, which was incorporated in 2012 by a consortium of public and private sector entities to address gaps faced by Singapore-based companies in the project and structured asset-backed finance markets. Clifford Capital provides direct loans to offshore marine and infrastructure projects on a senior, mezzanine or junior basis as well as by making equity investments in similar types of projects.

Domestic loan incentives, subsidies and loan guarantees are available in certain countries for both domestic and foreign-owned investors. An example is the US Department of Energy's Loan Guarantee Program, established under Title XVII of the Energy Policy Act of 2005, which provides a mechanism for US federal support of clean energy (including nuclear) projects that use innovative technologies as well as investments in new and innovative technologies. Under this programme, the Secretary of Energy is authorised to make loan guarantees to support qualified projects. In Japan, the Ministry of Economy, Trade and Industry (METI) helps foster foreign direct investment into Japan. METI supports foreign companies by matching them with Japanese companies interested in establishing business partnerships, and by inviting and assisting individuals from abroad in establishing companies in Japan.

These programmes and entities, while not directly tied to exports or development, provide project developers with other options for officially backed credits where the requirements for and considerations of ECA or multilateral funding may not otherwise be met.

4. Typical ECA credit facilities

4.1 Guarantees, insurance policies and direct loans

Almost all ECAs offer credits in support of trade or investment which are tied credits – so that the amount and required use of the credit are limited to a maximum percentage of the value of the exported goods and services from the ECA's home country, plus related finance charges (normally interest during construction), or to the value of the relevant home country private sector investment overseas. ECAs typically offer these types of credits in the form of guarantees of third party debt and/or in the form of direct loans. Such home country sourcing requirements are in most instances the key factors when deciding which ECA to approach.

The calculation of eligible tied content of goods and services requires detailed preparation in conjunction with the exporters of goods and services sourced from the country of the relevant ECA. The relevant sponsor will often be assisted in the preparation of an application to the relevant ECA by the relevant exporters of such goods or services and by a financial adviser with working knowledge of the procurement rules and documentation requirements of that ECA. The criteria for eligibility for tied content varies from ECA to ECA. Common factors include:

- the source of the content;
- the timing of the shipping of content compared with the application process;
- the national flag of the vessel shipping the exported content;
- whether the content is sourced from a related party to the sponsors and, if so, whether sourcing is on arm's length terms; and
- the nature of the goods or service (eg, whether it is a capital cost, a finance charge, a contingency built into the contract value relating to the service or goods to be financed). In addition to goods and services sourced from the country of the ECA, a percentage of eligible local costs, such as onshore construction costs and operating costs (during construction), can typically also be co-financed by the same ECA.

Traditionally, most ECAs have not provided direct funding of projects and investments; they provide guarantees or insurance policies to eligible commercial lenders, which provide funding through covered loan facilities. A multi-sourced project may involve a number of covered facilities from different ECAs; the overall financing structure will normally include a common terms agreement and an intercreditor agreement binding all lenders (but not normally the ECAs).

The distinctions between direct loans and debt guarantees are exactly as the names imply. ECAs that are able to make direct loans are able to fund directly to project companies, in the case of tied facilities, upon confirmation that the proceeds of such loans will be used to satisfy (or reimburse the borrower for) the above-described sourcing requirements. For other ECAs, due to internal liquidity restrictions, direct funding of a loan is not an option – for these entities, the mechanism for providing official funding credits in support of exports is through the provision of debt guarantees (as further described below) to third party commercial lenders who provide loan advances directly to the project company. The Italian ECA – Servizi Assicurativi del Commercio Estero (SACE) – is an example of the latter type of ECA, insofar as its primary mechanism for providing export credits is by guaranteeing loans granted by commercial banks to foreign borrowers to finance Italian exports or civil works executed overseas by Italian companies or their foreign subsidiaries. Other forms of credit support offered by SACE include political risk insurance policies and the issuance of surety bonds on behalf of Italian suppliers.

4.2 Political and comprehensive risk coverage

ECA debt guarantees include both guarantees against political risks and guarantees against all risks – commercial and political (ie, comprehensive guarantees). Historically, political risk guarantees were the staple long-term credit product of many ECAs. This is because many ECAs supported private sector transactions involving the sale of goods and/or services from the developed country of origin to a developing and emerging market, where private sector capital has historically been unavailable due to its inability to absorb political or country risks perceived to be greater in such markets than in the developed world. While there are important differences among individual ECAs, political risk debt guarantees generally cover private sector lenders against loss resulting from:

- currency conversion, availability or transferability restrictions;
- war and politically motivated violence;
- prolonged strikes that are country or industry wide; and
- expropriation or nationalisation of the project or its assets.

Coverage can also be extended to include breach of contract or contract repudiation where the counterparty to a key agreement or contract in the relevant transaction is an agency of the host government (such as a state-owned power purchaser or a state-owned concession grantor).

Political risks that are not typically covered include:

- currency devaluation;
- increased taxes (except for breach of contract coverage of the type described above in cases where an implementation agreement or investment agreement between a sponsor and a host government exists and provides change-in-law or change-in-tax protection for the investor);
- legal system risk; and
- strikes that are not country or industry wide.

Some ECAs, such as the Export-Import Bank of Korea (K-Exim) and Korea Trade Insurance Corporation (K-sure), provide comprehensive products that cover both political and commercial risks, normally for major international projects. K-Exim provides guarantees to co-financing lenders to protect such lenders from any borrower default and, upon the occurrence of an event of default, will repay the co-financing lenders to the extent of their outstanding principal and interest then due and payable. Similarly, K-sure provides buyer credit cover, or export credit insurance, to banks lending to firms purchasing Korean-sourced products, which covers political or country risk as well as commercial risks stemming from borrower payment and insolvency default. Many comprehensive guarantees (whether for political or commercial risks) do not cover 100% of the co-financing lenders' commitments – co-lenders are often left with an uncovered exposure of 5% or more.

ECA debt guarantees (whether against political or comprehensive risks) generally provide for payment by the ECA guarantor if a borrower cannot pay scheduled interest or principal on the guaranteed debt as a result of any of the covered risks. In certain cases, the guarantee may be triggered by other, unscheduled payment failures resulting from a covered risk (eg, a failure to make a mandatory prepayment), although this is less common and it is generally the rule that such guarantees extend only to the stipulated covered percentage of scheduled principal and (non-default) interest thereon. Increased costs, funding losses and general indemnification obligations are not generally covered by ECAs. If a borrower defaults in the payment of a covered amount, ECA guarantees will often provide for waiting periods before payments may be made and then only require payment by the ECA to the guaranteed lender of the specific covered amount which the borrower failed to pay, rather than the payment of the entire guaranteed debt.

The fees charged to lenders for comprehensive cover or debt guarantees are usually required to be paid up front on inception of the cover as a precondition to (or from) the first utilisation of the debt facilities.

4.3 Political risk insurance

Political risk insurance (PRI) is another mechanism to mitigate political risks for the benefit of international investors. There is in addition a commercial market for PRI; many government providers encourage investors to look first to commercial markets before seeking to obtain policies from official sources. The primary source of political risk cover across the globe has, however, historically been the ECAs. These policies are similar to political risk debt guarantees in terms of the covered political risk events; the availability of PRI can often facilitate an equity investor's ability to obtain financing – whether from commercial or official funding sources – on more favourable terms. The policy goals of the ECA providing a PRI policy will normally dictate the extent to which such policies can be made available to the relevant investor, and many of the same policy requirements that apply to direct loan and debt guarantee products are applicable to PRI policies issued by ECAs.

4.4 Working capital facilities

Certain ECAs will sometimes offer credits for working capital facilities intended to be made available to potential exporters. The EDC Supplier Financing Program is one example where EDC will buy promissory notes issued to a small- or medium-sized exporter by a foreign buyer related to the sale of Canadian goods and services. Doing so reduces the risk of non-payment and increases access to cash. The EDC Supplier Financing Program is available for contracts with relatively simple payment terms and with repayment terms of up to two years. EFIC offers a similar programme through its Working Capital Guarantee Program that is extended to Australian companies seeking working capital funds to expand their business activities, but who are unable to obtain such funds on their own from the commercial bank market. EFIC guarantees the working capital obligations owing to the commercial banks extending funds to the Australian exporter or borrower, and the borrower is required to apply monies utilised to hire additional staff, buy raw materials, manufacture products or otherwise facilitate meeting the requirements of its international sales contracts. Another similar example of an ECA support programme is US Exim's Working Capital Guarantee Program. These working capital loans, made by commercial lenders and backed by US Exim Bank's guarantee, enable US exporters to obtain loans that facilitate the export of goods or services. Generally, US Exim Bank guarantees 90% of the bank loan (including principal and interest) with typical loan terms of one to three years. Exporters may use the guaranteed financing in a variety of different ways, including:

- to pay for raw materials, equipment, supplies, labour and overheads to produce goods and/or provide services for export;
- to cover standby letters of credit;
- to finance foreign receivables; or
- to purchase finished products for export.

US Exim Bank has also established the Global Credit Express Program, which provides short-term working capital loans to small business exporters. Through the Global Credit Express Program, US Exim Bank seeks to finance the business of exporting rather than specific export transactions, marking a clear shift in US Exim Bank's lending policy.

4.5 Other ECA product offerings

In recent years, ECAs have expanded the scope of their product offerings to include the provision of equity investments, fund investments and project bond guarantees. JBIC has been particularly active in this area, and now includes equity participations in qualified projects, guarantees for corporate bonds issued by overseas subsidiaries and affiliates of Japanese entities[2] and targeted sector fund investments as part of its current product offerings. K-Exim has also received parliamentary authorisation to provide equity investments in project finance transactions.

5. The OECD consensus

5.1 The arrangement

In order to provide for a common framework for the orderly use of ECA credits, and to provide for fairness as between sponsors for different jurisdictions in international trade competition (so that awards are based on price and quality of the exported goods and not on the terms and conditions of related country ECA support), the Organisation for Economic Cooperation and Development (OECD) in 1978 adopted the 'Arrangement on Export Credits' (the Arrangement), which is often referred to as the 'OECD Consensus'. As at March 2014, the participants in the Arrangement are: Australia, Canada, the European Community (all 28 member states), Japan, Korea, New Zealand, Norway, Switzerland and the United States. The Arrangement is a voluntary gentleman's agreement among its participants, with provisions for information-sharing and monitoring among such ECAs being intended to promote transparency and ensure compliance. A participating ECA may deviate from the Arrangement rules to match financial and other terms offered by another ECA, or the participants can collectively agree to offer a common line in relation to a specific transaction. In such cases, the Arrangement includes procedures to ensure consultation and agreement.

The Arrangement does not have the force of law. It has, however, introduced discipline into the marketplace and has assisted in limiting many of the more severe international trade distortions resulting from government subsidy. The Arrangement

2 See JBIC – Financial Instruments, available at www.jbic.go.jp/en/finance.

applies to ECA credits with a maturity of two years or more and establishes:

- minimum down payment requirements on supported sales of goods and services;
- maximum permitted levels of support for export and local costs;
- maximum principal repayment periods;
- required commencement dates for repayment of principal;
- minimum interest rates; and
- minimum risk-based premium fees.

The basic rules of the Arrangement require that:

- the first principal repayment and the first payment of interest must occur within six months of the starting point of credit;
- interest ceases to be capitalised after the starting point of credit;
- (subject to limited exceptions) equal instalments of principal in respect of the credit are repaid no less frequently than every six months;
- interest is repaid no less frequently than every six months; and
- the credit has a maximum weighted average life not to exceed:
    - in the case of exports to sovereign buyers (or exports guaranteed by a sovereign), four-and-a-half years where the export destination is a high income country and five-and-a-quarter years where the export destination is a non-high income country;
    - in the case of exports to non-sovereign buyers which are not guaranteed by a sovereign, five years where the export destination is a high income country and six years where the export destination is a non-high income country;
    - in the case of non-nuclear power plants (regardless of whether a sovereign is involved and regardless of the country of destination), six-and-a-quarter years; and
    - in the case of nuclear power plants (regardless of whether a sovereign is involved and regardless of the country of destination), nine years.

Additionally, the Arrangement allows on an exceptional and duly justified basis export credits to be provided on terms different from those described above.

The Arrangement:

- requires a minimum 15% down payment on supported sales of goods and services;
- limits the covered percentage of an export to 85% of the related export contract value (including third country supply but exclusive of local content); and
- allows for support of local costs associated with the export (up to 30% of the value of the export contract, with prior notification to other participants if such support for local content exceeds 15% of the export contract value).

The Arrangement stipulates that the maximum principal repayment period is five years for exports to high income countries (with the possibility of extending to eight-and-a-half years if prior notification requirements are followed) and 10 years for exports to non-high income countries. However, for exports relating to non-nuclear power plants the maximum principal repayment period is 12 years and for exports relating to nuclear power plants the maximum principal repayment period is 18 years.

The rules for nuclear power plants were added to the Arrangement in 2010. The maximum repayment period for credits extended in respect of the initial nuclear fuel load is four years from delivery, with credits in respect of subsequent re-loads having a maximum repayment period of two years from delivery. Additionally, the maximum repayment term for credits relating to spent fuel disposal is two years, and the maximum repayment term for credits in respect of fuel enrichment or other fuel management is five years.

Over the years, OECD ECAs came to recognise that certain of the Arrangement rules were not easy to comply with in relation to limited recourse project financings. As a consequence, revisions to the basic Arrangement rules described above have been implemented for limited recourse project financings in order to allow an OECD ECA more flexibility in structuring the first principal repayment date, the maximum principal repayment term and the overall principal repayment profile, to mirror more closely the cash flows applicable under limited recourse project financings. The limited recourse project financing regime allows an OECD ECA to offer a project company a maximum repayment term of 14 years, together with repayments of principal that are less frequent than semiannual and are in uneven amounts (such that mortgage-style amortisation would be permissible), so long as:

- the weighted average life of the export credit is no longer than seven-and-a-quarter years;
- the first repayment of principal due is within two years of the starting point of credit; and
- no single principal repayment or series of principal repayments within any six-month period is more than 25% of the principal sum of the credit.

5.2 Starting point of credit

The 'starting point of credit' referred to in the Arrangement will vary depending on the nature of the transaction being financed. In pure export transactions, the credit period generally starts at the time of delivery of goods. In the case of projects involving a turnkey construction arrangement, the starting point of credit may be the day on which care, custody and control of the project is handed over to the project company. In projects where the importer is obliged to assemble and commission the equipment, the starting point of credit may be the day the equipment is ready for commissioning.

5.3 Commercial interest reference rate

The Arrangement additionally sets minimum interest rates to be charged by OECD ECAs. In general, OECD ECAs providing fixed-rate export credits are required to fix interest rates at a level not less than the 'commercial interest reference rate' (CIRR rate) applicable to the currency in which the ECA credit is denominated. The CIRR rate is established for each currency of the participants to the Arrangement and is reset monthly. The CIRR rate may also be established for a non-participating country currency. According to the Arrangement, the CIRR rate should represent the current fixed rate of interest which corresponds, as closely as possible, to the fixed rate charged by commercial lenders to first-class borrowers in the country in question. Each OECD ECA is required to designate one of two base rates for its CIRR rate, either:

- the three-year government bond yield for credits having a repayment term of up to five years, the five-year government bond yield for credits having a repayment term of up to eight-and-a-half years and the seven-year government bond yield for credits having a repayment term in excess of eight-and-a-half years; or
- the five-year government bond yield for credits of all maturities. A 100-basis point margin is added to the applicable base rate in order to arrive at the applicable ECA's CIRR rate.

For repayment terms in excess of 12 years a surcharge of 20 basis points is added. OECD ECAs are not precluded by the Arrangement from offering support for floating rate export loans, and frequently do so, but may not offer support based on the lower of a fixed CIRR rate and a short-term floating rate. Finally, the Arrangement sets minimum risk premia which may be charged by OECD ECAs based on objective criteria relating to the country that is the export destination.

Although the Arrangement is designed to ensure level pricing across participating ECAs, those ECAs that are able to provide direct lending have a potential advantage over those which simply issue loan guarantees that support loans from banks with higher funding costs than the sovereign cost of funds of the ECAs themselves.

5.4 Helsinki Package

In 1991 the participants to the Arrangement agreed to the 'Helsinki Package' of rules regarding the use of tied aid. 'Tied aid' is governmental support which is tied to trade and may take the form of financing provided by ECAs or their governments on concessionary terms that oblige the recipient to procure goods or services from the provider country. 'Untied aid' is aid which includes loans or grants whose proceeds are available to finance procurement from any country, the use of which is outside the terms of the Arrangement. Tied support may take the form of credits or grants. Although part of the overall Arrangement, the Helsinki Package of rules deals specifically with tied aid or government support.

There are two key tests of project eligibility for tied aid. The first is whether the project lacks capacity to generate cash flow sufficient to cover operating costs and to service the debt. The second is whether it is reasonable to conclude that it is unlikely that the project can be financed on market terms. The Helsinki Package also established baseline rules precluding the granting of any tied aid to high income nations and established minimum levels of concessionality. Under the Agreement, the participants are prohibited from providing tied aid that has a concessionality level of less than 35%, or 50% if the beneficiary country is a least developed country. Concessionality relates to the value of the subsidy being provided for any individual loan. If a country receives a grant of $50 million for a $100 million project, the concessionality level would be 50%; a grant of $35 million combined with traditional export credit for the remaining $65 million would result in a concessionality level of 35%.

In 2005 Ex Ante Guidance for Tied Aid was issued in relation to the two tests of project eligibility for tied aid originally established in the Helsinki Package. In addition to the two key tests of project eligibility for tied aid described above, the Ex Ante Guidance provides specific guidance and recommendations for various types of projects, including power plants, transmission facilities, transportation projects and manufacturing facilities.

5.5 Berne Union and the Prague Club

The International Union of Credit and Investment Insurance (otherwise known as the Berne Union) is made up of public and private providers of export credit and investment insurance. The association works closely with the OECD and the World Bank. It is an international, non-profit organisation dedicated to facilitating worldwide cross-border trade and investments by fostering international acceptance of sound principles in export credits and investments insurance, and by providing a forum for professional exchanges among its members.[3] The Berne Union promotes uniform principles for export credit and investment insurance through organised meetings of members, ad hoc seminars and workshops, and the exchange of information and experiences among the insurers. In accordance with the message included in its Value Statement, members of the Berne Union declare their commitment to operate in a financially responsible manner, to be respectful of the environment and to demonstrate high ethical values.

The Prague Club is another ad hoc group of relevance. It is made up of insurers in the public sector who do not meet the entrance requirements for the Berne Union but broadly share the same goals. The aim of the Prague Club is to work out an information exchange forum for newly established credit and investment agencies as well as encouraging international trade development by supporting unified rules both for export credit insurances and foreign investments. A number of Prague Club members have gone on to meet the requirements for full Berne Union membership, but remain active members of the Prague Club.

6. Loan structures

6.1 A and B loan structures

Co-financings of loans among commercial banks and multilaterals have become standard in the project finance market. While in many cases multilaterals and commercial banks will lend side by side, certain multilaterals have developed A and B loan structures which allow such multilaterals to leverage available liquidity from commercial banks while acting as lender-of-record on the loan. EBRD, IFC and the

3 See Value Statement of Berne Union, available at www.berneunion.org/about-the-berne-union/our-principles/.

IADB, for example, have structured their B loan programmes so that they enter into a loan agreement with the borrower in relation to a particular project, but then enter into a participation agreement with a syndicate of commercial banks which provides liquidity for a portion of such loan called the 'B loan'. Under this type of structure, EBRD/IFC/IADB administers the loan and collects all payments from the borrower, while also committing to distribute payments pro rata between itself and the commercial banks. This structure has the benefit of allowing the multilateral to commit more funds to a project in order to achieve its development priorities, while also providing participating banks with the ability to hold an economic interest in loans that are effectively being administered by the multilateral. B loan lenders are provided with limited voting and contractual rights in B loan structures, but practical protection is provided to B loan lenders simply by lending alongside a multilateral.

Commercial bank lenders often take practical comfort from the participation of multilaterals in the financing of a project. Finance documentation normally, however, contains explicit provisions excluding any inference that such multilaterals are acting in any type of governmental capacity. Commercial banks involved in multi-sourced projects are often required to acknowledge that they have entered into the transaction exercising their own credit judgement and without reliance on the decisions taken by the co-financers (similar to the acknowledgement given by the participating banks to an agent bank) and any non-express responsibility or duty on the part of the multilateral to the commercial banks is excluded.

6.2 Preferred creditor status

An issue has arisen over the past two years in relation to multilateral agencies which enjoy preferred creditor status. Multilaterals with preferred creditor status enjoy preferential access to foreign exchange from member governments if the host country experiences a foreign exchange crisis. These multilaterals are excluded from general country debt restructurings and are not subject to new money obligations under any restructurings. Preferred creditor status also typically exempts the relevant multilateral from in-country taxation, including in respect of withholding taxes. In most cases, preferred creditor status is recognised as a matter of practice, rather than as a matter of law.

The general rule in multi-sourced financings is that available cash in the event of partial payment default is shared between all lenders equally. Preferred creditor status creates an exception to this rule. Some ECAs and commercial lenders take the view that the involvement of multilaterals with preferred creditor status leaves them at a disadvantage to the extent that the multilateral does not pass along the benefit of its preferential access to foreign exchange to the other lenders in the financing group. In a sovereign default scenario, for example, the concern of ECAs is that they will not be treated equally with multilaterals and will remain exposed to foreign exchange risk and thus payment risk while entities benefiting from preferred creditor status will be given preferential access to foreign currency (and, in turn, the opportunity for debt repayment). While preferred creditor status regimes are an innovative means for attracting investment in the world's least developed nations, lenders (including ECAs) participating in financings side-by-side with multilaterals that benefit from preferred creditor status often seek a balanced approach in order to maintain consistent risk profiles and ensure equal treatment among all lending groups to the greatest extent possible.

7. Common funding issues

7.1 Documentation

Much of the documentation for an ECA or multilateral-funded loan will appear familiar to those who are experienced in traditional project financing structures. In a direct loan context, the lending institution will enter into a credit agreement with the borrower which will set forth the basic terms and conditions relating to the loan. Most institutions have their own form of loan agreement or rely heavily on precedents from prior transactions, although the documentation requirements and reliance on precedent may differ substantially from institution to institution. The extent to which ECAs and multilaterals will agree to covenant packages which are common among commercial lending institutions in their loan documents will vary, although (as further discussed below) there has recently been a trend where certain agencies have become more and more comfortable looking to the commercial markets for guidance on covenant packages. ECA and multilateral documentation normally contains extensive environmental and social and anti-corruption/bribery commitments. Where ECAs and multilaterals subscribe to a common covenant package with other lenders, the substance of such environmental and social and anti-corruption/bribery provisions normally appear for the benefit of all lenders in the common terms documentation.

Multi-sourced financing facilities are normally structured around a common terms agreement. This sets out common conditions, representations, covenants, and other loan terms and conditions which apply to each of the loans being extended to the project company. Separate loan agreements will be required in relation to each facility. These include terms and conditions that are specific to such facility, including in relation to pricing, tenor, yield protection, and other specific covenants and events of default. Harmonising the different requirements of each loan facility and ensuring that each individual agency's requirements have been addressed in a manner that is satisfactory to the project company and the other lenders in the transaction is a key concern for all parties. Where A or B loan structures are used, negotiations often occur between the B lenders and the relevant agency to ensure acceptable voting rights for each of the applicable credit providers. In general, ECAs and multilaterals will share in any project security on an equal basis.

7.2 Pro rata lending

Often in multi-source financings, loan drawdowns may not occur on a pro rata basis across all facilities (primarily because certain loans may only be permitted to be used for specific eligible costs). In these financings, project companies and their advisers need to pay close attention to drawdown schedules as well as construction and/or delivery schedules to ensure that loan proceeds can be sourced from the appropriate lender or group of lenders in a timely manner while also satisfying each applicable

ECA's sourcing requirements. Project companies additionally need to monitor the impact any such non-pro rata drawdown schedule may have on loan repayment schedules and the voting rights of different groups of lenders. In general, ECAs have come to accept non-pro rata drawdowns necessitated by sourcing requirements and the timing of acquisition of disparate project components.

7.3 Voting rights and other intercreditor matters

Transactions involving more than just a single ECA or a single multilateral will often involve intercreditor arrangements which need to be designed to consider special ECA/multilateral rights on key issues. The suite of special rights may relate to issues such as environmental and social matters, minimum offtake requirements (eg, where an ECA may require that a minimum percentage of project production be sold to companies based in the relevant ECA's home country – often a requirement in mining and commodities projects), minimum equity ownership requirements (eg, where an ECA requires that a minimum threshold of the project company's equity be owned by companies from the ECA's home country and maintains a consent right for any equity sales by such companies outside of pre-agreed and often limited parameters), or continued membership in the applicable multilateral by the country in which the project is being developed. Where applicable, the impact of preferred creditor status will need to be agreed. Special veto rights may also be considered where the applicable ECA or multilateral has identified core or fundamental events (often relating to matters such as political risks or developmental goals) which could conflict with such institution's policies or cause substantial political embarrassment for the applicable institution.

Significant intercreditor issues often arise in the context of multi-sourced financings that include ECAs, multilaterals and commercial lenders as a result of the different policy goals which may influence the response by different parties to problems arising in relation to a financing. The varying credit perspectives of the different institutions that may be involved in a single financing may result in lender perspectives differing when it comes to addressing major transactional issues. In the context of events of default, certain lenders may favour efforts to work out any issues with the project company and enable the project company to take steps to rectify the circumstances leading to the default while other lenders, particularly commercial lenders, may seek to extract high waiver fees from the project company or to enforce rights against the project company in a much more aggressive manner. Where A or B loan structures are being used, these issues may become more pronounced in the context of negotiating participant rights for those commercial banks providing liquidity under a B loan package – in general B loan participants have very limited voting rights. Multilaterals which adopt A or B loan structures have an acute need, however, for the liquidity B loan lenders provide. In practice, these multilaterals will be careful not to exercise their strict legal rights in their A loans which will reduce the value of their B loans to B loan participants.

7.4 Environmental and social considerations

Most multilaterals and ECAs adopt some form of the performance standards developed and implemented by the IFC. In developing its performance standards, the IFC's objective was fourfold:

- to identify and assess social and environmental impacts, both adverse and beneficial, in the project's area of influence;
- to avoid or, where avoidance is not possible, minimise, mitigate or compensate for adverse impacts on workers, affected communities and the environment;
- to ensure that affected communities are appropriately engaged in issues that could potentially affect them; and
- to promote improved social and environmental performance of companies through the effective use of management tools.

To meet these objectives, the IFC has established a programme titled 'Assessment and Management of Environmental and Social Risks and Impacts' (the Management System) applicable to projects with social or environmental risks and impacts that need to be managed, beginning in the early stages of project development and continuing on an ongoing basis through to project completion. The Management System incorporates the following elements:

- establishing an overarching policy that considers the environmental and social objectives and principles that guide the project to achieve sound environmental and social performance;
- creating a process to identify the environmental and social risks and impacts of the project;
- creating a management programme consisting of a combination of operational policies, procedures and practices, effectively to mitigate negative externalities and improve performance;
- establishing an organisational structure that defines roles, responsibilities and authority to implement the management programme;
- establishing and maintaining an emergency preparedness and response system for accidents and emergency situations associated with the project to prevent and mitigate harm to people and/or the environment;
- reporting, monitoring and measuring the effectiveness of the management programme, including site inspections and audits; and
- engaging stakeholders in analysis and planning, disclosure and dissemination of information, consultation and participation, grievance mechanisms and ongoing reporting.

Commercial lenders manage the environmental and social considerations of projects and project finance-related services through voluntary adoption of the Equator Principles, a set of ten environmental and social guidelines which primarily serve as an industry benchmark to assess and manage environmental and social risks and set forth due diligence standards to support decision making. The Equator Principles require that financial institutions work with borrowers for projects and undertake the following:

- categorising projects based on whether they have potential significant,

diverse, irreversible or unprecedented adverse environmental and social risks and/or impacts;
- conducting an assessment of the relevant environmental and social risks and impacts of the project, including any specialised studies which should be undertaken;
- evaluating compliance with IFC Performance Standards on Environmental and Social Sustainability (Performance Standards) and the World Bank Group's Environmental, Health and Safety Guidelines (EHS Guidelines), or host country laws, as appropriate;
- developing an Environmental and Social Management Plan (ESMP) for the project;
- demonstrating effective stakeholder engagement by making certain assessments of the project (including ESMPs) in a local language and in a culturally appropriate manner to affected communities;
- establishing a grievance mechanism to facilitate resolution of issues pertaining to the project's environmental and social performance;
- appointing an Independent Environmental and Social Consultant to carry out a review of any assessment documentation to assess compliance with the Equator Principles when applicable;
- including covenants in the financing documents which state that the borrower will comply with the ESMPs and the Equator Principles during the construction and operation of the project, provide periodic reports that document compliance with the ESMPs and the Equator Principles, comply with local environmental and social laws, regulations and permits and, at the end of the project's useful life, decommission the project facilities in accordance with an agreed plan;
- appointing an external expert to verify monitoring information for the life of the loan; and
- making certain assessment documentation available online and publicly reporting greenhouse gas emission levels for projects above a certain size.

Currently, 79 financial institutions adhere to the Equator Principles and commit to assessing projects' effects on their surrounding communities, including environmental and social impact reporting and mitigation. This serves to enhance their reputation for corporate social responsibility and tracks the standards pledged by ECAs and multilaterals.

7.5 Monitoring requirements

Monitoring requirements are mandated by multilaterals to ensure compliance with environmental action plans throughout the course of the project, from inception through to project completion. For example, the Environmental Policy of the EBRD states that: "operations are monitored on an on-going basis by an operation team ... throughout the Bank's relationship with the project". EBRD uses a host of monitoring mechanisms for projects that it finances, including "review of periodic environmental reports and other progress reports, monitoring visits by the Bank's environmental specialists or consultants and periodic third party audits to ensure that the sponsor is implementing agreed programs, policies, and actions" as set forth in the underlying legal documents. Although broadly applicable, EBRD defines a specific monitoring programme for each project, based upon due diligence and public consultation. The negotiation and implementation of these programmes often require significant negotiation and documentation to ensure that the standards being applied are properly enforced throughout the term of the loan. Other multilaterals similarly require comprehensive monitoring of projects in order to assess social and environmental impacts, including, for example, the IADB, the AfDB and the EIB. ECAs often apply similar standards, although monitoring requirements can differ substantially from institution to institution.

8. Recent trends

While global commercial markets have improved significantly since the global financial crisis, a number of recent developments have indicated the staying power of ECA and multilateral funding sources as part of the project finance landscape for the foreseeable future.

9. Non-OECD ECAs

Although ECAs have traditionally been based in OECD and other developed countries, recent growth in a number of developing countries has encouraged the development of ECAs in places that have historically been the target, rather than the source, of ECA funding. While this development evidences growth in these regions and should be encouraging from a development perspective, it is worth noting that many of these newer ECAs often do not adhere to common agreements such as the OECD Arrangement that are intended to ensure that ECA funding does not constitute unfair subsidisation of home country exporters. A hot topic of discussion in recent years has been the stratification between those ECAs that bind themselves to these normative standards and those that do not, and the ensuing trade imbalances created and the benefit provided to firms from certain countries over others. In its 2013 annual report, US Exim Bank highlighted the critical importance of this issue by stating that:

> *ECAs of non-OECD countries, such as China, Russia and Brazil, operate by a different set of rules. Their exporters are accustomed to advantages not available to exporters from OECD countries, such as borrow-now-buy-later drives (financing now for benefits later) and other forms of untied export credit. Such practices disadvantage American exporters and distort export finance.*

In order to compete effectively with ECAs that do not adhere to the Arrangement, certain ECAs have established funds to enable them to offer additional financing options in order to prevent market distortions that may occur when official funding is offered to projects on terms that are not consistent with consensus protocols. US Exim Bank's Tied Aid War Chest, for example, is a programme that was designed to counter situations where there is a reasonable basis for determining that a foreign government is unfairly supporting home exporters in a manner that does not comply with the Helsinki Package. Part of the purpose of the programme is to defend US exporters from foreign government financing that may create long-run trade advantages for foreign exporters to the detriment of US exporters.

10. Fund investments and ECA bonds

A further recent trend has been the partnering of ECAs and investment fund vehicles in order to finance limited scope – namely green energy or renewable energy – projects in specially designated markets. As an example, China Eximbank (CHEXIM) and the IADB have partnered in recent years to fund an infrastructure facility and public–private investment fund to be deployed in Latin America and the Caribbean. With the ability to deploy a variety of investment types and currencies, including the Chinese yuan, the fund supports investments that "bring together Chinese and international investors with producers in Latin America and the Caribbean". Similarly, JBIC partnered with IADB in 2013 to establish a fund to invest in renewable energy and energy-efficient projects in Mexico. JBIC plans to invest up to $40 million in the fund as part of its GREEN operations initiative. On a related front, K-Exim has entered the bond market directly with a Green Bond issuance, the proceeds of which are earmarked for projects that "address the transition to a low carbon and climate resistant growth".[4] As the market for project bonds expands, the provision of project bond guarantees will likely present an additional opportunity for ECAs.

11. Local currency funding options

Given the recent turmoil in currency markets and investors' demands to limit the potential for currency risk exposure, certain multilaterals have begun to provide local currency funding options. The IADB, for example, has recently begun offering local currency facilities to project companies, which not only helps mitigate the risk of currency shocks and potential mismatches between asset values and project liabilities, but also acts to strengthen local capital markets by encouraging local currency investments in projects that have all the traditional stability of multilateral support. The participation of local investors can also help mitigate political risks, as local governments may be less inclined to interfere in investments where local participation has provided crucial funding for project development. There is evidence to suggest that ECAs are also exploring ways in which to provide local currency funding.

12. Residual risk arrangements

An additional recent trend, which is expected to grow in the coming years as smaller agencies seek to leverage expertise and resources, is residual risk arrangements. Residual risk arrangements are agreements between ECAs and commercial banks pursuant to which the commercial bank will take documentation risk and agreed residual risk on the relevant borrower. While a residual risk quantum in the 10% range has been common in these arrangements to date, recent discussion has

---

4 See 'K-Exim issues the first USD Green Bond out of Asia attracting investors from three continents', February 27 2013, available at http://sebgroup.com.

evolved around whether the amount should increase to 20% or 30%. Finnerva plc (Finnerva) of Finland offers a finance guarantee product for credit institutions granting export credit to qualified exporters. The guarantee protects against repayment risks, though not risks related to a foreign buyer or such buyer's home country, and allocates a to-be-agreed residual risk (ie, a portion of the quantum of the debt) to the commercial lender.

13. The post-global financial crisis era and beyond

While ECAs and multilaterals have always constituted a major source of potential financing for investors and developers, recent events have thrust these institutions into an even more central role in the funding of major projects. Over the past few years there have been virtually no major project financings in non-OECD countries that have not involved at least one ECA or multilateral, and a substantial portion of what has been financed has included two or more of these types of entities. In addition to providing a constant source of liquidity and credit protection, the presence of ECAs and multilaterals has proven to be a major attraction for commercial banks, as these institutions have been perceived to provide stability in an otherwise unstable market. Without even considering the hard and soft political support an ECA or a multilateral can bring to the table, commercial lenders have grown comfortable with the extensive diligence and technical expertise that these entities offer. Given the prevalence of these funding sources over the past few years, many in the commercial market have come not only to invite agency participation but also to expect it.

On the agency side, after many years of developing their expertise working side-by-side with commercial lenders in a variety of projects markets, many ECAs and multilaterals have become accustomed to their role not just of providing competitive economic terms but also of leading negotiations in respect of the general terms and conditions for the multi-source transactions in which they are involved. More and more often, these covenant packages reflect standards that have been commonplace in the commercial project finance market for many years. Indeed, many ECAs have not only embraced these standards, but also taken structural steps to adopt commercial bank covenant standards as their own and to participate in financings in regions that were not traditionally designated for official credits. Other public institutions have also expanded their mandates to address demand for ECA-style funding in developed as well as developing nations. Both JBIC and EKF have recently made forays into the US domestic project finance market in support of Japanese and Dutch exporters, respectively, and this trend (at least as it pertains to ECAs from Asia) is expected only to continue as investors flock to North America to procure newly harnessed oil and gas resources. These institutions are able to provide a full spectrum of support for the companies they seek to promote, from initial investment structuring to analysis of funding alternatives, all the way through to financial closing.

Notwithstanding the above, it is important to note frequent recent discussion about the potential for ECAs to crowd out commercial banks in the project finance market. While the provenance of much of this debate may simply be that commercial lenders – who had previously taken a step back from the project finance market and now, in the post-recession era and with enhanced liquidity, are re-emerging as market players – are being forced to compete with the attractive loan terms being offered by ECAs and multilaterals, it will be important to further analyse this tension as traditional commercial lenders in the project finance world seek a return to centre stage. This tension aside, ECAs and multilaterals have, in short, become key financing providers to the projects marketplace. As the market continues to rely on the levels of diligence and technical capability – not to mention the attractive loan terms – offered by these official funding sources, it is to be expected that both ECAs and multilaterals will continue to play a leading role as credit providers to the project finance market for many years to come.

Appendix 1: List of export credit agencies (by country)

Country	Name	Abbreviation
Argentina	Banco de Inversión y Comercio Exterior	BICE
Australia	Export Finance and Insurance Corporation	EFIC
Austria	Oësterreichische Kontrollbank AG	OeKB
Belgium	Office National du Ducroire	ONDD
Brazil	Banco Nacional de Desenvolvimento Econômico e Social-Exim	BNDES-Exim
Canada	Export Development Canada	EDC
China	China Export and Credit Insurance Corporation The Export-Import Bank of China China Development Bank	SINOSURE CHEXIM CDB

continued on next page

Country	Name	Abbreviation
Colombia	Segurexpo de Columbia	Segurexpo
Croatia	Croatian Bank for Reconstruction and Development	HBOR
Czech Republic	Export Guarantee and Insurance Corporation Czech Export Bank	EGAP CEB
Denmark	Eksport Kredit Fonden	EKF
Ecuador	Corporación Financiera Nacional Fondo de Promoción de Exportaciones	CFN/Fopex
Finland	Finnvera plc Finnish Export Credit Ltd Finnfund	Finnvera FEC Finnfund
France	Compagnie Française d'Assurance pour le Commerce Extérieur Direction des Relations Economiques Extérieures (Ministere de L'Economie)[5] Promotion et Participation pour la Coopération Économique[6]	COFACE DREE PROPARCO

continued on next page

5 This entity may more appropriately be classified as a bilateral agency rather than an ECA.
6 This entity may more appropriately be classified as a bilateral agency rather than an ECA.

Country	Name	Abbreviation
Germany	Deutsche Investitions- und Entwicklungsgesellschaft mbH Euler Hermes Kreditversicherungs-AG KfW IPEX Bank[7]	DEG Hermes KfW
Greece	Export Credit Insurance Organization	ECIO
Hong Kong	Hong Kong Export Credit Insurance Corporation	HKEC
Hungary	Hungarian Export Credit Insurance Ltd Hungarian Export-Import Bank	MEHIB Eximbank
India	Export Credit Guarantee Corporation of India Ltd Export-Import Bank of India	ECGC I-Eximbank
Indonesia	Asuranski Ekspor Indonesia	ASEI
Iran	Export Guarantee Fund of Iran	EGFI
Israel	Israel Foreign Trade Risks Insurance Corporation Ltd	ASHRA
Italy	Servizi Assicurativi del Commercio Estero (SACE SpA)	SACE

continued on next page

7 While still nominally tied to the German government, this entity operates more as commercial bank rather than as an ECA.

Country	Name	Abbreviation
Japan	Japan Bank for International Cooperation Nippon Export and Investment Insurance	JBIC NEXI
Korea	The Export-Import Bank of Korea Korea Trade Insurance Corporation	KEXIM K-sure
Luxembourg	Office du Ducroire	ODD
Malaysia	Malaysia Export Credit Insurance Berhad	MECIB
Mexico	Banco National de Comercio Exterior SNC	BANCOMEXT
Netherlands	Nederlandse Financierings-Maatschappij Voor Ontwikkelingslanden N.V. Atradius	FMO Atradius
New Zealand	New Zealand Export Credit Office	NZECO
Norway	The Norwegian Guarantee Institute for Export Credits	GIEK
Oman	Export Credit Guarantee Agency	ECGA
Philippines	Philippine Export-Import Credit Agency	PhilEXIM

continued on next page

Country	Name	Abbreviation
Poland	Korporacja Ubezpieczén Kredytów Eksportowych Spólka Akcyjna	KUKE
Portugal	Companhia de Seguro de Créditos, S.A.	COSEC
Romania	EXIMBANK Romania	EximBank
Russia	Export-Import Bank of the Russian Federation Export Insurance Agency of Russia	Eximbank EXIAR
Singapore	Export Credit Insurance Corporation of Singapore Ltd	ECICS
Slovak Republic	Export-Import Bank of the Slovak Republic	Eximbank SR
Slovenia	Slovene Export Corporation	SEC
South Africa	Credit Guarantee Insurance Corporation of Africa Ltd	CGIC
Spain	Compañía Española de Seguros de Crédito a la Exportación, S.A. Secretaría de Estado de Comercio (Ministerio de Economía)	CESCE MCX
Sri Lanka	Sri Lanka Export Credit Insurance Corporation	SLECIC
Sweden	Exportkreditnämnden Svensk Esportkredit	EKN SEK

continued on next page

Country	Name	Abbreviation
Switzerland	Swiss Export Risk Insurance	SERV
Thailand	Export-Import Bank of Thailand	Thai Exim
Trinidad & Tobago	Export-Import Bank of Trinidad & Tobago	Eximbank
Turkey	Export Credit Bank of Turkey	Türk Eximbank
Ukraine	State Export Import Bank of Ukraine	Ukreximbank
United Kingdom	Export Credits Guarantee Department	ECGD
United States	Export-Import Bank of the United States Overseas Private Investment Corporations	US Exim Bank OPIC
Uzbekistan	Uzbekistan National Export-Import Insurance Company	Unic
Zimbabwe	Credit Insurance Zimbabwe	Credsure

About the authors

Erlend B Bakken
Lawyer, Michelet & Co
ErlendBakken@micheletlaw.com

Erlend Bakken is one of the founders of Michelet & Co, a law firm with fully integrated offices in Oslo and London. Michelet & Co provides legal and strategic advice to a range of clients within the oil and energy sector. Erlend has more than 15 years' experience advising oil and gas companies, investors, financiers and investment banks on corporate projects and corporate finance transactions. He regularly acts for both issuers and investment banks in bond issues. Erlend has a law degree from the University of Oslo and an LLM from the University of California.

Kerion Ball
Counsel, Ashurst LLP
kerion.ball@ashurst.com

Kerion Ball is a counsel in the derivatives and structured products practice of the securities and derivatives group of Ashurst LLP, based in London. Kerion advises banks, funds, other investment firms and corporates on a wide range of derivative products, with a focus on corporate equity and commodities derivatives, prime brokerage, structured funding transactions, regulatory capital driven structures and hedging solutions. Kerion regularly advises on netting, collateral and security issues as well as clearing and other regulatory matters associated with such transactions.

Kerion has recently advised on mezzanine financing linked to future projected oil production in connection with a secured borrowing base facility and related hedging of projected oil production in connection with the borrowing base facility, as well as hedging arrangements on a number of public authority sponsored project finance transactions. His experience also includes advising on an innovative structured energy derivative.

Nacim Bounouara
Senior associate, Ashurst LLP
nacim.bounouara@ashurst.com

Nacim Bounouara is a senior associate in the energy, transport and infrastructure department of Ashurst LLP, based in London. He specialises in project development and financing of energy and infrastructure projects, acting for lenders and sponsors across Europe, Africa and the Middle East.

Nacim's recent experience includes advising ACWA Power on the three phases of the Noor solar projects in Ouarzazate (Morocco) and the lenders on the development and financing of the Dublin Waste-to-Energy project.

Hege Dahl
Senior lawyer, Arntzen de Besche Advokatfirma AS
hda@adeb.no

Hege Dahl is a senior lawyer in the corporate and M&A department of Arntzen de Besche. She assists with questions related to corporate law, capital market transactions, securities law and financial markets regulation. Hege assists companies and investment banks in connection with stock exchange listings, in restructurings of companies and in takeover bids for listed shares. Hege also provides legal advice on regulatory requirements for investors, investment firms, funds, financial institutions and insurance companies.

Hege has worked as a lawyer at the Oslo Stock Exchange. She also has experience as a deputy judge as well as a senior adviser at the Ministry of Finance. Hege has been a member of and secretary for several government-appointed law commissions, in particular related to security law.

Tom Dimitroff
Partner, Infrastructure Development Partnership LLP
tdimitroff@infradev.co.uk

Tom has over 20 years' experience as a lawyer, risk analyst and business strategist.

Tom has been a core member of negotiating teams that have delivered globally significant energy projects, including the 1 million bpd BTC oil pipeline and the parallel 10 bcma SCP gas pipeline and he led the negotiation of the government agreements for the 10 bcma TAP gas pipeline. He has advised governments as well as companies and has led cross-functional teams delivering commercial structuring, financing and strategy advice for energy projects across Africa, the Middle East and North America. Prior to IDP, he was regional adviser to BP plc for Africa, the Middle East, Russia, the Caspian and Turkey.

Recently, Tom authored a study on global cross-border oil and gas pipelines under a grant from the Association of International Petroleum Negotiators (July 2014) and was consulting editor for *Risk and Energy Infrastructure*, published by Globe Law and Business (London, 2011).

Geir Evenshaug
Lawyer, Michelet & Co
GeirEvenshaug@micheletlaw.com

Geir Evenshaug is one of the founders of Michelet & Co which has fully integrated offices in Oslo and London. Michelet & Co provides legal and strategic advice to a range of clients within the oil and energy sector. Geir has more than 15 years' experience advising oil and gas companies, investors, financiers and investment banks on corporate projects and corporate finance transactions. He has been involved in most of the major corporate oil and gas transactions in Norway during recent years. He also has considerable experience in cross-border bond loan issues and complex restructurings. Geir has a law degree from the University of Oslo and an LLM from the University of Cambridge, England.

Barry Irwin
Partner, Allen & Overy LLP
Barry.Irwin@Allenovery.com

Barry Irwin is a partner in Allen & Overy, based in Singapore, and specialises in advising clients in the energy and resources sector, with a focus on mining, oil and gas, renewable energy and related infrastructure. He has advised clients throughout the Asia-Pacific and Africa on a range of cross-border transactions including structuring new projects, project acquisitions and disposals, joint ventures, farm-ins, offtake arrangements, mining services, and sales and marketing. Barry is recognised in independent directories as one of the leading global mining and oil and gas lawyers. He is a member of the Mining Law Committee of the International Bar Association, and the President of the Asian chapter of the Australian Mining and Petroleum Lawyers Association.

Barry is one of the authors of *Minerals and Mining*, published by Globe Law and Business, a contributing author to the World Bank Institute's *Guide to Key Documentation and Governance for*

Extractive Industries, and a contributor to *Long Term Contracts*, published by the Federation Press, on the practical, commercial and legal operation and effect of long-term commodities supply agreements.

Anthony Martinez
Associate, Clifford Chance LLP
anthony.martinez@cliffordchance.com

Anthony Martinez is an associate in the corporate practice of Clifford Chance LLP, specialising in private mergers and acquisitions, joint ventures and private equity transactions, particularly in the energy sector and emerging markets. He is a member of the firm's energy and infrastructure sector group and advises on a variety of transactions, including corporate and asset-level acquisitions and disposals as well as project development work across the energy value chain.

He has advised both private and public sector entities in various regions, particularly the former Soviet Union, Africa, the Middle East and Latin America, and was recently seconded to the energy regulatory agency of a Latin American government, where he advised on upstream oil and gas agreements, including production-sharing contracts and licences, joint operating agreements and farm-ins.

Nikhil Markanday
Partner, Ashurst LLP
nikhil.markanday@ashurst.com

Nikhil Markanday is a partner at Ashurst LLP, based in London. He specialises in the project development and financing of energy projects, in particular in the oil and gas sector. Nikhil is a finance specialist with significant expertise in acting for both sponsors and lenders on complex multi-sourced financings across the energy sector, including projects involving project bonds. He has advised clients on the project financing aspects of a number of LNG projects, pipeline, refinery and thermal power projects. Nikhil has also spent time on secondment to the European Investment Bank where he worked in the legal directorate.

Clive Ransome
Partner, Milbank, Tweed, Hadley & McCloy LLP
cransome@milbank.com

Clive Ransome is a partner in the projects, energy and infrastructure group of Milbank, Tweed, Hadley & McCloy LLP, based in London. He has specialised in oil and gas, power and infrastructure projects and other project-financed transactions for over 20 years while based in London and the Far East.

Clive was a member of the Linklaters team that advised the 214 bank lending syndicate on the UK France Channel Tunnel project. He is currently advising Mitsubishi Heavy Industries, Itochu and EnGie on the Sinop nuclear power plant project in Turkey. He has also worked on the $12 billion Sadara and $7 billion PetroRabigh petrochemicals projects in Saudi Arabia – two of the largest project financings in the market in recent years.

Clive was a contributor to *The International Legal Guide to: Project Finance 2013* (OUP); the UK chapter in *Guide to Financing Oil and Gas Projects* (Euromoney); and frequently contributes articles on finance and energy to legal magazines.

Nick Ross-McCall
Senior associate, Ashurst LLP
Nicholas.Ross-McCall@ashurst.com

Nick Ross-McCall is a senior associate in the resources and utilities group of Ashurst LLP, and is based in London. He specialises in the financing and development of energy projects, in particular upstream and power financings, with over 10 years' experience.

He has advised lenders and sponsors on numerous reserve-based lending transactions and other upstream finance products, including of assets in the North Sea, South East Asia, Russia, the Middle East and Africa.

Nick speaks regularly at conferences on energy matters and has authored many chapters and articles on upstream financing and other energy issues.

Antony Skinner
Partner, Ashust
Antony.skinner@ashurst.com

Antony is a partner in the corporate projects team of Ashurst based in London. He specialises in renewable and thermal power with respect to development, financing and M&A in the UK, Europe and Africa. Antony has advised sponsors and lenders, purchasers and vendors in a range of transactions in relation to renewables and power generation developments and in connection with a number of renewable portfolio acquisitions and financings. Antony advised the developer in connection with the development, equity raising and financing of a 60MW wind farm in Kenya. Antony has also advised Infinis in connection with the development and financing of over 300MW of onshore wind farms in the UK. Antony also advised the lenders in connection with the financing of the Carrington 884MW combined cycle gas turbine project in the UK.

Anna-Marie Slot
Partner, Ashurst LLP
anna-marie.slot@ashurst.com

Anna-Marie Slot is the head of high yield at Ashurst and a partner in the finance practice. She is currently based in Hong Kong. She has extensive experience acting for banks and other companies in a wide range of corporate finance and securities transactions, including high-yield debt offerings, tender offers, debt buybacks, refinancings, and numerous securities transactions such as Rule 144A and Regulation S offerings, as well as mezzanine debt investments and senior credit facilities. Her practice also includes advising companies on US securities law matters.

She has represented the underwriters in the first clean energy company out of India to issue a high yield bond, the underwriters in an offering by an Indonesia conglomerate with oil and gas interests in Indonesia, and MIE Holdings, an upstream oil and gas company, on its high yield issuances.

Anna-Marie is described by clients as "our first choice of adviser for complex matters" in *Chambers 2015 Asia Pacific* for China: high yields products.

Huw Thomas
Partner, Ashurst LLP
Huw.Thomas@Ashurst.com

Huw Thomas is a partner in the resources and utilities group of Ashurst LLP, based in London. He has specialised in energy and natural resources financings for over 25 years, with a particular emphasis on upstream oil and gas financings.

Huw has led Ashurst teams on a number of leading upstream oil and gas financings, including the $4 billion borrowing base facility for Lundin Petroleum AB, the up to $1.7 billion corporate facility for EnQuest plc and the $340 million borrowing base facility for Oranje-Nassau Energie BV, among many others.

Huw has also advised on Norwegian high yield bond issuances for several UK-headquartered oil and gas exploration and production companies, including Xcite Energy Resources plc, Salamander Energy plc and Iona Energy Co (UK) plc.

Huw speaks regularly at conferences on oil and gas financing and is a regular author on upstream oil and gas financing topics.

Philip Thomson
Partner, Ashurst LLP
philip.thomson@ashurst.com

Philip Thomson is a partner in Ashurst LLP, based in London. Philip specialises in the development and financing of large-scale projects in the energy sector. He acts for project sponsors, borrowers, lenders and host governments. His experience also includes joint ventures, commercial contracts, M&A transactions and restructuring transactions in the energy sector. He has a particular focus on the LNG industry and has worked on numerous transactions across all segments of the LNG value chain. Earlier in his career, he spent several months on secondment to BG Group based in Bolivia working exclusively on a natural gas liquefaction project. Philip has recently returned from four years working out of the Singapore office on transactions across the Asia-Pacific region.

David Wadham
Partner, Ashurst LLP
David.wadham@ashurst.com

David Wadham is a partner in the utilities and resources group of Ashurst LLP, based in London. He is global head of the firm's utilities practice and has previously worked in the Middle East and Paris. David specialises in the development and financing of large-scale energy and infrastructure projects.

In particular, David advises sponsors and funders (including export credit agencies) on the development and financing of independent power projects (IPPs). He also advises on commercial agreements, such as power purchase and gas supply agreements, construction and operating sub-contracts, as well as conventional and Islamic financing documentation.

David has advised on power projects in developing markets across the Middle East and Africa, as well as in fully liberalised markets such as the United Kingdom. His experience spans conventional forms of generation such as gas and oil, renewables, including wind and solar, as well as nuclear power projects.

Peter Wilkes
Partner, Allen & Overy
Peter.wilkes@allenovery.com

Peter Wilkes is a partner in the project, energy and infrastructure group of Allen & Overy, based in Perth. He holds a Bachelor of Jurisprudence and Bachelor of Laws. Peter specialises in financing and project development in the energy and resources sector. He has over 25 years' experience acting for sponsors and banks on the financing techniques relevant to the mining sector including project financing, syndicated bank facilities, hybrid funding, loan notes issued in the international capital markets and farm-ins and joint ventures.

Peter led the team that acted for Fortescue Metals Group on its $2 billion secured project bond in 2006 as well as the Allen & Overy team which acted for Fortescue Metals Group on its $5bn senior secured term loan facility, winner of the ALB Australasia Law Awards, Debt Market Deal of the Year 2013.